# Coral Reefs of the Southern Gulf of Mexico

*Harte Research Institute for Gulf of Mexico Studies Series*
*Sponsored by Texas A&M University—Corpus Christi*
*John W. Tunnell Jr., General Editor*

# Coral Reefs of the Southern Gulf of Mexico

*Edited by* **John W. Tunnell Jr.,**

**Ernesto A. Chávez,** *and* **Kim Withers**

*Foreword by* Sylvia Earle

Texas A&M University Press
*College Station*

The paper used in this book meets the minimum requirements of the
American National Standard for Permanence of Paper for Printed Library Materials,
Z39.48-1984. Binding materials have been chosen for durability.
⊗

**Library of Congress Cataloging-in-Publication Data**

Coral reefs of the southern Gulf of Mexico / edited by John W. Tunnell Jr., Ernesto A.
Chávez, and Kim Withers ; foreword by Sylvia Earle. — 1st ed.
    p.  cm. — (Harte research institute for Gulf of Mexico studies series)
  Includes bibliographical references and index.
  ISBN-13: 978-1-58544-617-9 (cloth : alk. paper)
  ISBN-10: 1-58544-617-3 (cloth : alk. paper)
  1. Coral reef ecology—Mexico, Gulf of.  2. Coral reefs and islands—Mexico, Gulf
of.  I. Tunnell, John Wesley.  II. Chávez, Ernesto A., 1942–  III. Withers, Kim.
  QH107.C67    2007
  577.7′89364—dc22
                                  2007008223

*In memory of Carl R. Beaver, Ph.D.*

# Contents

# Foreword

Shades of orange and gold streaked the darkening horizon as I climbed into the snug seat of the one-person submersible *Deep Rover* and prepared to realize a lifetime dream: to spend the night, sunset to sunrise, getting to know the under-sea residents of a coral reef by becoming a temporary resident myself. With guidance from Dr. J. W. Tunnell, senior editor of this volume, a site was chosen near Santiaguillo Reef just offshore from Veracruz, one of Mexico's largest, busiest industrialized ports. It seems an unlikely place to find reefs prospering, with tall pillars of coral, mounds of sponges, and a dazzling array of small fish right there, in plain view of a shoreline glittering with city lights, laced with tall buildings. But there they are, part of a system of wondrously rich and diverse reefs that arc along parts of the Gulf's southern and western coasts, from coastal waters north of Veracruz to the broad Campeche Bank reefs bordering the western Yucatán Peninsula, each reef an undersea "city" far more complex and diverse than any human metropolis.

Swept by clear, blue-green waters, crowned with forests of coral and hosting thousands of variations on the theme of starfish, urchins, sea lilies, crabs, lobsters, shrimp, anemones, mollusks and other less-obvious forms of ocean wildlife, Mexico's southern Gulf reefs are largely unknown except to those living nearby. Worldwide, coral reefs are called the "rainforests of the sea," owing to their extraordinary diversity and beauty, but the phrase could well be reversed, with forests of the land praised for their similarities to coral reefs. Although rarely acknowledged, far greater biological diversity is contained within marine systems than their terrestrial counterparts. Nearly all of the 32 or so phyla of animals occur within coral reef systems; only about half have representation anywhere on the land. Once, on a single small rock taken from 200 meters depth in the Caribbean Sea, I counted eleven phyla of animals and three divisions of plants—not including microscopic organisms that would likely outnumber all the other species combined.

As I sat cocooned in my underwater sphere more than a kilometer offshore from Isla Santiaguillo and 30 meters down, light faded and the "changeover" between day and night creatures began—the emergence of squirrel fish, morays, large snappers, and other night-active carnivores, coincident with the retreat of grazers to their overnight resting places—parrotfish, surgeonfish, butterfly-fish, along with filefish, small wrasses, and puffers. Looking closely at the great mounds of coral, I could see the tentacles of individual coral animals extending, and watched as a basket starfish unfurled its lacy branches to capture small crustaceans and other planktonic creatures.

I savored the night, shared with a fair cross section of most of the major forms of life on Earth, many endowed with bioluminescence—the ability to flash, sparkle, or glow with fireflylike brilliance. To photograph the reef, I had to turn on the sub's lights, with a single flick of a switch becoming the most luminous of all creatures on the reef that night. In so doing, the sub became the center of attention for a blizzard of minute shrimp, polychaete worms, arrow worms, jellies, and hosts of other small beings who in turn attracted fast-moving squid and a massive school of small, silvery fish that swirled around the sub, a roving banquet where it was hard to distinguish who was eating from who was being eaten.

As vibrant and rich as the reef area seemed, I was struck by the absence of lobsters, large grouper, large snappers, or sharks of any size. Sediment blanketed much of the reef and there were large areas where dead coral mounds and branches occupied far more space than living coral. Without knowledge of the state of the reefs in times past, it might seem that all was well. But as this volume demonstrates, much has changed in the past century, and the pace is accelerating.

The deep historical origins, present condition, and precarious future of Mexico's southern reefs are documented here with eloquence and understanding born of decades of careful observation by scientists endowed with rare passion and an uncommon ability to inspire others to take notice—and care about these enduring but vulnerable living treasures. This thoughtful summation of the knowledge concerning the reefs of the southern Gulf is especially valuable at this point in time, given the swift and sharp changes that are taking place in the region, a reflection of trends happening in the ocean worldwide. The reefs portrayed here have been developing over hundreds of millennia, but it has taken less than a half century for them to precipitously decline owing to the impacts of pollution from near and far, coupled with the consequences of overfishing—the extraction of more of the ocean's wild creatures than can be replenished.

According to recent studies by Canadian scientists, in half a century, the oceans globally have lost 90% of the large, predatory fish that have been targeted for large-scale taking by humans, notably sharks, tunas, marlin, groupers, snappers, halibut, and cod, among others. The disastrous consequences to coral reefs and other ocean systems relate to food chains—the result of not maintaining a healthy balance among the plants and grazers and the large carnivorous creatures that feed upon them.

In the Gulf of Mexico and throughout the greater Caribbean region, the decline of large herbivores—manatees, sea turtles, parrotfish, and certain large conchs—has contributed further to the disruptions. Complicating these impacts is the flow of noxious substances from the land to the sea, and from the skies above, coupled with a global warming trend that adversely affects coral health. The gradual acidification of the ocean, a direct consequence of increased carbon dioxide in the atmosphere, looms as another reason to be concerned about the survival of limestone-loving creatures such as coral, coralline algae, many mollusks, and numerous planktonic organisms.

These issues are not just something to worry about relative to the fate of Mexico's treasured southern reefs or even of coral reefs worldwide. Among the most important discoveries of the 20th century was the recognition that the ocean is vital to all life, ourselves included. The ocean, we now know, generates most of the oxygen in the atmosphere, absorbs much of the carbon dioxide, shapes planetary chemistry, drives climate and weather, and provides 97% of the space on Earth occupied by living things. If the ocean is in trouble, so are we. When coral reefs are in trouble, it is an indication that our personal life-support system is ailing, a signal that actions are needed to remedy what's wrong.

In fact, as this volume makes known, positive actions are being taken. Some critical areas, including the reefs near Veracruz, are now protected, and there are some promising indications of recovery. Policies are being developed to address pollution issues, to eliminate unsustainable fishing practices, and to recognize and integrate the vital "free services" provided by a healthy ocean to the economic and social balance sheet.

As never before, we now know enough to see the trends, understand the significance, and recognize the importance of doing whatever is necessary to restore and maintain health to these undersea treasures. As the 21st century begins, we have a chance to ensure that they will continue to be an enduring legacy for Mexico and for the world.

—Sylvia A. Earle

# Preface

Billy Causey introduced me to scientific diving at Seven and One-half Fathom Reef, offshore from Padre Island, Texas, and the coral reefs of Veracruz, Mexico, in the late 1960s. Billy and I went on to study the fish and mollusks, respectively, of Seven and One-half Fathom Reef for our master of science degrees at Texas A&I University (now Texas A&M University–Kingsville) in Kingsville, Texas. Subsequently, we both were accepted at the University of South Florida (USF) to work on our doctoral degrees together, continuing our love of scuba diving and reef research. Billy went on to Tampa–St. Petersburg and USF, but I got drafted into the U.S. Army. After two good years of enjoying the California coast from my duty station at Fort Baker, located at the northern foot of the Golden Gate Bridge, I joined Billy at USF. Eventually Billy went off to the Florida Keys, where he now is the superintendent of the Florida Keys National Marine Sanctuary, and I headed back to Texas A&M University (TAMU) for my Ph.D., studying the coral reefs of Veracruz for my dissertation.

I have had the good fortune and misfortune of studying the Veracruz reefs over the past three decades of my career from Texas A&M University–Corpus Christi (TAMU–CC). The good fortune was seeing and studying these beautiful reefs in the 1970s, teaching a graduate class in coral reef ecology with a field trip to these reefs, advising seven master's students (Roberts 1981; Allen 1982; Henkel 1982; White 1982; Stinnett 1989; Nelson 1991; Choucair 1992) and one doctoral student (Lehman 1993) on their thesis/dissertation projects on the biota of these reefs, and establishing lifelong Mexican colleagues concerning these reefs and other studies in Mexico. The misfortune, or bad fortune, was chronicling the environmental demise of these beautiful reefs in the 1980s and 1990s.

For my dissertation study (Tunnell 1974) on the ecological and geographical distribution of mollusks on Lobos and Enmedio reefs, Jim Ray, another TAMU Ph.D. student, put me in touch with Ernesto Chávez, a Mexican coral reef professor at the Instituto Politécnico Nacional in Mexico City. Ernesto helped me get my first scientific permit for working in Mexico, and we immediately became scientific colleagues, and later, personal friends. Ernesto had already been taking students to Isla de Lobos Reef, as well as conducting research there, in the late 1960s.

Being a field-oriented marine scientist, I knew when I arrived at my first job as a young assistant professor at TAMU–CC in 1974 that I wanted to take students for field experiences to the reefs of Veracruz. I had been "introduced to the marine tropics" by Donald R. Moore, University of Miami, on a molluscan cruise to the Bahamas on the research vessel *Gerda,* and it was a career-focusing experience. I wanted to do the same for our students at TAMU–CC. During 1976 and 1977 our two-week field trip was to Isla de Lobos Reef because it was in northern Veracruz state and closer to Corpus Christi (Plate 1). However, the difficult logistics, required paperwork, and riding a rented shrimp boat for four hours one-way to Lobos from Tuxpan proved too much. So in 1978 we elected to drive the extra day on to Veracruz city and use our own Zodiac and Boston Whaler and local small fishing boats (*pangas*) to get to and around the reefs for study. Most of the years from 1978 to 1993 we camped on Enmedio Island about five miles offshore of Antón Lizardo, a small fishing village just south of the city of Veracruz (Plates 2–9).

During the academic year 1985–86, I received a Fulbright Scholar Award to study the coral reefs of the Yucatán Peninsula. There, at Centro de Investigacion y Estudios Avanzados (CINVESTAV) in Mérida, Yucatán, I joined Ernesto Chávez, who was director of the marine ecology program at that time and also studying coral reefs around the Yucatán Peninsula. This experience gave me the opportunity to visit most of the Campeche Bank reefs and islands, and it gave me the broader picture of all southern Gulf of Mexico reefs. Ernesto and I vowed at that time to some day do a book on the reefs of the southern Gulf.

As the coral reefs of all southern Veracruz continued to decline, I decided we had to take the coral reef class to the healthier reefs of the Yucatán Peninsula. The Campeche Bank reefs would have been great, but they were too remote and difficult to reach with a class. So, in May 1992, I took an advanced group of coral reef students (ones who already had the coral reef class) to the fringing-barrier reef system of Placer, southern Quintana Roo (the Mexican Caribbean near Belize). Since the long, difficult drive would have been too much for a larger, inexperienced class, we went back to Enmedio one more time in 1993. In 1994, I sent a van to Quintana Roo loaded with our heavy equipment (scuba tanks, compressors, Zodiacs, outboard motors, etc.), and we flew the students into Cancun and made our way down the coast into the Sian Ka'an Biosphere Reserve. However, our study site at Casa Redonda, owned by the Casa Blanca fishing lodge on Punta Pájaros, again proved to be too remote and difficult logistically, although it was a great place to study. We spent the next year trying to determine where to go in Quintana Roo and in 1996 settled on our present site. Rancho Pedro Paila is owned by my friend Peter Watson from Minneapolis, Minnesota, and is located near the famous fishing lodge and inlet, both named Boca Paila. This site and the combination of driving the heavy equipment and flying the students work great, and it is still used as our study site today. We have completed 11 master's thesis projects at this new site, with more students taking an interest in learning about and helping to conserve coral reefs.

After I left the Yucatán in the mid-1980s, David Liddell, a coral reef geologist-ecologist, received a Fulbright Scholar Award also and studied the Yucatán reefs. Following that, several new colleagues began studies on the Veracruz reefs: Juan Manuel Vargas from the Universidad Veracruzana in Jalapa, Guillermo Horta-Puga from Universidad Nacional Autónoma de México in Iztacala, and Juan Pablo Carricart with the Mexican Navy's Instituto Oceanográfico in Veracruz and now at El Colegio de la Frontera Sur (ECOSUR) in Chetumal, Quintana Roo.

Carl Beaver did his master's thesis project at our study site at Placer, Quintana Roo, and assisted in teaching the coral reef class and lab while working on his Ph.D. and postdoc; he drove the van to and from Rancho Pedro Paila for many years. Carl then went to work for the state of Florida's coral reef monitoring and assessment program. Tragically, during the final copyediting phase of this book, Carl was killed in a motorcycle accident on December 18, 2006. His passion for life and his love and dedication to studying and saving coral reefs was infectious and inspired many students, family members, and coworkers. We dedicate this book to Carl's memory.

Roy Lehman took the coral reef class after receiving his master's degree and while teaching junior high school science in Corpus Christi. He returned to Enmedio Reef for many years as my assistant, studying marine algae and eventually deciding to return for his Ph.D. at TAMU. Roy is now a professor at TAMU–CC and teaching part of the class. I told him I still wanted to do the field trip part! May 2005 was the 30th year.

Finally, in 2002, during the design and development of our new Harte Research Institute (HRI) for Gulf of Mexico Studies at TAMU–CC, I had the opportunity to develop and participate in a research cruise to the Veracruz reefs (Plates 10–11). Sylvia Earle, with our HRI, the National Geographic Society, and Conservation International, along with Alberto Vázquez de la Cerda with the Mexican Navy and Universidad Veracruzana, assisted in planning and participating in the cruise. This Veracruz Reefs Expedition became a part of the 2002, year-five expedition of the Sustainable Seas Expedition (SSE), a partnership with the National Geographic Society and the Richard and Rhoda Goldman Fund, using mini-submersibles (*Deep Worker* and *Deep Rover* of Nuytco Research Ltd.), and the U.S. National Oceanic and Atmospheric Administration. Sylvia was lead scientist on the SSE program, and Alberto arranged for us to use the Mexican Navy's Oceanographic Institute's research ship *Antares*. Weather cooperated in late August–early September, and we had an almost perfect reef expedition and cruise. Kip Evans, a National Geographic photographer, was there to document it all, even documenting for the first time mass coral spawning at Santiaguillo Reef (Beaver et al. 2004).

In summary, my love for Mexico, her people and biodiversity, and especially her coral reefs, along with all the friendships and collaborations just mentioned, stimulated this book. Most of us scientists would just like "to do our science" and forget about the rest of the world. However, during the 1980s and particularly the 1990s, coral reef scientists around the world realized that we must do more than just science if we are going to make a difference in saving particular environments or natural areas that we love. This book is a result of such a drive. Our desire is to make the information more readily available for resource managers, students, scientists, and policy makers and to raise the awareness of coral reefs and their plight, so that the general public will become more aware and better stewards of these most amazing public natural resources.

Kim Withers, research scientist and editor at the Center for Coastal Studies at TAMU–CC, joined Ernesto and me to assist in the final editorial process. She participated in our field trip for the coral reef ecology class most of the past 10 years, and she advised or co-advised a number of our graduate thesis projects at the Sian Ka'an Biosphere Reserve study site. Her editorial abilities and field experience in Mexico made her a natural for joining our team and assisting in our effort.

—John W. Tunnell Jr.

# Acknowledgments

We have all benefited greatly from our mentors, colleagues, and students who went with us to the field, discussed many varying topics, and assisted us over the years to learn about and better understand the coral reefs of the southern Gulf of Mexico. They are too many to name here, but we gratefully acknowledge their friendship and collaboration over the years.

We attempted to have two reviewers per chapter, and we sincerely thank each of them for their time and commitment to making this book more accurate: Francisco Arreguin, Steve Cairns, Juan P. Carricart-Ganivet, Billy Causey, Quenton Dokken, Darryl Felder, Walter Jaap, John Ogden, Steve Gittings, Guillermo Horta-Puga, Judy Lang, David Liddell, Pedro Ardisson, Ian McIntyre, Jack Morelock, Patricia Moreno, Nancy Ogden, Margorie Reaka-Kudla, Peter Sale, Julio Sanchez, Alberto Vazquez, Enriqueta Velarde, Ernesto Weil, Michael Wynne, and Jorge Zavala.

When John Odgen reviewed two chapters, he asked, "What is the percentage of southern Gulf of Mexico coral reefs to the rest of the Gulf?" This was a challenging question, since there was no single source and many opinions. We finally put together a table of data (Table 1) from the acknowledged experts (Pedro Alcolado, Cuba; Billy Causey and Brian Keller, Florida Keys; Bob Halley, Pulley Ridge; Walt Jaap, Florida Middle Grounds; and G. P. Schmahl, Flower Gardens). Thank you, gentlemen.

Lastly, we would like to specifically thank Suzanne Bates for early coordination of the volume style and format, as well as the many figures. Shannon Davies at Texas A&M University Press was always encouraging and helpful with details. Gloria Krause and Jennifer Pearce assisted with manuscript details and editing. Carl Beaver and Jennifer Davidson assisted in the compilation of the species checklist, which is presented on the Internet at www.gulfbase.org. Others who were helpful with specific chapters are Guadalupe Barba, Aurora U. Beltrán-Torres, Susanne Janecke, Marion Nipper, Joel Pederson, and José Luis Tello. Ernesto Chávez holds a fellowship from COFAA-EDI, IPN.

Without permission from the various and numerous agencies in the Mexican government, we could not have performed the research presented over the past thirty-five years. We gratefully acknowledge their permission (primarily SEMARNAT, "Pesca," and "Exterior Relations" and their predecessors).

Coral Reefs of the Southern Gulf of Mexico

# Introduction

JOHN W. TUNNELL JR.

Coral reefs are among the most biologically diverse, productive, and complex ecosystems on earth. They are economically important as sources of food and medicinal products and they protect fragile shorelines from storm damage and erosion. Coral reefs are a source of cultural value and great natural beauty, and they provide vast revenues in tourism dollars. However, since the late 1970s and early 1980s, people around the world have become increasingly concerned about the degradation and loss of this ecologically and economically valuable marine habitat. Coral reefs are being destroyed at an alarming rate in the Gulf of Mexico and throughout the world. The latest report on the status of coral reefs of the world indicates that "coral reefs are probably the most endangered marine ecosystem on Earth" (Wilkinson 2004). According to the Global Coral Reef Monitoring Network (Wilkinson 2004), the world has lost an estimated 20% of coral reefs. It predicts that 24% of the world's reefs are under imminent risk of collapse from human pressures, and another 26% are under a longer-term threat of collapse.

Coral reefs are tropical, shallow-water ecosystems primarily restricted to the low latitudes, between 30°N and 30°S. Globally, they are far more abundant and display greater biodiversity in the Indo-Pacific Region, from eastern Africa and the Red Sea to the central Pacific. Second in worldwide distribution and diversity of coral reefs is the Western Atlantic Tropical Region, including the Caribbean Sea and Gulf of Mexico. Recent evidence indicates a definite, consistent, and long-term decline in the status of Caribbean coral reefs (Wilkinson 2004; Burke and Maidens 2004). The regional decrease in coral cover is alarming, declining 80% in the past 25 years (50% average in coral cover in 1977 to 10% in 2001). Documentation gathered for this book corroborate these numbers for the Gulf of Mexico. Like other coral reef regions of the world, the Gulf of Mexico exhibits a wide range of coral reefs of varying environmental status. Typically, reefs in the Gulf that lie offshore (Fig. 1), away from human populations and development and away from the influence of continental drainage, are in good condition (for example, the Flower Garden Banks in the northwestern Gulf, with about 50% cover, i.e., corals covering 50% of the bottom, and the Campeche Bank reefs in the southeastern Gulf). However, reefs close to mainland population centers and continental drainage reveal moderate to high impacts (for example, the Florida Keys in the eastern Gulf and the reefs off Veracruz in the southwestern Gulf).

Greatest coral reef development in the Gulf of Mexico occurs in the far eastern region, in the Dry Tortugas, Florida Keys, and Cuba, with a lesser amount in the southern Gulf off the state of Veracruz and on the Campeche Bank (Table 1). Approximately 15% of the coral reefs in the Gulf of Mexico lie in the southern region. Of the 46 named coral reefs in the southern Gulf of Mexico, 31 occur

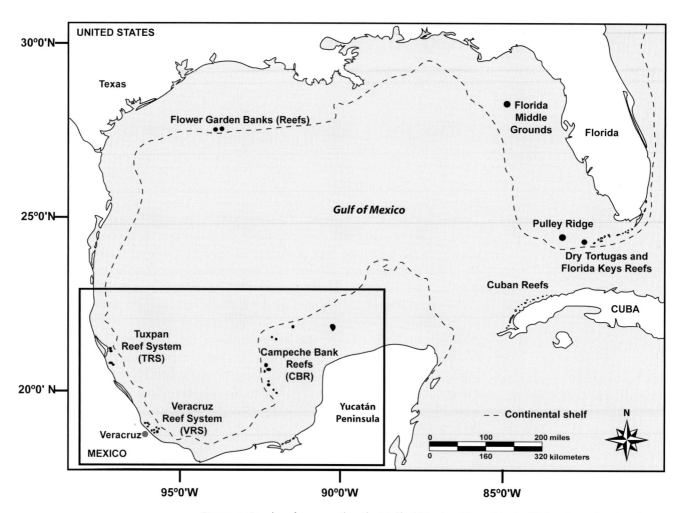

**Figure 1.** Coral reef areas within the Gulf of Mexico. The subject of this volume (enclosed area on map) includes the southern Gulf of Mexico from the Tuxpan Reef System through the Campeche Bank reefs off the northern Yucatán Peninsula.

on the narrow, terrigenous continental shelf in the southwestern quadrant and 15 on the broad, carbonate shelf in the southeast (Rezak and Edwards 1972; Tunnell 1992; Figs. 2.1–2.9, this volume). Although almost all reefs have been studied to some extent, Alacrán Reef on the northern Campeche Bank, and the southern Veracruz reefs, particularly La Blanquilla and Enmedio, have received the most attention.

The purpose of this book is to synthesize, summarize, and chronicle the knowledge on the coral reefs of the southern Gulf of Mexico (extending from Cabo Rojo, Veracruz, through the Yucatán Shelf of northern Yucatán Peninsula). This body of knowledge appears in several languages and spans more than 100 years. The intended audience is scientists, students, natural resource managers, and the environmentally conscious public. An extensive Literature Cited guides interested scientists to the more technical scientific literature. Major topics addressed in this book are the history of research on coral reefs in the southern Gulf of Mexico; their distribution, geologic origin, and development; the climate and oceanography of the reefs; the ecology and zonation of Veracruz and Campeche Bank reefs; major biota of the reefs and their associated islands; natural and anthropogenic impacts on coral reefs; and the conserva-

**Table 1. Extent of coral reef coverage within the Gulf of Mexico.**

| Reef or reef system | Reef coverage (ha) | Percent coverage (%) |
|---|---|---|
| Flower Gardens | 268[a] | 0.1 |
| Southern Gulf of Mexico | 38,483 | 14.6 |
| Tuxpan Reefs | 261[b] | <0.1 |
| Veracruz Reef System (North) | 1,045[b] | <0.4 |
| Veracruz Reef System (South) | 3,617[b] | 1.4 |
| Arcas, Arenas, Nuevo/Obispos, Triángulos | 1,060[b] | <0.4 |
| Alacrán | 32,500[b] | 12.3 |
| Cuba (Havana to Cabo San Antonio, western tip) | 59,000[c] | 22.3 |
| Florida | 166,258 | 63.0 |
| Florida Keys, Dry Tortugas | 125,000[d] | 47.3 |
| Pulley Ridge | 26,936[e] | 10.2 |
| Florida Middle Ground | 14,322[f] | 5.4 |
| Total | 264,009 | 100 |

[a]G. P. Schmahl, Flower Garden Banks National Marine Sanctuary, personal communication.

[b]Calculated from hydrographic charts and Logan (1969a, 1969b), Rezak and Edwards (1972), Carricart-Ganivet and Horta-Puga (1993) and Dahlgren (1993).

[c]Burke and Maidens (2004); Pedro Alcolado, Institute of Oceanology, Havana, Cuba, personal communication.

[d]Spalding et al. (2001).

[e]Bob Halley, U.S. Geological Survey, St. Petersburg, Fla., personal communication.

[f]Walt Jaap, Florida Marine Research Institute, St. Petersburg, Fla., personal communication.

tion and management of reefs. It is also the hope of the authors of this book to raise awareness of the poor condition of the Veracruz reefs and encourage broad involvement and participation by the public, scientists, resource managers, and policy makers in efforts to correct the environmental problems and begin restoration of this once highly productive ecosystem.

**1.** Coral reef ecology class from Texas A&M University–Corpus Christi (TAMU-CC) on field trip to Isla de Lobos, June 1976. **(a)** On board the transport vessel *Gina Letticia II* at dock. **(b)** Camp on Isla de Lobos. **(c)** Diver holding onto propeller of sunken ship on southwestern edge of reef, 20 feet deep. Photographs by J. W. Tunnell.

**2.** Right: Coral reef ecology class from TAMU-CC on field trip, traveling to Isla de Enmedio. **(a)** Crossing the Rio Pánuco at Tampico, June 1985. **(b)** Roadside stop along Rio Tuxpan, June 1984. **(c)** Fixing the boat trailer, June 1988. **(d)** Unloading gear on the beach at Antón Lizardo for five-mile boat trip to Isla de Enmedio, June 1985. Photographs by J. W. Tunnell.

**3.** Coral reef ecology class from TAMU-CC on field trip to Isla de Enmedio. **(a)** Group photograph, June 1978. The lighthouse keeper, Pancho, is standing between the two men with red caps; his wife, Esther, and daughter Carmela are at right. **(b)** Camp during rainy season, June 1990. **(c)** Siesta time, June 1978. **(d)** Too much sun, June 1987. **(e)** Boats on shore, June 1978. **(f)** Returning Pancho's boat, June 1983. Photographs by J. W. Tunnell.

**4.** Coral reef ecology class from TAMU-CC on field trip, during diving operations. **(a)** From boat off Isla de Enmedio, June 1987. **(b)** "Dive locker" tree, June 1987. **(c)** Filling tanks, June 1990. Photographs by J. W. Tunnell.

**5.** Coral reef ecology class from TAMU-CC on field trip, during scientific diving operations. **(a)** Line point-intercept transects, June 1987. **(b)** Quadrat photographs, June 1990. **(c)** Coring for coral history of Veracruz reefs and former climate of the region by Harold Hudson of the Florida Keys National Marine Sanctuary, June 1991. Photographs by J. W. Tunnell.

**6.** Coral reef ecology class from TAMU-CC on field trip, during excursion from Isla de Enmedio to Topatillo Reef and island offshore. **(a)** Resting between dives, June 1983. **(b)** Note shrinking size of island, June 1987. The island disappeared by 2002, probably due to the death of *Acropora palmata* and *A. cervicornis* corals that once surrounded and protected the island. **(c)** Snorkeling off island, June 1983. **(d)** scuba diving in windward canyon, June 1990. Photographs by J. W. Tunnell.

**7.** Lighthouse on Isla de Enmedio. **(a)** March 1965. Photograph by Bart German. **(b)** June 1988. Note the increase in vegetative cover. Photograph by J. W. Tunnell.

**10.** Sustainable Seas Expedition sponsored by the Richard and Rhoda Goldman Fund, in cooperation with the National Geographic Society and the Harte Research Institute for Gulf of Mexico Studies, on the Mexican Navy's oceanographic ship *Antares* to the Veracruz coral reefs. **(a)** *Antares* at anchor east of Anegada de Afuera Reef, September 2002. **(b)** Coral mass spawning at 10 m on leeward side of Santiaguillo Reef, August 29, 2002 (Beaver et al. 2004). Photographs by © Kip Evans, National Geographic Society.

**7.** Lighthouse on Isla de Enmedio. **(a)** March 1965. Photograph by Bart German. **(b)** June 1988. Note the increase in vegetative cover. Photograph by J. W. Tunnell.

8. The Veracruz coral reefs are one of the few places in the world where you can stand on a coral reef and see a snow-capped mountain. **(a)** Isla de Enmedio Lighthouse with Pico de Orizaba in the background between the lighthouse and palm tree at right (June 1984). **(b)** Pico de Orizaba from a closer land view (May 1991). Photographs by J. W. Tunnell.

**9.** Sunrise (**a**, August 1980) and sunset (**b**, June 1989) on Isla de Enmedio. Photographs by J. W. Tunnell.

**10.** Sustainable Seas Expedition sponsored by the Richard and Rhoda Goldman Fund, in cooperation with the National Geographic Society and the Harte Research Institute for Gulf of Mexico Studies, on the Mexican Navy's oceanographic ship *Antares* to the Veracruz coral reefs. **(a)** *Antares* at anchor east of Anegada de Afuera Reef, September 2002. **(b)** Coral mass spawning at 10 m on leeward side of Santiaguillo Reef, August 29, 2002 (Beaver et al. 2004). Photographs by © Kip Evans, National Geographic Society.

**11.** Above: Submersibles used on the Sustainable Seas Expedition on Veracruz coral reefs during August–September 2002: **(a)** *Deep Worker* and **(b)** *Deep Rover*. Photographs by © Kip Evans, National Geographic Society.

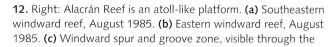

**12.** Right: Alacrán Reef is an atoll-like platform. **(a)** Southeastern windward reef, August 1985. **(b)** Eastern windward reef, August 1985. **(c)** Windward spur and groove zone, visible through the deep blue water in foreground, August 1985. Photographs by David Liddell.

**13.** The Trans-Mexican Neovolcanic Belt reaches the coast near Punta Boca de Loma about 100 km north of Veracruz city, March 1977. **(a)** View to southwest of mountains from the rocky shore. **(b)** Volcanic sandy beach. Photographs by J. W. Tunnell.

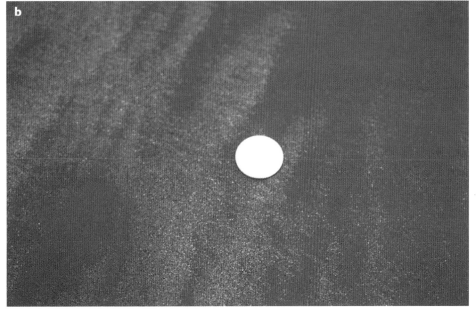

**14.** Volcanic rocky shores to the north (100 km, November 1977) and south (150 km, August 1976) of Veracruz city: **(a)** Punta del Morro and **(b)** Boca Andrea to the north. **(c)** Playa Escondido and **(d)** Montepio, San Andres Tuxtlas Mountains, to the south. Photographs by J. W. Tunnell.

**15.** Offshore oil operations in the Campeche oil fields in the Gulf of Mexico north of Ciudad del Carmen. **(a)** Production platform complex, November 2001. **(b)** Oil terminal northwest of Cayos Arcas, August 1985. Photographs by David Liddell.

**16.** Leeward slope of selected Veracruz Shelf reefs. **(a)** Spur and groove zone on upper slope of Santiaguilla Reef, June 1987. **(b)** Large "field" of massive coral heads (*Montastraea annularis*) at Santiaguilla Reef, June 1987. **(c)** Large "field" of massive coral heads (*M. annularis*) at Isla de Lobos Reef, June 1977. Photographs by J. W. Tunnell.

**17.** Satellite image of the Tuxpan Reef System, which extends along the coastline of northern Veracruz state. Cabo Rojo is the point of land in the upper part of the image, with Laguna de Tamiahua to the left and Blanquilla, Medio, and Isla de Lobos reefs offshore, north to south, respectively, in the Gulf of Mexico. The city of Tuxpan and Rio Tuxpan appear at the bottom of the image, with Tanguijo, Enmedio, and Tuxpan reefs offshore. Image courtesy of NASA Visible Earth.

**18.** Satellite image of the Veracruz Reef System in the Gulf of Mexico off Veracruz city (upper left) and Punta Antón Lizardo (center). Image courtesy of NASA Visible Earth.

**19.** Outer reefs in the northern group of the Veracruz Reef System off the city of Veracruz, August 2002. **(a)** View to the northwest over Anegada de Adentro Reef (note old shipwreck to the right). **(b)** View to the northwest over La Blanquilla Reef. **(c)** View to the north over Isla Verde Reef and island. Photographs by © Kip Evans, National Geographic Society.

**20.** Inner reefs in the northern group of the Veracruz Reef System off the city of Veracruz, August 2002. **(a)** View to the southwest over Pájaros Reef toward Isla Sacrificios and Veracruz city. **(b)** View toward the southwest over the leeward side of Pájaros Reef toward Isla Sacrificio and Veracruz city. **(c)** View of the leeward (western) side of Isla Sacrificios. Photographs by © Kip Evans, National Geographic Society.

**21.** Northernmost reefs in the northern group of the Veracruz Reef System located off the Port of Veracruz, August 2002. **(a)** View over Galleguillo Reef toward the southwest and the port. **(b)** View to the northwest over the port's earthen landfill on top of Gallega Reef. Photographs by © Kip Evans, National Geographic Society.

**22.** Outer reefs in the southern group of the Veracruz Reef System, off the fishing village of Antón Lizardo, August 2002. **(a)** View to the northeast over Anegada de Afuera Reef. **(b)** View to the west over the southern end of Anegada de Afuera Reef.

**(c)** View to the northwest over the reef platform of Anegada de Afuera Reef. Note the "blue hole" in the reef flat at bottom right. **(d)** View of Santiaguillo Reef to the north. Photographs by © Kip Evans, National Geographic Society.

**23.** Chopas Reef, the largest and southernmost in the Veracruz Reef System, August 2002. **(a)** View to the northwest, along the windward forereef over the southern end of the reef. **(b)** View to the north, over the northwestern leeward reef. Photographs by © Kip Evans, National Geographic Society.

**24.** Isla de Enmedio Reef platform and island, the most studied reef in the Veracruz Reef System. **(a)** View to the northeast, over the leeward side of the island, August 2002. Photograph by © Kip Evans, National Geographic Society. **(b)** View to the northwest over the island, August 2002. Photograph by J. W. Tunnell). **(c)** Photograph of a postcard (circa 1965–70) in similar location to that shown in (b). Note the large size of the island in the postcard and the eroded southern end of the island in both (a) and (b).

ISLA DE ENMEDIO, VER.

**25.** Isla de Lobos Reef. **(a)** View from the southwest. Photograph by Juan Manuel Vargas-Hernández. **(b)** View to the northeast from the lighthouse, June 1976. Photograph by J. W. Tunnell.

**26.** Right: Elkhorn coral (*Acropora palmata*) on the upper windward forereef of Topatillo Reef. **(a)** Living coral, June 1984. **(b)** Dead coral, covered with turf algae, June 1985. Photographs by J. W. Tunnell.

**27.** Windward forereef slope at Cabezo Reef, June 1987. **(a)** Massive coral heads of *Montastraea annularis* at mid-reef depths. **(b)** "Shingle shaped" (flat plate) corals in the deepest reef zones. This is the same species, just a different, flattened, growth form, due to the low light levels. Photographs by J. W. Tunnell.

**28.** Sea lilies (or sea feathers) (*Davidaster rubiginosa*), characteristic of the deepest reef zones among *Montastrea cavernosa*, June 1977. Photograph by J. W. Tunnell.

**29. (a)** Reef flat of Isla de Enmedio Reef, with abundant sea urchins (*Echinometra lucunter*) throughout, and knobby brain coral (*Diploria clivosa*) in the middle ground, June 1989. **(b)** "*Diploria* pavement" (Rigby and McIntire 1966) on Isla de Lobos Reef at the north point of the platform, *Diploria clivosa* and *Acropora prolifera* (branched form), June 1973. Photographs by J. W. Tunnell.

**30. (a)** Seagrass meadows of turtle grass (*Thalassia testudinum*) in the reef lagoon of Isla de Lobos Reef. Knobby brain coral (*Diploria clivosa*) in the middle ground, with coarse coral rubble and algal nodule substrate, June 1977. **(b)** Pure, dense turtle grass in soft substrate area, Isla de Lobos, June 1977. **(c)** Aerial view of Isla de Enmedio lagoon seagrass beds (dark areas) and "zone of the patches" (mixed seagrass, coral rock, and sandy bottom; Gutiérrez et al. 1993), September 2002. Photographs by J. W. Tunnell.

**31.** "Gorgonian garden" of soft corals on the upper leeward patch reef west of Isla de Enmedio, June 1989. **(a)** Close-up view. **(b)** Distant view, showing great density. Photographs by J. W. Tunnell.

**32.** Staghorn coral (*Acropora cervicornis*) "cemetery" on the upper leeward slope of Topatillo Reef. **(a)** Dead branches covered with encrusting red coralline algae, June 1983. **(b)** Dead branches covered with coralline red algae and filamentous algae in the foreground and some new staghorn coral recruits in the background, June 1985. **(c)** Dead branches covered mainly with filamentous algae and fleshy brown algae (*Dictyota* sp.), June 1993. Photographs by J. W. Tunnell.

**33.** Staghorn coral (*Acropora cervicornis*) on the upper slope of Topatillo Reef, June 1978. **(a)** Distant view in the shallows. **(b)** Close-up view. **(c)** Distant view at mid-slope, June 1983. Photographs by J. W. Tunnell.

**34.** Unique structural features of selected reefs of the Veracruz Reef System. **(a)** Reef cut at the Isla de Enmedio northeastern reef platform (reef flat), September 2002. **(b)** "Blue hole" on the south- eastern reef platform (reef flat) of Isla de Enmedio Reef, September 2002. **(c)** Coral pillar on the windward reef slope of Anegada de Afuera Reef, September 2002. Photographs by J. W. Tunnell.

# 1    Research History

JOHN W. TUNNELL JR.

The first scientific account of coral reefs in the southern Gulf of Mexico was made by an expedition of scientists from the Academy of Natural Sciences of Philadelphia (now Philadelphia Academy of Sciences) in the early months of 1890. Expedition leader and academy director Professor Angelo Heilprin described the purpose of the expedition as "to investigate the natural history of the Yucatán Peninsula and Mexico." Publications resulting from the expedition related for the first time the tropical nature of marine biota of the southern Gulf of Mexico (corals and coral reefs, Heilprin 1890; echinoderms, Ives 1890; mollusks, Baker 1891; crustaceans, Ives 1891).

Professor Heilprin (1890) suggested that other scientists had not previously searched the area for coral reefs for two reasons. First, Darwin's classical work (1842) on the structure and distribution of coral reefs failed to mention reefs in the southern Gulf of Mexico. Second, scientists had feared contracting yellow fever in the Gulf. Heilprin discusses seven of the reefs and islands off the city of Veracruz, mentions 12 species of corals and 1 gorgonian, notes the "vast quantity of coral" used in construction (piers, seawall, and ancient houses), and includes figures of two old maps showing the reefs, dated 1806 and 1885 (Figs. 1.1 and 1.2). The magnificent old 16th-century castle, Fort San Juan de Ulúa, also made of coral, sits on the western (leeward) side of Gallega Reef, a nearshore reef now attached to the mainland by a land bridge (earthen fill). Ganivet (1998) listed six species of massive scleractinian corals used to construct the Fort San Juan de Ulúa: *Siderastrea radians*, *Porites astreoides*, *Diploria* spp., *Colpophyllia natans*, *Montastraea annularis*, and *M. cavernosa*.

In the southeastern Gulf of Mexico, the first biological accounts were of nesting seabirds on the islands of Alacrán and on Triángulos reef by the early English adventurer William Dampier (1699), who first visited the area in 1675. More than a century passed before others mentioned the vegetation, seabirds, sea turtles, and West Indian monk seal associated with these and other Campeche Bank islands (Smith 1838; Marion 1884; Ward 1887; Agassiz 1888).

In 1912, Joubin published a map of coral reefs that included the Gulf of Mexico (Fig. 1.3), but not until the 1950s was further research conducted on reefs in the southern Gulf. Smith (1954) utilized Joubin's (1912) map, Heilprin's (1890) work, and other unpublished sources and nautical charts (Table 1.1) to prepare an updated coral reef distribution map and list of coral species. Blanquilla Reef, the most northerly emergent reef in the western Gulf of Mexico, was briefly visited in 1955 by Donald R. Moore (1958). He described some of the invertebrate fauna of the reef, listing 44 species, including 11 stony corals, 3 gorgonian corals, 17 gastropods, 7 bivalves, 3 echinoids, 1 asteroid, and 1 holothuroid.

In a much larger and collaborative effort, Kornicker et al. (1959) studied Alacrán Reef, the most northerly reef on the Campeche Bank, which is just north

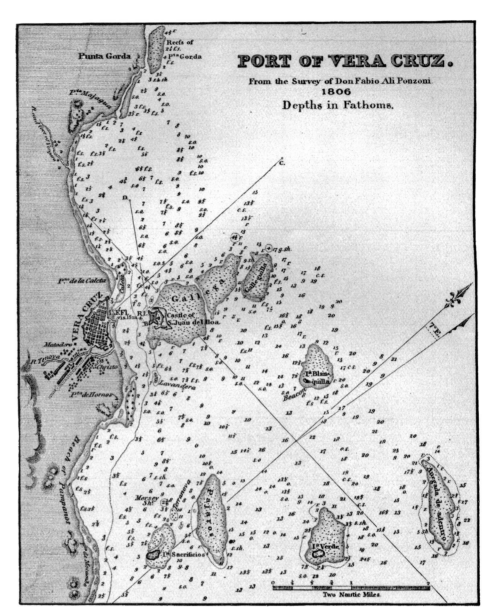

**Figure 1.1.** Historic navigation chart (1806) of the port city of Veracruz, Mexico (from Heilprin 1890).

of the Yucatán Peninsula. With funding primarily from the National Science Foundation, scientists from a number of different institutions participated in a productive expedition that quickly made Alacrán Reef one of the best-known Gulf reefs. The main focus of the expedition was the geology of Alacrán Reef, but a number of biological studies were published also, including descriptions of algae, island vegetation, foraminiferans, mollusks, fish, and birds (Tables 1.2 and 1.3).

In 1956, Emery (1963) sampled sediments offshore from the city of Veracruz and compared those reefs to reefs he had studied in the Pacific. His work was published in both English and Spanish in an international journal, raising the level of scientific interest in this unique geographic and geologic setting for coral reefs.

During the 1960s, interest and research on southern Gulf of Mexico coral reefs expanded to reefs throughout the Gulf. Researchers conducted field studies of coral reef systems during extended expeditions to remote locations. In their

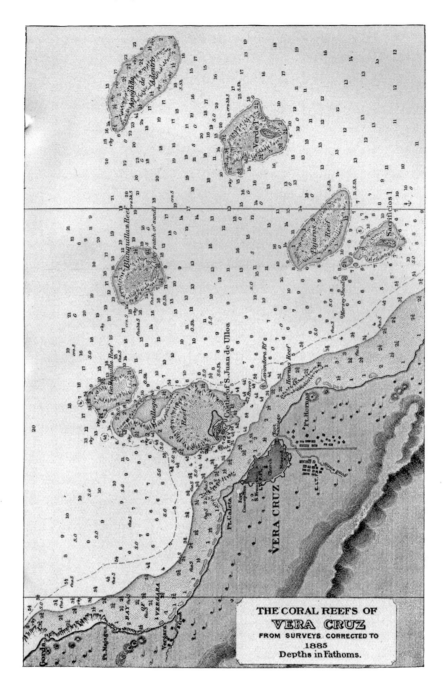

**Figure 1.2.** Historic map (1885) of the coral reefs of Veracruz, Mexico (from Heilprin 1890).

studies of the northern reefs of Veracruz state, Huerta M. and Barrientos (1965) reported on the marine benthic algae of Blanquilla and Isla de Lobos reefs, and Rigby and McIntire (1966) presented the first detailed information on the geology and ecology of Isla de Lobos Reef. Chamberlain (1966) recorded gorgonians from Lobos during the same expedition (Brigham Young University with Rigby and McIntire) and spent six weeks in the field studying Isla de Lobos Reef while staying on Lobos Island. Hidalgo (Hidalgo and Chávez 1967) and Chávez (Chávez et al. 1970; Chávez 1973; Bautista-Gil and Chávez 1977) both studied Isla de Lobos Reef during multiple expeditions with students from the Instituto Politécnico Nacional in Mexico City.

In the southwestern Gulf offshore from the city of Veracruz in southern Veracruz state, a number of students from the Universidad Nacional Autónoma de

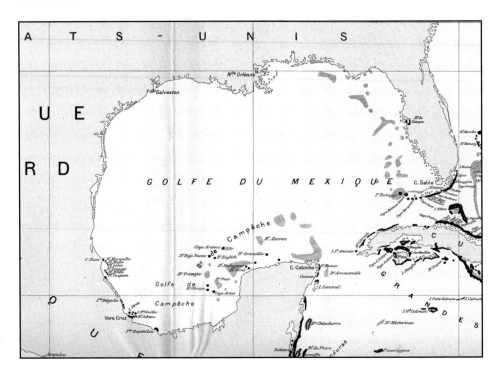

**Figure 1.3.** Historic map (early 20th century) of coral reef distribution in the Gulf of Mexico (from Joubin 1912).

Mexico conducted their "professional thesis" (a significant project produced by students in Mexican universities at the end of a bachelor of science degree). Primarily under the direction of Dr. Alejandro Villalobos, these projects on various topics within the Veracruz reef system were subsequently published: marine flora, sponges, pteropods, copepods, *Gecarcinus lateralis,* chaetognaths, appendicularians, plankton, hydrology, and meteorology (Tables 1.2 and 1.3). Villalobos summarized much of this work in the proceedings of an international symposium on investigations and resources of the Caribbean Sea and adjacent regions (1971) and in a subsequent journal review article (1980). Two other contributions to the knowledge of southern Veracruz reefs were studies of algae (Huerta M. 1960) and foraminiferans (Lidz and Lidz 1966).

During the 1960s, three geologic studies were conducted on the southern Veracruz reefs: Morelock and Koenig (1967), Edwards (1969), and Freeland (1971). All three focused on the unique environmental setting of terrigenous sediments surrounding shallow-water coral reefs.

On the Campeche Bank or Yucatán Shelf in the southeastern Gulf, a major, multi-year study by the Department of Oceanography at Texas A&M University contributed greatly to the knowledge of carbonate sediments (Logan et al. 1969a, 1969b) and all coral reefs of the region (Logan 1962; Logan et al. 1969a, 1969b). This project, which was collaboratively funded by the National Science Foundation, the American Petroleum Institute, the Office of Naval Research, Shell Development Company, and Mobil Oil Company, extended from 1959 to 1963 and was the longest and most productive reef study in the southern Gulf to that date. It was an extension and expansion of the Kornicker et al. (1959) Alacrán Reef studies mentioned earlier. In addition, as a side project, one of the other Campeche Bank reefs, Cayo Arenas, was studied in more detail (Busby 1966). Fishes of Triángulos and Cayo Arenas reefs were first reported in the 1960s (H. Chávez 1966).

From the 1970s through the 1990s, three institutions were primarily responsible for the research, reports, thesis and dissertation projects, and publications

**Table 1.1.** *Nautical charts of emergent coral reefs in the southern Gulf of Mexico.*

| Chart no. | Chart name (Scale) | Charting agency* | Reefs charted (north to south) |
|---|---|---|---|
| No. 411 | Gulf of Mexico (1:2,160,000) | NOAA | All |
| N.O. 28030 | Tampico to Progresso (1:1,023,400) | USN | All, southern Gulf |
| N.O. 28320 | Tampico to Punta del Morro (1:250,000) | USN | Blanquilla, Medio, Isla de Lobos, Tanguijo, Enmedio, Tuxpan |
| N.O. 28321 (H.O. 1577) | Plans on the East Coast of Mexico Inset: Isla de Lobos (1:20,000) | USN | Isla de Lobos |
| N.O. 28301 | Punta del Morro to Puerto de Alvarado (1:100,000) | USN | Galleguilla, La Gallega, La Blanquilla, Anegada de Adentro, Verde, Pájaros, Sacrificios, Anegada de Afuera, Topatillo, Santiaguillo, Anegadilla, Enmedio, Chopas, Blanca, Cabezo, Rizo |
| N.O. 28302 (H.O. 2760) | Veracruz Harbor and Approaches (1:18,000) | USN | Galleguilla, La Gallega, La Blanquilla, Anegada de Adentro, |
| S.M. 823 | Veracruz y Proximidades (1:25,000) | MN | Verde, Pájaros, Sacrificios |
| N.O. 28303 | Port of Veracruz (1:6,250) | USN | La Gallega, Pájaros, Hornos, |
| S.M. 824 | Portulano de Veracruz (1:7,500) | MN | Sacrificios |
| S.M. 825 | Fondeadero Anton Lizardo (1:25,000) | MN | Anegada de Afuera, Topatillo, Santiaguillo, Anegadilla, Enmedio, Chopas, Blanca, Cabezo, Rizo |
| H.O. 1233 | Plans de Banco Campeche Insets: Cayos Arcas (1:18,156) Alacrán Reef (1:145,141) Cayo Arenas (1:24,321) Triángulos (1:36,481) | USN | Cayos Arcas (Centro, Este, Oeste) Alacrán Cayo Arenas Triángulos (Este, Sur) |

* USN = U.S. Navy; MN = Mexican Navy; NOAA = National Oceanic and Atmospheric Administration.

on southern Gulf of Mexico coral reefs: Secretaría de Marina, Dirección General de Oceanografía; Texas A&M University–Corpus Christi (formerly Corpus Christi State University); and the Universidad Nacional Autónoma de México. In addition, in the late 1980s and 1990s, two institutions, Universidad Veracruzana in Jalapa and Centro de Investigación y Estudios Avanzados (CINVESTAV)–Unidad Mérida of the Instituto Politécnico Nacional, began research on the Veracruz reefs and Alacrán Reef, respectively. Most research during this timeframe focused on southwestern Gulf reefs.

The northern Veracruz reefs, due to their remoteness, are the least studied in the southwestern Gulf region. Of the six northern reefs, Isla de Lobos received the most attention in the form of studies of polychaetes, mollusks, crabs, and fish (Tables 1.2 and 1.3).

In the extreme southwestern Gulf, more than 20 coral reefs lie in two separate but adjacent groups, one offshore from the city of Veracruz and one offshore from the fishing village of Antón Lizardo. Because both these reef groups are more easily accessible than the northern Veracruz reefs, they have received much

**Table 1.2.** *Principal literature on coral reefs/islands of the southern Gulf of Mexico, listed by reef/island counterclockwise from Alacrán in east to Blanquilla in west.*

| Reef/island location | Publication (Topic) |
|---|---|
| Alacrán | Marion 1884 (island vegetation), Millspaugh 1916 (island vegetation), Kornicker et al. 1959 (geology and biology), Múzquiz 1961 (algae), Fosberg 1961, 1962 (island seabirds and vegetation), Bonet and Rzedowski 1962 (island vegetation), Kornicker and Boyd 1962a, 1962b (geology), Folk 1962 (island sediments), Rice and Kornicker 1962 (mollusks), Hoskin 1963, 1966, 1968 (geology), Davis 1964 (foraminiferans), Folk and Robles 1964 (island sediments), Hildebrand et al. 1964 (fish), Bonet 1967 (geology), Folk 1967 (island seabirds, vegetation, sediments), Folk and Cotera 1971 (island sediments), Macintyre et al. 1977 (geology), Boswall 1978 (sea birds), Tunnell and Chapman 1988, 2001 (seabirds), Solís 1990 (benthic communities), Bosscher and Schlager 1992 (reef growth model), Martínez-Guzmán and Hernández-Aguilera 1993 (stomatopods and decapods), Torruco et al. 1993 (spatial distribution), González-Gándara et al. 1999 (fish), González-Gándara and Arias-González 2001a, 2001b (fish), Liceaga-Correa and Euan-Avila 2002 (bathymetric mapping), Aranda et al. 2003 (gastropods), Brulé et al. 2003 (grouper), González-Gándara et al. 2003 (fish) |
| Cayo Arenas | Busby 1966 (geology) |
| Triángulos and Cayo Arenas | H. Chávez 1966 (fish), Carricart-Ganivet and Beltrán-Torres 1993 (coral), Hernández 1997 (sponges) |
| Cayos Arcas | Farrell et al. 1983 (coral diversity and zonation), Salas de León et al. 1992 (meteorology) |
| Enmedio | Rannefeld 1972 (stony corals), Tunnell 1974, 1977 (mollusks), Huerta M. et al. 1977 (algae), Rickner 1975, 1977 (crabs), Tunnell and Dokken 1979 (Ixtoc 1 oil impacts), Baca et al. 1982 (Ixtoc 1 oil impacts to seagrasses), Allen 1982 (crabs), Henkel 1982 (echinoderms), White 1982 (shrimps), Lubel 1984 (ciliates), Stinnett 1989 (sponges), T. J. Nelson 1991 (coral zonation), Lehman and Tunnell 1992b (algae), Riley and Holt 1993 (fish), Choucair 1992 (fish), Lehman 1993 (algae) |
| Isla Verde | Morales-García 1986 (stomatopods and decapods), Horta-Puga and Ramírez-Palacios 1996 (lead pollution), Mateo-Cid et al. 1996 (algae) |
| Sacrificios | Morales-García 1987 (stomatopods and decapods) |
| La Blanquilla | Rodríguez and Fuentes 1965 (hydrography), Reséndez-Medina 1971 (fish), Villalobos 1971 (ecology), Green 1977 (sponges), Santiago 1977 (coral ecology), Horta-Puga and Carricart-Ganivet 1989 (bleaching) |
| Isla de Lobos | Huerta M. and Barrientos 1965 (algae), Chamberlain 1966 (gorgonians), Rigby and McIntire 1966 (geology and ecology), Chávez et al. 1970 (benthic communities), Ray 1974 (crustaceans), Tunnell 1974, 1977 (mollusks), Márquez-Espinoza 1976 (fish), Bautista-Gil and Chávez 1977 (foraminiferans), Roberts 1981 (polychaetes), Allen 1982 (crabs) |
| Blanquilla | Moore 1958, Huerta M. and Barrientos 1965 (algae) |

more study, and therefore, more information about them is available. Though most studies focused on individual reefs, some cover multiple reefs or the entire reef complex. Perhaps the most studied of all reefs in this region is Enmedio Reef. Gutiérrez et al. (1993) compared the coral reefs of the Veracruz region to those within the Sian Ka'an Biosphere Reserve of Quintana Roo along the Mexican Caribbean. For this book, we have categorized and listed the extensive studies in this region by reef (Table 1.2) and by topic (Table 1.3).

The oceanographic program within the Mexican Navy (Instituto de Investigación Oceanográfica del Golfo y Mar Caribe) has contributed significant infor-

**Table 1.3.** *Principal literature on coral reefs of the southern Gulf of Mexico, listed by subject area.*

| Subject area/topic | Publication (Location) |
| --- | --- |
| Mexican coral reefs | Smith 1954, Rezak and Edwards 1972, Ferré-D'Amaré 1985, Chávez and Hidalgo 1988, Tunnell 1988, Wells 1988, Dahlgren 1989, 1993, Carricart-Ganivet and Horta-Puga 1993, Lang et al. 1998, Jordán-Dahlgren 2002; Jordán-Dahlgren and Rodríguez-Martínez 2003, Jordán-Dahlgren 2004 |
| Veracruz coral reefs (Southwestern Gulf) | Heilprin 1890, Moore 1958 (Blanquilla), Emery 1963, Rigby and McIntire 1966 (Isla de Lobos), Morelock and Koenig 1967, Chávez et al. 1970 (Isla de Lobos), Villalobos 1971, Rannefeld 1972 (Enmedio), Kühlmann 1975, Chávez and Hidalgo 1988, Tunnell 1988, Montes 1991, T. J. Nelson 1991 (Enmedio and Cabezo), Jordán-Dahlgren 1992, Lara et al. 1992, Vargas-Hernández et al. 1993, 2002, Ricono 1999, Horta-Puga 2003 |
| Campeche Bank/Yucatán coral reefs (Southeastern Gulf) | Kornicker et al. 1959 (Alacrán), Logan 1969a, 1969b, Logan et al. 1969, Farrell et al. 1983 (Cayos Arcas), Chávez et al. 1985, Dahlgren 1993, Chávez 1997, Blanchon and Perry 2004 |
| Geology | Kornicker and Boyd 1962a, 1962b (Alacrán), Emery 1963 (Veracruz), Hoskin 1963 (Alacrán), Busby 1966 (Arenas), Hoskin 1966 (Alacrán), Bonet 1967 (Alacrán), Morelock and Koenig 1967 (Veracruz), Hoskin 1968 (Alacrán), Edwards 1969 (Veracruz), Logan 1969a, 1969b (Campeche Bank), Freeland 1971 (Veracruz), Macintyre et al. 1977 (Alacrán), Bosscher and Schlager 1992 (Alacrán), Novak et al. 1992 (Alacrán), Blanchon and Perry 2004 |
| Meteorology | Salas de León et al. 1992 (Arcas) |
| Islands—seabirds | Kennedy 1917, Fosberg 1961, 1962 (Alacrán), Folk 1967 (Alacrán), Boswall 1978 (Alacrán), Tunnell and Chapman 1988 (Alacrán), Howell 1989, Tunnell and Chapman 2001 (Campeche Bank) |
| Islands—vegetation | Marion 1884 (Alacrán), Millspaugh 1916 (Alacrán), Fosberg 1961, 1962 (Alacrán), Bonet and Rzedowski 1962 (Alacrán), Folk 1967 (Alacrán), Flores (1984), Tunnell and Chapman 2001 |
| Islands—sediments | Fosberg 1961, 1962 (Alacrán), Folk 1962, 1967 (Alacrán), Folk and Robles 1964 (Alacrán), Folk and Cotera 1971 (Alacrán) |
| Plankton | Coto 1965 (Veracruz), D. Rodriguez 1965 (Veracruz), Súarez-Caabro 1965 (Veracruz) |
| Algae | Huerta M. 1960 (Veracruz), Múzquiz 1961 (Alacrán), Huerta M. and Barrientos 1965 (Blanquilla and Isla de Lobos), De la Campa 1965, Huerta M. et al. 1977 (Enmedio), Lehman and Tunnell 1992b (Enmedio), Huerta-Múzquiz et al. 1987 (Campeche Bank), Lehman 1993 (Enmedio), Mateo-Cid et al. 1996 (Verde) |
| Seagrasses | Lot-Helgueras 1971 (Veracruz) |
| Foraminiferans/protozoans | Davis 1964 (Alacrán), Lidz and Lidz 1966 (Veracruz), Bautista-Gil and Chávez 1977 (Lobos), Lubel 1984 (Enmedio) |
| Sponges | Green 1977 (La Banquilla), Stinnett 1989 (Enmedio) |
| Polychaetes | Roberts 1981 (Lobos), Granados-Barba et al. 2003 |
| Corals | Tunnell 1988, Montes 1991 (Veracruz), Jordán-Dahlgren 1992 (Veracruz), Beltrán-Torres and Carricart-Ganivet 1993 (Isla Verde), Carricart-Ganivet 1993 (Isla Verde), Horta-Puga and Carricart-Ganivet 1985, 1993, Carricart-Ganivet 1994, Carricart-Ganivet and Beltrán-Torres 1994, 1997, Beltrán-Torres and Carricart-Ganivet 1999, Vargas-Hernández and Román-Vives 2002, Cruz-Piñon et al. 2003, Horta-Puga 2003, Carricart-Ganivet 2004 |
| Gorgonians | Chamberlain 1966 (Isla de Lobos), Nelson et al. 1988 (Veracruz), Tunnell and Nelson 1989 (Veracruz), Dahlgren 1993, Jordán-Dahlgren 2002 |

(*continued*)

**Table 1.3.** *(continued)*

| Subject area/topic | Publication (Location) |
| --- | --- |
| Mollusks | Baker 1891 (Veracruz), Rice and Kornicker 1962, 1965 (Alacrán), Tunnell 1974, 1977 (Lobos and Enmedio), Sevilla et al. 1983 (Lobos), Gónzalez-Solís et al. 1991 (Campeche Bank reefs), Aranda et al. 2003 (Alacrán) |
| Crustaceans | Ives 1891 (Veracruz), Aguayo 1965 (Veracruz), Cabrera 1965 (Veracruz), Krutak 1974 (Veracruz), Ray 1974 (Isla de Lobos), Rickner 1975, 1977 (Veracruz), Rickles 1977 (Veracruz), Krutak and Rickles 1979 (Veracruz), Allen 1979, 1982 (Lobos and Enmedio), White 1982 (Enmedio), Martínez-Guzmán and Hernández-Aguilera 1993 (Alacrán) |
| Chaetognaths | Rodriguez 1965 (Veracruz) |
| Echinoderms | Ives 1890 (Veracruz), Henkel 1982 (Enmedio) |
| Fish | Hildebrand et al. 1964 (Alacrán), H. Chávez 1966 (Triángulos), Reséndez-Medina 1971 (La Blanquilla), Márquez-Espinoza 1976 (Isla de Lobos), Castro-Aguirre and Márquez-Espinoza 1981 (Isla de Lobos), Garduño-Andrade 1988 (Campeche Bank reefs), Choucair 1992 (Enmedio), Riley and Holt 1993 (Enmedio), González-Gándara et al. 1999 (Alacrán), Garduño and Chávez 2000 (Campeche Bank reefs), González-Gándara 2001 (Alacrán), González-Gándara and Arias-González 2001a, 2001b (Alacrán), Brulé et al. 2003 (Alacrán), Vargas-Hernández et al. 2003 (Veracruz) |
| Fisheries | Chávez 1994 (Yucatán), Vargas-Hernández et al. 2003 (Veracruz) |
| Benthic communities | Chávez et al. 1970 (Isla de Lobos), Solís 1990 (Alacrán), Quintana y Molina 1991 (Veracruz), Torruco et al. 1993 (Alacrán) |
| Environmental impacts | Tunnell and Dokken 1979 (Enmedio), Baca et al. 1982 (Enmedio), Jernelov and Linden 1981, Villalobos-Figueroa 1981, Chávez and Hidalgo 1988, 1989, Tunnell 1992, Chávez and Tunnell 1993, Vargas-Hernández et al. 1993 (Veracruz), Horta-Puga and Ramírez-Palacios 1996 (Verde), Ganivet 1998 (Veracruz), Carricart-Ganivet and Merino 2001 (southern Gulf of Mexico) |
| Management and conservation | Chávez and Tunnell 1993 |
| Status | Lang et al. 1998, Horta-Puga 2003 (Veracruz), Jordán-Dahlgren 2004 |

mation on the Veracruz Reef System, as well as on reef biology, over the past 25 years. This program first operated from a small station (Estación Oceanográfica) in the city of Veracruz but is now housed within a new institute building just south of the Mexican Naval Academy at Antón Lizardo.

In the southeastern Gulf on the Campeche Bank, great distance from shore continued to limit the number of reef studies. Apparently, only one paper was published on these reefs during the 1970s: a report on the thickest recorded Holocene reef section, located on Alacrán Reef (Macintyre et al. 1977). During the 1980s, researchers characterized coral diversity and zonation on Cayo Arenas Reef, reviewed all Mexican Atlantic coral reefs, presented environmental problems and human impacts on southern Gulf and Caribbean coral reefs, and published the distribution of the fish fauna associated with all Campeche Bank reefs (Tables 1.2 and 1.3).

During the 1990s, studies continued on both Campeche Bank and the Veracruz Reef System. Organismal and biological studies covered algae, sponge-associated fauna, corals, mollusks, stomatopods, decapods, and fish. Ecological studies covered benthic communities, zonation and community structure, eco-system connectivity, and marine resources. Other studies focused on reef sediments and a computer simulation model of reef growth (Tables 1.2 and 1.3).

Most recently, a number of fish studies have appeared, especially on Alacrán Reef from the laboratory of Ernesto Arias-González at CINVESTAV in Mérida. Some biological studies include several on *Montastraea annularis* growth rates, gorgonian diversity and connectivity, polychaetes, mollusks, and nesting seabirds associated with Campeche Bank reef islands. Other recent studies have been on geologic facies through time on Campeche Bank reefs and the utilization of Landsat Thematic Mapper data for mapping coral reef bathymetry (Tables 1.2 and 1.3).

Jordán-Dahlgren and Rodríguez-Martínez (2003) provide one of the latest summaries of all Mexican coral reefs within the Gulf of Mexico and Caribbean in the excellent book on all Latin American coral reefs (Cortés 2003). Most recently, Jordán-Dahlgren (2004) provided a brief environmental diagnosis or status report on southern Gulf reefs. Overall, the reefs in the extreme southern Gulf that lie off the city of Veracruz and village of Antón Lizardo have been most impacted and those on the Campeche Bank least impacted. The reefs near Tuxpan in northern Veracruz are intermediate. Chapters 5, 6, 12, and 13 provide further details.

# 2 Reef Distribution

JOHN W. TUNNELL JR.

There are 46 named coral reefs in the southern Gulf of Mexico. Of these, 31 are the Veracruz Shelf reefs (VSR) in the southwestern Gulf off the state of Veracruz, and 15 are the Campeche Bank reefs (CBR) in the southeastern Gulf (Table 2.1, Fig. 2.1). Other named and unnamed shoals and banks have yet to be explored; these likely have coral communities as well. Dahlgren (1993), for instance, lists approximately 10 named and more than 25 unnamed banks (topographic highs and reefs) on the Campeche Bank for which there is little or no scientific information.

Coral reefs in the southwestern Gulf are typically located nearshore (<200 m) to mid-shelf (22 km) on a narrow terrigenous continental shelf (Morelock and Koenig 1967). The climate here is subhumid to humid and has high rainfall and substantial mainland drainage. In the southeastern Gulf, reefs are located on a wide carbonate shelf, primarily along the 55 m contour on the outer shelf, and range from 130 to more than 200 km offshore (Tunnell 1992). In contrast to the southwestern Gulf, the climate here is semiarid. The southeastern Gulf reefs are surrounded by oceanic Caribbean waters from the Yucatán Channel and are not affected by mainland drainage. The southern Gulf reefs are submerged "mountain-like" structures scattered across the continental shelf, in contrast to the scattered patch reefs in nearby low-energy coastal areas such as the Florida Keys and Belize, where mangroves line the shoreline and seagrasses predominate as submarine vegetation nearshore. Mainland shorelines are moderate-energy sandy beaches or rocky shores (volcanic) in the southwestern Gulf and low-energy sandy beaches or rocky shores (limestone) in the southeastern Gulf.

The southwestern Gulf coral reefs are clustered in two systems, each within two subgroups: the Tuxpan Reef System (TRS) and Veracruz Reef System (VRS). To the north there are six emergent platform reefs in the TRS, three of which are grouped off Cabo Rojo and three northeast of Tuxpan (Fig. 2.2). Isla de Lobos Reef is the only one in the TRS that has an island, and consequently is the best known because the island has served as an adequate base camp for extended expeditions (e.g., Rigby and McIntire 1966; Chávez et al. 1970; Ray 1974; Tunnell 1974; Roberts 1981; Allen 1982). Blanquilla Reef is the most northerly emergent coral reef in the western Gulf of Mexico (Moore 1958).

The VRS in the far southwestern Gulf of Mexico comprises 25 coral reefs in two subgroups, one consisting of smaller reefs nearshore and one with mostly larger reefs extending farther offshore (Fig. 2.3). The first, or northern, group of 13 reefs lies offshore from the city of Veracruz (Fig. 2.4) and is composed of eight emergent platform reefs (Gallequilla, Anegada de Adentro, La Blanquilla, La Gallega, Pájaros, Isla Verde, Tierra Nueva, and Isla Sacrificios), two submerged bank reefs (or submerged patch reefs Bajo Mersey and Lavandera), and three fringing reefs (Punta Gorda–Punta Majahua, Hornos, and Punta Mocambo).

**Table 2.1.** *Data on southern Gulf of Mexico coral reefs.*

| Reef name | Reef type[1] | Size[2] | | Distance[3] to mainland (km) | Islands[4] | Geographic position[5] | | Depth[6] (m) |
|---|---|---|---|---|---|---|---|---|
| | | Length (m) | Width (m) | | | Latitude | Longitude | |
| *Tuxpan Reef System (southwestern Gulf)* | | | | | | | | |
| Blanquilla | EP | 739 | 500 | 5 | 0 | 21°30'14" | 97°10'39" | 0–45 |
| Medio | EP | <500 | – | 8 | 0 | 21°30'02" | 97°10'30" | 0–45 |
| Isla de Lobos | EP | 1,950 | 1,100 | 11 | 1 | 21°20'18" | 97°10'21" | 0–45 |
| Tanguijo | EP | <500 | – | 9 | 0 | 21°00'41" | 97°10'44" | 0–24 |
| Enmedio | EP | <500 | – | 9 | 0 | 21°00'27" | 97°10'36" | 0–24 |
| Tuxpan | EP | <500 | – | 11 | 0 | 21°00'08" | 97°10'11" | 0–24 |
| *Veracruz Reef System (southwestern Gulf)* | | | | | | | | |
| *Northern Reefs (off city of Veracruz)* | | | | | | | | |
| Punta Gorda– Punta Majahua | F | 3,800 | 375 | 0 | 0 | 19°14'33" | 96°10'34" | 0–4 |
| Galleguilla | EP | 1,000 | 375 | 2 | 0 | 19°13'53" | 96°07'24" | 0–18 |
| Anegada de Adentro | EP | 1,870 | 500 | 8 | 0 | 19°13'35" | 96°03'22" | 0–36 |
| La Blanquilla | EP | 625 | 625 | 4 | 1 | 19°13'35" | 96°05'49" | 0–24 |
| La Gallega | EP | 2,370 | 1,125 | 0 | 0 | 19°13'23" | 96°07'39" | 0–12 |
| Isla Verde | EP | 1,120 | 750 | 5 | 1 | 19°12'09" | 96°03'58" | 0–27 |
| Pájaros | EP | 1,870 | 750 | 3 | 0 | 19°11'18" | 96°05'22" | 0–18 |
| Hornos | F | 1,000 | 250 | <0.5 | 0 | 19°11'30" | 96°07'20" | 0–3 |
| Lavandera | SRB | <250 | – | <0.5 | 0 | 19°11'35" | 96°07'18" | 3–5 |
| Bajo Mersey | SRB? | <200 | – | 1 | 0 | 19°11'02" | 96°05'56" | 4–13 |
| Tierra Nueva | EP | 160 | 110 | 1 | 0 | 19°10'56" | 96°05'43" | 0–18 |
| Isla de Sacrificios | EP | 1,000 | 500 | 1 | 1 | 19°10'35" | 96°05'30" | 0–14 |
| Punta Mocambo | F | 2,500 | 625 | 0 | 0 | 19°08'49" | 96°05'27" | 0–7 |
| *Southern Reefs (off Antón Lizardo)* | | | | | | | | |
| Anegada de Afuera | EP | 4,370 | 1,125 | 16 | 0 | 19°09'25" | 95°51'15" | 0–45 |
| Topatillo | EP | 375 | 100 | 17 | 0 | 19°08'36" | 95°50'06" | 0–45 |
| Santiaguillo | EP | 375 | 250 | 20 | 1 | 19°08'32" | 95°49'28" | 0–45 |
| Anegadilla | EP | 625 | 125 | 21 | 0 | 19°08'14" | 95°47'43" | 0–45 |
| Aviso | EP | 250 | 100 | 6 | 0 | 19°07'07" | 95°56'38" | 0–24 |
| Polo | EP | 500 | 500 | 5 | 0 | 19°06'30" | 95°58'38" | 0–24 |
| Isla de Enmedio | EP | 2,250 | 1,800 | 6 | 1 | 19°06'21" | 95°56'18" | 0–24 |

(*continued*)

**Table 2.1.** (continued)

| Reef name | Reef type[1] | Size[2] | | Distance[3] to mainland (km) | Islands[4] | Geographic position[5] | | Depth[6] (m) |
|---|---|---|---|---|---|---|---|---|
| | | Length (m) | Width (m) | | | Latitude | Longitude | |
| Chopas | EP | 5,000 | 1,625 | 3 | 2 | 19°05'17" | 95°58'06" | 0–24 |
| Blanca | EP | 875 | 500 | 3 | 0 | 19°05'13" | 95°59'56" | 0–18 |
| Cabezo | EP | 6,200 | 2,500 | 15 | 1 | 19°04'26" | 95°50'43" | 0–24 |
| El Giote | SRB | 500 | 300 | <1 | 0 | 19°03'58" | 95°59'54" | 0–2 |
| El Rizo | EP | 2,870 | 875 | 5 | 0 | 19°03'50" | 95°55'40" | 0–18 |
| *Campeche Bank Reefs (southeastern Gulf)* | | | | | | | | |
| Alacrán | EP | 25,000 | 13,000 | 137 | 5 | 22°29'15" | 89°42'00" | 0–36 |
| *Cayo Arenas Complex* | | | | | | | | |
| Northeast Reef Wall | EP | 2,400 | <750 | 167 | 2 | 22°07'25" | 91°23'24" | 0–30 |
| West Reef Wall | EP | 300 | 50 | 169 | 1 | 22°07'08" | 91°23'32" | 0–30 |
| Southeast Reef Wall | EP | 610 | 50 | 167 | 1 | 22°06'44" | 91°23'08" | 0–30 |
| Bajo Nuevo | EP | – | – | ~194 | – | 21°50'00" | 92°05'12" | 0–30 |
| Bancos Ingleses | SRB | – | – | ~181 | 0 | 21°45'48" | 91°55'36" | 9–36 |
| Triángulo Oeste | EP | 656 | 300 | 193 | 1 | 20°57'00" | 92°14'00" | 0–18 |
| *Triángulos Este-Sur Complex* | | | | | | | | |
| Triángulo Este | EP | 2,370 | 547 | 187 | 2 | 20°55'15" | 92°12'29" | 0–18 |
| Triángulo Sur | EP | 2,100 | 990 | 189 | 6 | 20°54'17" | 92°13'54" | 0–18 |
| Banco Pera | SRB | – | – | ~151 | 0 | 20°45'00" | 91°55'36" | 16–44 |
| Bajos Obispos | SRB | 3,000 | – | ~140 | 0 | 20°30'00" | 92°10'36" | 5–?18 |
| Banco Nuevo | SRB | – | – | ~173 | – | 20°30'36" | 91°50'24" | 0–30 |
| *Cayos Arcas Complex* | | | | | | | | |
| Cayo del Centro | EP | 2,630 | 1,640 | 128 | 1 | 20°13'12" | 91°58'22" | 0–18 |
| Cayo del Oeste | EP | 900 | 240 | 128 | 1 | 20°12'39" | 91°59'10" | 0–18 |
| Cayo del Este | EP | 1,010 | 580 | 128 | 1 | 20°12'05" | 91°5848 | 0–18 |

*Source:* Hydrographic charts in Logan (1969), Rezak and Edwards (1972), Carricart-Ganivet and Horta-Puga (1993), and Dahlgren (1993).

[1] Reef type: EP = emergent platform; F = fringing; SRB = submerged reef bank.
[2] Size: Length and width are measured from the hydrographic charts or taken from the listed literature.
[3] Distance is calculated from the hydrographic charts.
[4] Number of islands is obtained from hydrographic charts (Triángulo Este and Sur) or personal observation by J. W. Tunnell Jr.
[5] Geographic position is taken from the most central position of each reef platform or bank from the hydrographic chart or from the listed literature.
[6] Depth is taken from the listed literature or the hydrographic charts.

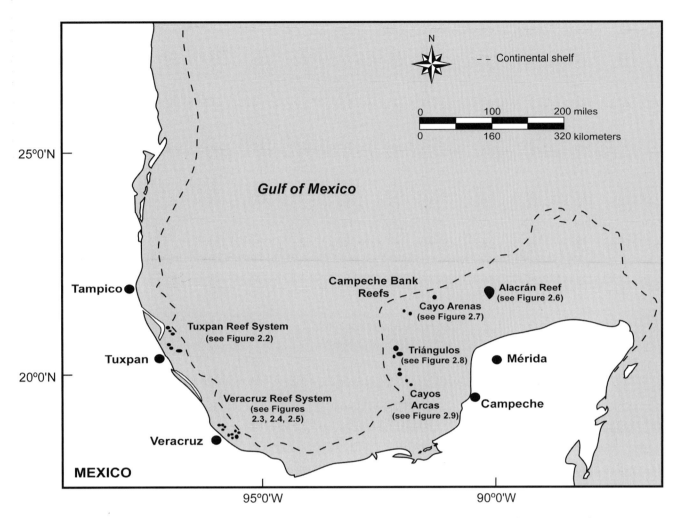

**Figure 2.1.** Geographic distribution of coral reefs within the southern Gulf of Mexico. The Tuxpan and Veracruz Reef Systems are in the southwestern Gulf of Mexico and the Campeche Bank reefs are in the southeastern Gulf of Mexico.

It is important to note that one historical reef, Punta Caleta, a fringing reef, was destroyed during the development of the Port of Veracruz, and in the 1600s, part of La Gallega Reef was used to build Fort San Juan de Ulúa for protection of the city and harbor. Subsequently, at the beginning of the 20th century, a land bridge was extended from Punta Caleta on the mainland to the fort on La Gallega Reef to partially enclose the Port of Veracruz on the north side (compare the historical maps in Figs. 1.1 and 1.2 to Fig. 2.4).

Three of the reef platforms in the northern VRS are associated with islands: La Blanquilla, Isla Verde, and Isla Sacrificios (Fig. 2.4). La Blanquillas island is a sandy cay, always changing shape and size, whereas Isla Verde and Isla Sacrificios are densely vegetated and fairly stable. Isla Verde's vegetation is low and mostly natural, although transplanted almond trees provide a shady canopy over part of the island. Isla Sacrificios has a large, important lighthouse, a public visitors' area, and many exotic transplants among the natural vegetation (see chapter 11 for more information on island biota).

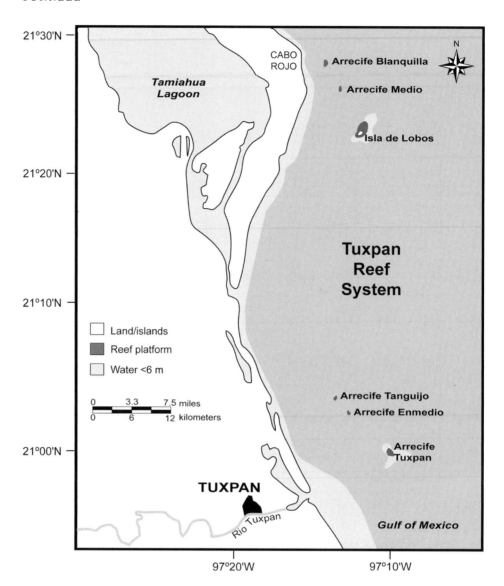

**Figure 2.2.** The Tuxpan Reef System (TRS), which consists of six emergent platform reefs, three off Cabo Rojo and three northeast of Tuxpan, Veracruz, Mexico.

The second, or southern, group of reefs in the VRS lies offshore from the fishing village of Antón Lizardo and is composed of 12 emergent platform reefs: Anegada de Afuera, Topatillo, Santiaguillo, Anegadilla, Polo, Isla de Enmedio, Aviso, Blanca, Chopas, El Rizo, Cabezo, and El Giote (Fig. 2.5). This group contains the three largest reefs in the southwestern Gulf—Afuera, Chopas, and Cabezo—of which Cabezo is the largest. Some smaller reefs in this group are "satellite" reefs of larger ones (e.g., Aviso Reef near Isla de Enmedio Reef and Polo Reef near Chopas Reef). El Giote Reef is the smallest and nearest to shore and has a navigational light stand located on it.

Four of the reef platforms in the southern group off Antón Lizardo feature islands: Santiaguillo, Cabezo, Isla de Enmedio, and Chopas. Chopas Reef actually has two islands, Isla Salmedina on the southeast end and Isla Blanca on the northeast end. Both islands have only low natural vegetation. Isla de Enmedio has low natural vegetation as well as a dense canopy of transplanted shade trees. El Aguila (on Cabezo) and Santiaguillo islands have no vegetation except for

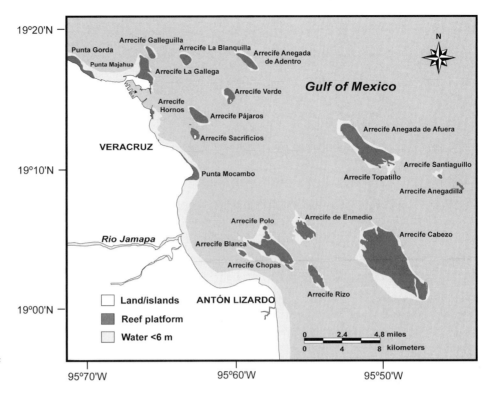

**Figure 2.3.** The Veracruz Reef System (VRS), which consists of reefs offshore from the city of Veracruz and the fishing village of Antón Lizardo, Veracruz, Mexico.

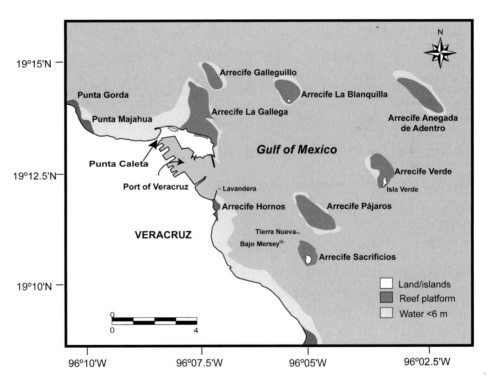

**Figure 2.4.** The northern group of reefs, showing islands associated with the reefs, in the Veracruz Reef System (VRS) located offshore from the city of Veracruz.

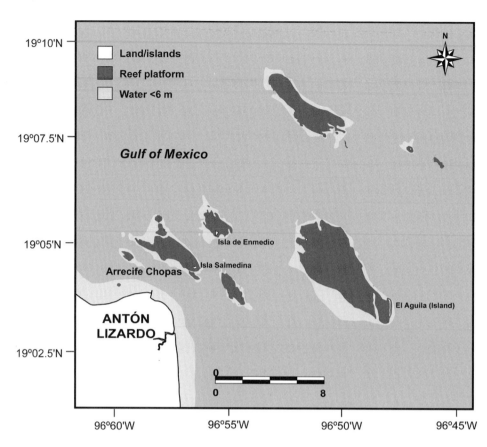

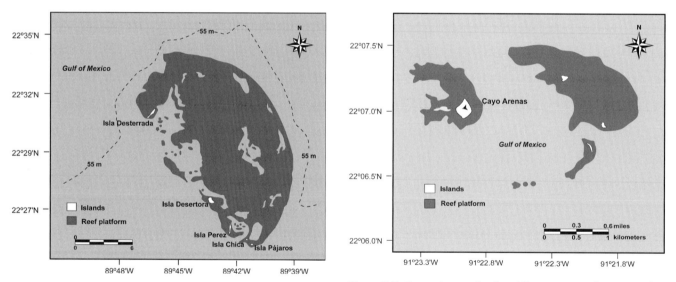

**Figure 2.5.** The southern group of reefs, showing islands associated with the reefs, in the Veracruz Reef System (VRS) located offshore from the fishing village of Antón Lizardo.

**Figure 2.6.** Alacrán Reef and associated islands.

**Figure 2.7.** Cayos Arenas Reef and three unnamed associated islands.

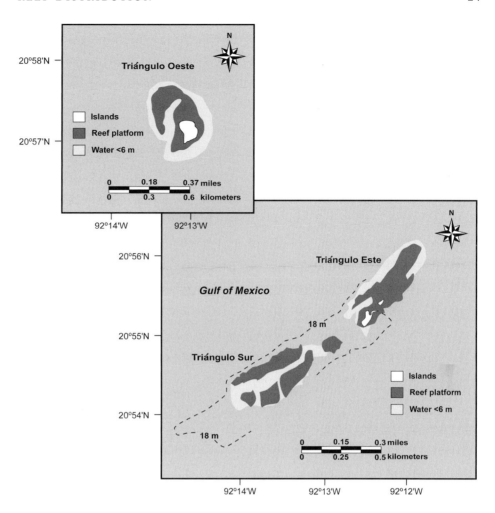

**Figure 2.8.** Triángulos Reefs (Oeste, Este, and Sur) with associated islands.

*Sesuvium* sp. (sea purslane) on the latter. Both islands on Cabezo and Santiaguillo reefs are composed almost totally of coral rubble (no sand). Topatillo Reef once had a coral rubble cay (*Acropora cervicornis* [staghorn coral] rubble only), which no longer exists. It is believed that stands of *Acropora palmata* (elkhorn coral) on the windward side and *A. cervicornis* on the leeward side formerly protected Isla Topatillo. After the death of these two species in the late 1970s and early 1980s (Tunnell 1992), this small island began to erode because no living *Acropora* protected it from wave action. By 2002, Isla Topatillo had disappeared completely (J. W. Tunnell Jr., personal observation).

The southeastern Gulf of Mexico comprises 11 named emergent platform reefs and four named submerged bank reefs (these do not reach the surface) along the outer continental shelf of the Campeche Bank (Fig. 2.1). Of these reefs, Alacrán Reef (Fig. 2.6) is the largest (25 × 13 km) and most northerly in the entire southern Gulf of Mexico; Cayo Arenas (Fig. 2.7), Triángulos (Fig. 2.8), and Cayos Arcas (Fig. 2.9) are all considered complexes, having multiple emergent platforms and islands. Nuevo Reef has a single emergent platform and ephemeral island, and Bancos Ingleses, Banco Pera, Banco Nuevo, and Bajos Obispos are all submerged reef banks (Table 2.1).

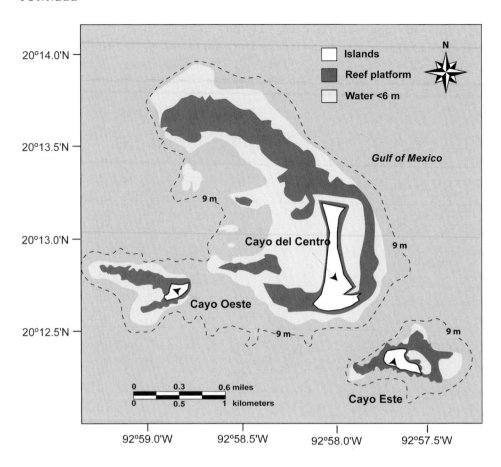

**Figure 2.9.** Cayos Arcas and associated islands.

Manned lighthouses are found on four of the reef islands: Isla Perez of Alacrán, Cayo Arenas, Triángulo Oeste, and Cayo del Centro of Cayos Arcas. Alacrán Reef has five vegetated islands (islas): Desterrada, Desertora, Perez, Chica, and Pájaros. Cayo Arenas has one large named vegetated island, Cayo Arenas, and three smaller, unvegetated, and unnamed coral rubble cays. Triángulos has at least two islands, Triángulo Oeste and Triángulo Este. Finally, Cayos Arcas has three vegetated islands, Cayo del Centro, Cayo del Oeste, and Cayo del Este.

# 3 Origin and Geology

W. DAVID LIDDELL

**Overview**

**Gulf of Mexico Basin** The Gulf of Mexico is a roughly circular basin encompassing parts of the southeastern United States and eastern Mexico. It is some 1,500 km in diameter, up to 3,700 m deep, and has been filled with 10–15 km of Mesozoic and Cenozoic sediments (Salvador 1991a). Its boundaries are the Florida Escarpment and Platform to the east, the Campeche Escarpment and Platform to the south, the Sierra Madre Oriental to the west and the Gulf Coastal Plain to the north and northwest (Fig. 3.1). These boundaries reflect Mesozoic-Cenozoic carbonate platform growth (Florida and Yucatán platforms), Laramide compression (Sierra Madre Oriental), and progradation (Gulf Coastal Plain) (Ewing 1991). While the transition between the basin and the Florida and Yucatán platforms is abrupt, the transition to the coastal plain to the north and west is gentle. The coastal plain is much broader (>500 km) to the north and narrower (<50 km) to the west. The deep, central part of the basin is underlain by oceanic crust, while the Gulf Coastal Plain and the Florida and Yucatán platforms are underlain by continental or transitional (rifted continental) crust. As the emphasis of this volume is on the southern Gulf of Mexico, this discussion will largely be restricted to two areas, the Yucatán Platform and the western Gulf Coastal Plain.

**Yucatán Platform** The Yucatán Platform includes the subaerially exposed Yucatán Peninsula and associated submerged shelf (dominated by the Campeche Bank). The platform is composed of flat-lying, predominantly carbonate sediments dating back to the Late Cretaceous (Table 3.1) and reaching some 3–4 km in thickness. Lesser amounts of evaporitic sediments also occur. Average rainfall on the northern peninsula is <70 cm/yr (Ferré-D'Amaré 1985), considerably less than that of the Tampico-Veracruz area along the western Gulf. Relief on the peninsula is low, on the order of 100 m or less, and the landscape is dominated by karst topography. Thus, there is little surface drainage and limited terrigenous sediment is transported to the waters adjacent to the peninsula. There is the possibility of freshwater discharge into the coastal areas of the Gulf through the karst system, as suggested by Ferré-D'Amaré (1985) for the eastern coast of the Yucatán Peninsula.

The shelf is broad to the north and west, reaching some 240 km in width, and narrow to the east along the boundary with the Caribbean. The broad northern and western portion is known as the Campeche Bank, which is the site of numerous bank reefs (sensu Logan 1969b) and at least one atoll or "atoll-like" structure (see Figs. 2.1, 2.6–2.9; Plate 12). It is bounded to the west by the steep Yucatán Escarpment, a product of Cretaceous and later platform growth, to the north by the Yucatán Terrace and to the east by the Yucatán Channel (Bryant et al. 1991). The shelf-slope break occurs between 180 and 270 m. A submarine

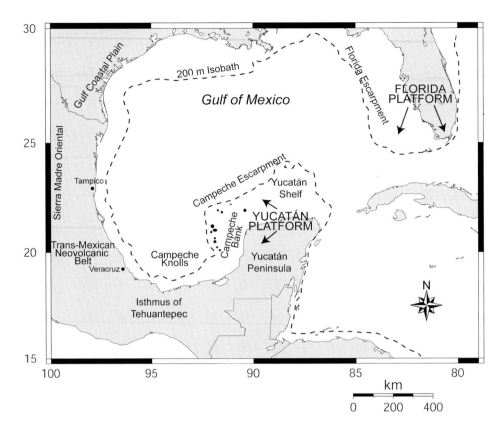

**Figure 3.1.** Gulf of Mexico showing prominent topographic features (from Salvador 1991a).

terrace between 90 and 135 m corresponds to the late Wisconsinian sea-level lowstand, and additional terraces at 50–64 m and 33–36 m likely represent still-stands, or pauses, in sea-level change (Logan 1969a).

**Western Gulf Coastal Plain**　This section of the Gulf coast extends southward from Tampico to Veracruz and the Isthmus of Tehuantepec (Fig. 3.1). The Sierra Madre Orientál orogenic belt is a Laramide feature (latest Cretaceous to early Tertiary) and forms the western boundary of the plain. The Isthmus of Tehuantepec is bordered on the east by the Yucatán Platform. This portion of the western Gulf Coastal Plain can be subdivided into three physiographic "embayments" (the Tampico, Veracruz, and Isthmus of Tehuantepec) that are separated by highlands, such as the Trans-Mexico Neovolcanic Belt (Plate 13). These embayments correspond to structural basins that have received thick fills of terrigenous sediment.

Rainfall is high on the coastal plain, 100–150 cm/yr, and several major rivers, namely (from north to south) the Moctezuma-Panuco, Tuxpan, Tecolutla, and Papaloapan, cross the plain. These have been responsible for the delivery of considerable quantities of fine-grained terrigenous sediment to the Gulf. Subsidence in the Gulf since at least the Late Jurassic has resulted in a gentle, basin-ward slope by these sediments (Bryant et al. 1991). Reefs do occur along this portion of the coastal plain (see Figs. 2.1–2.5), despite the heavy terrigenous sediment input. Cretaceous carbonate rocks are exposed in the foothills and highland areas bordering the coastal plain. Volcanic rocky shores occur in the Punta del Morro–Punta Delgado region (Plate 14a, b) approximately 100 km north of Veracruz city and in the San Andres Tuxtlas region (Plate 14c, d) about 150 km south of Veracruz (J. W. Tunnell Jr., personal communication).

**Table 3.1.** *Geologic time scale, after Geological Society America (Palmer and Geissman 1999).*

| Eons | Eras | Periods (Epochs) |
|---|---|---|
| PHANAEROZOIC 543 Ma–present | Cenozoic 65 Ma–present | Quaternary *1.8 Ma–present* (Holocene *0.01 Ma–present*) (Pleistocene *1.8–0.01 Ma*) Tertiary *65–1.8 Ma* |
| | Mesozoic 248–65 Ma | Cretaceous *144–65 Ma* Jurassic *206–144 Ma* Triassic *248–206 Ma* |
| | Paleozoic 543–248 Ma | Permian *290–248 Ma* Carboniferous *354–290 Ma* Devonian *417–354 Ma* Silurian *443–417 Ma* Ordovician *490–443 Ma* Cambrian *543–490 Ma* |
| PROTEROZOIC 2.5–0.54 Ga | Neoproterozoic 0.9–0.54 Ga | |
| | Mesoproterozoic 1.6–0.9 Ga | |
| | Paleoproterozoic 2.5–1.6 Ga | |
| ARCHEAN 3.8–2.5 Ga | | |
| HADEAN ~4.6–3.8 Ga | | |

*Note:* Ma = mega-annum (million years ago); Ga = giga-annum (billion years ago).

## Geologic History

**Basin Formation**   The Gulf of Mexico originated in the Late Triassic (c. 220 Ma) with the rifting of Pangea and the separation of the North American, South American, and African plates. Initial activity (Late Triassic through Middle Jurassic) was characterized by subsiding rift basins that were filled with thick packages of volcanic rocks and nonmarine terrigenous sediments such as "red beds." Extensive salts were deposited in marginal basins (graben) separated from the open ocean during the Middle Jurassic. During the Late Jurassic, shelves were established around the margins of the basin, which continued to subside (Salvador 1991b). The shelves were the site of deposition of marine limestones to the south and east and shales to the west.

Although tectonically stable since at least the Late Jurassic, simple subsidence of the Gulf basin has been modified by nonorogenic salt movement (T. H. Nelson 1991). Vast quantities of salt, principally halite (NaCl), were deposited during the Middle Jurassic in the newly opened Gulf of Mexico. With subsequent

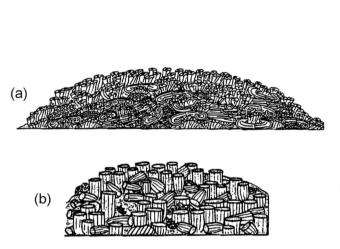

(a)

(b)

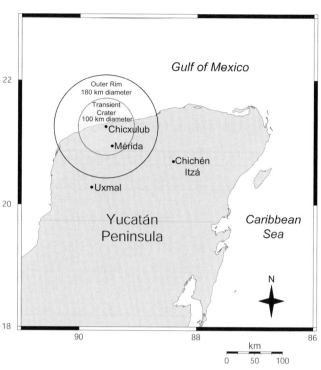

**Figure 3.2.** Cretaceous rudist reefs (from Kauffman and Sohl 1974) in which frameworks are dominated by **(a)** erect and recumbent forms and **(b)** largely erect forms.

**Figure 3.3.** Cretaceous-Tertiary impact crater on the Yucatán Peninsula. The impact was centered on the current village of Chicxulub.

burial to modest depths (2–3 km for fine terrigenous sediment, less for carbonates), the salt flowed upward, producing salt structures (salt-cored anticlines and plugs) at widely scattered locations around the Gulf of Mexico. Such salt movement may have occurred as early as the Late Jurassic (Salvador 1991b). In the case of the Flower Garden Banks in the northern Gulf of Mexico, diapiric salt structures produced shallow-water habitat for reef development surrounded by depths inhospitable for reef-building corals (Rezak et al. 1985).

Basinward slippage of salt may produce listric-normal faults (growth faults), which are gently curving faults formed in poorly consolidated sediment. These are responsible for basinward movement of sediment along a slip surface that soles out above the basement (T. H. Nelson 1991). Such faults are important in compartmentalizing hydrocarbon reservoirs. Basinward movement of salt may also produce salt-cored fold and thrust belts.

Salt structures may produce structural traps for petroleum. Much of the early (c. 1901–22) exploration for hydrocarbons in the Gulf was associated with salt structures (Nehring 1991). The Campeche Knolls diapir province hosts the important Campeche oil fields, which are offshore Ciudad del Carmen (Plate 15a) (Ewing 1991). An offshore oil terminal has been constructed at Cayos Arcas (Plate 15b) for shipping of the field's production.

**Cretaceous Reefs** During the Cretaceous Period (144–65 Ma), reefs in the southern Gulf of Mexico and worldwide were increasingly dominated by a group of bivalves known as rudists (subclass Heterodonta, order Hippuritoida). These strongly inequivalved bivalves were typically attached to the seafloor and often gregarious. The group encompasses several families including the Caprinidae, Hippuritidae, and Radiolitidae. They exhibit a variety of growth forms, including spiraled, recumbent and erect, cone-shaped forms (Fig. 3.2). Some had extremely thick walls and reached sizes up to 2 m in length.

The rudists provided a sediment-trapping framework, underwent well-defined succession (Kauffman and Sohl 1974), and dominated most shelf environments by the Late Cretaceous. It is possible that some rudists may have possessed a symbiotic relationship with algae, as do modern zooxanthellate scleractinian corals (Stanley 1987). This widespread and successful group went extinct at the end of the Cretaceous Period.

Rudist reefs represent some of the earliest known reef formers from the southern Gulf of Mexico. In the Early Cretaceous, rudist reefs built up the Yucatán Platform margin. This margin is now represented by the steep, submerged Campeche Escarpment. Along the western Gulf Coastal Plain, the Tuxpan Platform was also fringed by rudist reefs and developed a steep margin with associated deep-water breccia deposits. The formation containing these reefs, the El Albra, is part of the famous petroleum-producing trend known as the Golden Lane (Salvador 1991c). Such rudist reefs are much less prominent in the Late Cretaceous of the Yucatán and Tuxpan platforms.

**Impact at the End of the Cretaceous** A highly significant late Mesozoic (65 Ma) event was the probable impact of a 10 km asteroid or comet on the northern edge of the present Yucatán Peninsula. This event coincides with, and is perhaps responsible for, the boundary between the Mesozoic and Cenozoic eras of the geologic time scale. The impact made an egg-shaped crater some 180 km across, center upon the village of Chicxulub in the state of Yucatán (Fig. 3.3). The impact crater is now buried beneath some 1,000 m of younger marine carbonate sediments, but it appears on gravity surveys and may influence the distribution of cenotes (sinkholes) along the northern Yucatán Peninsula (Hildebrand et al. 1995; Fig. 3.3). PEMEX exploratory wells drilled in the 1950s penetrated the impact layer and encountered rocks indicative of shock metamorphism, but these were initially thought to be igneous in nature.

The occurrence of an impact event at the Cretaceous-Tertiary (K-T) boundary has been well documented and evidenced by numerous features such as an iridium (platinum group element) anomaly, shocked (high pressure) quartz, carbon from global wildfires, and tsunami deposits. However, the effect of such an impact upon the earth's biota has been far more controversial. Alvarez et al. (1980) proposed the idea that debris ejected into the atmosphere by the impact caused a sudden cooling of the earth ("nuclear winter") that was responsible for the extinction of the dinosaurs and many other terrestrial and marine organisms at the end of the Cretaceous. Since the initial paper, authors have proposed other negative consequences of an impact, such as acid rain from the vaporized evaporitic rocks of the Yucatán Platform (MacDougall 1988) or intense global wildfires (Melosh et al. 1990). Other authors have placed greater emphasis on slower (tectonically driven) climate change (Stanley 1984) or, in the case of the dinosaurs, the effects (disease, predation, competition) of intercontinental migration (Bakker 1986). Further, various authors have shown that foraminiferal (Keller 1989) and molluscan (Kauffman 1979; Hansen et al. 1987) faunas exhibited fluctuations in diversity that are not synchronous with the terminal impact event, suggesting that other factors may have also played a role in the K-T extinctions. Cowen (2000) provides a good discussion of the evidence for, and possible consequences of, a large impact at the K-T boundary.

**Pleistocene Sea-Level Fluctuations** During the Pleistocene Epoch (c. 1.8–0.01 Ma), sea level underwent numerous oscillations in response to advances and retreats of the ice caps (glacioeustasy). During the last glacial interval (the late Wisconsinian) sea level had dropped to 100–125 m below the present datum by 20–17 ka (Hallam 1992), leaving any reefs from before that time "high and dry." This lowering of sea level is also responsible for a common break in slope at about 100 m depth around much of the Caribbean and Gulf of Mexico (90–135 m terrace on the Campeche Bank; Logan 1969a).

During the sea-level lowstand, wind-blown deposits of carbonate sediments (eolianites) were deposited upon the exposed shelves, often forming elongate ridges, as documented for the northeastern Yucatán Peninsula by Ward (1985a, 1985b). Logan (1969a) suggested that lithified banks on the 51–64 m terrace on the northwestern and northeastern portions of the Yucatán Shelf are also eolian dunes. McKee and Ward (1983) noted that eolianites are not restricted to lowstand intervals and may, apparently, also form during highstands.

Pauses in the dropping of sea level (stillstands) may result in the formation of wave-cut terraces at various depths, resulting in a steplike underwater morphology. On the Campeche Bank, such terraces occur at 90–135 m, 51–64 m, and 33–36 m (Logan 1969a).

With the reduction of the ice caps at the end of the Pleistocene, sea level rapidly rose to within 5–7 m of modern levels by 5 ka (Lighty et al. 1982; Fairbanks 1989). Modern reefs became established after flooding of the insular and continental shelves; thus, the reefs we can dive upon today are only a few thousand years old. Through excavation and dating of Holocene reefs at Jamaica, Land (1974) determined that reef growth on the order of 0.6–1.0 m/ky has occurred since their establishment. Goreau and Land (1974) pointed out that modern Jamaican reefs are relatively thin veneers of less than 10 m thickness mantling preexisting Pleistocene topography. Such appears to be the case for many of the reefs of the southern Gulf of Mexico as well. Logan (1969b) noted that most or all reefs on the Campeche Bank were established on relict, presumably eolian features located near the 55 m isobath. These structures may rise up to within 30 m of the sea surface. It should be mentioned that high rates of carbonate accretion are known for some Campeche Bank reefs (e.g., Isla Perez; Macintyre et al. 1977).

## Modern Reefs of the Southern Gulf of Mexico

**Characteristics of Modern Reefs** The reefs that appeared after the Cretaceous mass extinctions were essentially modern in character and dominated by colonial scleractinian corals (James 1983). Modern coral reefs consist of a framework, principally zooxanthellate (symbiont-bearing, reef-building) scleractinian corals, that traps sediment produced by the processes of skeletogenesis and bioerosion. Corals and calcareous green algae, such as *Halimeda*, are typically the most important contributors to reef sediment. Significant bioeroders include parrotfish (Scaridae), grazing echinoids (*Echinometra*), clionid sponges (*Cliona*), lithophagid bivalves (*Lithophaga*), and endolithic algae. The sediment generated is then bound by inorganic and organic interstitial cements and by the overgrowth of crustose coralline algae (Rhodophyta) and encrusting foraminifera, such as *Gypsina*. Along with the high growth rates of the zooxanthellate scleractinians, the possession of an internal framework enables reefs to build upward into shallow water and resist the destructive power of waves.

Modern western Atlantic reefs are highly diverse communities, containing numerous corals (e.g., 64 species are known from Jamaica; Goreau and Wells 1967; Wells and Lang 1973), gorgonians, sponges, algae, and other species. These reefs are host to numerous fish and other invertebrates. The biota display zonation, reflecting their response to declining wave energy and light levels with increasing depth (e.g., Goreau 1959; Goreau and Goreau 1973; Graus et al. 1984). For a description of the reef zonation and biota inhabiting the southern Gulf of Mexico reefs, refer to Logan (1969b), Farrell et al. (1983), Ferré-D'Amaré (1985), and additional chapters in this volume.

**Campeche Bank Reefs** Campeche Bank reefs occur in a broad arc running from the north-central portion of the bank (Alacrán Reef) to the southwest (Cayos Arcas). The reefs occur near the shelf edge, some 100–200 km from the coastline of the Yucatán Peninsula (see Fig. 2.1). Reefs are largely absent on the northeastern portion of the shelf, possibly due to upwelling of cold (17°–180°C) water along the northeastern shelf (Logan 1969b; Glynn 1973).

Fringing or barrier-type reefs are conspicuously absent from the northern and western coastal areas of the Yucatán Peninsula. These reef types are extensively developed along the eastern (Caribbean) side of the Yucatán Peninsula and southward into Belize. The general absence of reefs along the Gulf coastal areas of the Yucatán Peninsula may be due to low winter temperatures (8°–100°C air temperatures; Ferré-D'Amaré 1985), the effects of which would be more pronounced along the coastline than farther out on the shelf where the bank reefs occur. As noted earlier, there is also the possibility of freshwater discharge through the Yucatán karst system into coastal areas.

Logan (1969b) subdivided the Campeche Bank reefs into geomorphic categories, the principal subdivision being between submerged reef banks (e.g., Banco Ingleses and Obispo Shoals, located between Triángulo Sur and Cayos Arcas; see Fig. 2.1) and emergent reef banks or "walls." The latter are further subdivided into (1) solitary reef knolls (Nuevo and Triángulo Oeste [see Fig. 2.8]), (2) linear reef walls (Triángulo Este-Sur [see Fig. 2.8]), (3) crescent reef walls (e.g., windward reef at Alacrán Reef [see Fig. 2.6, Plate 12] and parts of Cayo Arenas and Cayos Arcas [see Figs. 2.7 and 2.9]), and (4) reef complexes with multiple emergent walls (e.g., Cayo Arenas and Cayos Arcas). The majority of these reefs form arcs that are convex to the northeast, reflecting the prevalent northeast-southwest wave progression (Logan 1969b).

At some 11 × 22 km, Alacrán Reef is by far the largest reef in the southern Gulf of Mexico. It has an extensive lagoon, reaching 22 m in depth and containing numerous small patch reefs. There are also five islands situated along the leeward (southwestern) side of the reef. Alacrán Reef is the best known of the Campeche Bank reefs and has been the subject of numerous geological and biological studies (see Tables 1.2, 1.3, and 3.2). A core taken from Isla Perez, one of the leeward islands, indicated some 30 m of Holocene reef growth (principally by the coral *Acropora cervicornis*). This translates into deposition rates of 12 m/ky (Macintyre et al. 1977). This rate is considerably higher than the accretion rates previously described for Jamaica by Land (1974). The cored Holocene reef was situated on top of a similar-appearing pre-Holocene reef that extended from 33 m down to 50–60 m and the shelf platform (Bonet 1967).

In addition to the "true" reefs mentioned above, organic structures lacking scleractinian frameworks also occur on the Campeche Bank (Logan 1969b). These hard banks or biostromes form relatively thin veneers over relict topography, particularly in the 18–60 m depth range. These veneers consist of concentrically layered nodules, 1–18 cm in diameter, produced by the crustose coralline algae *Lithophyllum* and *Lithoporella*. They are often encrusted by the foraminiferan *Gypsina plana* and the alga *Lithothamnium*. These nodular crusts are

**Table 3.2.** *Principal studies dealing with the geology of the southern Gulf of Mexico.*

| Reef/Island location | Publication |
| --- | --- |
| **Campeche Bank** | |
| Alacrán Reef | Kornicker et al. (1959) |
| | Kornicker and Boyd (1962b) |
| | Folk (1962, 1967) |
| | Hoskin (1962, 1963, 1966, 1968) |
| | Folk and Robles (1964) |
| | Bonet (1967) |
| | Folk and Cotera (1971) |
| | Macintyre et al. (1977) |
| | Novak (1992) |
| | Novak et al. (1992) |
| Cayo Arenas | Busby (1966) |
| Campeche Shelf | Logan (1962, 1969a) |
| | Macias-Zamora et al. (1999) |
| **Veracruz-Tampico** | |
| Isla de Lobos Reef | Rigby and McIntire (1966) |
| Veracruz Reef System | Emery (1963) |
| | Morelock and Koenig (1967) |
| | Edwards (1969) |
| | Freeland (1971) |
| | Hernandez (1987) |

most common on the northern shelf and are much less well developed on the western shelf, perhaps due to the increased terrigenous sediment input there.

**Tuxpan-Veracruz Reefs**    Reef development along the western Gulf Coastal Plain is largely confined to two areas: the Tuxpan Reef System in the north (see Fig. 2.2) and the Veracruz Reef System in the south (see Figs. 2.3–2.5). Most of these reefs are relatively small (only a few square kilometers), exhibit low relief, and are located near shore (Ferré-D'Amaré 1985). There are six emergent platform reefs in the Tuxpan area (see Fig. 2.2), Isla de Lobos Reef being the best known. There are 25 emergent platform reefs in the Veracruz area, including three small fringing reefs (Tunnell, chapter 2, this volume). Winter low temperatures range from 8°–10°C (air) at Veracruz down to 0°C (air), infrequently, at Tampico (Ferré-D'Amaré 1985). Reefs are also absent to the north of the Tuxpan Reef System, most likely due to low winter temperatures. Reefs are absent to the south of the Veracruz Reef System, perhaps due to upwelling (Ferré-D'Amaré 1985).

As noted for the northern and western Yucatán Peninsula, the western Gulf Coastal Plain also lacks extensive barrier and fringing reefs. The Tuxpan-Veracruz areas are subject to low winter temperatures, terrigenous sedimentation, and, during the rainy season, lowered salinities in some areas (e.g., 18.3 psu at Veracruz [Ferré-D'Amaré 1985; Tunnell 1988]).

**Sediment Composition**  Numerous studies have examined the composition of Holocene reef sediment from the southern Gulf of Mexico, particularly Alacrán Reef (Table 3.2). Not all of these are quantitative. Studies of certain areas, notably Cayos Arcas and Triángulos on the Campeche Bank and the Tuxpan-Tampico portion of the western Gulf Coastal Plain, are lacking. Although both geographic and bathymetric variation in sediment composition does occur, some generalizations may be made.

Campeche Bank (Open Shelf)  Logan (1969a) provides the most complete description of Campeche Bank sediments. Terrigenous material is largely lacking, except in the southwestern part of the shelf where material is transported from the Bay of Campeche. A blanketlike sedimentary deposit, ranging in thickness from a few centimeters to perhaps 1 m, occurs above the 90 m isobath. Four Holocene lithofacies were distinguished: (1) pelagic ooze on the outer shelf and slope below the 45 m isobath, (2) calcisiltites with pelagic tests on the western slope below 36 m, (3) molluscan-algal sands on the eastern and northwestern shelves above the 45 m isobath, and (4) reef and associated environments described below. In order of importance in providing skeletal grains for the sands are mollusks, foraminifera, coralline (Rhodophyta) and calcareous (Chlorophyta) algae, echinoids, bryozoans, anthozoans, and arthropods. Nonskeletal grains are provided by, in order of importance, calcareous ovoid pellets, ooids, mud lumps, and limestone lithoclasts.

Logan (1969a) noted the presence of relict (pre-Holocene) grains on the shelf and the mixing of these and more modern allochems. This implies relatively slow sedimentation rates and resulting time averaging of the sediment on the shelf. This is in stark contrast to the rapid accretion rates found at Isla Perez on Alacrán Reef (Macintyre et al. 1977).

Campeche Bank Reefs  Logan (1969a) noted that sediments from reefs and associated environments (e.g., lagoons) were dominated by coral, coralline and calcareous algae, and foraminifera. In contrast to the open shelf, mollusks, echinoids, and bryozoans were less important sediment constituents on the reefs.

In a pioneering study, Kornicker and Boyd (1962b) provided a general overview of the sedimentology and biotic zonation of Alacrán Reef and lagoon. They noted that considerable lateral variation occurred in the organisms present and in the bottom character around the reef complex.

Folk and Robles (1964) studied Isla Perez, the largest leeward island on Alacrán Reef. They noted six populations of sediment, based on size and composition. The general composition of the sand-sized fraction was 60% *Halimeda*, 25% coral, and 15% foraminifera and other grains. Coarser fractions were dominated by coral (e.g., coral stick ramparts generated by storms). Folk (1967) and Folk and Cotera (1971) focused on the origin, geomorphology, and size-sorting of sands occurring on sand cays off the leeward side of Alacrán Reef. He noted that these were areas of intense organic sediment production.

Seventeen environments were characterized on Alacrán Reef based on sediment composition and size (Hoskin 1963). These were (from east to west): windward shelf, lower windward slope, upper windward slope, surge channels, boulder rampart, windward reef flat, moat, *Thalassia* beds, cellular reef surface, cellular reef deep, pinnacle reef, lagoon proper, patch reefs, shallow sand, leeward reef surface, lower leeward slope, and leeward shelf. *Halimeda*, coral, and fecal pellets were the dominant components of the sand-sized sediment fraction.

**Table 3.3.** *Composition of Alacrán Reef sediment in percentage abundance of grains.*

| Location | Back reef | | | Forereef South | | | | Forereef North | | |
|---|---|---|---|---|---|---|---|---|---|---|
| Depth (m) | 1 | 2 | 4 | 7 | 11 | 12 | 17 | 3 | 10 | 17 |
| Sample size (n) | 8 | 2 | 2 | 2 | 2 | 2 | 2 | 2 | 2 | 2 |
| Coral | 23.1 | 50.6 | 27.6 | 56.6 | 53.8 | 32.0 | 32.6 | 64.2 | 61.2 | 50.2 |
| *Halimeda* | 43.5 | 22.0 | 47.0 | 28.2 | 20.4 | 40.5 | 47.0 | 8.4 | 10.0 | 26.8 |
| Coralline algae | 11.0 | 5.4 | 2.6 | 4.8 | 9.4 | 11.4 | 6.2 | 13.8 | 13.6 | 10.0 |
| *Homotrema* | 0.4 | 0.0 | 0.0 | 0.2 | 0.0 | 0.0 | 0.0 | 1.0 | 0.2 | 1.6 |
| *Gypsina* | 0.5 | 0.2 | 0.2 | 0.4 | 0.4 | 0.0 | 0.0 | 0.4 | 0.0 | 0.0 |
| Miliolina | 7.9 | 7.8 | 8.6 | 0.2 | 2.8 | 5.2 | 1.6 | 1.4 | 1.8 | 1.4 |
| Textulariina | 1.8 | 0.6 | 1.2 | 0.8 | 0.2 | 1.4 | 0.4 | 0.2 | 0.6 | 1.0 |
| Rotaliina | 0.3 | 0.2 | 0.4 | 0.0 | 0.4 | 0.2 | 0.0 | 0.0 | 0.2 | 0.0 |
| Bivalve | 7.6 | 4.8 | 6.8 | 5.0 | 6.8 | 6.0 | 5.4 | 6.2 | 7.0 | 5.6 |
| Gastropod | 2.6 | 5.8 | 2.2 | 1.4 | 2.6 | 1.6 | 4.6 | 0.8 | 2.0 | 1.8 |
| Echinoderm | 0.4 | 0.6 | 1.0 | 0.8 | 1.4 | 0.8 | 0.4 | 2.2 | 1.0 | 0.6 |
| Gorgonian | 0.0 | 0.0 | 0.2 | 0.0 | 0.2 | 0.0 | 0.0 | 0.0 | 0.0 | 0.0 |
| Sponge spicule | 0.1 | 0.2 | 0.4 | 0.0 | 0.8 | 0.6 | 0.4 | 0.0 | 0.0 | 0.2 |
| Bryozoan | 0.2 | 0.0 | 0.0 | 0.0 | 0.0 | 0.0 | 0.0 | 0.0 | 0.0 | 0.0 |
| Pelloid | 0.2 | 0.0 | 0.0 | 0.6 | 0.0 | 0.2 | 0.0 | 0.4 | 1.0 | 0.2 |
| Cryptocrystalline | 0.1 | 0.6 | 0.0 | 1.0 | 0.4 | 0.2 | 0.2 | 0.2 | 0.4 | 0.2 |
| Unidentified | 1.0 | 1.2 | 1.8 | 0.0 | 0.4 | 0.4 | 1.4 | 0.8 | 1.0 | 0.4 |

*Note:* Sample measurements based on thin-section counts of 300 points per sample (after Novak et al. 1992).

*Halimeda* was most abundant on the windward and leeward reefs, coral reached its peak abundance on the tops of lagoon pinnacle reefs, and fecal pellets were most abundant in deeper lagoonal areas. Foraminifera, coralline algae, mollusks, and aggregate grains showed little variation across these environments.

Near-surface diagenesis occurs on pinnacle reefs in the Alacrán Reef lagoon (Hoskin 1966). Diagenetic processes observed included pelletization of lagoon floor muds, macroboring of coral by lithophagid bivalves, microboring of coral and mollusk fragments by endolithic algae, aragonite cementation in cavities, and recrystallization of coral grains.

Novak (1992) and Novak et al. (1992) provided a quantitative description of reef sediment from Alacrán Reef (Table 3.3). For all samples, coral, the calcareous green alga *Halimeda,* and coralline algae constituted well over 70% of all grains by volume. The distribution of allochems was similar to the distribution of the living, sediment-producing organisms. Coral grains were relatively more abundant in forereef samples and *Halimeda* grains in back-reef samples. In contrast to the findings of Hoskin (1963), Novak et al. (1992) found that fecal pellets were relatively minor sedimentary constituents of their samples and coralline algae were fairly important. It should be noted that the back-reef samples studied by Novak et al. (1992) were from the shallower, eastern portion of the lagoon; the deeper, pellet-rich lagoon areas and the pinnacle reefs sampled by

Hoskin (1963) were not sampled by Novak et al. (1992). Cluster analysis delineated three Alacrán Reef lithofacies: back reef, shallow forereef (<10 m), and deep forereef (>10 m).

Tuxpan-Veracruz Reefs   Relatively little is known about the geology of these reefs. Although primarily concerned with the biotic communities, Rigby and McIntire (1966) noted the importance of substrate character (stable or unstable, sandy or rocky) in determining the distribution of community types on Isla de Lobos Reef near Tuxpan. The seafloor north and south of the reef is dominated by reef-derived calcareous sand, whereas the seafloor to the west of the reef displays an admixture of reef-derived and terrigenous material. The latter included quartz, ferromagnesium minerals, volcanic rock fragments, and obsidian and were presumably transported by the Rio Tuxpan or Rio Panuco. The seafloor immediately east of the reef was dominated by rocky reef debris. Finally, they postulated that the linear trend of Isla de Lobos, Medio, and Blanquilla reefs might reflect their establishment on a relict Pleistocene or older topography.

Emery (1963), Edwards (1969), and Freeland (1971) examined the mixed terrigenous-carbonate sediments off the city of Veracruz (see Figs. 2.3 and 2.4). Morelock and Koenig (1967) studied the reefs located at Antón Lizardo to the south of Veracruz, where eight reefs rise from 15–45 m on the shelf (see Figs. 2.3 and 2.5). All of these reefs are located parallel to the shoreline and perpendicular to the approach direction of prevailing waves. They are strongly influenced by storm waves and are largely barren of sandy sediment on the windward portion where there are well-developed boulder ramparts. The authors concluded that the reefs have been established on antecedent Pleistocene dunes. Further, the terrigenous sand and gravel present on the shelf are late Pleistocene (Wisconsinian) in age and present-day terrigenous sedimentation rates are very low, allowing the reefs to develop. Carbonate sediments accumulated only in the immediate area of the coral reefs and even these samples rarely exceeded 50% calcium carbonate by weight.

**Conclusions**

Modern marine environments in the southern Gulf of Mexico reflect the interplay of events occurring over a span of some 220 my. For example, some of the reefs on the Yucatán Shelf were established on Pleistocene eolian dunes formed during a sea-level lowstand. The dunes themselves occur on a Cretaceous and younger carbonate platform that grew outward into the newly opened Gulf of Mexico basin. The development of reefs along the Tuxpan-Veracruz coast is limited by climatic factors (winter low temperatures), but also by the abundant supply of terrigenous sediment being shed from the Sierra Madre Orientál and Trans-Mexican Neovolcanic Belt.

The history of the southern Gulf of Mexico spans an interval from the Late Triassic to the present and comprises an area that is some 1,500,000 km². However, the scope of this chapter is necessarily limited. The reader is referred to the excellent *Geology of North America, Volume J: Gulf of Mexico Basin* (Salvador 1991), for more detailed information on the geologic framework of the Gulf of Mexico. The reader is also referred to Logan (1969a, 1969b) for more information on the geology of the Campeche Bank.

# 4    Climate and Oceanography

LAURA CARRILLO, GUILLERMO HORTA-PUGA,
AND JUAN PABLO CARRICART-GANIVET

The climate and oceanography of coral reef areas within the southern Gulf of Mexico (SGM) are the result of large-scale water circulation (i.e., the Loop Current and associated large anticyclonic gyre) and mesoscale features interacting within the slope and shelf (cyclonic or anticyclonic gyres, tropical cyclones, and other meteorological events called *nortes*). Local conditions (such as freshwater inflow by river discharge, total volume ~ $187.6 \times 10^9$ m$^3$ yr$^{-1}$ in the case of the Campeche, Veracruz, and Tuxpan reef areas or negligible in the case of the Yucatán Peninsula; Carricart-Ganivet and Merino 2001), precipitation, and local wind also affect the area. In this chapter, we summarize the knowledge of these oceanographic and climatic conditions in the coral reef areas of the southern Gulf of Mexico. We discuss the general surface circulation by dominant processes in the Loop Current region, deep western Gulf, Bay of Campeche, Tamaulipas-Veracruz shelf, and Campeche Bank. Local weather and continental influence (freshwater inflow) in the different coral reef areas are also discussed.

## General Surface Circulation

The general long-term circulation in the southern Gulf is dominated by two semipermanent large-scale features (Behringer et al. 1997): (1) the Loop Current in the eastern Gulf, which is a component of the Gulf Stream current system, and (2) a large anticyclonic gyre in the western Gulf, with its characteristic Western Boundary Current (Fig. 4.1). The Loop Current intrudes the Gulf of Mexico with variability in its broad spectral band (Molinari et al. 1977; Sturges and Evans 1983). Early studies suggested that the Loop Current (LC) intrudes farther northwest during summer and minimumally during winter (Leipper 1970; Nowlin and Hubertz 1972; Maul 1977), but phasing with this seasonal cycle varies considerably (Molinari et al. 1977; Sturges and Evans 1983). Although the nature of the Loop Current oscillations is not clear, it has been suggested that the oscillations could be related to the variability of the Yucatán Current (Ichiye 1962; Cochrane 1963; Reid 1972; Maul et al. 1985; Molinari and Morrison 1988; Bunge et al. 2002). On the other hand, it has been demonstrated that the instability processes and topography of the bottom play an important role in the Loop Current variability (Maul 1977; Hurlburt and Thompson 1980).

The Loop Current is characterized by shedding anticyclonic eddies at intervals of 3 to 17 months (Elliott 1982; Maul and Vukovich 1993; Sturges and Leben 2000). These anticyclonic eddies have a periodicity of 3–35 months and width of ~300 km (Monreal Gómez and Salas de León 1997; Leipper 1970; Maul 1977; Behringer et al. 1977; Hurlburt and Thompson 1980; Elliott 1982). Detached eddies travel westward with a velocity of 2.1–4 km day$^{-1}$ (Elliott 1979; Vukovich and Crissman 1986; Johnson et al. 1992) interacting with the slope and shelf (Merrell and Morrison 1981; Brooks and Legeckis 1982; Elliott

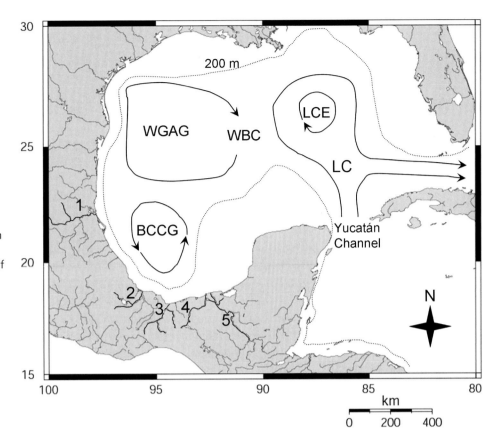

**Figure 4.1.** Large-scale circulation features and rivers in the Gulf of Mexico. The largest southern Gulf of Mexico rivers are (1) Pánuco, (2) Papaloapan, (3) Coatza-coalcos, (4) Grijalva, and (5) Usumacinta. BCCG = Bay of Campeche cyclonic gyre; WBC = Western Boundary Current; WGAG = western Gulf anticyclonic gyre; LCE = Loop Current eddy; and LC = Loop Current (from Zavala-Hidalgo et al. 2002).

1982; Merrell and Vázquez de la Cerda 1983; Vidal et al. 1994a) and with the Western Boundary Current (Sturges and Blaha 1976; Blaha and Sturges 1981; Sturges 1993). Occasionally, the anticyclonic gyre (detached from the Loop Current) collides with the western Gulf shelf off Tamiahua, Veracruz. This interaction with the topography can split the gyre into a new eddy that can interact with the old one. This anticyclonic/cyclonic pair, or a tripolar cyclonic/anticyclonic/cyclonic gyre system, was detected by hydrographic data or satellite images and by numerical simulations (Merrell and Morrison 1981; Vidal et al. 1992; Vidal et al. 1994b). It is important to consider that these gyres transport a volume of water with oceanic characteristics from slope to the shelf, that is, about one-third of the total anticyclonic volume (Monreal Gómez and Salas de León 1997). As a result, two currents that flow parallel to the coast northwardly and southwardly are formed. There are also cross-shelf jets associated with eddy pairs (Monreal Gómez and Salas de León 1997). Elliott (1982) showed that the anticyclonic gyres could substantially contribute to the water formation of the Gulf of Mexico Subtropical Underwater because intense vertical mixing, mainly during winter, affects the water in the first 200 m.

Mixing is one of the mechanisms for the formation of the Gulf Common Water with 36.4 psu and 22.5°C (Elliot 1982). However, this mixing affects only the surface layer. The other identified mechanism is the mixing induced by the collision of the anticyclonic gyre against the slope and shelf at the western side of the Gulf (Vidal et al. 1992, 1994b, 1994c), allowing the dilution of the Caribbean Subtropical Underwater with the lower-salinity surface layer of the thermocline (Vidal et al. 1992). Cochrane (1972) and Vázquez de la Cerda (1975) suggested that the Western Gulf Anticyclone Gyre (WGAG) (Fig. 4.1) is renewed periodically by detached gyres from the Loop Current. However, it has been suggested that wind stress together with the geometry and dimensions of the basin enhance this anticyclonic circulation (Sturges and Blaha 1976; Zavala-Hidalgo et al. 2003b).

Another semipermanent eddy-like circulation in the southern Gulf is observed over Bay of Campeche (Fig. 4.1). This region is characterized by cyclonic circulation that consists of a semipermanent cyclonic cold gyre of ~150 km in diameter (Vázquez de la Cerda 1993), which is smaller than the WGAG and has higher velocities (Monreal Gómez and Salas de León 1997). Climatological wind-stress information suggests that the Bay of Campeche cyclonic gyre is forced by the cyclonic wind-stress curl (Vázquez de la Cerda 1993; Gutiérrez de Velásco and Winant 1996).

On the northeastern Campeche Bank, cyclonic eddy generation takes place. Recently, by analyzing Topex/Poseidon sea-surface height anomaly data from January 1993 to March 2000, Zavala-Hidalgo et al. (2003a) reported the formation of eight cyclonic eddies generated on the northeastern Campeche Bank. These Campeche Bank cyclonic eddies were always generated in the same region. They were not periodic but had a timed relationship with the formation of major anticyclonic eddies from the LC (Zavala-Hidalgo et al. 2003a).

On the eastern section of the Campeche Bank (along the eastern slope of the Yucatán Shelf), there is an upwelling of cool, nitrate-rich water (Furnas and Smayda 1987; Merino 1997), preventing coral reef development. This water moves westward and apparently leaves the shelf to the north to Alacrán Reef (Merino 1997).

Small-scale circulation immediately around southern Gulf coral reefs is still not known. This is an important issue to be considered for future studies. Most of the studies in the southern Gulf of Mexico have been focused on processes that occur mainly offshore from the shelf, and only a few of them refer to circulation on the Tamaulipas-Veracruz shelf or on the Campeche Bank. Data reports of currents 30 km offshore of Tuxpan and the Port of Veracruz on the Tamaulipas-Veracruz shelf (Gutiérrez de Velásco et al. 1992, 1993), as well as high-resolution numerical simulation, historical hydrographic data, sea-level data, and satellite images (Zavala-Hidalgo et al. 2003b), showed that there is a seasonal reversal of the along-shelf current that reaches a monthly mean speed of 0.70 m s⁻¹. This along-shelf current is downcoast from September to March and upcoast from May to August (Fig. 4.2). In the fall and winter, the downcoast current reaches the southern Bay of Campeche. On the Campeche Bank, a westward coastal current has been suggested (Monreal-Gómez et al. 1992; Vázquez de la Cerda 1993; Merino 1997). Recently, from numerical modeling, the circulation has been observed on the Campeche Bank upcoast throughout the year (Fig. 4.2). However, in the middle of the shelf the transport has a maximum in July that drops almost to zero in September and remains weak until March, increasing slowly until June (Zavala-Hidalgo et al. 2003b).

While most of the circulation on the outer shelf is influenced by eddies (Merrell and Morrison 1981; Brooks and Legeckis 1982; Elliott 1982; Merrell and Vázquez de la Cerda 1983; Vidal et al. 1994a) and the WBC (Sturges and Blaha 1976; Blaha and Sturges 1981; Sturges 1993), currents on the shallow shelf respond quickly to changes of wind stress. Thus, the main forcing over the western shelf of the Gulf is the along-coast wind-stress component.

Offshore transport is expected in regions where opposing along-shelf currents meet. There is a confluence region in the southernmost part of the Bay of Campeche, observed from September to March. These offshore currents are

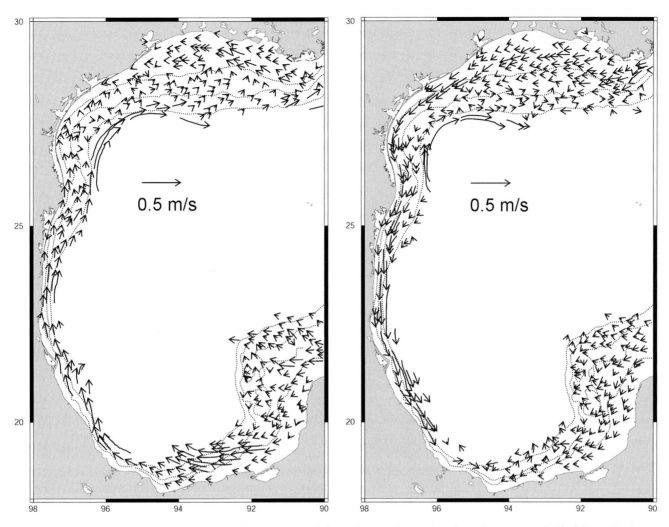

**Figure 4.2.** Mean surface currents from model data for June (left) and December (right) along the western shelf of the Gulf of Mexico. Shown are the isobaths of 25, 50, and 200 m (modified from Zavala-Hidalgo et al. 2003b).

clearly observed in satellite images because of their associated high chlorophyll *a* content and strong thermal fronts.

## Freshwater Inflow and Continental Influence

The central Gulf of Mexico, like most of the Caribbean Sea, has clear oligotrophic waters suitable for coral reef development. However, discharge from numerous rivers changes coastal conditions locally (Fig. 4.1), precluding the development of coral reefs along most of the Gulf coastline. Within the southern Gulf, the Grijalva-Usumacinta river system discharges ~$105.2 \times 10^9$ m$^3$ yr$^{-1}$ into the southeastern corner; whereas along the western coast of the Gulf the most important discharges are due to the Pánuco (~$18.9 \times 10^9$ m$^3$ yr$^{-1}$), Papaloapan (~$41.1 \times 10^9$ m$^3$ yr$^{-1}$), and Coatzacoalcos rivers (~$22.4 \times 10^9$ m$^3$ yr$^{-1}$) (Carricart-Ganivet and Merino 2001). Continental influence by river discharge within the southern Gulf is reduced on the Campeche Bank, since the Yucatán Peninsula is karstic and there is no surface runoff (Merino et al. 1990; Merino 1997). This is reflected on the spatial distribution of salinity. Salinity values on the western side of the Campeche Bank are characteristically higher than in Tuxpan and Veracruz (mean values of >36.35 psu vs. 35.96 psu; Table 4.1), reflecting the fact that runoff is minimal with respect to evaporation-precipitation.

**Table 4.1.** *Sea-surface temperature (SST), surface air temperature (SAT), salinity, precipitation, and wind speed and direction at six reef areas in the southern Gulf of Mexico.*

| Reef area | Annual average (SST °C) | Maximum (SST °C) | Minimum (SST °C) | Annual average (SAT °C) | Maximum (SAT °C) | Minimum (SAT °C) | Annual average salinity (PSU) | Pluvial precipitation (mm yr⁻¹) | Wind speed (m s⁻¹) | Wind direction (degrees) |
|---|---|---|---|---|---|---|---|---|---|---|
| Tuxpan | 26.4 | 29.7 | 21.9 | 25.5 | 29.4 | 19.8 | 35.93 | 835.1 | 5.49 | 239.31 |
| Veracruz | 26.6 | 29.4 | 22.9 | 26.0 | 29.2 | 21.8 | 35.98 | 821.4 | 5.51 | 220.68 |
| Arcas | 26.7 | 29.4 | 23.5 | 26.1 | 29.0 | 22.1 | 36.28 | 372.2 | 6.12 | 256.54 |
| Triángulos | 26.6 | 29.4 | 23.4 | 26.2 | 29.2 | 22.5 | 36.26 | 425.6 | 6.17 | 262.31 |
| Arenas | 26.5 | 29.6 | 23.3 | 25.9 | 29.3 | 21.9 | 36.46 | 384.9 | 6.29 | 269.04 |
| Alacrán | 26.6 | 29.4 | 23.6 | 25.9 | 29.0 | 22.3 | 36.38 | 391.4 | 6.21 | 264.41 |
| Average | 26.6 | 29.5 | 23.1 | 25.9 | 29.2 | 21.7 | 36.22 | 538.4 | 5.97 | 252.05 |
| Standard deviation | 0.10 | 0.13 | 0.64 | 0.24 | 0.16 | 0.98 | 0.21 | 225.2 | 0.36 | 18.51 |

*Notes:* SST, SAT, and wind data are from the Comprehensive Ocean Atmosphere Data Set (COADS) (Slutz et al. 1985; http://ingrid .ldeo.columbia.edu/SOURCES/.COADS/). Temperature and wind data were for 2° latitude-by-longitude squares associated with each area, covering the period January 1967 to December 1992. Wind directions were calculated using zonal and meridional wind data. Salinity and precipitation data are from the *Atlas of Surface Marine Data 1994* (DASILVA) (Da Silva et al. 1994; http://ingrid.ldeo.columbia.edu/ SOURCES/.DASILVA/). Salinity and precipitation data were for 1° latitude-by-longitude squares associated with each area, covering the period January 1945 to December 1993.

Figure 4.3 shows the seasonal salinity fluctuation in different coral reef areas. In general, lower salinity values are observed during summer when river discharge peaks than during the spring dry season. A correlation value of 90% was obtained between salinity values and precipitation for each reef area. Differences between reef areas are expected because of the different dominant processes within each region (i.e., Campeche Bank, Bay of Campeche, and Tamaulipas-Veracruz shelf). Thus, a similar behavior of the salinity was observed between Tuxpan and Veracruz, Cayos Arcas and Triángulos (Bay of Campeche), and Cayo Arenas and Alacrán reefs.

On the southwestern coast of the Gulf, despite the presence of numerous small rivers, coral reef formations are found in two groups between the Pánuco and Papaloapan rivers: some reefs are located off Tuxpan, but most formations are located farther south, off Veracruz. This second group, the Veracruz Reef System, includes the most developed reefs of the area (Carricart-Ganivet and Horta-Puga 1993). River runoff, mainly due to the discharge from the Jamapa-Atoyac river system creates suboptimal conditions for zooanthellate corals in this group (Horta-Puga and Carricart-Ganivet 1990). Within the Veracruz Reef System, continental influence, measured in terms of the distribution of bottom terrigenous sediments and salinity, is higher on the reefs located near the mouth of the Jamapa-Atoyac rivers and substantially decreases toward the north due to prevailing water circulation (Hernández-Rosario and Tinoco-Blanco 1988).

Coral reefs in the southern Gulf are exposed to a variable degree of continental influence. Because this gradient is caused mainly by river discharge, the influence is higher inshore, decreasing with distance from the coastline. Within the western half of the Campeche Bank, due to the discharge from the Grijalva-Usumacinta river system and prevailing water circulation, continental influence, measured in terms of the distribution of suspended terrigenous sediments, decreases toward the northeast of the mouths of these rivers (Carranza-Edwards et al. 1993).

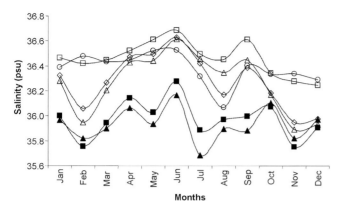

**Figure 4.3.** Average monthly salinity by reef area: Tuxpan (▲), Veracruz (■), Cayos Arcas (◇), Triángulos (△), Cayo Arenas (□), and Alacrán (○). Data from the *Atlas of Surface Marine Data 1994* (DASILVA) (de Silva et al. 1994; http://ingrid.ldeo.columbia.edu/SOURCES/.DASILVA/. Data are for 1° latitude-by-longitude squares associated with each area, covering the period January 1945 to December 1993.

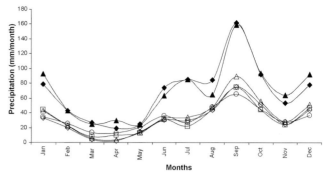

**Figure 4.4.** Average monthly precipitation by reef area. Tuxpan (▲), Veracruz (◆), Cayos Arcas (◇), Triángulos (△), Cayo Arenas (□), and Alacrán (○). Data from the *Atlas of Surface Marine Data 1994* (DASILVA) (de Silva et al. 1994; http://ingrid.ldeo.columbia.edu/SOURCES/.DASILVA/. Data are for 1° latitude-by-longitude squares associated with each area, and covering the period January 1945 to December 1993.

## Climate of the Southern Gulf of Mexico

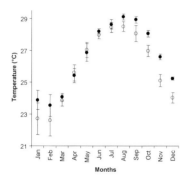

**Figure 4.5.** Average monthly sea-surface temperature (•) and surface air temperature (○) in the southern Gulf of Mexico. Error bars are standard deviations from the mean. Data are from the Comprehensive Ocean Atmosphere Data Set (COADS) (Slutz et al. 1985; http://ingrid.ldeo.columbia.edu/SOURCES/.COADS/). Data were for 2° latitude-by-longitude squares associated with six reef areas, covering the period January 1967 to December 1992.

The Gulf of Mexico is at the transition between the subtropical and tropical climate zones. Its climate on a seasonal timescale is modulated by the meridional change in position of the Intertropical Convergence Zone (Nobre and Shukla 1996; Landsea et al. 1999; Giannini et al. 2000; Marshall et al. 2001; Jáuregui 2003). Hence, seasonal variability is less pronounced in the tropical southern half of the Gulf, where the tropical easterlies are the prevailing winds all during the year, and the temperature gradient is weaker than in the subtropical northern half. Although there is precipitation during all seasons, summer is the rainiest season (Fig. 4.4). Based on the average for all reef areas, the rainy season lasts from June to October, with a maximum precipitation in September of 104.2 mm month$^{-1}$. Spring is the dry season, and April the driest month with an average precipitation of 12.8 mm month$^{-1}$. Comparing the different reef settings, the Veracruz Reef System, with a total annual precipitation average of 821.4 mm yr$^{-1}$, has a wetter climate than the Campeche Bank reefs, which average 393.5 mm yr$^{-1}$ (Table 4.1). This agrees with higher cloudiness in lower latitudes within the southern Gulf of Mexico.

The strength and position of the high pressure cells, formed at mid-latitudes, causes frontal incursions of cold air outbreaks (*nortes*), with increased frequency during winter. Additional atmospheric variability is primarily due to penetration of tropical weather systems that propagate and can intensify to become tropical storms and hurricanes. Perhaps one of the most important causes of interannual climatic variability is El Niño–Southern Oscillation (ENSO), which also influences the western tropical Atlantic (Nobre and Shukla 1996; Enfield and Mayer 1997; Saravanan and Chang 2000). ENSO events are more significant in terms of the change in the precipitation patterns resulting in coastal river streamflow and sediment production. Other important causes of interannual climate variability is the intraseasonal Madden-Julian Oscillation, associated with an increase in tropical storm frequency in the Gulf of Mexico, which is linked to wind changes in the lower troposphere of the eastern Pacific (Maloney and Hartmann 2000).

## Sea Surface and Air Temperature

The climate of the southern Gulf, as expected for tropical latitudes, is fairly homogenous, with hot summers and cool winters. Figure 4.5 presents monthly mean surface air temperature (SAT) and sea-surface temperature (SST) calculated for all reef areas in the southern Gulf. Atmospheric SAT is higher in August, averaging 28.5°C, and lower in February, with a mean of 22.6°C (Fig. 4.5). The SST follows the same pattern, with averages of 29.1°C in August and 23.5°C in February (Fig. 4.5). The difference in surface air temperature between the hottest and coolest months is ~5.9°C; the average annual SST was ~0.7°C higher (26.6°C) than the average annual SAT (25.9°C) (Table 4.1). There is no considerable difference between the maximum values for SST in all coral reef areas; however, differences up to 1.7°C are observed between Tuxpan and Alacrán.

## Winds

In general terms, the easterly tradewinds are the prevailing winds in the southern Gulf of Mexico. However, the direction of the winds in the Gulf responds to the seasonal position of the high-pressure systems; during the fall and winter, high-pressure systems move from the northwest continental United States into the Gulf, generating northeasterly winds in the western Gulf (Table 4.1) (Zavala-Hidalgo et al. 2003b). During summer, intensification and westward displacement of the semipermanent high-pressure system known as the Bermuda High, and the warming of the continental United States, generate southeasterly winds (Zavala-Hidalgo et al. 2003b). Average wind speed in the reef areas is ~6.0 m s$^{-1}$ (Table 4.1). However, wind speeds are higher at the Campeche Bank, averaging 6.2 m s$^{-1}$, and lower in Veracruz and Tuxpan, at 5.5 m s$^{-1}$ (Table 4.1). From autumn to spring several cold fronts (*nortes*) derived from artic air masses may attain speeds up to 33 m s$^{-1}$. Generally there are more than 30 *nortes* each fall and winter, which may cause a drop of air temperature up to 10°C. Heavy surge is also associated with the nortes and potentially may cause the same damage as wind-generated waves of tropical storms. During a strong norte, gale force winds may cover a large portion of the Gulf for a period of 1 to 3 days, with wave heights reaching 9 m in central and southern areas.

## Tropical Cyclones

The Gulf of Mexico is located in the main path of tropical cyclones that form in the North Atlantic. The hurricane season spans June to November, with August, September, and October the months with the highest incidence. On average, 9–10 tropical cyclones (tropical storms and hurricanes) form each season, and 5–6 develop into hurricanes (>117 km hr$^{-1}$). Tropical cyclones usually develop west of 50°W and move westward or west-northwestward at speeds less than 27 km hr$^{-1}$ in the lower latitudes. After moving into the Caribbean Sea, they usually either move toward the Gulf of Mexico or recurve and accelerate into the North Atlantic. Some will recurve after reaching the Gulf of Mexico, while others will continue westward to landfall. Additionally, tropical cyclones may form along old frontal boundaries that drift into the Gulf of Mexico or coastal Florida. Damage caused to southern Gulf of Mexico reefs are documented elsewhere in this book (see chapter 12).

# Reef Zonation and Ecology: Veracruz Shelf and Campeche Bank

ERNESTO CHÁVEZ, JOHN W. TUNNELL JR.,
AND KIM WITHERS

For decades, the ecology and zonation of coral reefs have dominated ecological studies in tropical regions of the world. Along with the geologic history of an area, physical environmental parameters govern ecological and geographical distribution of reef organisms. Benthic habitats and communities are usually similar and typical in various geographic regions, but understanding the reef types characteristic of any given region can be critical to understanding the ecological processes. Platform reefs are the characteristic reef type in the southern Gulf of Mexico.

Coral reefs are generally classified by their shape and proximity to the shoreline. Major types include atoll reefs, shelf or platform reefs, fringing reefs, and barrier reefs. Atolls are the common reef structure in the central Pacific Ocean. These reefs are typically ring-shaped with a central lagoon and develop on igneous rock emerging from the deep ocean. Atolls often have emergent margins (reef flats and islands that are also known as keys or cays) and may also have patch reefs in their sediment-dominated lagoons. A shelf or platform reef is a reef bank emerging from a continental shelf rather than the deep ocean. Located near or far from the mainland coast, the reef platform may include a shallow lagoon with sand keys. In cross section, these reefs look like flat-topped mountains (Fig. 5.1), and when viewed from above, their outline is often ellipsoidal. Fringing reefs are found on or near the shoreline and are composed of only a reef front or forereef slope.

A barrier reef can be a simple offshore barrier or it can be a complex system of reefs that may include all the reef types described above. Barrier reefs protect island and mainland coasts from the direct impact of wave action and erosion. There are only two major barrier reef systems, the Great Barrier Reef in eastern Australia and the Meso-American Barrier Reef System (MBRS), running south from northeastern Yucatán to Honduras in the eastern Caribbean Sea. The northern part of the MBRS is a series of fringing-barrier reefs along the Quintana Roo, Mexico, coastline with fringing reefs occurring at rocky headlands and barrier reefs occurring between the headlands along coastal embayments. To the south, off Belize and Honduras, the MBRS becomes a more typical offshore barrier reef. Because the MBRS is outside the Gulf of Mexico, its description is beyond the scope of this book. However, the MBRS is linked to Gulf of Mexico reefs, particularly as a larval source (Jordán-Dahlgren 2002; Jordán-Dahlgren and Rodríguez-Martínez 2003).

In the strictest sense, there are no atolls in the Gulf of Mexico or Caribbean Sea. Although superficially similar to Pacific atolls, Banco Chinchorro, Glover's Reef, Lighthouse Reef, and Turneffe Atoll (MBRS) are not built on igneous rock. Alacrán Reef, a platform reef on Campeche Bank, has been considered an

**Figure 5.1.** Bottom profile between Progreso, Yucatán and Alácran Reef, showing typical shape of platform reef (adapted from Kornicker et al. 1959).

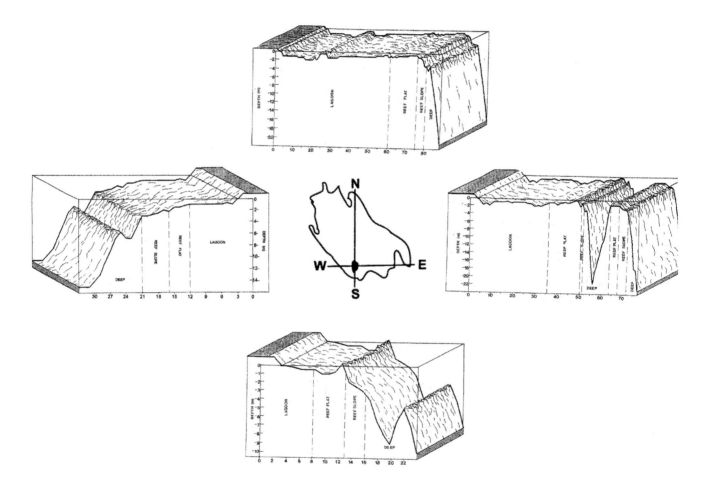

**Figure 5.2.** Profiles of Isla de Enmedio Reef radiating from four cardinal compass directions starting at Enmedio Lighthouse (adapted from Lehman 1993).

atoll or "atoll-like" because of its shape (Fosberg 1962), but its geological origin is quite different (see Liddell, chapter 3, this volume).

Most coral reefs in the Gulf of Mexico are platform reefs. The actively growing portion of Gulf platform reefs is oriented toward the northeast, east, or southeast, depending on geographic location, and faces the dominant wave swell, where a well-defined reef crest outlines the reef front. Although some are well enough developed to have a reef lagoon and small cays (e.g., Isla de Enmedio Reef, Alacrán Reef, Cayos Arcas), many are just shallow platforms without a lagoon (e.g., Topatillo, Anegadilla). The length of the emergent reef crest ranges from a few hundred or thousand meters in the Tuxpan Reef System (TRS) and

Veracruz Reef System (VRS), to about 22 km on Alacrán Reef, the largest reef in the Gulf of Mexico. All but Anegada de Afuera, Cabezo and Chopas (southern VRS), and Alacrán Reef are small reefs, less than 4 km long. There are only three fringing reefs in the western Gulf of Mexico, all located in the VRS: Punta Gorda–Punta Majahua, Hornos, and Punta Mocambo reefs. In these reefs, the reef front may reach depths of nearly 20 m. Cabo Catoche is on the northeasternmost corner of the Yucatán Peninsula where the Caribbean Sea meets the Gulf of Mexico. Contoy Island, southeast of Cabo Catoche, is the first fringing reef in the MBRS.

Accurate maps of southern Gulf of Mexico coral reefs are lacking, except the instances of Isla de Lobos Reef (Rigby and McIntire 1966), Isla de Enmedio Reef (Rannefeld 1970), and Alacrán Reef (Kornicker and Boyd 1962a, 1962b). This is one of the great needs within the region. Likewise, accurate reef profiles are also scarce, although numerous schematics have been presented. One exception is the accurate distance and depth profiles measured and created by the Secretaría de Marina on several Veracruz reefs. Isla de Enmedio Reef, one of the most studied in the region, is presented in four compass-heading profiles in Figure 5.2. These profiles reveal the characteristic shallow lagoon and fairly steep-sided windward and leeward forereefs.

## Reef Habitats and Zonation

Examination of the species distribution and reef structure reveals three general habitats (moving from east to west): the windward reef, a lagoon, and the leeward reef (Fig. 5.3). Differences in zonation patterns between leeward and windward slopes are the result of adaptation of species to wave action, while the patterns observed with depth primarily reflect changes in light intensity (Chávez et al. 1985). Variations observed on some reefs are most likely the result of different stages of reef development, the relative effects of the main driving forces, and maturity of the coral community. Environmental driving forces shape the reef structure, and their effect has led to the establishment of the same type of associations along gradients of light and energy intensities. The persistence of these gradients over evolutionary times allowed the maximum expression of interspecific competition, stimulating the increase of biodiversity (Chávez et al. 1985).

**Windward Reef**   The windward reef is the most dynamic portion of the coral reef and is characterized by a spur and groove system. The contour of the windward side of reefs in the Gulf of Mexico follows a wide curve that is more pronounced along the southeastern side. Fast-growing, branching forms like

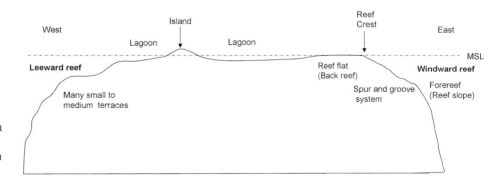

**Figure 5.3.** Schematic profile of a typical southern Gulf of Mexico platform coral reef. MSL = mean sea level.

elkhorn coral (*Acropora palmata*) dominate the spurs and are broken down by wave action, then calcareous algae cement fragments of broken coral into the reef structure. Smaller, unconsolidated fragments are transported downslope through the grooves and are deposited in low areas on reef terraces of the reef slope. These fragments may be further broken down and transformed into coral sand and eventually reach the continental shelf surrounding the reef base.

Most reefs exhibit a well-defined, subsurface reef crest running along the east and southeastern upper margin. This crest is the result of the balance between reef construction by corals and coralline algae, and reef destruction by wind and waves (Quintana y Molina 1991). The reef crest is very high energy, and breaking surf is common; it is the shallowest zone and may be covered by only a few centimeters of water at lowest tides (Tunnell 1988). Common organisms in this zone include the hydrocoral *Millepora alcicornis*, zoanthids (e.g., *Palythoa*), particularly on nearshore reefs, the sea urchin *Echinometra lucunter*, the green alga *Caulerpa racemosa*, and encrusting coralline red algae (Tunnell 1988; Lara et al. 1992).

Below the crest, which nearshore is up to 12 m wide and offshore up to 40 m wide (Lara et al. 1992), the forereef is dominated by the spur and groove system. The spurs jut out of the reef and up into the water column and are densely covered by corals and calcareous algae. Coarse sand and abundant coral fragments are found in the bottoms of the grooves. Initially, the forereef slopes gently, generally <20° (Jordán-Dahlgren and Rodríguez-Martínez 2003), but at Veracruz, 20°–30° (Tunnell 1988). From sea level to ~10 m, there is typically a fringe of elkhorn coral that protects the reef from wave action (*Acropora palmata* zone; mostly dead now). On the southeastern margin, this fringe was well developed and colonies expanded into large palmate "fronds" 2–4 m in width. Major spur-builder species include *Acropora palmata* in shallow areas and *Montastraea annularis* in deeper sections (Jordán-Dahlgren and Rodríguez-Martínez 2003).

The slope of the reef increases greatly below the *Acropora palmata* zone, sometimes reaching the bottom as vertical walls or overhangs (Tunnell 1988). At mid-depths, which at Veracruz is up to 17 m (Tunnell 1988) and at Campeche Bank is ~25 m (Rezak and Edwards 1977), massive or encrusting stony corals are dominant, primarily *Diploria strigosa*, *Montastraea annularis* (species complex), and *Porites astreoides*. On deeper reef slopes, which at Veracruz are 15–40 m (Lara et al. 1992; Jordán-Dahlgren and Rodríguez-Martínez 2003) and at Campeche >25 m (Rezak and Edwards 1972; Jordán-Dahlgren and Rodríguez-Martínez 2003), light diminishes and "shingles" or flattened, platy coral heads are characteristic to the bottom (Tunnell 1988). Common species include *M. cavernosa*, *Agaricia* spp., and *P. astreoides*.

**Lagoon and Leeward Reef**  Unlike the windward reef, the protected leeward (western) side of the southern Gulf of Mexico reefs is relatively calm. There is no reef crest or breaking surf and, on the reef slope, no well-defined spur-groove zone. The leeward habitats are the most variable areas of the reef (Lara et al. 1992). The degree of development of the leeward reef and the species present vary with distance from shore and concomitant changes in sedimentation rates (Gutiérrez et al. 1993). Terrigenous sedimentation can be high and waters may be turbid, especially nearshore. If a lagoon is present, it is found centrally and leeward of the crest. If a sand island is present, it is typically located in the southwestern part of the lagoon (Tunnell 1988). If a reef has an island, it may also have a zone of secondary coral growth and rocky rubble to the west of the island (e.g., Isla de Enmedio, Cayos Arcas)

Traversing westward from the windward reef, just behind the reef crest, the shallow (0.5–1.0 m) reef flat (back reef) slopes gently away (<10°; Gutiérrez et al. 1993) from the crest (Tunnell 1988). Storm-tossed boulders are conspicuous features on the windward side of the reef flat. Encrusting coralline algae are abundant and play an active role cementing broken coral fragments into the reef structure (Jordán-Dahlgren and Rodríguez-Martínez 2003). Corals include small heads of *Porites astreoides*, *P. porites*, *Siderastrea radians*, and encrusting *Diploria clivosa* (Tunnell 1988; Lara et al. 1992; Gutiérrez et al. 1993).

A wide reef lagoon is characteristic in well-developed or mature platform reefs in the southern Gulf of Mexico. Leeward of the reef flat, the bottom of the lagoon slopes gently from east to west. Bottom types range from hard substrate to coarse and fine sediment, and bottom communities and microhabitats represent many stages of development: bare sand, coral patches or pinnacles, coralline algae, green calcareous algae, and/or turtle grass (*Thalassia testudinum*). Dense turtle grass beds can be found in the lagoons of many reefs at Veracruz, but they are uncommon on Campeche Bank platforms, except Alacrán Reef.

Depth of the leeward reef slope ranges from 3 to 24 m at Veracruz (Lara et al. 1992) and the slope is steeper (>20°) than the windward side (Jordán-Dahlgren and Rodríguez-Martínez 2003). Although uncommon, the leeward slope of some reefs, such as Isla de Lobos Reef (TRS) and Santiaguillo (VRS, Plate 16), exhibit the spur and groove structure that is usually found only on the windward reef slope. Massive, stony corals such as *Montastraea*, *Diploria*, and *Siderastrea* are common in some places (Solís 1990; Lara et al. 1992; Gutiérrez et al.1993; Jordán-Dahlgren and Rodríguez-Martínez 2003). Prior to its die-off in the late 1970s and early 1980s, staghorn coral (*Acropora cervicornis*) formed dense thickets on the leeward slopes of many southern Gulf of Mexico reefs, almost like an understory beneath the massive corals. Old coral heads of *M. annularis*, some up to 5 m wide and extending 2–4 m into the water column, are common features on the leeward reef. The deeper portions of the leeward reef are quite similar to the deeper portions of the windward forereef below the spur-groove zone. Massive head corals are typically dominant on the deeper leeward reef slope, and in the deepest areas, platy or shingle coral growth is found.

**Zonation**   Zonation of the main components of the reef community of Holocene Jamaican reefs and Pleistocene reefs in Barbados are similar (Jackson 1992) and have remained relatively constant over the past 200,000 years (Fig. 5.4). This pattern is similar in the southern Gulf of Mexico (Rigby and McIntire 1966; Chávez et al. 1970; Chávez 1973; Solís 1990), although zonation of windward and leeward sides often differs (Fig. 5.5). The most striking difference between the two slopes is that elkhorn coral is generally present only on the windward reef, and staghorn coral is generally found only in leeward reef habitats. Coral cover on the leeward slope, and hence zonation, is usually poorly developed on both mid-shelf and nearshore reefs due to the influence of freshwater and terrigenous sediment deposition (Lara et al. 1992). Figure 5.6 is a generalized diagram of reef zonation and the effects of wave energy, sedimentation, depth, and light penetration.

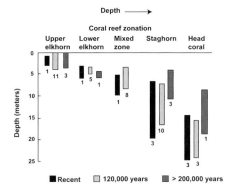

**Figure 5.4.** Relative abundance of dominant corals in elkhorn, staghorn, and head coral reef zones and depth distributions in Recent (Holocene) and Pleistocene Caribbean reef communities (after Jackson 1992). Numbers below bars are numbers of reefs sampled for each community.

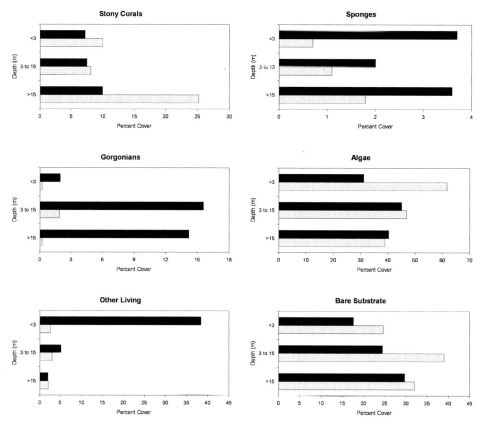

**Figure 5.5.** Comparison of coverage (%) by major benthic categories on windward (black bars) and leeward (patterned bars) reef slopes at Alacrán Reef (data from Solís 1990). Note differences in scale on axes showing percentage of cover.

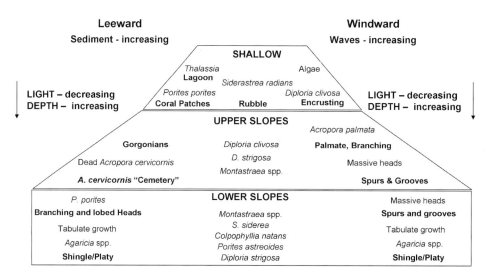

**Figure 5.6.** Generalized model of species composition by reef habitat and zone (modified from Lara et al. 1993).

## Development of Reef Communities

Coral reef community complexity in the Gulf of Mexico increases from the relatively depauperate reefs in the western Gulf to reefs with higher species diversity on Campeche Bank. This is the result of differences in environmental factors as well as proximity to larval sources such as the MBRS. Of particular importance are differences in environmental stability with respect to temperature and freshwater inflow (especially nutrient and sediment loading), the locations of reefs with respect to Gulf of Mexico currents and gyres, and the width of the continental shelf. The center of reef biodiversity in western tropical Atlantic appears to be Jamaica, with about 65 species of corals (Wells and Lang 1973). From this center, diversity of coral species decreases from 55 species on the MBRS, to 42 species in the Campeche Bank reefs, 36 in the Veracruz Reef System, and 29 in the Tuxpan Reef System (see Horta-Puga et al., chapter 8, this volume), with the fewest species (20) found on the Flower Garden Banks in the northern Gulf (Aronson et al. 2005).

The reefs in the southern Gulf of Mexico represent all stages of reef development from relatively immature (e.g., Topatillo) to mature (e.g., Alacrán Reef). The forereef is the first stage of reef development, which in its earliest phase would look like a small patch reef (Fig. 5.7). As reef growth proceeds, the forereef becomes more defined and prominent. Establishment and growth of branching corals such as *Acropora palmata* causes the reef front to expand seaward while coralline algae consolidate the substrate so that slower-growing massive corals (e.g., *Montastraea annularis, Diploria clivosa*) can become established in the deeper waters. In this stage of reef development, the coral reef is often dome-shaped, as are Bajo Nuevo and Obispos reefs on Campeche Bank.

Eventually the reef crest develops, and the protection it provides allows development of the reef flat. Under these conditions, massive corals are dominant in the protected leeward portions of the reef. Growth is more or less constant along the reef borders, but erosion by waves may lead to accumulation of coral fragments and debris, limiting coral growth in the central and back portions of the reef and imposing conditions of differential growth, with rates being more favorable on the upper forereef. Coral erosion on the reef crest and upper forereef provides a great deal of material that is transported to various parts of the

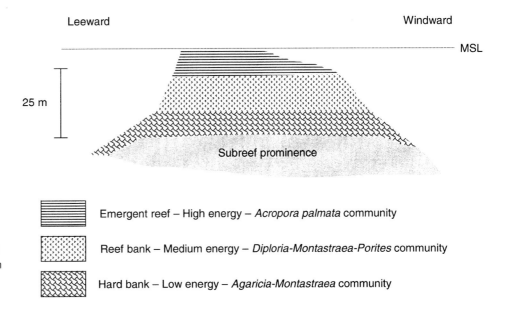

**Figure 5.7.** Generalized model of reef development (modified from Logan 1969). MSL = mean sea level.

reef. Small coral pieces are often cemented into the reef structure by the coralline algae or are transported to windward habitats. Larger pieces are broken down into gravel and are taken to deeper levels of the forereef through the groove system. Accumulation of sediment behind the reef flat reduces coral growth significantly and results in formation of a lagoon.

When upward growth approaches the surface, branching corals like the elkhorn coral attain the climax stage in the succession of the upper forereef community. This coral has the highest growth rate, and its development accelerates morphological differentiation of reef habitats, creating suitable conditions for the formation of a reef lagoon, where the sediment may be fine enough for the establishment of turtle grass and small, branched coral colonies (e.g., *Porites* spp.), well adapted to make use of the intense sunlight in the shallow water. In the southwestern Gulf of Mexico, turtle grass beds appear to be the climax stage of soft lagoon bottoms, where sedimentation is high. In other cases, sand and coral patches occupy lagoon floors.

## Veracruz Reefs

Coral reefs of the southwestern Gulf of Mexico, located off the state of Veracruz, are of three types: fringing, emergent platform, and submerged banks (see Table 2.1). They can be divided into two groups from north to south (see Fig. 2.1). The first group of six platform reefs, the Tuxpan Reef System (TRS), lies east and southeast of Cabo Rojo and comprises six small reefs between 21°00'04"N and 21°30'10"N, from north to south: Blanquilla, Medio, Isla de Lobos, Tanguijo, Enmedio, and Tuxpan (see Fig. 2.2, Plate 17). They are located on the continental shelf 5–11.2 km offshore.

The second group is known as the Veracruz Reef System (VRS). Near the city of Veracruz, the VRS includes 25 small to medium-sized coral reefs located between 19°14'33"N and 19°03'11"N (see Fig. 2.3, Plate 18). The VRS includes three coastal fringing reefs and two submerged reef banks (see Table 2.1), but most are platform reefs located on the continental shelf up to 20.5 km offshore. This group of reefs is further divided into northern and southern groups (Carricart-Ganivet and Horta-Puga 1993). The northern group is located offshore from the city of Veracruz and includes 13 reefs and banks, from north to south: Punta Gorda–Punta Majahua, Galleguilla, La Blanquilla, La Gallega, Anegada de Adentro, Isla Verde, Pájaros, Hornos, Lavandera, Tierra Nueva, Bajo Mersey, Isla de Sacrificios, and Punta Mocambo (see Fig. 2.4, Plates 19–21). The southern group, which lies south of the city of Veracruz and offshore from the fishing village of Antón Lizardo, includes the 12 remaining reefs, from north to south: Anegada de Afuera, Topatillo, Santiaguillo, Anegadilla, Aviso, Polo, Isla de Enmedio, Chopas, Blanca, Cabezo, El Giote, and El Rizo (see Fig. 2.5, Plates 22–24).

**Tuxpan Reef System** The TRS is located near the northernmost limit of the tropical belt. In general, these small reefs are in good shape and show little environmental degradation (Universidad Veracruzana 2003) even though they are close to shore (within 11.2 km). Detailed descriptions of Isla de Lobos Reef were completed in mid- to late 1960s (Rigby and McIntire 1966; Chávez et al. 1970; Chávez (1973) but have not been updated. The small reefs a few kilometers to the north-northwest of Isla de Lobos Reef, Blanquilla and Medio, have received only cursory attention (Moore 1958; Rigby and McIntire 1966). The three other coral reefs in this group, Tanguijo, Enmedio, and Tuxpan, which lie farther south and nearer the city of Tuxpan, are virtually unknown but are currently under study by personnel from Universidad Veracruzana in Tuxpan.

The general configuration of reefs in this system is a flame-shaped contour from an overhead view with the convex or windward side facing south and east. The southeast side is exposed to prevailing winds, and breaking surf is common on the reef crest. The reef crest defines the contour of the lagoon. There is a sand key and lighthouse in the lagoon of Isla de Lobos Reef (Plate 25), but not on other reefs in this group. Their positions are demarcated by monuments with automated lights, in addition to the breaking surf on their south and east sides. Behind the reef crest on Isla de Lobos Reef, the lagoon was densely covered by turtle grass in areas where sediment was fine, and *Halimeda opuntia*, a green calcareous algae, covered most of the hard bottom areas (Chávez et al. 1970; Chávez 1973). A well-defined, V-shaped spur and groove zone covered most of the upper slopes (10–13 m) of both windward and leeward reefs (Rigby and McIntire 1966). Massive corals, primarily *Montastraea annularis* and *Diploria strigosa*, dominated the coral community on both reef slopes.

On the smaller reefs, lagoons were not big enough to retain fine sediment, so grass beds were not well developed (Moore 1958; Rigby and McIntire 1966). Instead, much of the reef top was covered by coarse sand or coral debris cemented together by coralline algae. Although not surveyed extensively, coral communities appeared poorly developed on the windward slopes of these reefs. Development on the leeward slope seemed similar to that of Isla de Lobos Reef.

Isla de Lobos Reef is the largest and most well developed of the Tuxpan reefs. It has been well described, especially the lagoon. The main topographic features delineated were a flat lagoon, a deeply grooved leeward reef, a more complexly grooved but more uniform windward reef, a broad apron of calcareous sand to the south that includes the island, more sandy areas to the west and north of the reef, and a rocky slope to the east (Rigby and McIntire 1966; Fig. 5.8). Communities on the windward and leeward reef slopes were similar, and both reef slopes exhibited spur and groove structure (Fig. 5.9).

The windward reef crest on Isla de Lobos Reef was a ridge of coralline algae and associated cemented coral material (Rigby and McIntire 1966). Windward of the crest, to about 8 m, *Acropora palmata* was the dominant species, and an "undergrowth" of *Diploria clivosa* was present in shallow areas and *Diploria strigosa* in deeper areas. In the spurs and grooves between 8 and 17 m, massive hemispherical or sheetlike coral development dominated. The coral community consisted primarily of *Diploria strigosa* with *Siderastrea siderea*, *D. clivosa*, and *Montastraea annularis* in lesser amounts. Below 17 m, low hemispherical heads of coral, or sheetlike and/or encrusting growth was common. *Montastraea cavernosa* dominated. The base of the windward reef was described as "exceedingly cavernous," with corals growing as "arched heads and crusts."

The leeward reef crest was poorly defined except in the northern part of the lagoon (Rigby and McIntire 1966). The lagoon slopes westward and then drops off to the steep slope of the reef. *Acropora palmata* was dominant in depths to 3–6 m, and an understory of sheetlike *D. clivosa* existed in shallower areas and low-growing *D. strigosa* or *M. annularis* in deeper water. *Montastraea annularis* was dominant on the slope from below the *Acropora palmata* zone to about 17 m. As on the windward reef, *M. cavernosa* dominates in the deepest areas (~25 m) of the leeward reef and forms sheets and hemispherical heads.

At the shallow transition between the lagoon and windward or leeward reef crests, a belt of *Diploria clivosa* covers most of the rocky substrate. This belt was

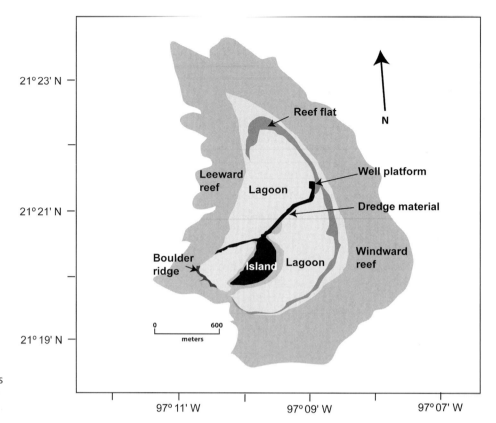

**Figure 5.8.** Physiographic features of Isla de Lobos Reef (after Rigby and McIntire 1966).

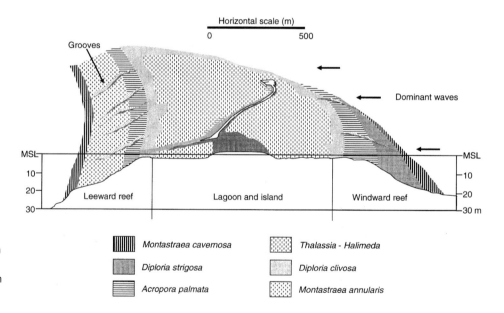

**Figure 5.9.** Bottom profile of Isla de Lobos Reef showing the dominant benthic communities in the various reef zones (modified from Chávez 1973). MSL = mean sea level.

wider in the east and west-central lagoon margins. Leeward of the windward reef crest, the reef flat was up to 30 m wide and consisted primarily of massive algal crusts and flattened heads of *D. clivosa* (Rigby and McIntire 1966). Other corals found in this zone were *D. strigosa, Siderastrea siderea,* and *Porites* spp. The hydrozoan *Millepora,* as well as various echinoids and anemones, were also observed.

The lagoon was generally within 0.6 m of low tide (Rigby and McIntire 1966) but reached 2 m in some areas (Chávez et al. 1970). A dredged ship channel runs

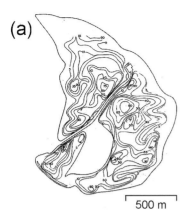

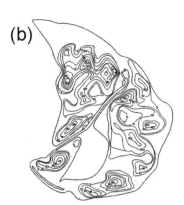

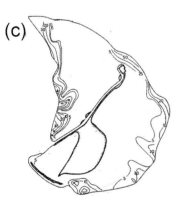

**Figure 5.10.** Distribution and abundance (percentage of cover) of **(a)** turtle grass (*Thalassia testudinum*); **(b)** the green calcareous alga *Halimedia opuntia*, and **(c)** brain coral (*Diploria clivosa*) on the Isla de Lobos Reef platform (modified from Chávez et al. 1970).

southwest to northeast, cutting the lagoon in two. The dredged sediment was piled in a ridge along the south and east side of the channel where a road was built connecting the island to a gas well platform on the northeastern side on the reef crest. This ridge prevented water from moving freely through the lagoon, leading to rapid sedimentation with fine sand, primarily in the western half. Fine sediment covers only the surface of the lagoon bottom, because the texture of sediment was basically gravel-sized mixed with sand in different proportions (Chávez et al. 1970). In the southwest end of the lagoon there was a narrow boulder ridge about 500 m long, emerging about 1 m above the sea surface (see Fig. 5.8).

In the center of the lagoon, the green calcareous alga *Halimeda opuntia* and the seagrass *Thalassia testudinum* predominated; at the periphery, *Diploria clivosa* was dominant (Fig. 5.10a–c). An estimate of net primary productivity of the seagrass bed in the Isla de Lobos Reef lagoon was 14.6 ×$10^6$ g/d (Chávez et al. 1970). Common animal species were *Ophiothrix* sp. and *Ophioderma* sp. (brittle stars), *Modulus modulus* and *Cerithium litteratum* (gastropods), *Clibanarius antillensis* (hermit crab), *Mithrax forceps* (spider crab), and *Diploria clivosa* (brain coral).

**Veracruz Reef System** More coral reefs are found in the vicinity of the city of Veracruz than anywhere else in the southern Gulf of Mexico. Unfortunately, most of these reefs have been profoundly impacted by land-use practices, urbanization, their proximity to the coastline, and their easy access (see Horta-Puga, chapter 12, and Chávez and Tunnell, chapter 13, this volume). In addition, natural terrigenous deposition in this area is high (Emery 1963) due to inflows from Rio Jamapa and Rio Papaloapan. The reefs nearest Veracruz city are smaller, closer to shore, and most heavily impacted; those offshore from Antón Lizardo are larger in size, extend farther offshore, and are generally in better condition.

The northern group of reefs (those nearest Veracruz city) consists of at least three small fringing reefs (Punta Gorda–Punta Majahua, Hornos, and Punta Mocambo), seven platform reefs (Galleguilla, Anegada de Adentro, La Blanquilla, La Gallega, Pájaros, Isla Verde, and Isla de Sacrificios), and three submerged reef banks (Lavandera, Bajo Mersey, and Tierra Nueva). La Gallega is now attached to the mainland as a result of dredging and filling activities associated with development of the Port of Veracruz (see Fig. 2.4). The other platform reefs range from 1.4 to 7.5 km away from the shore. The fringing reefs are on or very near shore and have very low scleractinian coverage, a maximum depth of 6–12 m, and large amounts of deposited and suspended sediment (Lara et al. 1992). There is virtually no habitat development on the leeward portion because it is essentially on the shore. Anegada de Adentro and Isla Verde, in addition to development on the windward side, have well-developed leeward slopes which have large gorgonian patches in shallow areas (Lara et al. 1992). The leeward slopes of La Blanquilla, Pájaros, Isla Sacrificios, Galleguilla, and La Gallega are poorly developed, having corals only in the shallow and deep extremes.

The platform reefs in the southern group lie 2.6–20.5 km offshore from Antón Lizardo (see Fig. 2.5). Some of these reefs have a sand key, and some seem to be a part of a larger reef system, as is the case of Anegada de Afuera, Topatillo, and the group comprising Chopas, Polo, and Blanca. The offshore group, Anegada de Afuera, Santiaguillo, Anegadilla, and the central and northwestern parts of Cabezo, have good coral development on both windward and leeward sides (Lara et al. 1992). Those reefs that are slightly nearer shore, Isla

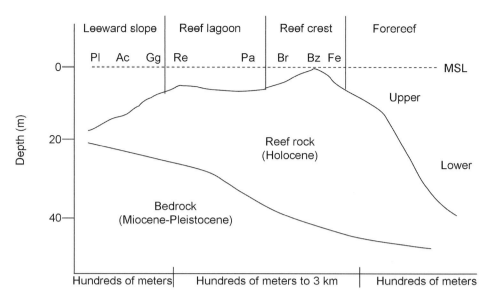

**Figure 5.11.** Zonation model of the coral reefs of the Veracruz Reef System showing four major zones and ten subzones (modified from Lara et al. 1992). Subzones: Fe = fore edge; Bz = breaker zone; Br = back reef; Pa = patch zone; Re = rear edge; Gg = gorgonian garden; Ac = *Acropora cervicornis* cemetery; Pl = platy zone; MSL = mean sea level.

de Enmedio, El Rizo, and the southeastern tip of Cabezo, have a relatively well-developed windward slope, but the leeward slope consists primarily of patchy coral heads on a sandy bottom. The remaining reefs located near shore are also relatively well developed on the windward side, but the leeward slope is poorly developed, with little coral.

The reefs of the VRS have been divided into four main zones and 10 subzones (Lara et al. 1992; Gutiérrez et al. 1993; Fig. 5.11): forereef (upper, lower), reef crest (fore edge, breaker zone, back reef), reef lagoon (patch zone, rear edge), and leeward slope (gorgonian garden, *Acropora cervicornis* cemetery, platy zone).

**Forereef**　In coral reefs of many other regions, the forereef is also known as the spur and groove zone. At fringing reefs such as Hornos and Mocambo, it ranges to depths of 12 m, but in outer reefs such as Anegada de Afuera, Anegadilla, Santiaguillo, and Anegada de Adentro, it may reach depths of 40 m. The forereef is divided into two depth-related subzones, upper and lower.

The upper forereef is characterized by a spur and groove zone on most reefs and is found in waters from 3 to 10 m deep with a slope of 20°–30°. Up to 18 coral species may be found, but *A. palmata* (Plate 26) was the dominant species prior to its decline in the 1970s and 1980s. This species was dominant because its branching growth form allowed it to withstand high-energy wave action and enhanced the capacity of its zooxanthellae to assimilate sunlight. Other common stony corals in this subzone are *Montastraea, Colpophyllia,* and *Diploria.* Other benthic components are the sponges *Calyspongia falax, Haliclona rubens,* and *Ircinia* sp., encrusting algae, and the gastropods *Morula nodulosa* and *Astrea tecta.*

The lower forereef ranges in depths from 10 to 40 m with a slope of 45°–90°. The lower spurs and grooves are well developed and sometimes reach the soft sediment of the continental shelf. The topography is very rough and cavernous, sometimes with cliffs up to 15 m, as in Anegada de Afuera, Cabezo, and Santiaguillo. Stony corals and encrusting algae constitute the majority of live cover. *Montastraea annularis* dominates, followed by *Siderastrea siderea* and *M. cavernosa.* Massive growth of large corals may be up to 2.5 m in diameter.

Shingle-shaped (platy or tabulate) forms occur on the sides of the spurs as well as on lowest slopes of the forereef (Plate 27). Sponges like *Ircina campana* and *Verongia fistularis* are common. The crinoid *Davidaster rubiginosa* (Plate 28) is found in this zone, as well as the bivalves *Malleus candeanus, Lima scabra,* and *Spondylus americanus.*

Reef Crest   The reef crest is the shallowest part of the reef. Turbulence from wind and waves is high, particularly from September to March, when strong north winds occur (Lara et al. 1992). Very dense aggregations of the sea urchin *Echinometra lucunter* are present throughout this zone. The reef crest has been divided into three subzones, windward to leeward: fore edge, breaker zone, and back reef (reef flat) (Lara et al. 1992; Gutiérrez et al. 1993).

The windward side of the reef crest, the fore edge (0–3 m depth), has a gentle to moderate slope (<30°) and is constantly exposed to wave action. On smaller reefs like Galleguilla, Polo, Aviso, Santiaguillo and Anegadilla, this is the only habitat in the upper forereef. This subzone is characterized by a dense carpet of turf algae, and on nearshore reefs, zoanthids (*Palythoa caribbaeorum* and *Zoanthus* sp.) are common. Stony corals grow as dispersed encrusting forms. In the lowest part of this subzone, *Acropora palmata* was dominant before dying off, mostly in the late 1970s and early 1980s (Tunnell 1992).

The breaker zone (reef crest proper) is the shallowest portion and may be partially exposed during lowest tides. This subzone is characterized by intense wave action and high illumination (Lara et al. 1992). Coralline algae predominate, and *Millepora alcicornis* is also characteristic. Encrusting stony corals are present as dispersed small colonies (<0.5 m), mainly *Siderastrea* sp., *Porites* spp., and *Diploria clivosa*. Large patches of the zoanthids *Palythoa caribbaeorum* and *Zoanthus* sp. are widespread, especially on nearshore reefs. The anemone *Stoichactis helianthus* is also a common element on the smaller reefs.

The back reef (reef flat) is the outer limit of the reef lagoon on its windward side (Plate 29). This subzone is characterized by a hard, flat substrate containing gravel from broken coral and scattered storm-tossed boulders, mainly on the most windward edge. There are abundant turf and coralline algae, sea urchins, and some mollusks such as *Cerithium litteratum, Astrea tecta,* and *Diodora cayennensis*. Stony corals are not common, and the main species are the encrusting forms of *Diploria clivosa, Porites astreoides,* and *Siderastrea radians. Porites porites* also occurs but in lower densities. The high-energy, smooth form of coralline algal nodules is common on the most leeward sections of the reef flat.

Lagoon   Low water movement, low wave energy, and shallow depths (0.5–2 m) characterize the reef lagoon. This is a habitat exposed to high light intensity. The bottom may be covered by turtle grass and/or algae, solitary coral heads, or small patches of coral, coral remains, and sand (Plate 30a, b). Two subzones are recognized (generally windward to leeward): the patch zone and the rear edge (Lara et al. 1992; Gutiérrez et al. 1993).

The patch zone is the shallowest portion of lagoons (0.5–1.0 m). This habitat is characterized by scattered patches of seagrass, rock, sand, and dead coral remains (Plate 30c). Live cover is typically <5%. Rocky patches are found mainly on larger reefs such as Anegada de Afuera, Cabezo, and Chopas. These generally consist of the remains of *Porites porites* mixed with *Siderastrea radians* and *Diploria clivosa*. Other common species include sponges such as *Haliclona* and *Tedania,* the sea urchins *Diadema antillarum* (before 1983), *Tripneustes ventricosus,* and *Echinometra lucunter,* and mollusks such as *Tridachia crispata* and *Cerithium litteratum.*

The rear-edge subzone is the transition from the lagoon to the leeward reef slope. It has a gentle slope, and fine and coarse sediments are abundant. Isolated small-branched corals such as *Acropora palmata, A. cervicornis* (before the die-off), and *Porites porites* as well as small heads of *Diploria* and *Siderastrea* are scattered throughout the zone (Gutiérrez et al. 1993). Other species, such as the sponges *Haliclona* and *Tedania,* the sea urchins *Echinometra lucunter* and *Tripneustes ventricosus,* as well as the gastropods *Cerithium litteratum* and *Astrea tecta,* can be locally common. The low-energy, branching forms of coralline algal nodules are common in some seagrass beds of leeward lagoons.

Leeward Reef   Low water movement, low wave energy, and the potential for high rates of terrigenous sedimentation characterize the leeward reef zone. Sedimentation is considered the main driving environmental force in this habitat, but it is dependent on distance from shore. Depth on the reef slope ranges from 3 to 24 m. The leeward reef slope is divided into three subzones, from shallower to deeper: the gorgonian garden, the *Acropora cervicornis* cemetery, and the platy zone (Lara et al. 1992; Gutiérrez et al. 1993).

The gorgonian garden starts at the outer edge of the lagoon and is found in water from 2 to 6 m deep. Its slope is gentle (<10°) and it generally receives a large amount of sediment. As its name implies, growth of soft corals can be profuse, especially on small leeward-protected patch reefs separated from the main reef and less subject to heavy sedimentation (Nelson et al. 1988; Tunnell and Nelson 1989; Plate 31). *Pseudoplexaura porosa* is often dominant; other common soft coral species include *P. acerosa, Plexaura flexuosa,* and *Eunicea* sp. In addition, the remains of *Acropora cervicornis* are prevalent in this subzone on several reefs in both the northern and southern groups: La Blanquilla, Anegada de Adentro, and Isla de Sacrificios in the northern group and El Rizo, Isla de Enmedio, Polo, and Aviso in the southern group. Other benthic elements include *Diploria* sp., encrusting sponges, and the sea urchins *Echinometra lucunter* and *E. viridis* (Gutiérrez et al. 1993).

The depth of the *Acropora cervicornis* cemetery (Plate 32) partially overlaps the gorgonian garden (3–15 m) and its slope may be up to 45°. Prior to the late 1970s and early 1980s, this zone was characterized by a dense, living thicket of *A. cervicornis* (Tunnell 1992; Plate 33). This zone seems to be the most biologically diverse habitat of all the reefs of the VRS (up to 13 genera and 17 species of stony corals), but coral coverage is now low (after the death of *A. cervicornis*), especially on reefs of the northern group. The most common stony corals are species of *Colpophyllia, Montastraea, Porites,* and *Diploria.* The fused remains of *A. cervicornis* provide substrate for a diverse community of sponges including *Ircinia, Calyspongia, Verongia,* and *Haliclona.* Sponge associates include brittle stars and sea urchins such as *Ophiocoma echinata, Echinometra viridis, Eucidaris tribuloides, Lytechinus williamsi,* and *Euapta lappa.* The mollusks *Cerithium litteratum* and *Lima scabra* are also common in the *Acropora cervicornis* cemetery.

The platy subzone occurs in depths of 10–24 m. The slope is not very pronounced and there are scattered fine sand patches. This habitat is well defined in the southern group, and in the northern group it is best developed on the reef system's extremities (north and south). The dominant living coral is *Montas-*

*traea annularis,* and *Agaricia* spp. is common in some areas. Dead remains of the stony corals *Montastraea* and *Sideastrea* provide substrate where the sponges *Verongia fistularis, Calyspongia falax, Ircinia campana, I. fasciculata,* and *I. strobilina* flourish. The crinoid *Davidaster rubiginosa* is also common.

Unique Features   There are several unique features on some of the Veracruz reefs that deserve biological and geological investigation: reef cuts (e.g., Isla de Enmedio Reef), "blue holes" (e.g., Isla de Enmedio Reef, Anegada de Afuera), and coral pillars.

REEF CUTS   Immediately behind the reef flat on the northeastern and southeastern extremities of Isla de Enmedio Reef, there are deep cuts extending into the reef platform (Fig. 5.12; Plate 34a). Locally, fishermen and others call these features *pozas azules* (blue holes) because of their deep blue color compared to the typical brownish bottom color of the adjacent reef flat (Rannefeld 1972). These structures are not round, like the true blue holes on the reefs of Belize, but are elongate structures extending from the continental shelf toward the reef's center. The northeastern cut extends about 250 m into the reef; the southeastern cut is slightly shorter (200 m). Both have steep-sided coral and rock walls where they cut the reef, then gently taper to barren, soft substrate bottoms. Prior to the *Acropora* die-off, the inner slopes were covered with thickets of *A. cervicornis* down to 6–8 m. Other reefs in the area with similar features include Anegada de Adentro, Anegada de Afuera, and Chopas.

BLUE HOLES   Distinctive, enclosed "blue holes" are found in reef flat areas of several reefs (Anegada de Afuera, Chopas, Isla de Enmedio, and Isla Verde) (Plate 34b). Two of these features are found on Isla de Enmedio Reef, one in the center of the reef flat and the other near the southeastern corner (see Fig. 5.12). Both features are irregularly circular, 25–30 m in diameter, and 10 m deep. They are steep-walled and feature large coral heads on the bottom or lower slopes. The leeward wall of the central blue hole is filled with caverns that reach far back into the reef flat.

CORAL PILLARS   Peculiar coral pillars or columns were observed within the deep forereef of the mid-windward bight of Anegada de Afuera during a research expedition in 2002 (Plate 34c). These pillars were of uniform diameter (approximately 0.5 m) and of varying height (1–4 m). Each was "capped" by a living (or sometimes dead) scleractinian coral (usually *Montastraea annularis* or *Siderastrea radians*). These pillars appear to have formed because the living coral cap was unable to clean or remove heavy sedimentation beyond an approximate 0.5 m diameter. Although rapid sedimentation seemed to be limiting peripheral growth, upward growth was not affected because other environmental parameters were favorable.

## Campeche Bank Reefs

Coral reefs on Campeche Bank lie north and west of the Yucatán Peninsula near the edge of the continental shelf 80–130 km offshore (see Fig. 2.1). There are eight reefs or reef groups, from west to east: Nuevo Reef, Bancos Ingleses, Bajos Obispos (Obispo Norte and Obispo Sur), Triángulo Oeste, Triángulos Este and Sur, Cayos Arcas, Cayo Arenas, and Alacrán Reef. Although they are generally larger than other southern Gulf reefs, all but Alacrán Reef are less than

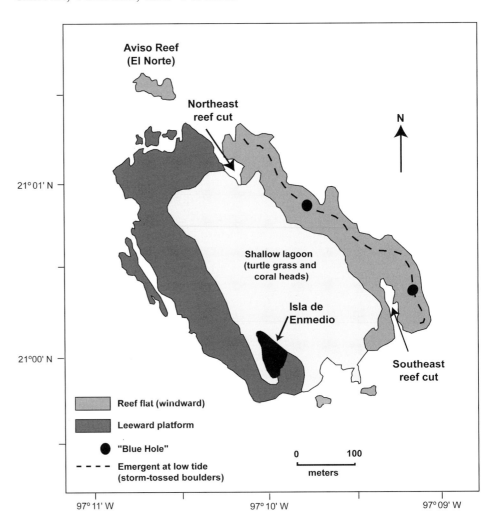

**Figure 5.12.** Aerial view of upper platform features of Isla de Enmedio Reef (after Rannefeld 1972).

3 km long. The five largest (Triángulo Oeste, Triángulos Este and Sur, Cayos Arcas, Cayo Arenas, and Alacrán Reef ) have at least one sand key. Logan (1969a, 1969b) provides extensive geological and biological descriptions of most Campeche Bank reefs. Nuevo Reef and Triángulo Oeste (Plate 35) are solitary reef knolls and are the simplest expression of emergent reefs on Campeche Bank (Logan 1969b). The Triángulos Este-Sur complex consists of two emergent reef masses on the summit of a narrow ridge that extends from Triángulo Oeste, about 8 km to the northwest. Bancos Igleses and Bajos Obispos are submerged reef banks that are intermediate in development between emergent reefs and hard bank deposits with no organic development. The Cayo Arenas reef group (Plate 36) contains three emergent reef masses and a fairly well developed lagoon. All share an extensive, shallow reef flat in the windward part of the reef (Jordán-Dahlgren and Rodríguez-Martínez 2003). Spurs and grooves occur on the windward slopes of most reefs, dominated by *Acropora palmata* (mostly dead now) in shallow areas and *Montastraea annularis* in deeper water. Unlike the others, Alacrán Reef has a small, deep (~20 m) lagoon on the southern edge of the platform, a vast shallow-water lagoonal complex of inner reefs and enough fine sediment for development of *Thalassia* over large areas. On most other Campeche Bank reefs, sandy areas are not colonized by seagrasses. An almost permanent sea current, a branch of the Yucatán Current running westward, constrains deposition of fine sediments and may limit seagrass devel-

opment. These reefs are in good condition (Jordán-Dahlgren and Rodríguez-Martínez 2003), probably due to their distance from shore (Tunnell 1992).

As in other southern Gulf of Mexico platform reefs, a series of common habitats characterize the structure of coral reefs on the Campeche Bank: a windward forereef with a spur and groove system, a central lagoon with various habitats, and a leeward reef. On the windward side, the upper forereef constitutes a zone where the branched elkhorn coral, *A. palmata*, grows actively toward the sea and protects the reef from the wave action. This upper slope or zone of *A. palmata* is characterized by the spur and groove structure. Below the *A. palmata* zone, the *Diploria-Montastraea-Porites* association (Rezak et al. 1985) is characteristic, rather than a zone of gorgonians as occurs on many Caribbean reefs. On some reefs, a terrace follows the buttress and grooves at 20–25 m, where skeletal remains of broken coral from the front reef accumulate and are gradually being transformed into sand.

The leeward side of the reef usually lacks the *A. palmata* zone. Wave action is low and coral growth is dominated by massive species rather than branching corals as on the windward side. On the upper levels, from 3 to 10 m, gorgonians are also very abundant and share the habitat with the association *Diploria-Montastraea-Porites*. Large sponges become dominant at 15–25 m. A sandy terrace replaces the slope at 25 m, where coral growth is scarce.

The reef crest and flat are found immediately behind the *A. palmata* zone, where the water is very shallow and where diagenesis, the process of reef coral destruction and formation of new hard substratum, is very intense. Growth of other species besides coralline algae is not significant, although *A. palmata* did grow on some deeper reef flat areas of southern Alacrán Reef.

Toward the center of the reef, there is a lagoon with a soft sediment bottom. In some cases, such as the southern Alacrán Reef platform, the lagoon may be as deep as 23 m. However, on most Campeche Bank reefs it is a shallow flat or depression no more than 4 m deep and is often covered by a dense carpet of turtle grass, mixed with small branching corals, soft corals, and some algae. The leeward side of the lagoon often transitions gently to the back slope of the reef.

**Alacrán Reef**   Alacrán Reef (Plate 37) is the largest reef on Campeche Bank and the most studied, including both early descriptions and more recent accounts. Alacrán Reef is roughly oval when viewed overhead and has five to seven small sand banks or islands on the western edge (see Fig. 2.1). The windward side forms a coral barrier that is well developed, emerging in many places at low tide and defining the reef complex to the north, east, and southeast. The lagoon reaches a depth of 23 m in its southernmost portion (Kornicker et al. 1959; Chávez et al. 1985). Much of the work on Alacrán Reef has been conducted on the southern end of the reef and/or in the vicinity of Isla Perez, where researchers have stayed during expeditions (Kornicker and Boyd 1962b; Chávez et al. 1985; Solís 1990; Novak et al. 1992; Torruco et al. 1993).

Researchers have identified several reef habitats representative of the zonation typical of most reefs in the Gulf of Mexico that are not in direct contact with the shoreline (Kornicker et al. 1959; Fig. 5.13): windward and leeward reef slopes (outer slope and reef front), reef crest (seaward margin) and reef flat, and reef lagoon and sand islands.

Windward and Leeward Reef Slopes   The lower forereef (outer slope) is where abundance of living coral and algae diminishes. The upper forereef (reef front)

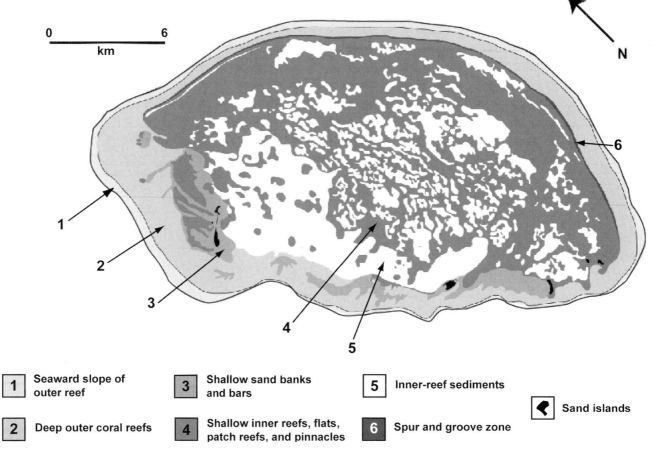

**Figure 5.13.** The main habitats of Alacrán Reef (redrawn from Kornicker et al. 1959).

| | | | | | | |
|---|---|---|---|---|---|---|
| **1** | Seaward slope of outer reef | **3** | Shallow sand banks and bars | **5** | Inner-reef sediments | |
| **2** | Deep outer coral reefs | **4** | Shallow inner reefs, flats, patch reefs, and pinnacles | **6** | Spur and groove zone | Sand islands |

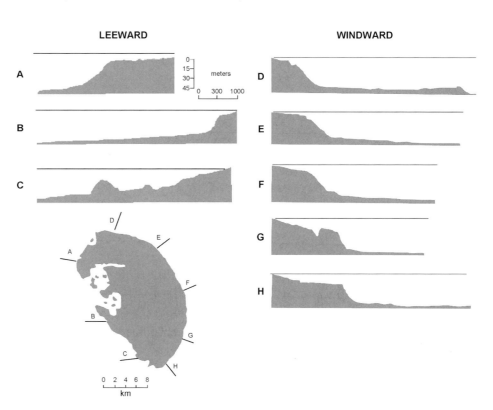

**Figure 5.14.** Selected bottom profiles at Alácran Reef (modified from Kornicker et al. 1959).

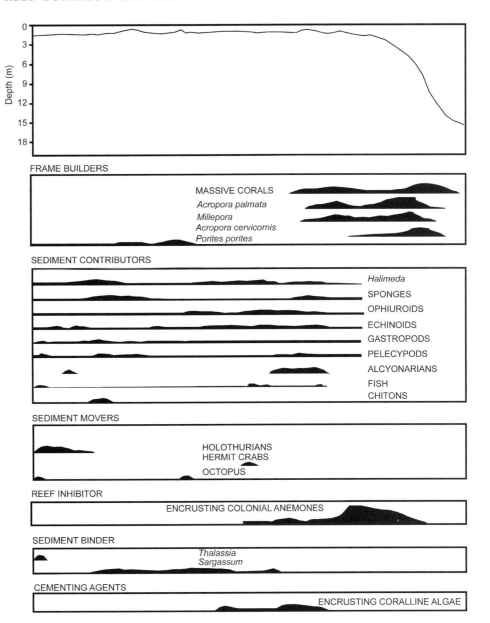

**Figure 5.15.** Profile of Alacrán Reef at the windward site known as "the boilers" (transect profile "E," Fig. 5.14), showing the relative abundance of the main components of the reef community (redrawn from Kornicker and Boyd 1962b).

is the upper seaward face of the reef, extending above the outer slope to the reef edge. On Alacrán Reef the transition from upper forereef to lower forereef is marked by an abrupt vertical drop-off between 10 and 15 m on the windward reef and between 7 and 10 m on the leeward reef (Logan 1969b; Kornicker et al. 1959; Fig. 5.14). This also coincided with the lower depth limit of *Acropora* on the windward side (Fig. 5.15). The leeward slope was relatively poorly developed, with discontinuous coral coverage (Chávez et al. 1985) on primarily patch reefs (Kornicker et al. 1959). Both windward (Fig. 5.15) and leeward (Fig. 5.16) communities consisted of *Acropora*, along with massive corals such as *Diploria* and *Montastraea*, gorgonians, *Millepora*, and *Halimeda*.

Both *Acropora palmata* and *A. cervicornis* were apparent in the upper windward forereef in the 1960s (Kornicker and Boyd 1962b; Logan 1969b). More recently, only *A. palmata* (probably dead) was observed in depths less than 15 m on the southern windward reef, and both species were observed on the southern leeward side at depths less than 3 m (Solís 1990). *Diploria strigosa,*

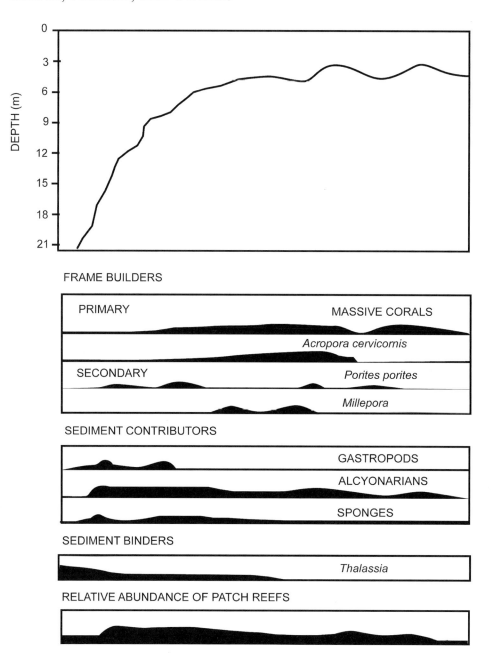

**Figure 5.16.** Profile of Alacrán Reef at the leeward side of the reef, showing the relative abundance of main components of the reef community (redrawn from Kornicker and Boyd 1962b).

*Montastraea* spp., and *Porites* spp. remained common members of the scleractinian community throughout the upper windward forereef, with increasing dominance by *Siderastrea radians* between 3 and 15 m. On the upper leeward forereef massive corals dominated the coral community, with the addition of *A. cervicornis* (probably dead) at depths <3 m. However, algae and bare substrate together represented the greatest percentage of cover in the upper forereef on both windward (~45%–70%) and leeward slopes (~85%) (Solís 1990).

The lower forereef encompasses depths below 10–15 m on both leeward and windward sides. This lower scarp is nearly vertical to depths of >40 m or more and exhibits extensive spur and groove topography in some places (Logan 1969b). Historically, the *Diploria-Montastraea-Porites* community covered the upper 10 m of the windward lower slope (Kornicker et al. 1959; Logan 1969b). Cover was estimated at 50% (Kornicker et al. 1959). On the leeward lower slope, corals and gorgonians covered about 65% of the substrate, clustered in closely spaced patches. However, algae dominated ( >40%) more recent estimates of living cover in both windward and leeward lower forereefs, which had only about 10% coral cover (Liddell and Ohlhorst 1988; Solís 1990). Solís (1990) reported nearly 30% bare substrate on both leeward and windward slopes. The coral community was dominated by *Montastraea cavernosa, M. annularis, Diploria strigosa,* and *Siderastrea siderea.* At 30 m depth, massive corals are important framework components, although much of the area is covered by sand.

Reef Crest (Seaward Margin) and Reef Flat   Breakers marked the reef crest, which extended above water at low tide (Kornicker et al. 1959). Coral boulders (up to 1 m in diameter) marked the windward edge of the reef, and *Acropora palmata, Millepora, Gorgonia,* and *Halimeda* were abundant below low tide level. Leeward of the crest, the reef flat contained considerable coral rubble, composed mainly of worn fragments of *Acropora,* and scattered coral boulders. *Echinometra lucunter* (sea urchin), *Astrea* sp. and *Strombus* sp. (gastropods), and *Halimeda* sp. (alga) were common. Coralline algae actively cement coral fragments on the reef flat, but they are less abundant on Alacrán Reef than on reefs in the VRS. The lagoonal boundary of the reef flat on the windward side was poorly defined in most places, grading into patch reefs in deeper water (<2 m) and extensive areas of coarse sand with *Thalassia* and *Halimeda* in shallow areas at the northern end of the reef. There are several channels (5–8 m deep) that extend parallel to the crest on the leeward edge of the reef flat. There is no surf zone, reef flat, or boulder zone on the leeward reef margin. Instead, from 1 to 6 m in depth there is a mixture of bottom types, including open sand, dense turtle grass beds, coral concentrations, and wide patch reefs containing some areas of *A. cervicornis* gravel and some a cobble pavement.

Reef Lagoon and Sand Islands   The lagoon between the windward and leeward reef slopes contained a mosaic of habitats ranging from sand islands along the western edge (see Tunnell, chapter 11, this volume) to patch reefs, a network of anastomosing inner reefs, particularly in deeper water on the northwest end, and beds of *Thalassia* and *Halimeda,* where sediments have been trapped (Kornicker et al. 1959). Maximum depth is ~25 m at the southern end near Isla Pérez. The lagoonal areas between the patch and pinnacle reefs typically consisted of unconsolidated sediment, seagrass beds, macroalgal beds, or areas of coral growth. There is an extensive subtidal flat west of Isla Pérez, where *Thalassia testudinum* and *Halimeda opuntia* occupy large areas (Fig. 5.17). Another important association was dominated by *P. porites,* also covering many areas of the shallow lagoon. On the lagoon side of the islands a pavement of fragments of *Acropora cervicornis* frequently covered the bottom.

Zonation   Zonation of the leeward and windward slopes of southern Alacrán Reef are different (see Fig. 5.5) and reflect adaptations by organisms to exposure to wave action (windward vs. leeward) and depth (light decreases with depth) (Solís 1990). Cover of stony corals ranged from 7% to 25%. Coral cover on the windward reef was consistently lower than on the leeward reef. Cover was also slightly higher in deeper areas on both slopes. Cover of sponges and gorgonians were greater on the windward side and at deeper depths. In shallow water (<3 m), algal cover was greater on the leeward slope, but at depths greater than 3 m, cover was similar on leeward and windward slopes. Of the other organisms,

■ Land (Isla Pérez)

▨ *Acropora cervicornis*

▧ *Acropora cervicornis* rubble

▨ *Acropora palmata*

▨ *Porites* – crustose coraline algal flats

▢ Dominantly sandy bottom (*Thalassia* and *Halimeda*)

◊ Massive coral heads

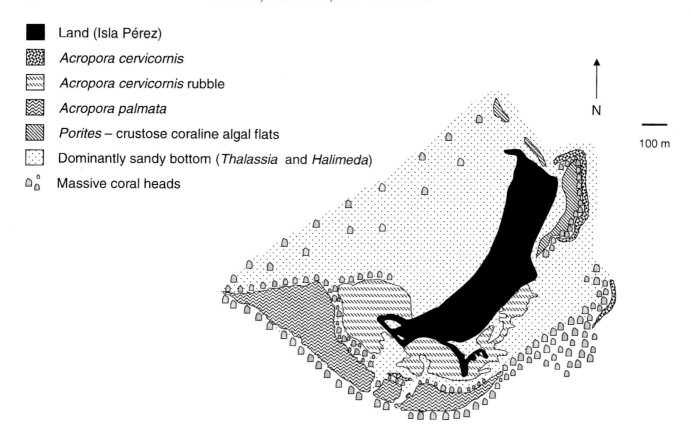

**Figure 5.17.** Reef habitats and bottom types surrounding Isla Pérez, on the leeward, southwestern side of Alacrán Reef (redrawn from Macintyre et al. 1977).

dense aggregations of the zoanthid *Palythoa* sp. were found in the shallow windward reef, but not at other depths. There was a greater amount of bare substrate in the leeward reef than in the windward reef, and bare area increased with depth in the windward reef.

**Cayos Arcas** The Cayos Arcas is a group of three coral and sand cays (Cayo del Centro, Cayo Oeste, and Cayo Este) that emerge from a shallow-water platform near the southwestern extreme of the Campeche Bank (Farrell et al. 1983; see Fig. 2.1 and Plate 38). This area is within the boundaries of Mexico's offshore petroleum fields, and a deepwater oil terminal was built near the reefs in the early 1980s. The reef platform has a roughly oval outline and is oriented north-south with an arcuate windward reef margin (Fig. 5.18). The cays enclose a small, protected lagoon up to 8 m deep. A shallow terrace of varying widths is found on the north, east, and south sides of the largest island, Cayo del Centro. Beyond this terrace, the slope increases abruptly to about 10 m depth, and a series of grooves spurs and grooves extends about 50 m toward the north-northeast. Spurs may reach to within 2 m of the surface and grooves to 5–12 m deep. In the deepest portions of the grooves another rocky terrace begins, becoming gradually deeper and sandy.

The most well developed reef on Cayos Arcas is the area to the northwest of Cayo del Centro (Farrell et al. 1983; Figs. 5.19 and 5.20). In 1981, its most striking feature was an extensive reef flat (~100 m wide) almost completely covered with dense, monospecific *Acropora cervicornis*. Farrell and his colleagues noted that Logan (1969b) had not remarked on this obvious feature and suggested

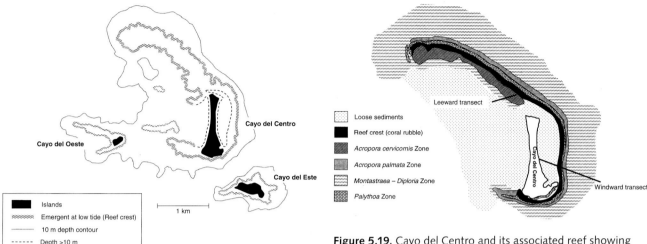

**Figure 5.18.** Cayos Arcas islands and reefs (redrawn from Farrell et al. 1983).

**Figure 5.19.** Cayo del Centro and its associated reef showing the approximate distribution of the major reef zones and locations of transects (modified and redrawn from Farrell et al. 1983).

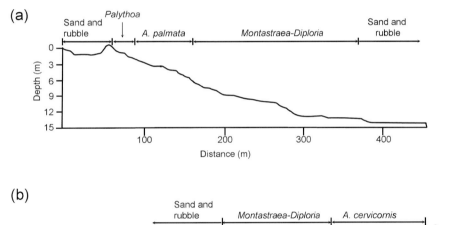

**Figure 5.20.** Windward **(a)** and leeward **(b)** transect profiles (see Fig. 5.19 for transect locations) on the Cayo del Centro reef, Cayos Arcas (redrawn from Farrell et al. 1983).

that it had developed in the intervening years. To the windward of the reef flat, the reef crest was not emergent and was composed of unconsolidated coral rubble encrusted with calcareous algae (Farrell et al. 1983). The forereef extended about 350 m from the crest and to a sandy bottom at a depth of 18 m. Zoanthids (*Palythoa carribeaorum* and *Zoanthus sociatus*) dominated in depths of 1–3 m, grading to *Acropora palmata* from 3 to 7 m. *Acropora palmata* cover was estimated at 75%. The lower forereef ( >7 m) was dominated by massive corals, *Montastraea* and *Diploria*. To the lee of the reef flat, the bottom sloped gently to about 3 m (Farrell et al. 1983). Cover on this slope ranged from 20% to 60% and consisted of a diverse assemblage of zooxanthellate scleractinian corals (primarily *Acropora, Montastraea,* and *Diploria*). Most of the bottom of the lagoon is covered with sand, scattered algal turfs, and scarce coral heads (J. W. Tunnell, personal observation).

**Declining Coral Cover**

Since the 1970s, declining cover of coral on reefs and the concomitant overgrowth of reef structures with noncoralline, fleshy, and filamentous macroalgae has become a worldwide phenomenon (Aronson and Precht 2001). Declining coral cover was first noted on the Veracruz reefs in the early 1970s (Rannefeld 1972), and cover has declined in many reefs in the southern Gulf of Mexico, especially in windward shallow reef zones (e.g., reef crest, upper forereef). Although crustose algae seem to be the dominant overgrowing organisms on many southern Gulf of Mexico reefs, overgrowth by filamentous macroalgae has also occurred, particularly on the reefs nearer shore (Jordán-Dahlgren and Rodríguez-Martínez 2003; Table 5.1). Both crustose algae and zoanthids are considered "consolidating" or "stabilizing" overgrowth, whereas filamentous or fleshy macroalgae are considered "nonconsolidating." Clearly, reefscape views from the 1970s to 1990s show a transition from a coral-dominated community to a fleshy algae–dominated community (Tunnell 1992; Plate 39), revealing a system completely out of balance.

Several workers have documented the continuing decline in coral cover in the VRS (Table 5.2). Overall coral cover in the mid-1960s appears to have been 40%–50% on windward forereefs (Kühlmann 1975), but by the mid-1980s percentages averaged in the mid-20% range (Secretaría de Marina 1978). By the late 1980s through the late 1990s, coral cover continued to decline into the teens (T. J. Nelson 1991; Horta-Puga 2003). By 2002, during the Harte Research Institute–Sustainable Seas Expedition to the Veracruz reefs, coral cover continued to decline, averaging between 4 and 6% on four reefs (Tunnell et al. in prep.). However, coral cover on TRS reefs nearest Tuxpan (Tanguijo, Enmedio, and Tuxpan) may still average near 40% (Veracruz ReefMonitor Update 2001); there is no current information on Isla de Lobos or the reefs in the northern group.

Coral cover has also declined on Alacrán Reef from estimates of 40%–50% in the late 1950s and 1960s (Kornicker et al. 1959; Kornicker and Boyd 1962b; Logan 1969b) to around 10% in the 1980s (Liddell and Olhorst 1988; Solís 1990). Algae, often macroalgae, dominated more recent benthic communities. Solís (1990) suspected that algal dominance could have been caused by the relatively intense human use of the area. Her study was conducted on the southern portion of the reef, the area that is most accessible to the northern Yucatán coast for fishing and some tourism.

Cover at Cayos Arcas when Farrell et al. (1983) conducted their study appeared to be about the same as had been reported by Logan (1969b). It is likely that some decline has occurred due the die-off of *Acropora*, but no current information is available. The remaining reefs on Campeche Bank have not been studied since Logan (1969b).

Although both nutrient enrichment and reduced herbivory may play roles in increased algal cover on reefs, coral mortality is also important because it provides the empty space needed for algal colonization (Aronson and Precht 2001). A major contributor to loss of coral cover was the large-scale die-off of *Acropora* that affected tropical Atlantic reefs in the 1970s and 1980s. Although both bleaching and hurricane damage have been implicated in the loss of *Acropora*, white band disease has been identified as the primary cause of *Acropora* mortality throughout the greater Caribbean, including the southern Gulf of Mexico (Aronson and Precht 2001; Jordán-Dahlgren and Rodríguez-Martínez 2003). In the late 1990s, recolonization by *A. palmata* was noted on many reefs on Campeche Bank, particularly Alacrán Reef and Cayo Arenas (Jordán-Dahlgren

**Table 5.1.** *Dominant species by reef or reef system and general zones, with condition of dominants and identity of overgrowing organisms, if present.*

| Reef zone | Reef or reef system | Dominant/Subdominant | Condition of dominant species | Overgrowth? |
|---|---|---|---|---|
| **Leeward reef** | | | | |
| | Isla de Lobos | *M. annularis/D. strigosa* | Diseased, dead | Filamentous algae, crustose algae |
| | TRS | *M. annularis/C. natans* | Healthy | None |
| | VRS | *A. cervicornis/M. cavernosa* | Dead | Filamentous algae |
| | CBR | Mixed corals/*M. cavernosa* | Healthy | None |
| | Alacrán | *M. annularis/M. cavernosa* | Healthy | None |
| **Lagoon/Flat** | | | | |
| | Isla de Lobos | *D. clivosa/P. furcata* | Healthy, diseased | Crustose algae, filamentous algae |
| | TRS | *D. clivosa/*Branched coral-algae | Healthy | None |
| | VRS | *D. clivosa/P. astreoides* | Healthy | None |
| | CBR | *A. palmata/M. annularis* | Dead | Crustose algae |
| | Alacrán | *M. annularis/*Other corals | Healthy | |
| **Reef crest** | | | | |
| | Isla de Lobos | *A. palmata/*Coral-crustose algae | Dead | Crustose algae, stabilizing zoanthids |
| | TRS | *A. palmata/*Coral-crustose algae | Dead | Crustose algae, stabilizing zoanthids, filamentous algae |
| | VRS | *A. palmata/*Coral-crustose algae | Dead | Crustose algae, filamentous algae |
| | CBR | *A. palmata/*Coral-crustose algae | Dead | Crustose algae, stabilizing zoanthids |
| | Alacrán | *A. palmata/*Coralline and fleshy algae | Dead | Crustose algae, stabilizing zoanthids |
| **Upper forereef** | | | | |
| | Isla de Lobos | *A. palmata/D. clivosa* | Dead | Filamentous algae |
| | TRS | *D. strigosa/M. faveolata* | Healthy | |
| | VRS | *A. palmata/M. annularis* | Dead | Crustose algae, filamentous algae |
| | CBR | Coral grounds/*D. strigosa* | Healthy | |
| | Alacrán | Coral grounds/*D. clivosa* | Healthy | |

*(continued)*

**Table 5.1.** (*continued*)

| Reef zone | Reef or reef system | Dominant/Subdominant | Condition of dominant species | Overgrowth? |
|---|---|---|---|---|
| **Leeward reef** | | | | |
| **Lower forereef** | | | | |
| | Isla de Lobos | *M. cavernosa/S. siderea* | Healthy | |
| | TRS | *M. faveolata/S. siderea* | Healthy | |
| | VRS | *C. natans/M. faveolata* | Healthy | |
| | CBR | *M. cavernosa/S. siderea* | Healthy | |
| | Alacrán | *M. faveolata/S. siderea* | Healthy | |

*Notes:* Modified from Jordán-Dahlgren and Rodríguez-Martínez (2003). TRS = Tuxpan Reef System, VRS = Veracruz Reef System, and CBR = Campeche Bank Reefs.

**Table 5.2.** *Percentage of coral cover through time on selected Veracruz coral reefs, 1965–99.*

| Date | Reef name | Coral cover | Reference |
|------|-----------|-------------|-----------|
| 1965–66 | La Blanquilla, Pájaros, Anegada de Adentro | 40%–50% (Up to 65% *Acropora palmata*) | Kühlmann 1975 |
| 1971 | Isla de Enmedio | 17%–53% (Over 65% *A. palmata*) (Up to 100% *A. cervicornis*) | Rannefeld 1972 |
| Mid-1980s | Isla de Sacrificios, La Blanquilla, Isla Verde, Anegada de Adentro, Isla de Enmedio, Anegada de Afuera | 19%–44% (Most in mid-20% range) (2.7% *A. palmata* at Isla de Enmedio) (4.7% *A. cervicornis* at Isla de Enmedio) | Secretaría de Marina 1987 |
| 1989 | Isla de Enmedio | 17% (1.4% *A. palmata*) | T. J. Nelson 1991 |
| 1989 | Cabezo | 12% (3.0% *A. palmata* at Cabezo) | T. J. Nelson 1991 |
| 1999 | Galleguilla, Isla Verde, Isla de Sacrificios | 17% (3% *A. palmata*) (<0.5% *A. cervicornis*) | Horta-Puga 2003 |
| 2002 | Anegada de Adentro | 0.5–8% | Tunnell et al. in prep. |
| 2002 | La Blanquilla | 1–8% | Tunnell et al. in prep. |
| 2002 | Anegada de Afuera | 1–13% | Tunnell et al. in prep. |
| 2002 | Enmedio | 4–6% | Tunnell et al. in prep. |

and Rodríguez-Martínez 2003). There are also indications that *A. palmata* has begun to recolonize TRS reefs (Universidad Veracruzana 2003). However, we still do not know whether these recolonizations represent the early stages of recovery by the species, or if these are short-lived, episodic events. The lack of any substantial recovery to date suggests that other factors may be preventing recovery. In addition, there have been no reports of recolonization by *A. cervicornis* on any reefs in the southern Gulf of Mexico. Nevertheless, past observations indicate that fast-growing species like *A. cervicornis* have the potential to recover rapidly and can dominate an area in a period of one to two decades, as noted by Farrell et al. (1983) on Cayos Arcas.

# 6    Reef Biodiversity

KIM WITHERS AND JOHN W. TUNNELL JR.

Coral reefs are known to harbor the highest biological diversity (biodiversity) of any habitat within the sea. Over 2,000 marine species and almost 300 terrestrial species have been reported from the southern Gulf of Mexico coral reefs and their islands, respectively (Table 6.1 and 6.2). Since a list of this size is beyond the scope of this book, we refer the reader to www.gulfbase.org (Nipper et al. 2004) for complete species checklists that include references, distributions, and habitats.

Few reefs anywhere in the world have a complete species list available for comparison, but regional comparisons for selected taxa are helpful in understanding regional biogeography. Generally speaking, for coral reef organisms, the number of species within a particular group decreases as one moves from the center to the periphery of the tropics. In the case of the Caribbean Sea, latitudinal gradients in species diversity (numbers of species) have been recognized as one makes the transition from Jamaica (center with high diversity) to the Bahamas and east coast of Florida (periphery with lower diversity). Likewise, moving westward into the semienclosed Gulf of Mexico, gradients exist in numbers of species from east to west and south to north. Temperature has been suggested as the single most important environmental factor governing these changes and limitations, but local factors, such as salinity, topography, depth, turbidity, and nutrients, among others, can also account for varying numbers of species or genera in any given locality.

For example, both stony corals (scleractinians) and soft corals (gorgonians), demonstrate this distributional pattern. Horta-Puga et al. (chapter 8, this volume) indicate that almost 70 zooxanthellate coral species are found in the Caribbean Sea, the Caribbean Biogeographic Subprovince (Veron 1995). Within the southern Gulf of Mexico 42 species have been recorded, and there appears to be a gradient from slightly more species on the Campeche Bank reefs to fewer on southern Veracruz reefs (Veracruz Reef System) and even fewer still on northern Veracruz reefs (Tuxpan Reef System). Notable Caribbean genera missing from the southern Gulf include *Cladocora*, *Dendrogyra*, *Isophyllia*, *Isophyllastrea*, and *Solenastraea* (Horta-Puga et al., chapter 8, this volume). Likewise, within the southern Gulf, the following species occur on Campeche Bank reefs but are absent from Veracruz reefs: *Diploria labyrinthiformis*, *Eusmilia fastigiata*, *Madracis mirabilis*, and *Mycetophyllia aliciae*. Among the milleporid hydrocorals, only *Millepora alcicornis* occurs throughout the southern Gulf, while *M. complanata* and *M. squarrosa* are found only on Campeche Bank reefs.

Among the gorgonians, or soft corals, this gradient or geographic limitation is even more evident. Jordán-Dahlgren (2002), who studied the northeastern Yucatán–Caribbean Sea gorgonians for two decades, clearly demonstrated two distinct gradients in the Gulf of Mexico: (1) a westward-decreasing gradient in

**Table 6.1.** *Number of marine species found in each division (plants) or phylum (animals) on the coral reefs of the southern Gulf of Mexico (Plates 40–46).*

| Taxon | | Number of Species |
|---|---|---|
| Division Cyanophyta (Blue-green algae) | | 17 |
| Division Bacillariophyta (Diatoms) | | 50 |
| Division Chlorophyta (Green algae) | | 116 |
| Division Phaeophyta (Brown algae) | | 50 |
| Division Rhodophyta (Red algae) | | 165 |
| Division Spermatophyta (Vascular plants, seagrasses) | | 5 |
| Phylum Granuloreticulosa (Foraminiferans) | | 130 |
| Phylum Ciliophora (Ciliates) | | 71 |
| Phylum Porifera (Sponges) | | 38 |
| Phylum Cnidaria (Corals, anemones, jellies) | | 102 |
| Phylum Annelida (Segmented worms, polychaetes) | | 45 |
| Phylum Mollusca (Seashells) | | 548 |
|     Chitons | (7) | |
|     Bivalves | (134) | |
|     Gastropods (Snails and conchs) | (405) | |
|     Cephalopods (Octopus) | (2) | |
| Phylum Arthropoda | | 257 |
|     Ostracods | (88) | |
|     Decapods: Shrimp | (63) | |
|       Lobsters | (3) | |
|       Crabs | (93) | |
| Phylum Sipunculida (Sipuniculids) | | 2 |
| Phylum Echinodermata (Echinoderms) | | 47 |
|     Sea lilies | (1) | |
|     Starfish | (5) | |
|     Brittle stars | (15) | |
|     Sea urchins, etc. | (14) | |
|     Sea cucumbers | (12) | |
| Phylum Hemichordata (Acorn worms) | | 1 |
| Phylum Chordata (Chordates) | | 413 |
|   Subphylum Tunicata (Tunicates) | (24) | |
|   Subphylum Vertebrata (Vertebrates) | (389) | |
|   Class Elasmobranchiomorphi (Sharks, rays) | (29) | |
|     Class Osteichthyes (Bony fish) | (347) | |
|     Class Reptilia (Sea turtles) | (4) | |
|     Class Mammalia (Marine mammals) | (9) | |
| Total Marine Species | | 2057 |

*Notes:* A full checklist of all species is at www.gulfbase.org (Nipper et al. 2004). Numbers in parentheses are subtotals for species of lower taxa and are included in the total for phyla.

**Table 6.2.** *Number of terrestrial species found in each division (plants) and phylum (animals) found on coral reef islands of the southern Gulf of Mexico (Plates 47 and 48).*

| Taxon | | Number of Species |
|---|---|---|
| Division Spermatophyta | | 86 |
| Phylum Arthropoda | | 79 |
| Crabs | (2) | |
| Insects | (60) | |
| Spiders | (17) | |
| Phylum Chordata | | 133 |
| Reptiles (Lizards) | (2) | |
| Birds | | |
| Nesting seabirds | (9) | |
| Trans-Gulf migrants | (121) | |
| Mammals | (1) | |
| Total Terrestrial Species | | 298 |

*Note:* Numbers in parentheses are subtotals for species of lower taxa and are included in the total for phyla.

**Table 6.3.** *Decreasing gradient in diversity of gorgonians (soft corals) from the northeastern Yucatán (Caribbean Sea) to the southern Gulf of Mexico.*

| | Region | | |
|---|---|---|---|
| Taxonomic group | Northeast Yucatán | Campeche Bank | Southwest Gulf of Mexico |
|---|---|---|---|
| No. of families | 5 | 5 | 3 |
| No. of genera | 15 | 14 | 7 |
| No. of species | 43 | 31 | 15 |

*Note:* Adapted from Jordán-Dahlgren (2002).

gorgonian diversity and abundance from the northeastern Yucatán to the southwestern Gulf (Table 6.3), and (2) a similar northward-decreasing gradient in the southwestern Gulf. The composition of the Campeche Bank gorgonian reef fauna is more closely related to northeastern Yucatán than the southwestern Gulf of Mexico. Major genera missing from the southwestern Gulf are *Gorgonia* (sea fans), *Muricopsis, Pterogorgia, Iciligorgia,* and *Lophogorgia.* The average number of gorgonian species per reef on the northeastern Yucatán reefs is 32; on Campeche Bank reefs, 20; and on southwestern Gulf reefs, 6 (Jordán-Dahlgren 2002).

A trend of decreasing gorgonian diversity to the north is also evident in the southwestern Gulf along coasts of the state of Veracruz. On the southernmost reefs off Antón Lizardo, 15 species have been found; at Tuxpan, 9 species; and at Isla de Lobos Reef, 5 species (Jordán-Dahlgren 2002). Gorgonians are generally scarce in the southwestern Gulf, making their study difficult and the possibility of overlooking colonies easy. However, one low-diversity but high-density gorgonian reef was reported adjacent to Isla de Enmedio Reef (Nelson et al. 1988; Tunnell and Nelson 1989), confounding the normal abundance of this group within the region.

The need for more taxonomic studies, or floral and faunal surveys, is evident from Table 6.1. Due to the few studies in the region, many minor phyla are missing from this list (e.g., comb jellies, flatworms, ribbon worms, round worms, bryozoans, brachiopods, and others), but they are most likely present within the region. Also, the need for circulation studies between and within reefs will assist in explaining dispersal, recruitment, and ecological connectivity within the southern Gulf of Mexico.

## Reef Invertebrates

Coral reef algae (Lehman, chapter 7), fish (Chávez and Beaver, chapter 9), and island birds (Tunnell, chapter 11) are each covered elsewhere in this volume; therefore, only the well-studied invertebrate groups are characterized in this chapter.

**Foraminiferans**  Foraminiferans are predominantly marine, amoeboid protozoans in the phylum Rhizopoda. All either construct a shell or "test" from secreted organic material or calcium carbonate or from cemented foreign material (Ruppert and Barnes 1994). Most foraminiferans have shells that are multichambered, like a gastropod's, and calcareous. The majority are benthic organisms, although there are also sessile and planktonic species. All are heterotrophic and use their pseudopodia (flowing extensions of cytoplasm) to capture prey, usually organisms such as bacteria, algae, and other protozoans, as well as small metazoans such as rotifers, copepod larvae, and nematodes. Foraminiferans are eaten by a variety of gastropods, echinoderms, and fish.

Species distributions of foraminiferans are used to reconstruct paleoenvironments. The chemical composition of their shell can be used to determine the chemistry of the water in which they grew, and its isotopic composition provides information about water temperature. In addition, they are used extensively as indicator species or assemblages in biostratigraphy, particularly by the petroleum industry during exploration. They have also been proposed as a bioindicator for coral reef assessment and monitoring because they have similar water-quality requirements to zooxanthellate corals, relatively short lifespans that allow differentiation between long-term water-quality decline and episodic stress events, are relatively easy to collect and analyze, and their collection has minimal impact on reefs (Hallock et al. 2003). This index relies primarily on the presence of larger foraminifers with algal symbionts. The ecology of these genera is very similar to that of zooxanthellate corals, and conditions that cause coral decline (e.g., nutrient enrichment) also cause the disappearance of foraminifers with algal symbionts. Thus, even if corals are absent—for instance, following a mass mortality event—the presence of these foraminifers are indicative of water quality that is suitable for coral recovery.

Researchers have identified 127 foraminiferan species from reefs in the southern Gulf of Mexico. Only the encrusting species, *Homotrema rubra*, was listed at Blanquilla (Tuxpan Reef System) by Moore (1958). At La Blanquilla (Veracruz Reef System), foraminiferans constituted about 5% of total zooplankton (Rodríguez and Fuentes 1965). Benthic foraminiferan communities have

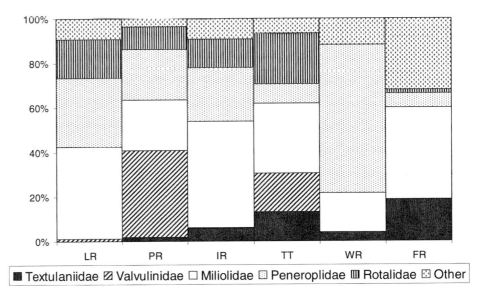

**Figure 6.1.** Relative abundance of foraminiferan families by habitat in sediments of Alácran Reef (modified from Davis 1964). LR = leeward reef; PR = lagoonal patch reefs; IR = inter-reef sediments (deep); TT = *Thalassia testudinum*, WR = windward reef; FR = forereef slope.

received the most attention. Reef lagoon sediments were sampled at 72 stations on Isla de Lobos Reef (Bautista-Gil and Chávez 1977). A total of 126 species were reported: 65 species representing 43 genera and 25 families and 61 unidentified species in 8 genera. The most frequently occurring, abundant species (and their maximum densities) were *Planorbulina* cf. *mediterranensis* (490,000/m$^2$), *Sorites* cf. *orbiculus* (319,000/m$^2$), *Amphisorus hemprichii* (114,200/m$^2$), *Cymbaloporetta squamosa* (140,000/m$^2$), and *Rotalia beccarii* (86,500 /m$^2$).

At Alacrán Reef, Davis (1964) identified 79 foraminiferan species in 43 genera and 17 families. Several habitats were represented: the leeward reef (31 species), lagoonal patch reefs (47 species), inter-reef sediments (see Fig. 5.13 in Chávez et. al., chapter 5, this volume) (39 species), *Thalassia* (20 species), windward reef (= *Acropora* zone; 12 species), and forereef slope (28 species). The proportion of foraminiferan tests in sediments varied from 16.2% in the coarse, poorly sorted sand of the reef front, to 22% in the medium-grained, better-sorted sand of the reef flat. Community composition (families) varied across habitats (Fig. 6.1). Miliolidae, Peneroplidae and Rotalidae were the most abundant families in all habitats. In the forereef, the high percentage of "other" families was due to the presence of planktonic species in the sample. This was the only habitat where planktonic species (e.g., *Globigerinoides rubra*) were relatively abundant. Species richness was lowest in the windward reef. The family Peneroplidae dominated, with *Archaias angulatus* accounting for more than 50% of individuals. The family Valvulinidae (17.2%) was abundant in the *Thalassia* sample but scarce or absent in other samples. This occurrence was considered anomalous because the family is not typical of coral reefs. Davis speculated that the family was ecologically associated with *Thalassia*.

**Ciliates**   The protozoan phylum Ciliophora, the ciliates, is the largest and most animal-like of the protozoan phyla (Ruppert and Barnes 1994). As their name implies, ciliates possess cilia or compound ciliary structures that are used for locomotion and/or food acquisition. Most also have a fixed cytostome, or cell mouth and a fixed cytoproct or cell anus. Ciliates are widely distributed in fresh and salt water as well as in the water films of soils. Ciliate food webs are similar to those seen in the macroscopic world, with food chains based on suspension feeding of unicellular algae or bacteria. There are also omnivorous and carnivorous ciliates. Ciliates were the dominant phytoplankton grazers in enclosure studies designed to determine effects of nutrients, zooplankton, and ctenophores on phytoplankton bloom dynamics (Turner and Granéli 1992). Planktonic ciliates and zooflagellates also appeared to be responsible for the majority of phytoplankton grazing in waters off coral reefs in Vietnam (Sorokin 1991).

Ninety-nine ciliate species have been documented from the reef lagoons on Isla Verde and Isla de Enmedio in the Veracruz Reef System. There have been no studies of the ciliates of the Tuxpan Reef System or Campeche Bank reefs. On Isla Verde, the epibiotic ciliates on the blades and basal portions of *Thalassia testudinum* leaves were examined (Alandro-Lubel and Martínez-Murillo 1999). Twenty-eight species were identified in six groups: folliculinids (7), licnophorids (1), stichotrichs (1), prostomatids (1), suctorians (6), and peritrichs (12). *Lagotia expansa* f. *depressa*, *Metafolliculina andrewsi*, *Parafolliculina trastanensis*, *Metacystis truncata*, *Acineta tuberosa*, *Cothurnia aplatita*, and *C. maritima* were the most frequently encountered species on the basal portion of the leaves. *Parafolliculina amphora* and *Vorticella campanula* were the most frequently found species on the leaf blades. Only two species were reported from the rhizomes: *Chaetospira mülleri* and *Cothurnia maritima*. Regardless of month, ciliate species richness was greatest on the basal portion of the leaves (12–20 species), where epiphytes were absent or present only in low densities. However, ciliate density on leaves and basal portions varied with month, with greater densities on the basal portion in August but the reverse in October and May. Increased densities on the leaves corresponded to periods of low epiphyte density. Competition for space with epiphytes appears to limit ciliate densities and affect species composition in ciliate communities in the Isla Verde reef lagoon.

The interstitial ciliates of the reef lagoon at Isla de Enmedio were described by Lubel (1984). Both vegetated and unvegetated sediments were sampled. A total of 71 species were identified, 63 from *Thalassia testudinum* and 26 from unvegetated areas. The most frequently encountered species in *Thalassia* sediments were *Parauronema acutum*, *Euplotes trisulcatus*, *Trachelostyla pediculiformis*, *Mesodinium acarus*, and *M. pulex*; most frequent in the unvegetated sediments were *P. acutum*, *M. pulex*, *E. moebiusi*, and *E. nana*. Seasonal variation was also seen, with the greatest species richness in both vegetated and unvegetated sediments during October.

There was no species overlap between the ciliates of interstitial sediments at Isla de Enmedio and the epibiotic ciliates at Isla Verde. At Isla de Enmedio, only 15 species (21%) were found in both vegetated and unvegetated habitats; at Isla Verde, 14 species (50%) were found on both leaves and basal portions of leaves. Ciliates appear to be very habitat specific (sediments vs. leaves) and exhibit microhabitat specificity as well, revealed by the relatively low species overlap between microhabitats within both studies.

**Sponges** The phylum Porifera is the most primitive of the metazoan phyla, and their cells are so highly independent that they resemble a colony of protozoans in some respects (Ruppert and Barnes 1994). These sessile organisms are predominantly marine and abundant wherever suitable substrate (e.g., coral, rocks) is available for attachment. Most sponges are found in relatively shallow water and range in size from a few millimeters to more than a meter high and wide. Sponges are filter feeders that primarily ingest organic particles that are too small to be seen by ordinary microscopy (i.e., pico- or nanoplankton), as well as bacteria, dinoflagellates, and other small plankton. In coral reef food webs, sponges link water-column productivity to benthic secondary producers (Gili and Coma 1998). In Caribbean coral reefs, 65%–93% of available particulate food is consumed by sponges, and bottom-up processes appear to control their distribution and abundance (Lesser 2006). Sponges possess physical (e.g., spicules) and chemical (e.g., exudates) defenses that result in low levels of predation, primarily by sea stars, fish, and sea turtles. In addition, sponges provide habitat for reef fishes, brittle stars, and shrimp (Díaz and Rützler 2001), provide nutritional advantages to some commensal organisms (e.g., sea cucumbers; Hammond and Wilkinson 1985), and increase coral survival, reef regeneration, and water clarity (Wulff 2006).

Thirty-six species in the class Demospongiea, representing six orders and 16 families, have been listed from reefs in the southern Gulf of Mexico. Demospongiea contains 90% of all sponge species and has a variable skeleton composed of spongin, siliceous spicules, or both (Ruppert and Barnes 1994). The reefs La Blanquilla and Isla de Enmedio in the Veracruz Reef System have received the most study, with 13 and 24 species, respectively. Only one species, *Neopetrosia* (= *Haliclona*) *longleyi*, was reported from Isla de Lobos in the *Thalassia-Halimeda* biotope (Chávez et al. 1970). Only two species have been reported from Campeche Bank reefs: *Callyspongia vaginalis* from Alacrán Reef (Chávez et al. 1985; Ardisson and Durán-Nájera 1997) and *Haliclona* sp. from Arenas Reef (Chávez et al. 1985).

Of the 13 species collected on La Blanquilla by Green (1977), all but *Neopetrosia longleyi* were found on the forereef slope. *Neopetrosia longleyi* was very abundant but collected only from the reef lagoon in water 1–1.3 m deep. *Haliclonia rubens* was also one of most abundant species and was the most widespread, occurring at a variety of depths. In addition, *Verongia fistularia* and *Callyspongia fallax* were very abundant between 5 and 15 m on the windward reef slope. Several relatively uncommon species were restricted to the upper forereef slope, between ~10 and 18 m: *Iricinia campana*, *Haliclona doria*, *Gelliodes areolata*, *Agelas sparsus*, and *Axinella manaspiculata*. *Callyspongia vaginalis* was only rarely encountered and appeared to be restricted to ~10 m.

Sponges from 20 species representing 6 orders and 11 families were collected from four habitats on Isla de Enmedio Reef (Stinnett 1989; Table 6.4): the lagoon in *Thalassia testudinum* (0.1–1.7 m), *Diploria clivosa* communities on both windward and leeward reef (1.5–4.0 m), the windward forereef (0.5–23 m), and the leeward gorgonian garden (4.0–8.0 m). The reef-crest and reef-flat habitat contained only boring clionid sponges and is probably not suitable for larval settlement due to its high energy. Several species were limited to only one habitat: *Ampimedon viridis* and *Adocia albifragilis* in *Thalassia testudinum*; *Placospongia* sp. and *Xetospongia caycedoi* in *Diploria clivosa*; and *Ulosa* (*Dictyonella*) *rutzleri*, *Raphidophlus juniperina*, *R. oxeotus*, *Ectyoplasia ferox*, *Agelas clathrodes*, and *Hyrtios* sp. in the gorgonian garden. More species (15) were identified from the gorgonian garden than from the other habitats; the fewest (6) were identified from the forereef. Nine species were found in all habitats.

**Polychaetes** Polychaetes are among the most important of the secondary producers, those organisms that convert detritus to biomass that is usable at higher trophic levels. They are also responsible for a great deal of nutrient regeneration and recycling due to their activities in the sediments. There is little information about the polychaetes that inhabit coral reefs, although they are important in the diets of many reef and reef-associated fishes (Díaz-Ruiz et al. 1998).

**Table 6.4.** *Distribution of sponges collected from four reef habitats at Isla de Enmedio Reef.*

| Species | Thalassia testudinum | Diploria clivosa | Forereef | Gorgonian garden |
|---|---|---|---|---|
| Hyrtios sp. | | | | X |
| Iricinia strobilina | X | X | X | |
| Aplysina fistularis | X | | X | X |
| Aiolochroia crassa | | X | X | |
| Adocia carbonaria | X | X | X | X |
| Adocia albifragilis | X | | | |
| Amphimedon compressa | X | | X | X |
| Amphimedon viridis | X | | | X |
| Niphates erecta | | X | | X |
| Xestospongia caycedoi | X | X | X | X |
| Xestospongia subtriangularis | | X | | |
| Raphidophlus juniperinus | | | | X |
| Raphidophlus oxeotus | | | | X |
| Desmapsamma anchorata | X | X | | |
| Ulosa rutzleri | | | | X |
| Ectyoplasia ferox | | | | X |
| Topsentia sp. | | | | X |
| Agelas clathrodes | | | | X |
| Placospongia sp. | | X | | |

*Note:* Modified from Stinnett (1989).

On southern Gulf of Mexico reefs, the only detailed account of the polychaete fauna is from Isla de Lobos (Roberts 1981), with a few incidental mentions of species on Isla de Enmedio (Tunnell and Nelson 1989) and Cabezo Reef (Tunnell and Nelson 1989; Nelson 1991). Overall, 42 species in 22 families have been listed from Isla de Lobos, although of these, 14 were identified only to genus. Those species mentioned from Cabezo Reef and Isla de Enmedio were the conspicuous members of the family Sabellidae: *Sabella melanostigma* and *Branchiomma nigromaculata* from both localities and *Sabellastarte magnifica* from Isla de Enmedio only. Members of the families Amphinomidae and Sabellidae constituted 53% of the collection at Isla de Lobos (Roberts 1981). Other common families were Orbiniidae, Cirratulidae, Syllidae, Eunicidae, Terebellidae, and Serpulidae.

Chávez et al. (1970) listed five species from the lagoon at Isla de Lobos: *Eurythoe complanata*, *Hermodice carunculata*, *Cloeia viridis*, *Eunice rubra*, and *Amphitrite ornata*. All five species were found in the *Thalassia-Halimeda* biotope, with *E. complanata* and *H. carunculata*, occurring in the *Diploria clivosa* biotope as well. Polychaetes were the third most abundant organism collected from the lagoon, with an estimated density of 33.5/m$^2$.

The 20 stations sampled by Roberts (1981) on Isla de Lobos can be divided into two broad habitats: reef and lagoon. The lagoon included *Thalassia* habitats containing varying amounts of coral (*Diploria* or *Porites*) or *Halimeda*, unvegetated habitats containing dredged material, artificial habitats such as a shipwreck, coral habitats (*Diploria, Acropora,* and *Montastraea*), and attached and drift macroalgae. The reef habitats included *Acropora,* rocks, a sunken ship, and sand at the base of the reef. Polychaetes were collected by hand and recovered from sediment samples. Soft sediment areas (e.g., *Thalassia,* dredge material) contained many burrowing forms (e.g., Cirratulidae), whereas boring and small cryptic forms (e.g., Syllidae) were found in holes and crevices of rocks and coral. Many juvenile and other small polychaetes were found in the macroalgae. Thirty-nine species were collected from habitats in the lagoon and 12 species in reef habitats. Eight taxa were found in both habitat categories: *Cirriformia punctata, Eurythoe complanata, Hermodice carunculata, Hypsicomus elegans, Lepidonotus, Eunice, Loimia,* and Nereididae. No species was found at every station. Characteristic species with the greatest contributions to similarity among lagoon stations were *Eurythoe complanata* (26.7%), *Sabella melanostigma* (13.8%), *Hermodice carunculata* (10.2%), *Eunice* sp. (9.2%), *Typosyllis* sp. (7.5%), *Naineris setosa* (6.3%), and *Spirobranchus giganteus* (5.4%). *Eurythoe complanata* (16.5%) was also characteristic of the reef habitat, as were *Lepidonotus* sp. (58.5%) and Nereididae (12.5%).

**Mollusks**  Mollusks are among the most diverse of all invertebrates, second only to the arthropods. Four of the seven classes—Polyplacophora (chitons), Gastropoda (snails and slugs), Bivalvia (clams, oysters, mussels, etc.), and Cephalapoda (squids and octopus)—are found in coral reef habitats from the water column above the reef (squid) to epifaunal and infaunal areas in both hard and soft substrates. Of the two most diverse groups on the reef, bivalves are filter feeders and gastropods range from herbivorous to carnivorous to omnivorous. They, in turn, are important food sources for other larger animals that have the ability to crush or open shell coverings (crabs, octopus, starfish, fish).

Some mollusks are very important fishery species to humans. The infaunal clams (*almejas*) *Codakia orbicularis* (primarily) and *Asaphis deflorata* are taken from lagoonal seagrass beds by artisanal fishers, primarily from Antón Lizardo in the Veracruz Reef System. Their destructive fishery method of seagrass disruption (raking, fanning, or prop washing) has greatly reduced seagrass bed coverage on many reefs (see Horta-Puga, chapter 12, this volume). Larger gastropods, primarily in the herbivorous family Strombidae, have been collected for food and ornamental seashells for decades. The larger queen conch (*Strombus gigas*), as well as the medium-sized milk conch (*S. costatus*) and the smaller hawk-wing conch (*S. raminus*), West Indian fighting conch *S. pugilus*), and Florida fighting conch (*S. alatus*), are all gastropod fishery species. These species were overfished to commercial extinction during the 1970s on southwestern Gulf reefs and on most Campeche Bank reefs during the 1980s and 1990s (J. W. Tunnell, personal observation). Other large carnivorous gastropods taken for food include the horse conch (*Pleuroploca gigantea*) and the West Indian chank (*Turbinella angulatus.*) These two large predatory gastropods are now rarely seen on the coral reefs.

There have been 548 species of mollusks found on or immediately adjacent to coral reefs within the southern Gulf of Mexico: chitons (7 species), bivalves (134), gastropods (405) and cephalopods (2). Two-thirds of these species are considered micromollusks (less than 10 mm) and are therefore generally overlooked by the casual observer. Collection and processing (picking micromollusks from sand under a microscope) produce large numbers of these small species that live on reef rock, in the sand, or symbiotically with other reef taxa such as algae, sponges, corals, other mollusks, or echinoderms.

Baker (1891) was the first to report on marine mollusks associated with coral reefs and other areas in the southern Gulf of Mexico. Nearly 70 years later, Moore (1958) briefly reported on the fauna of Blanquilla Reef, the most northerly emergent reef in the western Gulf. He reported 24 species of mollusks, and Chávez et al. (1970) listed 126 species at nearby Isla de Lobos Reef. Tunnell (1974) listed 290 species while studying the ecological and geographical distribution of mollusks from Isla de Lobos Reef and Isla de Enmedio Reef, both in the southwestern Gulf.

On the Campeche Bank, Rice and Kornicker (1962, 1965 addendum) reported and provided photographs for 149 species from Alacrán Reef. Vokes and Vokes (1983) published a list of almost 800 species from various Yucatán Peninsula areas, including 374 from Alacrán Reef and Cayos Arcas Reef. Their work included a photographic guide and geographic distribution of species. Boudreaux (1987) characterized the reef flat assemblages of Campeche Bank coral reefs, listing 57 species, and Gónzalez-Solís et al. (1991) studied molluscan distribution and species richness in various Yucatán Peninsula habitats, including coral reefs. There have not been any recent molluscan formal studies.

Ecological distribution of mollusks on Isla de Lobos Reef and Isla de Enmedio Reef shows habitat specificity for principal species in major reef zones (Tunnell 1974; Fig. 6.2): seagrass beds (*Thalassia testudinum* zone), reef flat (*Diploria clivosa* zone), upper forereef (*Acropora palmata* zone), and deeper reef areas (*Diploria-Montastraea* zone). On hard substrates in shallow-water shoreline areas, two distinct zones were recognized for mollusks (Tunnell 1974): an *Echinolittorina–Angiola lineata* (= *Littorina-Planaxis*) zone in calm water around dredge spoil piles and an *Echinolittorina/Littoraria angulifera–Tetraclita* (barnacle) (= *Littorina-Tetraclita*) zone on vertical concrete and metal surfaces (Fig. 6.3). Reef flat molluscan assemblages on Campeche Bank reefs included five species common to all reefs in this zone: *Tegula lividomaculata, Astraea caelata, Engina turbinella, Barbatia cancellaria,* and *Isognomon radiatus.* The first three were most commonly found on upper rock surfaces, while the latter were attached under rocks (Boudreaux 1987).

**Ostracods** Members of the crustacean class Ostracoda, the seed or mussel shrimp, are minute (<2 mm), widely distributed crustaceans that are found in both fresh and salt water (Ruppert and Barnes 1994). Their bodies are completely enclosed in a bivalve carapace composed of calcium carbonate. Many ostracods are benthic and associated with the upper layer of mud or detritus, but there are also planktonic, burrowing, interstitial, and epibiotic species. The majority of ostracods are filter- or suspension-feeding herbivores and detritivores, and their trophic role is that of secondary producer. They are consumed by a variety of organisms including fish, annelids and copepods (Delorme 2001). The fossil record of ostracods is extensive and they are often used to reconstruct coral reef and other marine/estuarine paleoenvironments because they are sensitive to changes in hydrologic parameters, such as salinity, water temperature, and dissolved oxygen (e.g., Bosellini et al. 2001; Dingle et al. 2001; Frenzel and Boomer 2005). In addition, ostracods are sensitive to pollution and other environmental stressors and are widely used as indicator species (e.g., Ruiz et al. 2000; Frenzel and Boomer 2005).

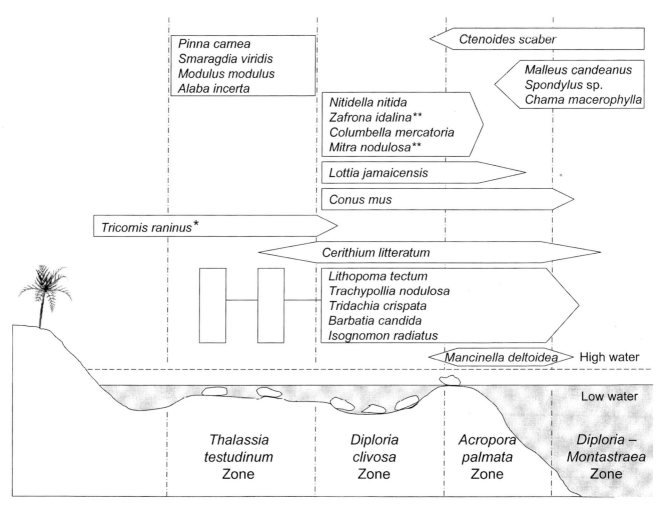

**Figure 6.2.** Distribution of dominant mollusks represented within windward lagoon and forereef biotic zones on Isla de Lobos Reef (modified from Tunnell 1974). * = species common on Isla de Lobos Reef but rare or absent at Isla de Enmedio Reef; ** = species common on Isla de Enmedio Reef but rare or absent at Isla de Lobos Reef.

Description of the ostracod fauna of reefs in the southern Gulf of Mexico is restricted to the Veracruz Reef System. All seven of the reefs nearest the city of Veracruz were sampled (northern group, 25 stations); only El Giote, Chopas, and Isla de Enmedio near Antón Lizardo (southern group, 8 stations) were sampled (Rickles 1977; Krutak and Rickles 1979; Krutak et al. 1980). No attempt was made to distinguish live ostracods from dead ones. Eighty-five species of ostracods were identified, with a mean of 26 species from stations in the northern group and 22 species from stations in the southern group. Seventeen species comprised 87.7% of the total collection (9,601 individuals; Table 6.5). These 17 species were common to both the northern and southern reef groups. Five species made up 66% of the total collection. *Loxocorniculum tricornatum* and *Morkhovenia inconspicua* were ubiquitous and *Loxocorniculum* cf. *postdorsoalata* was nearly ubiquitous (31 of 33 stations). Overall, *Loxocorniculum tricornatum* dominated collections in all but two stations in the northern group and *Loxocorniculum* cf. *postdorsoalata* dominated all sampling stations in the southern group.

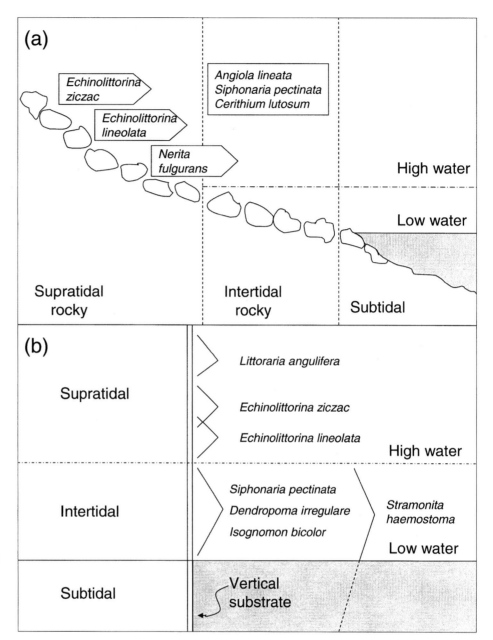

**Figure 6.3.** Mollusks associated with intertidal and subtidal hardsubstrates in the southwestern Gulf of Mexico. **(a)** *Echinolittorina* and *Angiola lineata* zones in calm water around spoil piles on Isla de Lobos. **(b)** *Echinolittorina/ Littoraria angulifera* and *Tetraclita* (barnacle) zone in rough water on metal well platform and shipwreck hull on Isla de Lobos and concrete pier on Isla de Enmedio (modified from Tunnell 1974).

**Decapods and Stomatopods** The crustacean order Decapoda (subclass Eumalacostraca) includes two suborders: Dendrobranchiata and Pleocyemata. The majority of decapods and all stomatopods (mantis shrimp, subclass Hoplocarida) are marine. Most are benthic, although many shrimp species are nektonic. Crustaceans, including decapods and other smaller crustaceans such as amphipods, serve many roles in the coral reef environment: as prey for many fish species (Díaz-Ruiz et al. 1998); as predators and scavengers (e.g., *Callinectes, Pagurus, Squilla*); as secondary producers (e.g., detritivores such as *Palaemonetes*, filter feeders such as *Callichirus*); as bioturbators and sediment modifiers (e.g., *Alpheus, Callichirus*); and as fish "cleaners" (e.g., *Periclimenes*). At least 146 species of decapods inhabit the coral reefs and adjacent waters in the southern Gulf of Mexico. The Dendrobranchiata (7 species) include shrimp in the fami-

**Table 6.5.** *Ostracod species comprising at least 1% of total collections from the Veracruz Reef System.*

| Species | Relative abundance (%) |
| --- | --- |
| *Loxocorniculum tricornatum* | 24.8 |
| *Loxocorniculum* cf. *postdorsoalata* | 19.9 |
| *Morkhovenia inconspicua* | 10.4 |
| *Xestoleberis* sp. 2 | 7.5 |
| *Cytherura elongata* | 3.2 |
| *Aglaiocypris croneisi* | 3.0 |
| *Orionina bradyi* | 2.9 |
| *Quadracythere* sp. 1 | 2.8 |
| *Xestoleberis* sp. 1 | 2.1 |
| *Aurila* sp. | 2.0 |
| *Haplocytheridea bradyi* | 1.9 |
| *Paracytheridea tschoppi* | 1.7 |
| *Perissocytheridea brachyforma* | 1.3 |
| *Hermanites transoceanica* | 1.1 |
| *Munseyella* cf. *minuta* | 1.1 |
| *Cushmanidea* cf. *ashermani* | 1.0 |
| *Puriana krutaki* | 1.0 |

*Note:* Modified from Krutak and Rickles (1979).

lies Penaeidae and Sergestidae. The majority of reef-associated decapods are in the suborder Pleocyemata, and are represented by five infraorders: barber pole shrimp (infraorder Stenopodidea, 3 species), true shrimp (infraorder Caridea, 45 species), hermit and porcelain crabs (infraorder Anomura, 16 species), true crabs (infraorder Brachyura, 67 species), ghost shrimp (infraorder Thalassinidea, 4 species), and lobsters (infraorder Palinura, 4 species). In addition, the mantis shrimp species (order Stomatopoda), a group of specialized, predatory crustaceans, are represented by 6 species.

Ives (1891) made the first surveys of crustaceans in Mexican Gulf waters, focusing on Veracruz harbor. He noted abundant corals in the area and reported six species of crabs. The decapods of the area received no further attention until the 1970s and 1980s when several studies were initiated on the Tuxpan and Veracruz reefs. A total of 124 decapods and 5 stomatopods have been reported from Isla de Lobos Reef (Chávez et al. 1970; Ray 1974; Rickner 1975, 1977; Allen 1982). In the Veracruz Reef System, Isla de Enmedio has received the most detailed study, with a total of 87 decapods reported (Ray 1974; Rickner 1975, 1977; Allen 1982; White 1982). On Alacrán Reef in Campeche Bank, Martínez-Guzmán and Hernández-Aguilera (1993) reported 68 decapod and four stomatopod species.

On Isla de Lobos, Chávez et al. (1970) studied various aspects of the reef lagoon and identified five biotopes in two zones, based on earlier work by Rigby and McIntire (1966). The surf zone of the island contained the rocky (dredge spoil) and sandy beach biotopes. In the sublittoral zone behind the reef crest were the mud bottom ("*Arenicola* [?]"), calcareous algae (*Rhipocephalus phoenix*), *Thalassia-Halimeda* meadow, and *Diploria clivosa* biotopes. Crustaceans, including small numbers of isopods, amphipods, and tanaids, were estimated at 55.2/m$^2$, and were the third most abundant invertebrate group. Thirteen of the 23 decapod species listed were found in the *Thalassia-Halimeda* meadow, as well as both stomatopod species. Overall, there was little overlap in species composition among habitats, with only five species found in more than one biotope. The xanthid crab, *Cataleptodius floridanus*, was the most widely distributed and was found in the mud bottom, calcareous algae, and *Thalassia-Halimeda* biotopes.

Isla de Lobos Reef and Isla de Enmedio Reef were chosen for studies of the reptant (crawling) decapod fauna (infraorders Anomura, Brachyura, and Palinura) because they represented the northernmost and southernmost reefs in Veracruz (Allen 1982). This study differed from that of Chávez et al. (1970) because it included both windward and leeward reef habitats. Five biotic zones were identified: (1) terrestrial zone, consisting of the islands at both reefs (and the rocky dredge spoil and sandy coast biotopes of Chávez et al. [1970]); (2) sand ribbon zone, the sandy area encircling both islands to a depth of 1 m; (3) *Thalassia-Halimeda* zone, in the lagoon of both reefs; (4) *Diploria clivosa* zone, on both windward and leeward reefs (but only leeward in Chávez et al. [1970]); (5) *Acropora* zone, on windward (*A. palmata*, both reefs) and leeward (*A. palmata*, Isla de Lobos; *A. cervicornis*, Isla de Enmedio) reefs; and (6) *Diploria-Montastraea* zone, on the forereef of both.

Isla de Lobos and Isla de Enmedio reefs had 37 reptant decapod species in common. Of the 49 species collected at Isla de Enmedio Reef, 12 were not found at Isla de Lobos. At Isla de Lobos Reef, 46 species were collected, of which nine were not collected at Isla de Enmedio. Overall, abundance was greatest in *Thalassia-Halimeda* and least in the deeper waters of the *Acropora* zone and the *Diploria-Montastraea* zone. The fauna of the *Diploria clivosa* zone was the most diverse. At least one species was exclusive to each zone on both reefs (Table 6.6). The most widespread species were *Calcinus tibicen* and *Stenorhyncus seticornus*, which were found in the *Thalassia-Halimeda*, *Diploria clivosa*, *Acropora*, and *Diploria-Montastraea* zones. No species was found in all zones.

White (1982) collected 34 species of shrimp from Isla de Enmedio reef habitats during January and June. Twenty-one species exhibited range extensions into the southwestern Gulf of Mexico. This collection included four species of penaeid shrimp (*Farfantepenaeus duorarum*, *Trachypenaeus similis*, *Sicyonia dorsalis*, and *S. parri*); the remaining were caridean shrimp. The most abundant species in the collection were *Sicyonia parri* (Penaeidae, 32.2%) and *Alpheus normanni* (Alpheidae, 26.4%). Penaeid shrimp species were collected only from *Thalassia* beds in the reef lagoon and were most active at night. Populations of *Alpheus normanni*, *Trachypenaeus similis*, *Sicyonia parri*, *Hippolyte curacoaensis*, and *Tozeuma carolinense* exhibited slight seasonal fluctuations based on January and June sampling. Two snapping shrimp (Alpheidae) were found in many reef habitats: *Alpheus formosus* and *Synalpheus fritzmuelleri*. Habitat preferences were noted for 23 species, and these were considered indicator species, which are those species that are found completely or predominantly within a specific habitat (Table 6.7).

Descriptions of the decapod and stomatopod fauna of Campeche Bank reefs are limited to one survey on Alacrán Reef that focused on the reef lagoon of Isla Perez (Martínez-Guzmán and Hernández-Aguilera 1993). Species richness was greatest in the families Alpheidae (9), Majidae (11), and Xanthidae (6). The

**Table 6.6.** *List of characteristic species of reptant decapods in each biotic zone on Isla de Lobos and Isla Enmedio reefs.*

**Terrestrial Zone**
*Coenobita clypeatus*
*Grapsus grapsus*
*Geocarcinus lateralis*
*Ocypode quadrata*

**Sand Ribbon Zone**
*Porcellana sayana*
*Petrochirus diogenes*
*Calappa gallus*
*Ebalia cariosa*
*Uhlias limbatus*
*Arenaeus cribrarus*
*Pinnixa* spp.

**Thalassia-Halimeda Zone**
*Pagurus brevidactylus*

**Diploria clivosa Zone**
*Dardanus fucosus*
*Petrolisthes jugosus*
*Petrolisthes galathinus*
*Pachycheles monilifer*
*Pseudocrytochirus corallicola*
*Eriphia gonagra*
*Paraliomera dispar*
*Paraliomera longimana*
*Pilumnus dasypodus*
*Platyactaea setigera*
*Peremon gibbesi*
*Macrocoeloma trispinosum nodipes*

**Acropora Zone**
*Domecia ancanthophora*

**Diploria-Montastraea Zone**
*Panilurus argus*

*Note:* Compiled from Allen (1982).

**Table 6.7.** *Indicator shrimp species of various reef habitats on Isla de Enmedio Reef.*

| Island and lagoon | Reef |
|---|---|
| **Thalassia beds** | **Windward reef front and flat** |
| *Farfantepenaeus duorarum* | *Alpheus bahamensis* |
| *Trachypenaeus similis* | *Alpheus cristulifrons* |
| *Sicyonia parri* | |
| *Leander tenuicornis* | **Crevices in lower windward reef front** |
| *Alpheus normanni* | *Alpheus peasei* |
| *Hippolyte curacaoensis* | |
| *Tozeuma carolinense* | **Leeward reef front and flat** |
| | *Synalpheus mcclendoni* |
| **Algal nodules** | *Synalpheus minus antillensis* |
| *Periclimenes americanus* | *Thor manningi* |
| **Rocky areas** | |
| *Alpheus armillatus* | |
| *Salmoneus* sp. | |
| **Intertidal rocks** | |
| *Automate gardineri* | |

*Note:* From White (1982).

majority of species were found in coral rubble (20) and *Thalassia* (18) habitats. Although collections were limited in this study, several species were found in unvegetated substrates (rocks, sand, coralline algae): *Cataleptodius floridanus*, *Panopeus occidentalis*, and *Leptodius parvulus*. The southern limits of *Processa vossi* and *Tyche emarginata*, previously reported as Florida, were expanded to Campeche Bank based on their collection during this study.

**Echinoderms**   Echinoderms, the sea stars, brittle stars, sea urchins, sea cucumbers, and crinoids, are among the most conspicuous members of the coral reef invertebrate community. They are frequently used to define and name the communities they inhabit due to their dominance and abundance (Kier and Grant 1965). Like the polychaetes, they are important components of coral reef food webs and a significant food source for carnivorous fish (Díaz-Ruiz et al. 1998). Perhaps most importantly, their foraging activities can significantly modify reef substrate (Kornicker and Boyd 1962), and they can play the role of keystone species. For example, the crown of thorns starfish (*Acanthaster planci*) is a voracious predator of coral polyps on reefs in the tropical Indo-Pacific and is capable of reducing living coral cover. In the Gulf of Mexico, tropical Atlantic, and Caribbean, the long-spined sea urchin (*Diadema antillarum*) was an important algal herbivore. The mass mortality of long-spined sea urchins in the 1980s, from which populations have not recovered, is one factor that contributes to increasing macroalgal growth on reefs throughout the Caribbean (Hughes et al. 1985; Carpenter 1990), Veracruz (Nelson 1991), and the rest of its range.

Few studies have focused on the echinoderms associated with reefs in the southern Gulf of Mexico. In his work in the harbor of Veracruz, Ives (1890) reported seven species. Caso (1961, cited in Henkel 1982) listed 25 species (exclusive of crinoids, class Crinoidea) from reefs in the southern Gulf of Mexico. In the Tuxpan Reef System, 12 species, including two sea stars (class Asteroidea), two brittlestars (class Ophiuroidea), four echinoids (class Echinoidea), and three sea cucumbers (class Holothuroidea) were collected by Chávez et al. (1970) on Isla de Lobos Reef. On Blanquilla (Tuxpan Reef System), Moore (1958) noted five species, and on La Blanquilla (Veracruz Reef System) Villalobos (1971) listed seven, including the crinoid *Nemaster mexicanensis* (= *N. rubiginosa*), and the basket star *Astrocaneum*. The echinoderm fauna of Isla de Enmedio Reef in the Veracruz Reef System was studied extensively by Henkel (1982), who listed a total of 41 species including 1 crinoid, 4 sea stars, 13 brittlestars, 14 echinoids, and 9 sea cucumbers. The sea urchins *Diadema antillarum*, *Lytechinus variegatus*, and *Echinometra lucunter* were found on Cabezo Reef (Nelson 1991). The reefs on Campeche Bank have received almost no attention. The sea star *Oreaster reticulatus* has been reported from Alacrán Reef (Ardisson and Duran-Najera 1997). Overall, a total of 46 echinoderm species have been listed for the reefs in the southern Gulf of Mexico, mostly from Isla de Enmedio. The most diverse groups are the brittlestars and sea urchins, with 14 species each, followed by the sea cucumbers (12), sea stars (5), and crinoids (1).

On Isla de Lobos, echinoderms, particularly brittlestars, were the most abundant organisms collected (Chávez et al. 1970). Total echinoderm abundance was estimated at 76/m², and was comprised of 94% brittle stars. Echinoderms were found only in the *Thalassia-Halimeda* (6 species) and *Diploria clivosa* (9 species) zones. The variable sea urchin (*Lytechinus variegatus*) and the sea cucumbers *Euapta lappa* and *Leptosynapta crassipatina* were found only in the *Thalassia-Halimeda* meadows; sea stars and brittlestars, as well as *Diadema antillarum* and *Eucidaris tribuloides*, were found only in the *Diploria clivosa* zone. *Tripneustus ventricosus* and *Echinometra luncunter* (echinoid) and the sea cucumber *Holothuria mexicana* were found in both habitats.

Echinoderms on La Blanquilla were found in two habitats: the lagoon and southwestern leeward forereef (Villalobos 1971). Only echinoids (*Diadema antillarum*, *Eucidaris tribuloides*, and *Tripneustus ventricosus*) were listed in the *Diploria* and *Thalassia* communities found within the lagoon habitat. In the leeward reef habitat, *Nemaster mexicanus* (= *N. rubiginosa*) and the basket star *Astrocaneum* were associated with the *Montastraea* zone. *Encope michelini* (echinoid) was found in the *Plexaurella* community.

Echinoderms at Isla de Enmedio were collected from five biotic zones: *Thalassia*, *Diploria clivosa*, *Acropora*, *Diploria-Montastraea*, and sand bottom (Henkel 1982). Species richness was greatest in the *Diploria clivosa* zone (22) followed by *Acropora* (20), *Thalassia* (19), *Diploria-Montastraea* (14), and sand bottom (10). Most species (19) were restricted to one habitat, primarily *Diploria clivosa* (4), *Diploria-Montastraea* (5), or sand bottom (6). Only three species, the echinoids *Diadema antillarum* and *Tripneustus ventricosus* and the sea cucumber *Isostichopus badionotus*, were found in all habitats.

**Appendicularians**   Appendicularians (Class Larvaceae or Appendicularia) are members of the subphylum Tunicata (tunicates), one of two "invertebrate" chordate subphyla. Although they do not possess backbones as do other chordates, at some time in their life cycle they exhibit a notochord, a dorsal hollow nerve cord, gill slits (pharyngeal clefts), and a postanal tail (Ruppert and Barnes 1994). The appendicularians are small (~5 mm), transparent, planktonic tunicates found near the surface of marine waters. As adults, they resemble an ascidian tadpole larva. Appendicularians live within a secreted mucous "house" and feed on plankton filtered from the water stream that flows through the house. They discard and secrete a new house every few hours (López-Urrutia et al. 2003). In tropical and temperate waters, appendicularian growth rates are nearly an order of magnitude higher than copepods of similar body weight, and they contribute from 10% to 40% of total mesozooplankton production (Hopcroft and Roff 1995; López-Urrutia et al. 2003). Predation plays a larger role in control of their communities than either food quantity or quality (Hopcroft and Roff 1998).

Appendicularians constituted 2%–30% of total zooplankton at La Blanquilla and were usually the second most abundant zooplankton after copepods (Vega Rodriguez and Arenas Fuentes 1965). Flores-Coto (1974) listed 21 species of from 12 stations located in waters surrounding the reef. The most abundant species (and their maximum densities) were *Oikopleura longicauda* (692/m$^3$), *Fritillaria borealis* f. *sargassi* (769/m$^3$), and *F. formica* (343/m$^3$). Eight species were found in at least three-fourths of stations, and *Oikopleura longicauda*, *O. cophocerca*, and *Fritillaria borealis* f. *sargassi* were found at all stations. Species richness ranged from 5 to 17 and density ranged from 58/m$^3$ to 870/m$^3$.

## Zoogeography

The zoogeographical affinities of selected noncoral invertebrate fauna of the reefs of the southern Gulf of Mexico include species that extend into the Carolina Region (warm temperate), which encompasses both the northern Gulf of Mexico and the Carolinian Province on the U.S. Atlantic Coast from about Cape Canaveral, Florida, to Cape Hatteras, North Carolina, and the Tropical Western Atlantic Region's Caribbean, West Indian, and Brazilian provinces (Briggs

1974; Fig. 6.4). Species whose distributions extend into the eastern Atlantic are considered "amphi-Atlantic," and "circumtropical" is used to describe those that occur worldwide in tropical waters. Overall, fewer than 10% of the species for which distributional data was compiled are restricted to the Caribbean Province (Table 6.8). The distributions of more than half extend into the West Indian, Brazilian, or Carolinian provinces, and about one-third extend into

Fig. 6.4. Zoogeographic regions and provinces referred to in the text (compiled from Briggs 1974).

**Table 6.8.** *Zoogeographical affinities of selected taxa collected on reefs in the southern Gulf of Mexico, primarily Isla de Lobos and Isla de Enmedio reefs (see Fig. 6.4).*

| Group | Number of species | Restricted to Caribbean Province | Extend into West Indian Province | Extend into Brazilian Province | Extend into Carolinian Province | Extend into northern Gulf of Mexico | Amphi-Atlantic | Circum-tropical |
|---|---|---|---|---|---|---|---|---|
| Mollusks | 235 | 21 | 117 | 144 | 119 | 62 | 9 | 5 |
| Crabs | 55 | 6 | 37 | 37 | 28 | 11 | 8 | 6 |
| Shrimp | 30 | 2 | 26 | 15 | 18 | 15 | 6 | 3 |
| Echinoderms | 42 | 3 | 32 | 23 | 13 | 22 | 8 | 5 |
| Total | 342 | 32 | 212 | 219 | 178 | 110 | 31 | 19 |

the northern Gulf of Mexico. It is likely that when the invertebrate faunas of the Campeche Bank reefs are more fully studied, the numbers of organisms restricted to the Caribbean Province will increase. In general, the invertebrate fauna of southern Gulf of Mexico coral reefs is tropical, although many species can also be found in warm temperate waters.

The molluscan fauna associated with southwestern Gulf of Mexico coral reefs is predominantly of Caribbean origin (Tunnell 1974). The fauna is depauperate compared to geographical areas located within the Caribbean proper. Taxa that are missing or low in numbers are the larger intertidal or shallow subtidal chitons; the typical, widespread families Trochidae, Turbinidae, and Conidae, of which there are only a few species; *Fissurella*, of which there is only one species compared to nine found within the Caribbean basin; and *Cittarium pica, Tectarius muricatus,* and *Nodilittorina tuberculata,* which are common in Caribbean reefs but are missing from southwestern Gulf reefs. Location of southwestern Gulf reefs near the edge or periphery of the tropics is the most likely reason for these missing or reduced more tropical elements.

Allen (1982) stated that all crabs collected at Isla de Enmedio and Isla de Lobos were wide-ranging, eurythermic tropical species. The majority of the shrimp also appear to be tropical, since most species' distributions (87%) extend into the West Indian Province. There were few decapods that were restricted to the Caribbean Province (Table 6.8). The echinoderm fauna of Isla de Enmedio contained the fewest species that were restricted to the Caribbean Province. Henkel (1982) described the zoogeographic affinities of the echinoderms as "complex," with 28 species restricted to tropical waters and 13 species also found in warm, temperate waters. Most (68%) were restricted to the waters of the western Atlantic, with only a few extending into the eastern Atlantic or considered circumtropical.

# 7

# Reef Algae

ROY L. LEHMAN

Coral reef algal communities include the zooxanthellae, symbiotic algae in the gastrodermis of the hermatypic (reef-building) corals, free-living, encrusting coralline algae, phytoplankton, mat-forming and boring micro-filamentous algae, and calcified, fleshy, and turf macroalgae. Coral reefs should probably be called tropical reefs, biotic reefs, or even algal reefs. Corals cannot build a reef single-handedly; algae contribute greatly to reef productivity and growth. Nutrients supplied to hermatypic corals by zooxanthellae allow them to grow and reproduce quickly enough to form reefs. Coralline algae contribute greatly to reef biomass, may deposit more calcium carbonate than the corals themselves (Littler and Littler 1984) and are the cement that holds the reef together. Reefs are formed as much by the accumulation of calcareous sediment as by the growth of corals. The spaces formed by coral fragments and large rubble fill with fine and coarse carbonate sediment. Encrusting calcareous algae grow over the sediment, cementing it into place. These algal reef builders also prevent erosion of the reef by waves by consolidating and cementing the substrate together. The stony substrate that is formed is tough enough to withstand waves that can destroy even the hardiest of corals.

The most significant of the attached primary producers on shallow reefs, like those in the southern Gulf of Mexico, are the red (division Rhodophyta), brown (division Ochrophyta, class Phaeophyceae), and green fleshy algae (division Chlorophyta). Many genera (e.g., *Sargassum*) bear a superficial likeness to higher plants but are distinguished by their lack of vascular tissues; they do not have true leaves, stems, and roots. Coral reef phytoplankton, the microscopic plants that float within the photic layer of the ocean, include golden algae (division Ochrophyta, class Chrysophyceae) and cyanobacteria (= blue-green algae, kingdom Monera, phylum Cyanophycota). Although the primary productivity of phytoplankton around reefs is small compared to that of the zooxanthellae and macroalgae, when the smallest phytoplankton, the picoplankton and nanoplankton, are included, abundance and productivity might be higher than earlier thought (Dawes 1998). Cyanobacteria are also important because they are nitrogen fixers and provide a substantial source of nutrients within the coral reef environment (Adey and Goertemiller 1987). They form surface mats or may bore into certain shells and skeletons of corals. Most notable is a free-living filamentous alga, *Calothrix* (Berner 1990). There is also evidence that some corals may have symbionts that can fix nitrogen, providing nutrients for the zooxanthellae.

**Algal Biodiversity on Southern Gulf of Mexico Coral Reefs**

There have been few studies of the algae associated with coral reefs in the southern Gulf of Mexico. A revised and expanded checklist of the fleshy macroalgae was assembled from a survey of literature that covers the coral reefs of the

**Table 7.1.** *Number of species of macroalgae reported from surveyed reefs in the southern Gulf of Mexico.*

| Coral reef | Rhodophyta | Phaeophyceae | Chlorophyta | Total |
|---|---|---|---|---|
| Blanquilla | 23 | 7 | 9 | 39 |
| Isla de Lobos | 20 | 6 | 16 | 42 |
| Isla Verde | 34 | 5 | 24 | 63 |
| Isla de Enmedio | 77 | 21 | 42 | 140 |
| Santiaguillo | 16 | 11 | 17 | 44 |
| Sacrificios | 20 | 6 | 13 | 39 |
| Alacrán | 34 | 11 | 28 | 73 |

*Note:* Numbers and totals are from the compilation of all known publications after corrections and revisions.

southern Gulf of Mexico (www.gulfbase.org) and contains 331 total species, including 165 species of red algae (division Rhodophyta), 50 species of brown algae (division Ochrophyta, class Phaeophyceae), and 116 species of green algae (division Chlorophyta). The list contains major taxonomic rearrangements, name changes, and author revisions and conforms primarily to the taxonomic arrangement and names used by Wynne (1998) and Littler and Littler (2000). Table 7.1 compares the number and percentage of algal species by higher taxonomic groups found on reefs of the southern Gulf of Mexico.

**Veracruz Reef System**  Huerta M. and Barrientos (1965) compared the marine algae of Tuxpan with those found at Blanquilla and Isla de Lobos reefs. They indicated that these reefs are similar in regard to the flora, as they are both offshore coral reefs with shallow, protected waters. They reported a total of 31 species of macroalgae at Blanquilla and 43 species at Isla de Lobos.

Isla de Enmedio Reef was studied by Huerta M. et al. (1977), Lehman and Tunnell (1992a, 1992b), and Lehman (1993). Together, they report the highest species richness (148) for any reef of the southwestern Gulf of Mexico. Lehman and Tunnell (1992b) and Lehman (1993) evaluated and collected samples from Isla de Enmedio Reef and adjacent reefs each June over a 10-year period. They reported a total of 91 species of macroalgae. Of these, 34 (including four forms) belong to the division Chlorophyta, 11 to Ochrophyta, and 46 to Rhodophyta. A comparison of species richness with the earlier list of Huerta M. et al. (1977) showed a slight difference in the total number of species identified (97). Lehman and Tunnell (1992b) reported fewer numbers of species in the divisions Ochrophyta (class Phaeophyceae) and Rhodophyta and greater number of Chlorophyta. Factors that may influence these differences include actual changes in species composition or differences in sampling techniques and the locations that were sampled or both. The systematic list from Huerta M. et al. (1977) also includes 41 species of epiphytic microalgae collected primarily from the lagoon; of those, only seven were included in the list of Lehman and Tunnell (1992b) and they were incidentally found on larger algae. The deepwater areas that require the use of scuba were not surveyed by Huerta M. et al. (1977), whereas Lehman and Tunnell (1992b) list 18 deepwater algae. The combination of both checklists resulted in a total of 148 algal species for Isla de Enmedio

Reef. The checklist for algae from Isla de Enmedio Reef listed only 140 species due to taxonomic rearrangements, name changes, and combinations that are integrated into the reevaluation of algal species from all the known checklists and literature of the primary reefs of the southern Gulf of Mexico. The total distribution of numbers of species for algae at Isla de Enmedio Reef is 77, 21, and 42 for the Rhodophyta, Ochrophyta (class Phaeophyceae), and Chlorophyta, respectively (Huerta M. et al. 1977; Lehman and Tunnell 1992a and later corrections).

The benthic marine flora of Isla Santiaguillo and Isla Sacrificios, Veracruz, Mexico, was reported by Mendoza-González and Mateo-Cid (1985). They reported a total of 44 marine algae from Isla Santiaguillo and the associated reef. The division Chlorophyta contained the highest number of species (17). The totals for the remaining two groups were Rhodophyta (16) and Ochrophyta (11). Isla Sacrificios had 19 Rhodophyta, 6 Ochrophyta, and 13 Chlorophyta for a total of 38 macroalgae for the reef.

The marine algae associated with Isla Verde, Veracruz, Mexico, were reported by Mateo-Cid et al. (1996). The study included information on seasonality, reproductive stage, tidal level, wave exposure, substrate, and epiphytism. They indicated that the algal flora associated with the coral reef was as expected, and they reported on the numbers of different groups of algae collected, Rhodophyta (37), Ochrophyta (8), and Chlorophyta (24).

A list of the littoral marine algae of the state of Veracruz was compiled by Múzquiz (1961). She collected samples from Tuxpan to Veracruz, Isla de Enmedio Reef, and south to Montepío and Coatzacoalcos. The species recorded included 25 Chlorophyta, 14 Ochrophyta, and 51 Rhodophyta.

**Campeche Bank Reefs**  The marine flora of Alacrán Reef was evaluated by Huerta M. (1961). The algae associated with this reef contained the second highest diversity of algal species (69) when compared to Isla de Enmedio Reef (148). Alacrán Reef, however, contained numerous species that were found at no other studied reef within the southern Gulf of Mexico. It lies closer to the more tropical waters of the Caribbean and its flora is slightly more diverse than the other reefs. Twenty-three species of algae (8 Rhodophyta, 5 Ochrophyta, and 10 Chlorophyta) were listed from Alacrán Reef that have not been reported from any other reef in the southern Gulf of Mexico. This may be the result of different collectors with different expertise in specific algal groups or the lack of time for collecting in different zones of the reefs. There are some macroalgae, however, that are more tropical (water quality may also be a factor), and we would expect to find those species primarily at Alacrán Reef. Among these algae are members from the families Sargassaceae (Ochrophyta) and Udoteaceae (Chlorophyta). The total distributions of algal divisions and species numbers were Rhodophyta (34), Chlorophyta (24), and Ochrophyta (11).

Huerta-Múzquiz et al. (1987) studied the presence of marine algae along the coast of the Yucatán and adjacent islands including Alacrán Reef. Because their report also included the marine algae from the Caribbean side of the Yucatán, it is therefore rich in diversity and species numbers. The results included a total of 386 species, of which 116 are Chlorophyta, 54 Ochrophyta, and 199 Rhodophyta.

## Algal Zonation and Ecology at Isla de Enmedio Reef

Studies of Isla de Enmedio Reef and adjacent reefs began in 1983 and continued each year until an extensive field study of Isla de Enmedio Reef was concluded in 1990–91 as part of a Ph.D. dissertation (Lehman 1993). This study, which contained descriptions of the reef, the articulation of four major ecological zones, and a comprehensive evaluation of the reef macroalgae, is being used as a reef algal "model" in this volume, in the absence of other comprehensive studies in the region.

**Lagoon**  The living bottoms of protected lagoons of the southern reefs of the Gulf of Mexico are predominantly covered by turtle grass (*Thalassia testudinum*—39% at Isla de Enmedio Reef), with manatee grass (*Cymodocea filiforme*) found in much lesser amounts (>1%) and only in the deeper areas of lagoons. The average water depth is 1.30 ms (with a range of 0.25 to 2.75 m) at Isla de Enmedio Reef (Lehman 1993). Turtle grass is probably the most important marine angiosperm found in the shallow waters in the entire Gulf of Mexico (Humm 1964). It functions as a primary producer, food source, and habitat for a host of invertebrates, as an attachment source for epiphytic algae, and as shelter for many marine animals (Voss and Voss 1955). Most of the remaining bottom is a combination of coral rubble (16.4%), sand (28.3%), and a hard substrate (6.0%) that in many cases is encrusting coralline algae at Isla de Enmedio Reef (Lehman 1993). The lagoon has the greatest species richness of all the zones, having a high species diversity of organisms, most of which are macroalgae (Lehman 1993). Brown algae that dominate lagoons include *Dictyota menstrualis* [*dichotoma* sensu *auct.*] and *Padina gymnospora*. *Dictyota* forms either dense mats or is loosely packed over bare substrate in protected areas of the lagoon. Large, dense clumps of *Padina gymnospora* are attached to rocky substrates in shallow water (1.08 m). The brown alga, *Padina gymnosperma*, has a rounded thallus with concentric white (calcium carbonate) and brown bands. The margin is enrolled so that the marginal meristematic cells are protected from herbivory and the effects of high energy. This species is found in the shallow waters of lagoons. It has been reported from many reefs in the southern Gulf of Mexico and is found in all zones, from the shallow lagoons, along the slope, and into areas of deep water. There are additional species (4 to 5) of *Dictyota* that are commonly found in the lagoons and shallow slope zones of the reefs. The brown alga *Cladosiphon occidentalis* is established in the lagoons as an epiphyte on other algae or more commonly on turtle grass, potentially becoming locally abundant in lagoons that are environmentally stressed by elevated levels of nutrients.

The red algae (Rhodophyta) are the largest and most diversified group of tropical algae. In addition, they are the most difficult group to identify because of species variability and because their morphology is difficult to distinguish visually. Thus, they usually require special preparation for analysis of reproductive structures in order to identify them. In the lagoon of Isla de Enmedio Reef, one commonly finds the red coralline algae in the forms of encrusting (crustose) layers overgrowing hard substrate areas, spherical knobby nodules, and articulated (geniculate) and nonarticulated branches These coralline red algae can grow 0.8–1.5 inches each year (Littler and Littler 1984). Species of *Amphiroa* are often found intermixed with other species of algae in seagrass beds or in rock crevices. They are usually attached lightly to hard substrates. These algae are fragile, calcareous, dense clumps with individual branches that divide dichotomously. Joints between the branch sections are uncalcified and flexible. *Galaxaura rugosa* is a bushy, loosely packed, rounded clump most often found in reef-protected areas, especially the lagoon. The plant is a reddish color and heavily calcified with articulated joints. Additional noncalcareous species commonly found on coral reefs include members of the genera *Chondria, Chondrophycus,* and *Laurencia.*

The most common green algae (Chlorophyta) in the lagoons are *Neomeris annulata, Caulerpa sertularioides, C. racemosa, Dictyospheria cavernosa,* and many species of the genus *Halimeda. Halimeda* species, especially *H. opuntia* (which has been reported from all the reefs surveyed from the literature) are major producers (along with red calcareous algae and coral skeletons) of carbonate sediments and sands of the reef (Goreau et al. 1979; Hillis-Colinveaux 1980). This green to dark green alga consists of hard, flattened "oatmeal"-shaped segments, which are articulated. The rounded or three-lobed thalli branch in all planes. In the process of converting all of its protoplasm into reproductive cells (= holocarpy), the thallus loses all its pigments and dies, leaving the white calcified walls. The resulting dead segments are the primary component of the calcareous sands found in lagoons. *Neomeris annulata* is also reported from the surveyed reefs in the southern Gulf of Mexico. It is a small, highly calcified fingerlike plant (diameter of 1–3 mm and height of 1–2 cm), with green, fuzzy apical filaments that grow in dense clusters.

Other calcareous green algae are *Rhipocephalus phoenix* and *Udotea spinulosa. Rhipocephalus phoenix* resembles a pinecone with a slender stalk. Flattened plates that make up the thallus are lightly calcified and radiate around the stalk, forming a small Christmas-tree shape. The plants are found throughout lagoons and are usually associated with marine grasses in shallow waters (an average of 1.34 m at Isla de Enmedio Reef). *Udotea spinulosa* has a highly calcified, erect, fan-shaped thallus supported by a thin stipe. It occurs most often in deeper waters (~3 m) on sandy, plainlike bottoms.

The most common noncalcareous green algae are members of the genus *Caulerpa.* From the checklist of literature surveyed from the southern Gulf of Mexico reefs, eight species of *Caulerpa* have been reported (Chávez et al. 1970; Huerta M. and Barrientos 1965; Múzquiz 1961; Huerta M. et al. 1977; Lehman and Tunnell 1992a; Lehman 1993; Mateo-Cid et al. 1996; Mendoza-González and Mateo-Cid 1985; Torruco et al. 1993). The plants consist of a siphonous stolon, which runs horizontally over the surface of the substrate and is anchored with clusters of rootlike rhizoids. At intervals along the stolons are highly differentiated erect branches called assimilators that have a characteristic morphology for each of the different species. These assimilators are the principal sites of photosynthesis. *Caulerpa sertularioides* is one of the most common algae found in the protected lagoons, growing on shallow, sandy substrates. It has featherlike assimilators. The common green alga *Caulerpa cupressoides* is found in areas of slightly higher energy. Its assimilators are tough, stiff, parallel columns of short branchlets. The rhizoids are attached to coral rubble or fragments or anchored directly into sandy substrates. *Caulerpa racemosa* is frequently found in large patches in areas of the reef that experience high-energy wave action. It is attached to hard substrates, including live coral heads. The rhizoids are adapted for firm attachment and at times will cover exposed living and dead coral rock. The assimilators are swollen spherical branchlets that can survive in heavy surf areas. For all species of *Caulerpa,* the morphology of the assimilator is variable and indicates the habitat in which the species survives.

One of the largest cells known to science is the green alga *Ventricaria ventricosa* [*Valonia ventricosa*]. The plant looks like large shiny marbles. The spherical cell is thin-walled and dark green in color with a reflective shine.

They are usually found as solitary individuals, but sometimes several may grow near each other or together. They are attached to the substrate by tiny, hairlike rhizoids.

*Dictyosphaeria cavernosa* is a light green alga that has a wall composed of small vesicular-like cells a single layer thick. It is commonly found in shallow, protected waters of lagoons attached by rhizoids to hard substrate. This alga may cover extensive areas, forming mats, and as it ages will frequently rupture, showing its hollow construction. This alga has been associated with areas having an overabundance of nutrients (primarily nitrogen) (Littler et al. 1989). Alacrán Reef has members of the family Siphonocladaceae (*Dictyosphaeria ocellata* and *Siphonocladus rigidus*) and the family Udoteaceae (*Halimeda incrassata, H. monile, Penicillus capitatus,* and *P. pyriformis*) that have not been reported from other southern Gulf of Mexico reefs (Chávez et al. 1970; Huerta M. and Barrientos 1965; Múzquiz 1961; Huerta M. et al. 1977; Lehman and Tunnell 1992b; Lehman 1993; Mateo-Cid et al. 1996; Mendoza-González and Mateo-Cid 1985; Torruco et al. 1993).

**Reef Flat and Crest**   The reef flat and crest become evident as the bottom of the lagoon rises to a shallow depth (an average of 1.16 m at Enmedio Reef; Lehman 1993). This zone is most obvious on the windward side of the reef where the waves and currents create a zone of high (stress) energy. In addition, the shallow water permits intense sunlight to heat the zone, killing many nontolerant organisms. The reef flat at Isla de Enmedio Reef has a low diversity (H' = 2.11; Lehman 1993), and only the most tolerant of species are found there, including the red coralline algae *Padina gymnospora* and *Halimeda opuntia*. The turbulence, along with wave action and shallow depth, results in a reduction of grazing by fish and other herbivores (Humm 1964).

The reef flat may be covered with a layer of encrusting coralline algae, which essentially functions as the bottom. Red algal nodules often occur on this substrate. In low-energy areas of lagoons, zones of nodules with elongated knobs may accumulate in depressions, whereas in high-energy areas such as windward reef flats, the nodules lack protuberances and are smooth. The swollen structures are unable to form on the nodules as they are rolled about by the waves on the hard red coralline algal substrate (Littler and Littler 1984). Their color is usually some shade of red but may range from violet to yellow to tan.

Red algae with fleshy thalli are also common. *Digenea simplex* is a pervasive noncalcareous red alga that has been described from many of the reefs in the southern Gulf of Mexico. The plant is a dark reddish-brown, stiff, wiry alga that is dichotomous or irregularly branched. It occurs on hard surfaces, in areas of high energy, and is often covered with filamentous epiphytes. This alga has been commonly associated with eutrophic waters. Also found with *Digenea simplex* is *Gelidium crinale*. This thick, wiry turf of a dark violet color is capable of withstanding considerable wave disturbances and comprises the majority of the thick mat found along the windward reef crest and slopes of the reefs.

**Reef Slope**   The reef slope (windward) is distinguished primarily by an increase in depth, a shift to a hard substrate bottom (58.61%), and an increase in the number of living corals (1.74%). This zone is characterized by a typical spur and groove construction, with remnant *Acropora palmata* found in the upper areas. Small, turf-forming filamentous algae are common. This "turf" is composed primarily of *Gelidium crinale, Ceramium, Centroceras, Polysiphonia,* and other species of very small filamentous red algae. These small, fleshy, or filamentous types grow in a short, thick turf along the reef flat and adjacent slope. A large number of fishes, sea urchins, mollusks, and other animals forage on these plants. Because this turf provides quality biomass and has a high growth rate, resulting in an extremely rapid biomass turnover rate, it provides an excellent source of food for herbivores. The primary production to biomass ratio of the algal mat turnover is very high—so high that this noncoralline algal mat may be responsible for the majority of the primary productivity that is channeled to organisms harvested by humans from coral reef communities (Adey and Goertemiller 1987).

Two common pelagic species of *Sargassum* (*S. fluitans* and *S. natans*) are often found trapped in lagoons or caught on corals and rubble along the reef slopes and are a major component of beach drift on islands associated with the reefs. Because Alacrán Reef is nearer to the Caribbean than the other reefs of the southern Gulf of Mexico, the flora takes on a more tropical Caribbean affinity. Members of the Sargassaceae, including *Turbinaria tricostata*, *T. turbinata*, *Sargassum polyceratium*, *S. ramifolium*, and *S. vulgare*, have been reported only from this reef.

**Deep Water**   In the deeper waters surrounding the reef, the articulate and nonarticulate red algae species *Jania adherens*, *Galaxura rugosa*, and *Amphiroa rigida* are common. *Amphiroa fragilissima*, and *Galaxaura rugosa* are common and have been reported from many of the reefs of the southern Gulf of Mexico (Chávez et al. 1970; Huerta M. and Barrientos 1965; Múzquiz 1961; Huerta M. et al. 1977; Lehman and Tunnell 1992b, Lehman 1993; Mateo-Cid et al. 1996; Mendoza-González and Mateo-Cid 1985; Torruco et al. 1993).

Deepwater rocky areas surrounding the reef are dominated primarily by two brown algae species, *Lobophora varigata* and *Dictyota menstrualis*. *Lobophora varigata* has three different growth forms that occur as a result of variations in depth and habitat type. These forms include the decumbent, crust, and ruffled forms (Littler and Littler 2000). In the deep zone of Isla de Enmedio Reef, the decumbent form is the dominant plant and form type. The thallus is compressed, prostrate, and in shelflike layers. These blades are fan-shaped, thin, and overlapping. The thallus is light brown and has faint concentric growth zones with fine hairs. *Dictyota menstrualis* is common in all zones at Isla de Enmedio Reef (Lehman 1993).

**Ecology**   If grazers are removed in large numbers, macroalgae can thrive and occupy the space that corals and other organisms held. In the reefs located near Veracruz, Mexico, herbivorous fish have become less numerous due to overfishing. As the numbers of fish are reduced, another important grazer, such as a sea urchin (e.g., *Diadema antillarum*), will become more prevalent. The urchins apparently may benefit from reduced competition with fish. Urchins appeared to take up the slack for the fishes, and algal populations remained more or less stable. In 1983, due to unknown causes, populations of the long-spined black urchin *Diadema antillarum* died throughout the Gulf of Mexico and Caribbean (Lessios et al. 1984). Macroalgae, freed from grazing pressure, became much more abundant on many reefs (Tunnell 1992). At Isla de Enmedio Reef, the algae have taken over the reef almost entirely, and the formerly rich coral reefs are now more seaweed beds than coral reefs. In addition, coastal development with increased human population has resulted in more intensive fishing,

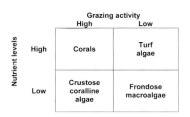

**Figure 7.1.** Diagrammatic representation of the relative dominance paradigm of algae types (Littler et al. 1991).

and there has also been an increase in the release of nutrients from sewage and agricultural fertilizer (Tunnell 1992). The macroalgal growth is enhanced by eutrophication at the same time that the grazers that keep them under control are removed. There is increasing evidence that this is a global threat to coral reefs (Littler and Littler 2000).

In addition to controlling how many macroalgae there are, grazers affect which particular types of algae live on the reef and where they are located. Coralline algae, for example, are abundant because the calcium carbonate in their tissues discourages grazers. Others produce noxious chemicals that are toxic or distasteful; these macroalgae tend to be more abundant (Fenical 1980). Grazing affects the growth rate, reproduction, and survival of macroalgae, and there is a strong relationship among grazing, nutrients, and the type of algal flora (Littler and Littler 1988). Grazing controls algal biomass, nutrients set the upper limits to that biomass, and both play a role in the type of species present. The existence of three morphological groups of algae (filamentous, fleshy, and calcareous) is dependent in part on the intensity of grazing and nutrient levels (Fig. 7.1).

# 8

# Reef Corals

GUILLERMO HORTA-PUGA, JUAN MANUEL VARGAS-
HERNÁNDEZ, AND JUAN PABLO CARRICART-GANIVET

*Editors' note—Coral reef zonation is discussed in chapter 5 and soft and hard coral biodiversity is discussed in chapter 6.*

Recent distribution of the shallow-water zooxanthellate Scleractinia extends to the greater Indo-Pacific (Pacific and Indian Oceans, Red Sea, and Persian Gulf) and the Atlantic, including the Gulf of Mexico. The greater Indo-Pacific is the most prominent and diverse biogeographic province; the Atlantic is far inferior to the greater Pacific in all aspects of species richness (Wells 1956, 1957; Stehli and Wells 1971; Veron 1995, 2000). During the Cenozoic, the Atlantic Province was physically and genetically connected with the eastern Pacific, sharing numerous coral species. However, by the Pliocene, the Central American Isthmus formed a barrier and separated the two ocean provinces, accelerating local extinction processes that have promoted substantial taxonomic differences between them. The Indo-Pacific is now by far the most diverse in terms of species, genera, and families of reef-building corals, with >700 species. This level of scleractinian diversity arose in a complex, geographically large, and highly heterogeneous environment, isolated from continental land masses that protected the region from the effects of multiple glacial periods. This produced, along with the reticulated evolution, a suite of suitable conditions for the appearance of numerous species since the end of the Mesozoic. The reef fauna that survived in the Atlantic, which is mainly composed of long-lived genera derived from the Tethys fauna, is less diverse today (Veron 1995).

The Atlantic Province is characterized by a coral fauna uniformly distributed within all reef areas. It is divided into three subprovinces, Caribbean, Brazil, and Eastern Atlantic, which are characterized mainly in terms of species diversity and/or endemicity (Veron 1995). The Caribbean subprovince contains well-developed reefs and is the most diverse, with approximately 70 hermatypic coral species. The other subprovinces have depauperate faunas and some endemic species (Veron 1995). The Gulf of Mexico, a region within the Caribbean subprovince, has lower scleractinian diversity, with only 40 recorded species and no endemic species. Nearly all Gulf of Mexico zooxanthellate corals are restricted to coral reefs, although some species of *Porites, Siderastrea,* and *Montastraea* have been seen thriving on nonreef environments, especially in intertidal rocky shores in the coasts of Veracruz, near Punta del Morro and Sontecomapan (G. Horta-Puga, personal observation).

## The Ecological Environment

Reef development in the southern Gulf of Mexico has been achieved in two different geological environments. The western area is a terrigenous sedimentary province. Sediments, derived from eroded materials of the nearby mainland and transported by rivers and streams, are deposited onto the narrow continental shelf (Tunnell 1988; Vargas-Hernández et al. 1993). This depositional environment precludes any significant nearshore reef development, but not on the adjacent continental shelf, where well-developed platform-type reefs occur. Despite the fact that other physical conditions are suitable for coral reef development, the Veracruz Shelf reefs have developed only in two areas, the Tuxpan Reef System (TRS), offshore near Cabo Rojo and Tuxpan, and the Veracruz Reef System (VRS), off the Port of Veracruz (Britton and Morton 1989; Carricart-Ganivet and Horta-Puga 1993). The TRS is comprised of six platform-type reefs: Blanquilla, Medio, Isla de Lobos, Tanguijo, Isla de Enmedio, and Tuxpan (Carricart-Ganivet and Horta-Puga 1993). The VRS is by far the most extensive reef area in the Gulf of Mexico, and it is divided into northern and southern groups by the outlet of the Jamapa River, which discharges its waters and suspended materials in the vicinity. The VRS includes three fringing reefs: Punta Gorda, Hornos, and Punta Mocambo and 17 platform-type reefs: Galleguilla, La Gallega, La Blanquilla, Anegada de Adentro, Isla Verde, Pájaros, Isla de Sacrificios, Anegada de Afuera, Isla de Enmedio, Blanca, Chopas, Rizo, Cabezo, Topatillo, Polo, Santiaguillo, and Anegadilla (Carricart-Ganivet and Horta-Puga 1993; Vargas-Hernández et al. 1993; Gutierrez et al. 1993). The eastern area of the southern Gulf comprises the Campeche Bank reefs, which lie on the wide, shallow continental shelf north and west off the Yucatán Peninsula. This is a carbonate depositional environment, not influenced by important river discharge, although very probably with some intrusions of groundwater. The eastern area includes four major and well-developed platform-type reefs, Alacrán, Cayos Arcas, Cayo Arenas, and Triángulos, as well as numerous small and poorly known submerged bank reefs (Ferré-D'Amaré 1995; Jordán-Dahlgren and Rodríguez-Martinez 2003; Jordán-Dahlgren 2004). For a more comprehensive description of the environmental conditions in the southern Gulf, see Carrillo et al., chapter 4, and Horta-Puga, chapter 12, in this volume.

## Scleractinian Biodiversity

The thorough revision of the stony corals of Mexico by Horta-Puga and Carricart-Ganivet (1993) and the more recent work on the stony corals of the Mexican Atlantic, by Beltrán-Torres and Carricart-Ganivet (1999), report that 40 scleractinian species are known in the southern Gulf. This number does not include a few species, such as *Favia favosa*, on Alacrán Reef (Kornicker et al. 1959), because this species is not part of the Caribbean Province. Other questionable species records include *Colpophyllia breviserialis*, *Cladocora arbuscula* (Farrell et al. 1983), and *Solenastrea* sp. (Logan et al. 1969b) at Cayos Arcas and *Mussismilia hartii* (Tunnell 1988), and *Isophyllia multiflora* (Villalobos 1971) at the VRS.

Several other species have undergone taxonomic revision in recent years. *Colpophyllia amaranthus* is now included in *C. natans* (*fide* Cairns 1982). It has been demonstrated that *Acropora prolifera* is an almost infertile hybrid of *A. palmata* and *A. cervicornis* (Vollmer and Palumbi 2002; Van Oppen et al. 2000). *Favia conferta* is a synonym of *F. gravida* (Vaughan 1901), which in turn is also a synonym of *F. fragum* (Zlatarski and Martínez-Estalella 1982). The last one, therefore, is the only recognized species that inhabits the southern Gulf. Some recently recognized species are now included in the species list are *Montastraea franksi*, *M. faveolata*, *Porites divaricata*, and *P. furcata*, following the criteria established by Weil (1992a, 1992b), Weil and Knowlton (1994), and Jameson (1995, 1997). *Porites branneri*, *Diploria labyrinthiformis*, and *Meandrina meandrites* were recorded in the Tuxpan Reef System (Moore 1958; Rigby and McIntire 1966; Chávez et al. 1970). However, Tunnell (1988) and Horta-Puga and Carricart-Ganivet (1993) considered these to be were misidentifications.

The 40 species of reef corals found in the southern Gulf belong to 19 different genera in 11 families and 6 suborders of the order Scleractinia (Table 8.1), following the classification of Veron (1993). Scleractinian corals are a taxonomically challenging group of modular-type organisms that have developed a high degree of morphological intergradation among sibling species, due to reticular evolutionary processes (Veron 1995). This renders identification difficult and makes the species status unclear if based only on skeletal features. For example, the status of the genera *Agaricia* and *Undaria* is controversial because their taxonomic status is based on morphometric data alone (Stemann 1991). Therefore, we assign all Gulf of Mexico agaricids, except *Leptoseris cucullata*, to the genus *Agaricia* (Table 8.1). It is possible that further genetic and molecular studies on Atlantic corals will change the number and status of scleractinian species, as has been recently demonstrated for *Montastraea* (Weil 1992; Weil and Knowlton 1994), *Porites* (Weil 1992a, 1992b; Jameson 1995, 1997) and *Acropora* (Van Oppen et al. 2000).

## Scleractinian Biogeography

Compared with the adjacent Caribbean region, which has about 70 recorded coral species, the southern Gulf of Mexico has a depauperate fauna, with only 40 species. More species should be discovered with more extensive future taxonomic surveys on the numerous submerged bank reefs of the Campeche Bank. Notably absent in the southern Gulf are some important genera such as *Cladocora, Dendrogyra, Isophyllia, Isophyllastrea,* and *Solenastrea,* which are present, even abundant, in the far eastern Gulf of Mexico off Florida and Cuba. Throughout the wider Caribbean, reef coral distribution is uniform, with little or no regionalization and with a generalized trend of a progressively lower diversity toward their geographic limits. For example, Bermuda, the most northern reef in the Atlantic, has only 20 coral species (Veron 1995). And, as can be seen from diversity data (Table 8.2), this trend also applies to the southern Gulf, which seems to be a marginal reef region of the Caribbean Biogeographic Subprovince.

Table 8.2 summarizes coral species recorded for each of the reef areas in the southern Gulf of Mexico. The total number of species is 40. Although there are some differences in the number of recorded species for the various reef areas in the southern Gulf, it is considered that almost all recorded coral species are widespread. Increased survey effort in the area may level these numbers out. The following assumptions are made for reef coral distribution in the southern Gulf of Mexico:

- Because a gap in distribution of any species is unlikely, it is assumed that the number of species in the Campeche Bank reefs is 40, the same total as the southern Gulf.
- *Diploria labyrinthiformis, Eusmilia fastigiata, Madracis mirabilis, Meandrina meandrites,* and *Mycetophyllia aliciae* are absent in the Veracruz Shelf reefs. This could be associated with an increase in water turbidity, due to a high load of suspended solids derived from river discharge, in nearshore seawater (Morelock and Koenig 1967; Tunnell 1992). This generally pre-

**Table 8.1.** *Scleractinian and milleporine reef corals from the southern Gulf of Mexico.*

### Classification and List of Species

Phylum Cnidaria

   Class Anthozoa

      Subclass Zoantharia

         Order Scleractinia (= Madreporaria) Bourne 1900

Suborder Archaeocoeniina Veron 1993

   Family Astrocoeniidae Koby 1890

      *Stephanocoenia intersepta* Milne, Edwards, and Haime 1848

   Family Pocilloporidae Gray 1842

      *Madracis decactis* (Duchasaing and Michelotti 1860)

      *Madracis mirabilis* (Duchasaing and Michelotti 1860)

   Family Acroporidae Verrill 1902

      *Acropora cervicornis* (Lamarck 1816)

      *Acropora palmata* (Lamarck 1816)

Suborder Fungiina Verrill 1865

   Family Agariciidae Gray 1847

      *Agaricia agaricites* (Linnaeus 1758)

      *Agaricia fragilis* Dana 1848

      *Agaricia lamarcki* Milne, Edwards, and Haime 1851

      *Leptoseris cucullata* (Ellis and Solander 1786)

   Family Siderastreidae Vaughan and Wells 1943

      *Siderastrea radians* (Pallas 1766)

      *Siderastrea siderea* (Ellis and Solander 1786)

Suborder Faviina Vaughan and Wells 1943

   Family Faviidae Gregory 1900

      *Favia fragum* (Esper 1788)

      *Diploria clivosa* (Ellis and Solander 1786)

      *Diploria strigosa* (Dana 1848)

      *Diploria labyrinthiformis* (Linnaeus 1758)

      *Manicina areolata* (Linnaeus 1758)

      *Colpophyllia natans* (Houttuyn 1772)

      *Montastraea annularis* (Ellis and Solander 1776)

      *Montastraea cavernosa* (Linnaeus 1767)

      *Montastraea faveolata* (Ellis and Solander 1786)

      *Montastraea franksi* (Gregory 1895)

   Family Mussidae Ortmann 1890

      *Scolymia lacera* (Pallas 1766)

      *Scolymia cubensis* (Milne, Edwards, and Haime 1849)

      *Mussa angulosa* (Pallas 1766)

*(continued)*

**Table 8.1.** (*continued*)

**Classification and List of Species**

      *Mycetophyllia aliciae* Wells 1973

      *Mycetophyllia danaana* Milne, Edwards, and Haime 1849

      *Mycetophyllia ferox* Wells 1973

      *Mycetophyllia lamarckiana* Milne, Edwards, and Haime 1848

Suborder Caryophylliina Vaughan and Wells 1943

  Family Caryophyllidae Gray 1847

    *Eusmilia fastigiata* (Pallas 1766)

Suborder Meandriina Veron 1993

  Family Oculinidae Gray 1847

    *Oculina diffusa* Lamarck 1816

    *Oculina valenciennesi* Milne, Edwards, and Haime 1848

    *Oculina varicosa* (Lesueur 1821)

  Family Meandrinidae Gray 1847

    *Meandrina meandrites* (Linnaeus 1758)

    *Dichocoenia stokesii* Milne, Edwards, and Haime 1848

Suborder Poritiina Veron 1993

  Family Poritidae Gray 1842

    *Porites astreoides* Lamarck 1816

    *Porites branneri* Rathbun 1888

    *Porites colonensis* Zlatarski 1990

    *Porites divaricata* Lesueur 1821

    *Porites furcata* Vaughan 1900

    *Porites porites* (Pallas 1766)

Class Hydrozoa

Order Capitata

  Family Milleporidae

    *Millepora alcicornis* Linnaeus 1758

    *Millepora complanata* Lamarck 1816

    *Millepora squarrosa* Lamarck 1816

*Notes:* Diversity data for the southern Gulf of Mexico were obtained only from reliable published literature. For the Tuxpan Reef System: Moore 1958; Rigby and McIntire 1966; Chávez et al. 1970; and Vargas-Hernández and Román-Vives 2002. For the Veracruz Reef System: Heilprin 1890; Villalobos 1971; Kühlmann 1975; Carricart-Ganivet and Horta-Puga 1975; and Tunnell 1988. For the Campeche Bank reefs: Kornicker et al. 1959; Kornicker and Boyd 1962; Logan et al. 1969; Farrell et al. 1983; Chávez et al. 1985; Román-Vives et al. 1989; and Carricart-Ganivet and Beltrán-Torres 1997. The majority of these data are summarized in the work by Beltrán-Torres and Carricart-Ganivet 1999.

**Table 8.2.** *Zooxanthellate scleractinian coral records for the southern Gulf of Mexico.*

| Species | TRS | VRS | VSR | CAC | TRI | CAE | ALC | CBR | SGM |
|---|---|---|---|---|---|---|---|---|---|
| *Stephanocoenia intersepta* | 1 | 1 | 1 | 1 | 1 | 1 | 1 | 1 | 1 |
| *Madracis decactis* | 1 | 1 | 1 | 1 | 1 | 1 | 1 | 1 | 1 |
| *Madracis mirabilis* | 0 | 0 | 0 | 0 | 0 | 0 | 1 | 1 | 1 |
| *Acropora cervicornis* | 1 | 1 | 1 | 1 | 1 | 1 | 1 | 1 | 1 |
| *Acropora palmata* | 1 | 1 | 1 | 1 | 1 | 1 | 1 | 1 | 1 |
| *Agaricia agaricites* | 1 | 1 | 1 | 1 | 1 | 1 | 1 | 1 | 1 |
| *Agaricia fragilis* | 1 | 1 | 1 | 0 | 1 | 0 | 1 | 1 | 1 |
| *Agaricia lamarcki* | 0 | 1 | 1 | 0 | 1 | 0 | 0 | 1 | 1 |
| *Leptoseris cucullata* | 0 | 1 | 1 | 0 | 0 | 0 | 0 | P | 1 |
| *Siderastrea radians* | 1 | 1 | 1 | 1 | 1 | 1 | 1 | 1 | 1 |
| *Siderastrea siderea* | 1 | 1 | 1 | 1 | 1 | 1 | 1 | 1 | 1 |
| *Favia fragum* | 0 | 1 | 1 | 1 | 1 | 1 | 1 | 1 | 1 |
| *Diploria clivosa* | 1 | 1 | 1 | 1 | 1 | 1 | 1 | 1 | 1 |
| *Diploria labyrinthiformis* | 0 | 0 | 0 | 1 | 1 | 1 | 1 | 1 | 1 |
| *Diploria strigosa* | 1 | 1 | 1 | 1 | 1 | 1 | 1 | 1 | 1 |
| *Manicina areolata* | 1 | 1 | 1 | 1 | 1 | 0 | 0 | 1 | 1 |
| *Colpophyllia natans* | 1 | 1 | 1 | 1 | 1 | 1 | 1 | 1 | 1 |
| *Montastraea annularis* | 1 | 1 | 1 | 1 | 1 | 1 | 1 | 1 | 1 |
| *Montastraea cavernosa* | 1 | 1 | 1 | 1 | 1 | 1 | 1 | 1 | 1 |
| *Montastraea faveolata* | 1 | 1 | 1 | 1 | 1 | 1 | 1 | 1 | 1 |
| *Montastraea franksi* | 1 | 1 | 1 | 1 | 1 | 1 | 1 | 1 | 1 |
| *Oculina diffusa* | 1 | 1 | 1 | 0 | 0 | 0 | 1 | 1 | 1 |
| *Oculina valenciennesi* | 0 | 1 | 1 | 0 | 0 | 0 | 0 | P | 1 |
| *Oculina varicosa* | 1 | P | 1 | 0 | 0 | 0 | 0 | P | 1 |
| *Meandrina meandrites* | 0 | 0 | 0 | 1 | 1 | 0 | 0 | 1 | 1 |
| *Dichocoenia stokesi* | 0 | 1 | 1 | 1 | 1 | 0 | 1 | 1 | 1 |
| *Mycetophyllia aliciae* | 0 | 0 | 0 | 1 | 1 | 0 | 0 | 1 | 1 |
| *Mycetophyllia danana* | 1 | 1 | 1 | 1 | 1 | 1 | 1 | 1 | 1 |
| *Mycetophyllia ferox* | 1 | 1 | 1 | 1 | 1 | 1 | 1 | 1 | 1 |
| *Mycetophyllia lamarckiana* | 1 | 1 | 1 | 1 | 1 | 1 | 1 | 1 | 1 |
| *Mussa angulosa* | 1 | 1 | 1 | 1 | 1 | 0 | 0 | 1 | 1 |
| *Scolymia lacera* | 0 | 1 | 1 | 0 | 1 | 0 | 1 | 1 | 1 |
| *Scolymia cubensis* | 1 | 1 | 1 | 0 | 1 | 0 | 0 | 1 | 1 |
| *Eusmilia fastigiata* | 0 | 0 | 0 | 1 | 1 | 1 | 1 | 1 | 1 |
| *Porites asteroides* | 1 | 1 | 1 | 1 | 1 | 1 | 1 | 1 | 1 |
| *Porites branneri* | 0 | 1 | 1 | 0 | 1 | 0 | 0 | 1 | 1 |
| *Porites colonensis* | 1 | 1 | 1 | 0 | 0 | 0 | 0 | P | 1 |
| *Porites porites* | 1 | 1 | 1 | 1 | 1 | 1 | 1 | 1 | 1 |
| *Porites furcata* | 1 | 1 | 1 | 0 | 0 | 0 | 1 | 1 | 1 |
| *Porites divaricata* | 1 | 1 | 1 | 1 | 0 | 1 | 1 | 1 | 1 |
| Species richness | 28 | 35 | 35 | 28 | 32 | 23 | 29 | 37 | 40 |

*Notes:* 1 = present, 0 = absent, P = probably present. TRS = Tuxpan Reef System; VRS = Veracruz Reef System; VSR = Veracruz Shelf Reefs; CAC = Cayos Arcas; TRI = Triángulos; CAE = Cayo Arenas; ALC = Alacrán; CBR = Campeche Bank Reefs; SGM = Southern Gulf of Mexico.

cludes the presence of the less sediment-resistant species. This distribution pattern has also been described for gorgonian corals by Jordán-Dahlgren (2002). It is also possible that some of these species were already present in the Veracruz Shelf reefs, and very recent localized extinction processes were the cause for their absence.

- It is possible that scleractinian diversity could be lower in the TRS, compared with the VRS, but a larger sampling effort in the TRS might reveal similarity to the VRS.

- Only one species of milleporid coral, *Millepora alcicornis*, is present on the Veracruz Shelf reefs. However, on the Campeche Bank reefs, *M. complanata* and *M. squarrosa* are also present.

# 9 Reef Fish

ERNESTO A. CHÁVEZ AND CARL R. BEAVER

Coral reefs are among the most biologically diverse ecosystems on the planet. Nowhere on the reef is this diversity as conspicuously displayed as in the reef's fish community. Between 66% and 89% of all marine fish species are found on coral reefs and reef-associated habitats (Moyle and Cech 1988). The tremendous diversity of reef-fish species is generally thought to be the result of a diversity of habitats found on the reef. The complexity of the reef provides fishes with a multitude of microhabitats or niches to populate.

Although diversity is generally high in undisturbed reef communities, reef-fish distribution is not homogeneous and, in fact, can be quite patchy. The heterogeneity of reef-fish distribution may be attributed to habitat characteristics (Hixon and Beets 1993), spatial distribution of food (González-Gándara et al.1999), and topographic complexity (Risk 1972; Nuñez-Lara and Arias-González 1998) among other factors.

Although diverse reef-fish communities exist throughout much of the western Gulf of Mexico, much work has concentrated on the commercially important fish and fishing grounds along the Campeche Bank (Hildebrand et al. 1964; H. Chávez 1966; Reséndez-Medina 1971; Garduño-Andrade 1988, 1989; Garduño and Chávez 2000; González-Gándara and Arias-González 2001a, 2001b). Despite being commercially important in their own right, the reef fishes off the states of Veracruz and Tamaulipas in the western Gulf of Mexico have received little quantitative analysis.

Because of the paucity of quantitative studies, the analysis presented here is based on three contributions. Two of these represent recent quantitative studies in the area (Garduño-Andrade 1988; Choucair 1992), and the other (Castro-Aguirre and Márquez-Espinoza 1981) is the only source paper written on the subject.

Because an in-depth description of all species is beyond the scope of this project, the analysis presented herein is based on dominant elements of the fish community within each reef area. For the reader requiring more information, a complete list of fish species observed at each reef is provided at www.gulfbase .org (Nipper et al. 2004).

In the Veracruz Reef System (VRS), quantitative data are available only for the reefs around Isla de Enmedio. However, because the Isla de Enmedio Reef is centrally located, and because the VRS reefs are concentrated within a relatively small geographic region, these data can be considered representative of the VRS as a whole. In all cases, observations were made in several habitats and from several depths, including zones in the windward reef areas, in protected or leeward reef areas, and in reef lagoonal areas.

Reef-fish distribution within the reefs of the southern Gulf of Mexico raises questions related to physiography. Is fish community structure the same in all reef areas? If not, how are the resources allocated among communities, populations, or guilds? If environmental driving forces are responsible for the differences in reef-fish distribution, do the physiographic features impose differences on reef-fish fauna, and do these driving forces lead to significantly different faunal components in an area? For answers to these questions, we review the abundance and distribution of dominant fish species on each reef in an attempt to describe the differences in these reef-fish assemblages.

## Species Abundance

Although a number of qualitative studies of southern Gulf of Mexico reef fishes have been done, few quantitative studies pertaining to the abundance of reef fish exist, and consequently, data are scarce. Despite this limitation, the information presented herein comes from only quantitative surveys.

Fish records of Isla de Lobos Reef include the work of Castro-Aguirre and Márquez-Espinoza (1981), who used diverse methods of collection, such as beach seine, gill nets, hook and lines, by hand and using a jar, and rotenone. Data from Isla de Enmedio Reef were reported by Choucair (1992), whose methodology included diving and counting fish within a virtual cylindrical area. Coral reefs of the Campeche Bank were sampled using rapid, timed visual-survey techniques conducted while diving (Garduño-Andrade 1988; Garduño and Chávez 2000).

**Isla de Lobos Reef**   The fish assemblage of this reef has approximately 76% of reef-fish species known to occur in the western Atlantic along the coast of Florida. Species richness recorded at Isla de Lobos Reef (88) is the second greatest in the southern Gulf of Mexico, surpassed only by Alácran Reef (Castro-Aguirre and Márquez-Espinoza 1981).

The reef-fish community at Isla de Lobos Reef is strongly dominated by Atlantic threadfin (*Polydactylus octonemus*) (1,800 caught). Five other species, spotfin mojarra (*Eucinostomus argenteus*), slippery dick (*Halichoeres bivittatus*), little-eye herring (*Jenkinsia majua*), and striped parrotfish (*Scarus iseri*), were caught in numbers ranging from 786 to 156 specimens. Nine other fish species were caught, ranging from 39 to 20 specimens each. An additional 69 species recorded at this reef are considered rare (Fig. 9.1).

The evident differences in fish composition at this reef may be an artifact of the sampling methodology. The use of a beach seine to sample reef-fish communities would likely bias the catch toward species commonly found in the water column, such as *P. octonemus,* while undersampling other species.

**Isla de Enmedio Reef**   Brown chromis (*Chromis multilineata*) and rainbow wrasse (*Halichoeres pictus*) dominated the reef-fish community at Isla de Enmedio Reef (Fig. 9.2). Counts of the next most abundant species declined abruptly. Dusky damselfish (*Stegastes dorsopunicans* = *Stegastes adustus*) and sergeant major (*Abudefduf saxatilis*) occupy this secondary level with counts around 1,000 each, followed by princess parrotfish (*Scarus taeniopterus*), doctorfish (*Acanthurus chirurgus*), and blue chromis (*Chromis cyanea*), all with approximately 500 fish observed per transect, followed by *H. bivittatus* with about 450 fish. Even less abundant is bluehead (*Thalassoma bifasciatum*), with less than 200 individuals observed in visual transects (Fig. 9.2).

Choucair (1992) suggests that low abundance and small size for many species can be explained by overfishing. Although overfishing has had a significant impact on the reef-fish community, it is likely that habitat loss and degradation of water quality have also had significant impact on the reef and its inhabitants.

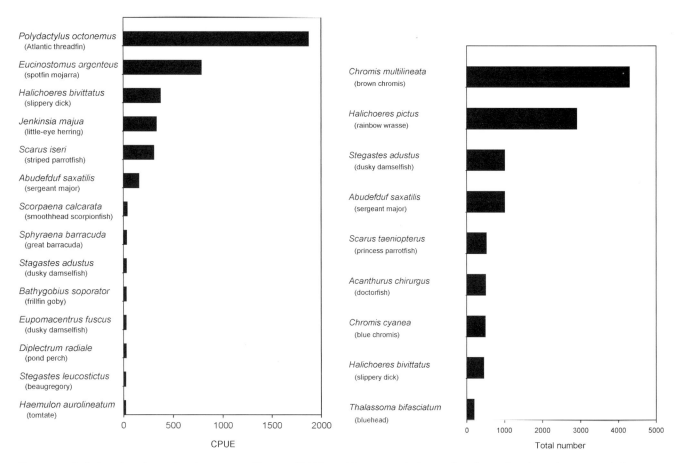

**Figure 9.1.** Relative abundance (catch per unit effort, or CPUE) of dominant fish species at Isla de Lobos Reef (after Castro-Aguirre and Márquez-Espinoza 1981).

**Figure 9.2.** Relative abundance (total numbers recorded in visual transects/cylinders) of dominant fish species at Isla de Enmedio Reef (after Choucair 1992).

**Triángulos Reef** Relative abundance of fish at this reef was sampled by using the modified rapid visual method adopted from Williams (1982). The technique consists of enumerating fish by means of a log-arithmetic scale that has the following ranges of abundance: 1 = 1; 2 = 2–5; 3 = 6–25; 4 = 25–125; 5 = 126–625; 6 = 626–3,125; and 7 = >3,125 (Garduño-Andrade 1988; Garduño and Chávez 2000). The results generated by this method apparently reflect a sampling deficiency, as evidenced by the stepped graphic display of Figure 9.3. According to Garduño-Andrade (1988), *S. taeniopterus*, yellowhead wrasse (*Halichoeres garnoti*), and ocean surgeon (*Acanthurus bahianus*) are the most abundant, with 150 fish observed per minute of swimming, followed by queen parrotfish (*Scarus vetula*), with 85 fish (Fig. 9.3). A group of six species occupy the next level, with each species having 75 fish counted per minute. Yellow goatfish (*Mulloides martinicus* = *Mulloidichthys martinicus*) and great barracuda (*Sphyraena barracuda*) occupy the next level of abundance, with 30 and 20 fish per minute observed, respectively. Six other species displayed an identical abundance of 18 individuals observed per minute.

**Cayos Arcas Reef** The establishment of a crude oil pumping station on one of the islands of Cayos Arcas Reef has had little apparent impact on the fish community of this reef, as evidenced by its similarity to the reefs surrounding adjacent undeveloped islands. This reef seems to support a highly diverse and

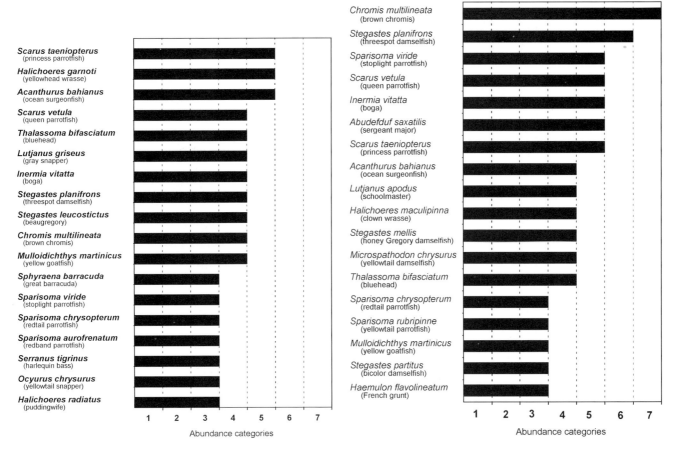

**Figure 9.3.** Relative abundance of dominant fish species at Triángulos Reef (after Garduño-Andrade 1988). Fish counts/minute were converted to abundance categories on a log-arithmetic scale representing the following ranges of abundance: 1 = 1; 2 = 2–5; 3 = 6–25; 4 = 26–125; 5 = 126–625; 6 = 626–3,125; 7 = <3,125.

**Figure 9.4.** Relative abundance of dominant fish species at Cayos Arcas Reef (after Garduño-Andrade 1988) Fish counts/minute were converted to abundance categories on a log-arithmetic scale representing the following ranges of abundance: 1 = 1; 2 = 2–5; 3 = 6–25; 4 = 26–125; 5 = 126–625; 6 = 626–3,125; 7 = <3,125.

dense reef-fish community (Garduño-Andrade 1988). The reef-fish community at Cayos Arcas Reef, as recorded by rapid visual technique (Garduño-Andrade 1988; Garduño and Chávez 2000), is dominated by *C. multilineata*. Threespot damselfish (*Eupomacentrus planifrons = Stegastes planifrons*) is the second most abundant species, followed by *S. taeniopterus*, *A. saxatilis*, boga (*Inermia vittata*), *S. vetula*, and stoplight parrotfish (*Sparisoma viride*) (Fig. 9.4). A group of eleven species displays lower levels of abundance, ranging from 75 to 10 individuals observed per minute. We suspect that reef-fish densities among the dominant populations at Cayos Arcas Reef may be influenced by seasonal upwelling along the Campeche slope.

**Cayo Arenas Reef**  Fish dominance at Cayo Arenas Reef is similar to that on Cayos Arcas. Despite the fact that abundance of dominant fish species at Cayo Arenas is an order of magnitude higher than at other coral reefs of the Campeche Bank, community structure is similar (Garduño-Andrade 1988). In terms of abundance, as sampled using the rapid visual technique (Garduño-Andrade 1988; Garduño and Chávez 2000), the dominant fish species is *C. multilineata*, followed by *T. bifasciatum*, *S. taeniopterus*, blue tang (*Acanthurus coeruleus*),

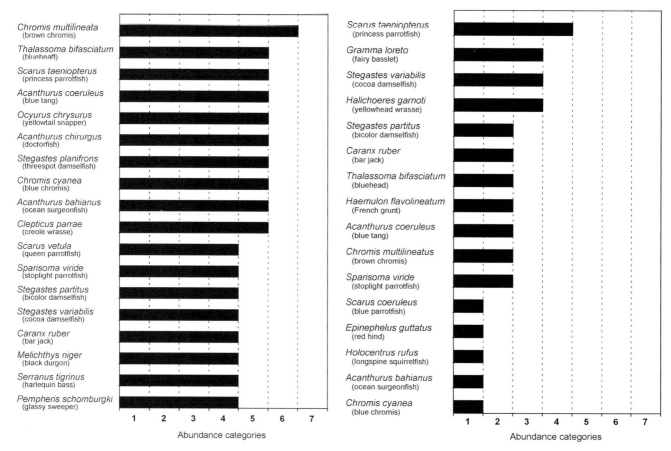

**Figure 9.5.** Relative abundance of dominant fish species at Cayo Arenas Reef (after Garduño-Andrade 1988). Fish counts/minute were converted to abundance categories on a log-arithmetic scale representing the following ranges of abundance: 1 = 1; 2 = 2–5; 3 = 6–25; 4 = 26–125; 5 = 126–625; 6 = 626–3,125; 7 = <3,125.

**Figure 9.6.** Relative abundance of dominant fish species at Alacrán Reef (after Garduño-Andrade 1988). Fish counts/minute were converted to abundance categories on a log-arithmetic scale representing the following ranges of abundance: 1 = 1; 2 = 2–5; 3 = 6–25; 4 = 26–125; 5 = 126–625; 6 = 626–3,125; 7 = <3,125.

yellowtail snapper (*Ocyurus chrysurus*), and *A. chirurgus* (Fig. 9.5). Observations of other species decreased in abundance from 200 to 25 observations per minute.

**Alacrán Reef**  The reef-fish community at Alacrán Reef is more complex than at any other reef in the southern Gulf of Mexico; it has greater species richness and low species dominance (Fig. 9.6). With the exception of *S. taeniopterus*, relative abundance was low among the 16 most common reef species at Alacrán Reef (Fig. 9.6). The remaining components of the fish community account for a significantly high species number, but are rare in occurrence (González-Gándara and Arias-González 2001a, 2001b). This high species richness and low abundance of reef fishes at Alacrán Reef may be indicative of high niche diversity and habitat heterogeneity. If it can be assumed that productivity is similar among reef-fish communities throughout the southern Gulf of Mexico, the relatively low fish abundance may be explained by a limited food resource available to residents of this reef system. Support of a highly complex and abundant reef-fish community requires both high habitat heterogeneity and an abundant and heterogeneous food resource. Alacrán Reef has a high level of habitat heterogeneity, leading to high species richness, but apparently population densities are limited by the quality and/or quantity of the food resource.

Although Alacrán Reef cannot maintain both high species abundance and high species diversity in its reef-fish community, it is no less important to other reef-fish communities in the southern Gulf of Mexico. Chávez and Tunnell (chapter 13, this volume) suggest that Alacrán Reef may be an important source of recruits to other reefs of the Gulf of Mexico. In the case of the Veracruz Reef System, the profound perturbation induced by economic development along the coast and intensive agricultural land use could be even greater without a permanent source of colonizers provided from "upstream" reef habitats such as Alacrán Reef. For this reason, Alacrán Reef deserves special protection of its ecological integrity to ensure that this process can be maintained in the long term.

**Toward an Integration of the Ecosystem**

**Fish and Reef Habitats**  Three main factors appear to limit reef-fish community development in the Gulf of Mexico as compared to the Caribbean: habitat diversity, limited reef area, and the distance from source populations (Dennis and Bright 1988). With the exception of Alacrán Reef, the reefs of Veracruz and Campeche Bank are generally small, and support a reduced habitat diversity, especially in zones deeper than 50 m (Logan 1969b). In comparison, many Caribbean reefs display high habitat diversity. As a result of this increase in habitat diversity, species diversity is greater on large Caribbean reefs (Garduño and Chávez 2000). Alacrán Reef is the largest reef in the southern Gulf of Mexico. Because of its size, Alacrán Reef supports a greater variety of habitats, along with more developed reef zones and seagrass beds. All other southern Gulf of Mexico reefs are relatively small with poorly developed leeward areas and lagoonal patch reefs, resulting in low habitat heterogeneity.

The relative consistency of the reef's physical environment significantly affects the fish community composition in that it favors long-term adaptive processes. As a result, species that are most abundant are those that have most successfully taken advantage of the physical habitat and food resources of the reef over the long-term. Trophic structure is determined by guilds of species sharing food preferences, rather than the presence or absence of rare species, whose role in the energy flow of a trophic web may be negligible. Consequently, variations in abundance of rare species may be expected to have little impact on the overall structure of a reef-fish community. The structure of guilds is probably conditioned by factors such as size and diversity of the habitat, which may determine the nature of the food supply (Williams and Hatcher 1983).

We can see this correlation between species diversity, habitat diversity, and reef size very clearly in a group of fishes commonly known as grunts. Grunts are represented by 12 species on large Caribbean reefs, 6 on Campeche Bank reefs, 3 from the Veracruz reefs (Castro-Aguirre and Márquez-Espinoza 1981), and only 2 species on the smallest of these reefs in the northwestern Gulf of Mexico (tomtate [*Haemulon aurolineatum*] and cottonwick [*Haemulon melanurum*]; Dennis and Bright 1988).

Finally, some differences in fish density may be striking to the reader. Particularly remarkable are the reported observations of *C. multilineata* at Cayos Arcas and Cayo Arenas, where observations per minute exceed 1,000. This is an order of magnitude higher than that recorded at most other reefs. Timing of the sampling, proximity to the continental slope, and the differential intensity of human perturbation in the area could possibly explain these differences.

**Trophic Structure**   Despite the similarities of fish communities observed among these reefs, we can observe some differences in the way trophic webs are organized, as indicated by the changes in relative abundance of dominant species at each reef, and in some particularly striking differences in fish densities. Relative abundance of fishes differs among reefs to such a degree as to suggest important quantitative and qualitative changes in the structure of trophic webs. Trophic structure comparisons indicate striking differences among coral reefs in guild composition as well as abundance.

Planktivores perform a critical function in the cycling of energy on coral reefs. Much of the energy flowing into coral reef systems comes in the form of nutrients released by large numbers of planktivorous fish living on the upper reefs (Hammer et al. 1988). Planktivorous fish glean energy and nutrients from the water column and deposit it on the reef in the form of detritus. Energy and nutrients are then available to a host of reef resident detritivores and plants, which in turn become food for other reef species.

The most abundant planktivorous fish, *C. multilineata*, was found at all reefs. The fish assemblage of zooplankton feeders in the Campeche Bank is quite similar to that at Flower Garden Banks, where *C. multilineata*, *T. bifasciatum*, and creole wrasse (*Clepticus parrae*) are dominant species grouped in mixed feeding schools at midwater with *I. vittata* and *O. chrysurus*.

Although found on all reefs along the western Gulf of Mexico, planktivores are not the most abundant fishes at all reefs. Cayos Arcas and Cayo Arenas reefs seem to support large numbers of piscivorous fish, such as the serranid groupers red hind (*Epinephelus guttatus*), rock hind (*E. adscensionis*), black grouper (*Mycteroperca bonaci*), and tiger grouper (*Mycteroperca tigris*) and *S. barracuda*.

Reef-fish assemblages are loosely structured (Sale 1982; Sale and Douglas 1984), with variation caused by differences in habitat heterogeneity. Reef size may lead to the expression of a higher diversity of habitats as in Alacrán Reef, allowing the possibility of a wider variety of niches to be exploited by fish.

Seasonal influence of freshwater runoff from the continent over the reefs at Veracruz and the west Campeche Bank, and the presence of a seasonal upwelling along the Campeche slope, result in water masses that cause changes in trophic pathways. Freshwater runoff most likely affects the reefs of the Veracruz Reef System and the southwestern portion of the Campeche Bank, while upwelling along the Yucatán Channel is more likely to influence Alacrán Reef. The influence of freshwater runoff in these areas seems to support the idea that because trophic structures respond to similar environmental influences in predictable ways, reefs displaying highly similar trophic structures may be influenced by similar environmental pressures.

Despite their limitations, available data may still provide a general view of reef-fish abundance, species distribution, and fish-community structure. Although differences in relative abundance were observed at each reef, it is evident that, as commonly occurs in natural communities, a few species exhibit strong dominance. A comparison of the number of species per trophic levels suggests there are some differences in trophic structure between reefs. Because the coral community is essentially the same, differences of microhabitat could account for these variations between reefs. Table 9.1 lists dominant species, trophic guild, and mean density (counts per minute) for reef fish of the Campeche Bank (after data from Garduño-Andrade 1988; Garduño 1989; Garduño and Chávez 2000). In addition, population parameter values for each dominant stock (after Opitz 1996) are included and are also shown in Table 9.2.

**Table 9.1.** *Relative density of reef-fish fauna on coral reefs of the Campeche Bank (mean of all reef fish, counts per minute).*

| Dominant species | Trophic guild* | Mean densities |
|---|---|---|
| *Holacanthus tricolor* (rock beauty) | SAP | 0.05 |
| *Pomacanthus paru* (French angelfish) | SAP | 0.05 |
| *Halichoeres maculipinna* (clown wrasse) | GC | 0.49 |
| *Haemulon flavolineatum* (French grunt) | GC | 1.28 |
| *Holocentrus rufus* (longspine squirrelfish) | GC | 0.45 |
| *Haemulon chrysargyreum* (smallmouth grunt) | GC | 0.05 |
| *Lutjanus apodus* (schoolmaster) | GC | 0.05 |
| *Anisotremus virginicus* (porkfish) | GC | 0.05 |
| *Haemulon aurolineatum* (tomtate) | GC | 0.05 |
| *Scarus taeniopterus* (princess parrotfish) | DH | 16.12 |
| *Scarus vetula* (queen parrotfish) | DH | 2.66 |
| *Sparisoma viride* (stoplight parrotfish) | DH | 2.47 |
| *Acanthurus bahianus* (ocean surgeonfish) | DH | 1.57 |
| *Acanthurus coeruleus* (blue tang) | DH | 4.05 |
| *Acanthurus chirurgus* (doctorfish) | DH | 2.00 |
| *Ocyurus chrysurus* (yellowtail snapper) | DH | 1.78 |
| *Scarus coeruleus* (blue parrotfish) | DH | 0.61 |
| *Sparisoma chrysopterum* (redtail parrotfish) | DH | 0.05 |
| *Gramma loreto* (fairy basslet) | EF | 15.67 |
| *Halichoeres garnoti* (yellowhead wrasse) | IP | 2.41 |
| *Haemulon sciurus* (bluestriped grunt) | IP | 0.05 |
| *Haemulon carbonarium* (caesar grunt) | IP | 0.05 |
| *Haemulon plumierii* (white grunt) | IP | 0.05 |
| *Eupomacentrus planifrons = Stegastes planifrons* (threespot damselfish) | OMNI | 6.13 |
| *Abudefduf saxatilis* (sergeant major) | OMNI | 2.42 |
| *Eupomacentrus mellis = Stegastes mellis* (honey Gregory damselfish) | OMNI | 0.50 |
| *Microspathodon chrysurus* (yellowtail damselfish) | OMNI | 0.41 |
| *Eupomacentrus partitus = Stegastes partitus* (bicolor damselfish) | OMNI | 2.03 |
| *Eupomacentrus variabilis = Stegastes variabilis* (cocoa damselfish) | OMNI | 2.64 |
| *Canthigaster rostrata* (sharpnose puffer) | OMNI | 0.05 |
| *Caranx ruber* (bar jack) | FF | 1.33 |
| *Epinephelus guttatus* (red hind) | FF | 0.59 |
| *Chromis multilineatus* (brown chromis) | ZOO | 17.42 |
| *Inermia vitatta* (boga) | ZOO | 4.31 |
| *Clepticus parrae* (creole wrasse) | ZOO | 4.72 |
| *Thalassoma bifasciatum* (bluehead) | ZOO | 6.12 |
| *Chromis cyanea* (blue cromis) | ZOO | 1.83 |

*SAP = sessile animal feeders, preying on corals and sponges; FF = ichthyophagous or fish feeders; IP = invertebrate predators or benthic feeders, whose diet consists of mollusks, crabs, and sea urchins; EF = ectoparasite feeders, specialized species preying upon fish ectoparasites; DH = detritus and plant feeders, with more than 50% plant and detrital material in stomach contents; OMNI = omnivorous fishes; ZOO = zooplankton feeders, preying mainly on zooplankton; GC = generalized carnivores, preying on a variety of motile benthic animals, such as crustaceans, worms, and small fish. Where a trophic guild was unknown, a species was assumed to belong to the same trophic guild as other members of the same family (Garduño and Chávez 2000). Trophic categories adopted from Randall (1967a, 1967b, 1983), and Gladfelter et al. (1980).

**Table 9.2.** *Population parameter values and density of fishes and other species with potential importance for fisheries and for developing trophic models at reefs of the Gulf of Mexico.*

| Family | Species name | Mean biomass (g/m²) | L (cm) | W (g) | K | −to | M |
|---|---|---|---|---|---|---|---|
| Balistidae | *Balistes capriscus* (gray triggerfish) | 0.002 | 31 | 611 | 0.383 | −0.1 | 0.94 |
| | *Balistes vetula* (queen triggerfish) | 0.917 | 45 | 2,586 | 0.57 | −0.1 | 2.6 |
| Carangidae | *Caranx ruber* (bar jack) | 31.581 | 56 | 3,160 | 0.56 | −0.1 | 0.59 |
| | *Seriola dumerili** (greater amberjack) | 0.258 | 194 | 80,000 | 0.118 | −0.1 | 0.26 |
| | *Seriola rivoliana** (almaco jack) | 0.077 | 97 | 24,000 | 0.97 | −0.1 | 0.79 |
| Carcharhinidae | *Carcharhinus acronotus* (blacknose shark) | 0.290 | 200 | 90,000 | 0.159 | −0.1 | 0.33 |
| | *Carcharhinus leucas* (bullshark) | 1.129 | 305 | 350,000 | 0.125 | −0.1 | 0.24 |
| | *Carcharhinus limbatus* (blacktip shark) | 0.374 | 247 | 116,000 | 0.139 | −0.1 | 0.28 |
| Ginglymostomatidae | *Ginglymostoma cirratum* (nurse shark) | 16.125 | 430 | 500,000 | 0.141 | 0.1 | 0.24 |
| Haemulidae | *Haemulon album* (margate) | 0.359 | 65 | 5,300 | 0.2 | 0.1 | 0.79 |
| | *Haemulon plumieri* (white grunt) | 5.309 | 42 | 1,360 | 0.345 | −0.1 | 1.77 |
| | *Haemulon sciurus* (bluestriped grunt) | 1.18668 | 41 | 1,185 | 0.26 | −0.1 | 0.68 |
| Lutjanidae | *Lutjanus analis* (mutton snapper) | 0.373 | 74 | 5,511 | 0.12 | 0.1 | 0.2 |
| | *Lutjanus synagris* (lane snapper) | 0.782 | 42 | 1,213 | 0.268 | 0.1 | 0.69 |
| | *Ocyurus chrysurus* (yellowtail snapper) | 25.328 | 75 | 3,570 | 0.25 | 0.1 | 0.6 |
| Megalopidae | *Megalops atlanticus** (tarpon) | 5.676 | 250 | 160,000 | 0.065 | 0.1 | 0.16 |
| Pomacanthidae | *Holacanthus ciliaris* (queen angelfish) | 6.541 | 46 | 1,988 | 0.136 | 0.1 | 0.43 |
| | *Pomacanthus arcuatus* (gray angelfish) | 8.042 | 60 | 12,407 | 0.23 | 0.1 | 0.63 |
| Rachycentridae | *Rachycentron canadum** (cobia) | 0.108 | 160 | 33,400 | 0.21 | 0.1 | 0.42 |
| Scaridae | *Scarus guacamaia** (rainbow parrotfish) | 74.917 | 99 | 23,000 | 0.293 | 0.1 | 0.61 |
| | *Scarus vetula** (queen parrotfish) | 19.718 | 54 | 5,558 | 0.599 | 0.1 | 1.09 |
| | *Sparisoma rubripinne* (yellowtail parrotfish) | 0.881 | 46.5 | 2,734 | 0.584 | 0.1 | 1.11 |
| Scombridae | *Scomberomorus cavalla** (king mackerel) | 1.216 | 137 | 34,285 | 0.180 | 0.1 | 0.4 |
| Serranidae | *Diplectrum formosum* (sandperch) | 0.002 | 31 | 550 | 0.287 | 0.1 | 0.78 |
| | *Epinephelus guttatus* (red hind) | 1.882 | 52 | 2,919 | 0.24 | 0.1 | 0.58 |
| | *Epinephelus morio* (red grouper) | 0.016 | 93 | 5,010 | 0.113 | 0.1 | 0.31 |
| | *Epinephelus striatus* (Nassau grouper) | 1.535 | 90 | 23,800 | 0.09 | 0.1 | 0.24 |
| | *Mycteroperca bonaci* (black grouper) | 5.805 | 120 | 90,000 | 0.16 | 0.1 | 0.37 |
| | *Mycteroperca venenosa* (yellowfin grouper) | 0.040 | 86 | 12,270 | 0.17 | 0.1 | 0.42 |
| Sphyraenidae | *Sphyraena barracuda* (great barracuda) | 22.368 | 156 | 57,800 | 0.113 | 0.1 | 0.27 |
| Sphyrnidae | *Sphyrna tiburo** (bonnethead) | 0.5805 | 150 | 18,000 | 0.110 | 0.1 | 0.27 |
| Mollusks- Octopodidae | *Octopus maya** (mayan octopus) | 28 | 23 | 2,864 | 3.154 | 0.1 | 4.73 |
| | *Octopus vulgaris** (octopus) | 28 | 30 | 10,850 | 0.72 | 0.1 | 1.09 |
| Strombidae | *Strombus gigas* (queen conch) | 39 | 25 | 1,460 | 0.500 | 0.1 | 0.18 |
| Crustacean (Palinuridae) | *Panulirus argus** (spiny lobster) | 0.09 | 53.6 | 3,698 | 0.244 | 0.1 | 0.37 |

*Notes*: Fish data after Opitz (1996). Estimated reef areas in km² are as follows: Blanquilla-Medio-Lobos = 0.679; Tanguijo-Medio-Tuxpan = 0.375; Veracruz Reef System (North) = 9.06; Veracruz Reef System (South) = 36.12; Cayos Arcas–Cayo Arenas-Nuevo-Obispos-Triángulos = 20; Alacrán = 264.

†Von Bertalanffy growth parameters: L = asymptotic, W = asymptotic weight, K = growth rate, *to* = ordinate to origin, M = natural mortality (per year).

*Other important reef fisheries species not exploited regularly at reefs of the Gulf of Mexico (with the probable exception of Alacrán Reef) are included here as reference.

**Concluding Remarks**

These comparisons of species abundance may include some bias because sampling methods were not uniform. For instance, at Isla de Lobos Reef a beach seine was used, while at the rest of the reefs visual counting using scuba was employed; however, data from Choucair (1992, cylinder technique) may reflect important differences from those provided by Garduño-Andrade (1988, line transects). We acknowledge the challenges associated with comparing results and methods, even in cases when two different divers use the same sampling method and site (Sale 1997). In addition, we believe the sparseness of the data, as well as the use of different methods to sample fish, make comparisons among these reefs quite difficult, and acknowledge that species richness is likely underestimated and that the use of different sampling procedures contributes different bias to samples (P. Sale, personal communication). Despite these shortcomings, these studies provide the best available information for development of a management strategy for the reef fishes of the southwestern Gulf of Mexico. Furthermore, we believe that, because of the current threats to these fisheries, it is preferable to use these data for devising management plans now rather than waiting for more extensive data.

# 10　Reef Fisheries

CARL R. BEAVER AND ERNESTO A. CHÁVEZ

From the Laguna Madre de Tamaulipas, south through the Bay of Campeche to the reefs and on the outer continental shelf of the Yucatán Peninsula, reef fishes are an economically and ecologically important resource. More than 100 species of reef fish are closely associated with coral reefs and other types of hard bottom habitats in the Gulf of Mexico. Maintenance of healthy reef-fish populations is important to the economic and ecological health of the region. Reef fish are important to different interest groups for a multitude of reasons. Reef-fish user groups have commercial, artisanal, recreational, and scientific interests. Important nonconsumptive uses for reef fishes, such as tourism, sport diving, education, and scientific study, can conflict with traditional consumptive uses such as commercial and subsistence fisheries.

Fishes provide significant ecological benefits to the reef system as well. Reef fishes have evolved numerous symbiotic relationships with other reef denizens, creating highly complex trophic structures that contribute to the ecological balance and diversity of reefs. Unfortunately, overfishing is a major concern for many reef-fish populations. Consequently, fishing may be one of the most important activities contributing to degradation of coral reefs in the southern Gulf of Mexico.

Mexico has a long history of fisheries exploitation in the southern Gulf of Mexico, dating back to the Maya. The Dresden Codex depicts fishes offered as sacrifice to the gods. The writings of the Spanish priest Diego de Landa in his book *Relación de las Cosas de Yucatán* describe such a ceremony (Baughman 1952).

Despite this history of exploitation, for most areas, solid statistical data have only been collected since the late 1970s (Schirripa and Legault 1999; NOAA 2002c). Growing human population has increased demand for reef-fish products because they are an inexpensive source of protein. This increased demand, along with improved fishing technology, means that many stocks of reef fishes are seriously overfished or at least fully exploited. Reef fishes are vulnerable to overfishing because many species are long-lived, slow growing, slow to mature, exhibit delayed reproduction, and are easy to capture (Schirripa and Legault 1999; NOAA 2002c). In many parts of the western Atlantic, traditional fisheries species such as grouper (Serranidae) and snapper (Lutjanidae) have all but disappeared, and other species are in decline.

Although much literature exists pertaining to stocks of exploited reef fishes, reef fisheries are not limited to finfish alone. Throughout the southern Gulf of Mexico, modern markets support commercial fisheries for reef crustaceans such as *Menippe* sp. (stone crab) and *Panulirus* sp. (spiny lobster) as well as species such as *Strombus* sp. (conch), *almeja* clams and *Octopus* sp. (octopus). There is also a small but growing trade in ornamental fish and invertebrates for the aquarium trade.

## Fisheries Regulation in Mexico

The Ley Federal de Pesca (Fisheries Law) and the Reglamento de la Ley Federal de Pesca (Regulation of the Fisheries Law) establish regulations governing the conservation, preservation, exploitation, and management of all aquatic flora and fauna in Mexico. The goal of fisheries management in Mexico is optimum economic yield aimed at satisfying national demand and assuring Mexico's competitiveness in the world market. These goals are to be obtained through responsible and sustainable fishing, while recognizing a future based in the conservation and preservation of aquatic resources.

The Secretaría de Agricultura, Ganadería, Desarrollo Rural, Pesca, y Alimentación (SAGARPA; Secretary of Agriculture, Cattle Ranching, Rural Development, Fisheries, and Food), has the regulatory authority over aquatic species through the Instituto Nacional de la Pesca (National Fisheries Institute), the technical consultant supporting the decision-making process. The major responsibility of SAGARPA is the regulation of fishing gear types and the establishment of catch quotas, fishing seasons, and size and weight limits of managed species.

Fisheries resources are managed by the issuance of concessions, permits, and authorizations. Fishing activities are further classified as developmental, educational, commercial, aquacultural, or recreational. All concessions, permits, and authorizations must be registered with the Registro Nacional de Pesca (National Fisheries Registry). Concessions and permits are granted according to technical, cultural, and economic considerations, taking into account conservation needs and the public interest (SEPESCA 1990a, 1990b, 1992).

Concessions provide for the use, exploitation, and development of the national waters or territorial seas. They are granted for a minimum of five years and a maximum of 20 years. Concessions for cultivated fisheries can be granted for 50 years. Under this agreement concession holders must, among other things:

1. Extract, capture, and cultivate authorized species exclusively in zones determined by SAGARPA;
2. Present annually to SAGARPA the status of the technical and economic projects associated with the concession, including a program and schedule of landings and a final report on the amount of fish captured;
3. Perform fishing activities with authorized and registered equipment and methods;
4. Engage in aquaculture activities using areas and methods authorized by the concession.
5. Comply with the technical and economic conditions for the exploitation of each species, group of species or zones established by the SAGARPA;
6. Assist the federal government in the preservation of the aquatic environment and the conservation and reproduction of species, including the development of programs for repopulating species in natural settings;
7. Allow observers, investigators, and scientific and technical experts authorized by SAGARPA to board all vessels and facilities associated with the fisheries activities (SAGARPA 2006).

Coral reef–related species that currently require a permit for harvest include stone crab, other crabs, spiny lobster, conch, corals (including black coral and pink coral), marine fishes (finfish and sharks), and octopus. A separate permit is required for each.

**Fisheries Reserves and Refuge Zones**   In addition to controlling the fisheries activities according to quantity, type, and method through the concessions, permits, and authorization programs, the establishment of special fishery reserves and refuge zones and the use of fishing bans to protect threatened or endangered species is the responsibility of another Ministry, the Secretaría de Medio Ambiente y Recursos Naturales (SEMARNAT; Secretary for the Environment and Natural Resources). Fisheries reserves or bans can be established according to species or zone and can be temporary or permanent. Fishing activities are prohibited in fishery reserves.

**National Harvest (Production) Levels**   In 1997, national harvest levels were reported to be ~1.6 million metric tons. This represents the greatest harvest of Mexico's fisheries in history. The most recent year for which harvest levels are available is 2000, when an estimated 1.3 million metric tons were harvested from Mexican waters (FAO 2004). Sardines represent 30% of this production while squids represent 7%. Most (97.2%) of the fisheries harvest were organisms landed from littoral waters of the Pacific, Gulf of California, Gulf of Mexico, and Caribbean Sea, while the remainder were obtained from waters beyond the continental shelf.

## The Reef Fishes

In the state of Veracruz, 25 out of the 248 reported reef-fish species are commonly targeted for harvest. These 25 species represent 12% of all fishes harvested from the reefs (Vargas-Hernández et al. 2002). However, reef species do not contribute significantly to the total commercial catch of the state. Although their contribution to local human consumption may be important, they are generally not included in statistical records because they are artisanal fisheries. The main species exploited by artisanal fishers are *Strombus pugilis* (*caracol canelo* or cinnamon conch) and *Octopus vulgaris* in Veracruz, and mostly *Octopus maya* on the Campeche Bank reefs (octopus or *pulpo*), several species of snapper or *pargo*, such as *Lutjanus synagris* (yellowtail), *cubera* and other haemulids, several *Caranx* spp. (jacks or *jureles*), *Epinephelus* spp. (groupers or *chernas* and *meros*), and *Sphyraena barracuda* (great barracuda). Other exploited shellfish include *Strombus gigas* (queen conch or *caracol rosado*), *Panulirus argus* (spiny lobster or *langosta*), and *Codackia orbicularis* (the clam or *almeja*). Even though *S. gigas* and *P. argus* were never abundant on these reefs, they became commercially extinct due to overharvest. Consequently, few fishermen recall their commercial exploitation. Some other stocks of invertebrates have been exploited for the ornamental or jewelry trade in Veracruz, including several species of gorgonians, in particular *Plexaura homomalla* (an octocoral) and *Antipathes* sp. (black coral).

On the Campeche Bank, only Alacrán Reef has been exploited, mostly for grouper, the queen conch, spiny lobster, and secondarily for the species mentioned above; consequently, local stocks may be overexploited. Other reefs in the area have historically been too remote for artisanal fishermen to access.

A brief description of the main fisheries associated with southern Gulf of

Mexico coral reefs and estimates of potential yields are given below. In an attempt to explore the stock size and potential yield, data taken mainly from Opitz (1996) on density for a series of reef-dwelling species were adopted, and a pseudo-cohort analysis (Gulland 1983; Sparre and Venema 1992) was made by assuming that all stocks have been exploited to their maximum capacity. Given parameter values and stock size, it was possible to apply the method of cohort dynamics, a determination of fishing mortality (F) values, age of first catch (tc), and the potential yield. Maximum yield (MY, formerly considered sustainable or MSY) is a limit reference point, and as a function of F and tc, was assessed by applying the catch equation to each one of the main stocks and reefs. The area of each reef was estimated, and for each stock, density values (g m$^{-2}$) were transformed into total biomass over the reef areas, estimated at 46,242,750 m$^2$ for all the reefs of Veracruz and 264,000,000 m$^2$ for Alacrán Reef.

**Octopus** Despite catches of over 20,000 metric tons, most of the octopuses harvested in the southern Gulf of Mexico originate on the Campeche Bank, and consequently, are not strictly associated with coral reefs. In Veracruz, catch data come mostly from the coral reefs, where during the last two decades, annual harvest has fluctuated between 50 and 80 tons (Hernández-Tabares and Bravo-Gamboa 2002).

On the Veracruz reefs, fishers wading the shallow upper reefs typically use an illegal hooking device to harvest octopuses. Reefs may be visited as frequently as every two or three days. In these areas fishing activity impacts mostly juveniles with a mantle length >120 mm. At the time of this writing, the minimum legal size for O. vulgaris is 110 mm of mantle length. There are two closed seasons, one from April to May and the other from August to September.

On Alacrán Reef, the only Campeche Bank reef with an established octopus fishery, O. maya is exploited by fishermen from northern Yucatán. For O. maya, minimum legal size is 110 mm of mantle length and annual harvest is approximately 9,000 metric tons. In this region, the closed season extends from mid-December through the end of July (Chávez 1998).

Stock density (28 g m$^{-2}$, after Opitz 1996) of octopuses exploited on Veracruz (O. vulgaris) and Alacrán reefs (mostly O. maya) corresponds to a maximum fishing intensity of F = 0.5 and 0.8, respectively, with an MY = 295 and 871 tons for the Veracruz Reef System and Alacrán Reef, respectively (Table 10.1). From these catch records, we conclude that the Veracruz stock is severely over-

**Table 10.1.** *Fisheries mortality (F), maximum sustainable yield (MY), and estimated stock density for five commercially exploited species at reef locations in the southern Gulf of Mexico.*

| Species | Common name | Location | F | MY (metric tons/yr) | Stock density (g/m²) |
|---|---|---|---|---|---|
| *Octopus vulgaris* | Octopus | Veracruz | 0.5 | 295 | 28 |
| *Octopus maya* | Mayan octopus | Alacrán | 0.8 | 871 | 28 |
| *Strombus gigas* | Queen conch | Alacrán | 0.45 | 168 | 39 |
| *Panulirus* spp. | Spiny lobster | Alacrán | 0.3 | 7.2 | 0.16 |
| *Epinephelus morio* | Red grouper | Alacrán | 0.3 | 0.7 | 0.016 |

exploited, and reduction of fishing effort should be applied in order to reduce harvest to a more sustainable level. If a significant reduction of fishing effort is strictly enforced, a recovery of the stock and, consequently, fishery yields may be expected. Likewise, catch data suggest a similar conclusion could be made for Alacrán Reef. Unfortunately, catch data do not distinguish between catch made on the reef or from other nonreef Campeche Bank habitats.

**Conch**   Historically, two species of conch were exploited. In the Veracruz Reef System, *Strombus pugilis* (cinnamon conch or *caracol canelo*) is still targeted for harvest. The *Strombus gigas* (queen conch) fishery was once an important fishery on the Veracruz reefs; however, overexploitation has lead to its extinction as a fishery. Other gastropod mollusks currently exploited, particularly at Alacrán Reef, are *S. costatus, Turbinella angulatus, Pleuroploca gigantea*, and *Busycon contrarium*. For all these species, abundance is low and their exploitation is artisanal (Basurto et al. 2002). The fishery and biology of *S. pugilis* on the Veracruz reefs is largely unknown; limited catch data are reported by Pech-Paat et al. (2002), who state that 98 conch/ha were harvested in recent years.

Queen conch is exploited along the west Campeche Bank today. However, conch is not caught on the coral reefs; rather, exploitation takes place along the shoreline, where extensive turtle grass flats occur. By contrast, to the north in the state of Yucatán, fishing for the queen conch has historically occurred only at Alacrán Reef, where the stock has apparently collapsed due to intense fishing pressure, prompting the local government to prohibit queen conch harvest after 1987. Catch records show that more than 300 metric tons per year were caught in northern Yucatán between 1979 and 1986. Catch declined dramatically in 1987, when only 10 tons were harvested and the fishery was closed (Rodríguez-Gil 1994; Basurto et al. 2002).

Controversy over the closure continues today. On one hand, the queen conch is approaching extinction. On the other hand, there remains a strong social demand for a resource that may be in recovery. Regardless of any controversy, the lack of local control has allowed illegal harvest of tons of conch meat per month.

Historical records of the queen conch caught at Alacrán Reef (Rodríguez-Gil 1994) were examined in the context of several stock assessment models and by simulation. Results suggest that despite the depleted condition of the stock at the time the fishery was closed, the remaining adult stock was adequate to allow recovery of the biomass to exploitable levels in less than a decade. Potential yield values indicate an assumed stock density of 39 g m$^{-2}$ (after Opitz 1996), which corresponds to a maximum fishing intensity of $F = 0.45$ and MSY $=168$ metric tons (Table 10.1). Another estimate, based on the application of an age-structured simulation model, suggests that under a well-managed fishery, Alacrán Reef could sustain a queen conch exploitation of nearly 200 tons (Fig. 10.1).

**Spiny Lobster**   Similar to other fisheries mentioned above, overexploitation of spiny lobster on the Veracruz reefs led it to its extinction as a fishery. On the Campeche Bank, catch of this organism takes place mostly on noncoral habitats on the continental shelf. For this reason it is difficult to determine the amount of the catch that is harvested from the coral reefs. Alacrán Reef may be the only Campeche Bank reef where a formal spiny lobster fishery occurs. The fishery in the Yucatán Peninsula began at Alacrán Reef in the 1950s (González-Cano et al. 2002). Records from northern Yucatán show annual catches in the 450–

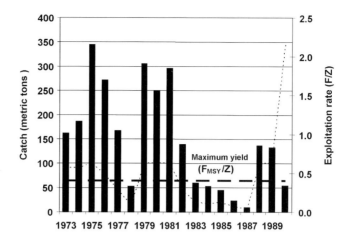

**Figure 10.1.** Reconstruction of the queen conch stock of Alacrán Reef by fitting a simulation model. Stock response suggests that maximum potential yield corresponds to a catch of 225 tons. Horizontal dashed line indicates the exploitation rate (F/Z) at the maximum yield ($F_{MSY}$/Z), or threshold of overexploitation. The thin dotted line shows the exploitation rate estimated each year; therefore, each time that this line is above the maximum yield ($F_{MSY}$/Z) line is interpreted as a condition of an overexploited stock. Vertical bars correspond to catch data, taken from Rodríguez-Gil 1994.

500 metric ton range for more than 10 years, and the stock seems to be stable. Despite limited attempts at using traps, harvest generally takes place mostly by divers using hookah. Management regulations specify a minimum cephalothorax length of 75 mm, a closed season from March to June, and a prohibition on retention of egg-bearing females. The number of annual permits issued is carefully controlled in order to avoid overexploitation of this fishery.

Stock biomass estimates of the spiny lobster taken from Alacrán Reef suggest a stock density of 0.162 g m$^{-2}$ (after data from González-Cano et al. 2002), which corresponds to a maximum fishing intensity of $F = 0.3$ and a MY = 7.2 metric tons (Table 10.1). Unfortunately, there is no evidence available concerning the current level of catch or fishing effort at the reef in order to assess the most likely prospects for the future of the fishery.

**Red Grouper**   Red grouper is one of the most commonly harvested fish of the southern Gulf of Mexico, and in particular on the Campeche Bank. Reported catch in Yucatán for the year 1999 was 8,300 tons. This fishery provides direct employment to over 16,000 fishermen. There are no catch records of red grouper from the coast of Veracruz, and as in other cases, its exploitation is not exclusive to the coral reefs. Alacrán Reef seems to be the only reef where there is a formal fishery for this species.

The southern Gulf of Mexico stock is considered overfished because its biomass is about 16% below the maximum biomass recorded in 1972. Regulations have been implemented to reduce catch quota by limiting the number of fishing licenses and a instituting a minimum legal size of 30 cm (Monroy et al. 2002).

An estimation of stock biomass and a diagnosis of potential catch on Alacrán Reef is based on a stock density of 0.0162 g m$^{-2}$ (after Opitz 1996), corresponding to a maximum fishing intensity of $F = 0.3$ and an MY = 0.716 tons (Table 10.1).

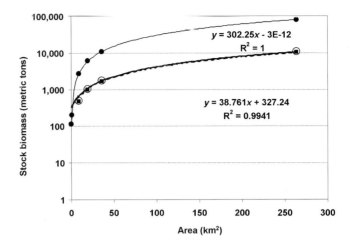

**Figure 10.2.** Potential total stock biomass (upper line, black dots) and maximum yield (lower line, open circles) as a function of reef area, as exemplified by the coral reefs of the southern Gulf of Mexico.

## Reef Potential Yield

Published sources (e.g., Opitz 1996) suggest that relative abundance of fishes may exist at an almost constant level in all reef areas of the Gulf of Mexico. Therefore, an attempt was made to synthesize and to explore the possible existence of a pattern between fish densities and maximum sustainable yield (MY) for all the reefs in the southern Gulf of Mexico. The 36 most abundant stocks were analyzed to estimate their biomass and MY values in reference to reef areas. Two findings deserve special comment. First, as usually occurs in natural communities, there exists a strong dominance by a few species. Consequently, it is probable that these species are captured most often. This does not mean, however, that these species are necessarily overexploited. Exploitation is more likely to impact slow-growing species with low densities, such as serranids, despite their frequency of capture.

The second interesting feature of these fisheries is the relationship between stock biomass (and therefore yield) and reef area (Fig. 10.2). Biomass increases almost exponentially with an increase in area between 0 and 50 km$^2$, after which the increase becomes decidedly linear. The exponential increase speaks to a minimum or threshold size for stock maintenance. Linear increases likely reflect the uniformity of primary productivity in reef waters across the region and the similar structural organization of reef-fish communities on western Caribbean coral reefs. Although we have herein examined a limited number of stocks, these patterns, if they are found to be true for other commercially exploited species, make a strong case for the need for strong regional management of fisheries in the southern Gulf of Mexico.

# 11 Island Biota

JOHN W. TUNNELL JR.

There are 25 islands associated with the 38 emergent reef platforms in the southern Gulf of Mexico (Table 11.1; see Figs. 2.2–2.9 for maps). The most conspicuous biota are island vegetation and birds, both seasonal migrants and nesting seabirds. Less conspicuous are the terrestrial or land crabs, insects, lizards, and nesting sea turtles. Most islands are low sandy cays, or they are mostly sand with some coral rubble and coral ramparts (rocks). A few small islands are composed of coral rubble only (mainly staghorn coral, *Acropora cervicornis*). Eight islands have "manned" lighthouses (Plates 7, 20b, 20c, 22d, 24, 25a, 49) that were first established in the late 1800s to early 1900s. Although there are no comprehensive geological papers collectively on the southern Gulf of Mexico coral reef islands, several detailed papers by Robert L. Folk and colleagues provide extensive information on sediment origin and composition, as well as morphology of the sand cays of Alacrán Reef (Folk 1962, 1967; Folk and Robles 1964; Folk and Cotera 1971).

## Vegetation

Six of the 25 islands have no vegetation, 11 islands have native vegetation only, and 8 have native vegetation and varying amounts of introduced vegetation (Table 11.1; Plates 50–53). The only thorough studies of island vegetation are those conducted on Alacrán Reef (Marion 1884; Millspaugh 1916; Fosberg 1961, 1962; Bonet and Rzedowski 1962; Folk 1967; Flores 1984, 1992; Tunnell and Chapman 2001). The most detailed studies, those of Bonet and Rzedowski (1962) and Flores (1984, 1992), demonstrate the dynamic conditions of these remote islands by comparing vegetational changes, along with changes in island shapes, through time, specifically, the years 1838 (Marion 1884), 1899 (Millspaugh 1916), 1961 (Bonet and Rzedowski 1962), and 1981 (Flores 1984). The five islands of Alacrán Reef (Islas Perez, Chica, Pájaros, Desertora, and Desterrada) demonstrate temporal vegetational succession, having passed through five phases, from (1) bare sand to (2) low vegetation of sea purslane (*Sesuvium*) and/or common purslane (*Portulaca*) to (3) low grassy dunes of either dropseed (*Sporobolus*) or sandbur (*Cenchrus*) to (4) vegetated flats or low dunes of beach sandmat (*Chamaesyce*) and/or saltwort (*Batis*) and, finally, to (5) thickets of sea rosemary (*Tournefortia*) and/or bay cedar (*Suriana*). The location and shape of all five islands at Alacrán have remained essentially the same since the 1950s. According to Flores (1984), however, all of the Alacrán Reef islands, except Isla Perez, did increase in size when compared to the previous studies over an 82-year time span. Subsequently, however, just a few years later (1986), Islas Pájaros, Chica, and Desertora were all significantly smaller (Tunnell and Chapman 2001).

**Table 11.1.** *List of southern Gulf of Mexico coral reef islands, with their composition, vegetation, and existence of colonial waterbird rookery.*

| Island name | "Manned" lighthouse | Composition[1] | Vegetation[2] | Presence of rookery |
|---|---|---|---|---|
| **Tuxpan Reef System** | | | | |
| Lobos | Yes | S | N, I | No |
| **Veracruz Reef System** | | | | |
| **Northern Reefs** (off city of Veracruz) | | | | |
| La Blanquilla | No | S | None | No |
| Verde | No | S | N, I | No |
| Sacrificios | Yes | S | N, I | No |
| **Southern Reefs** (off Antón Lizardo) | | | | |
| Santiaguillo | Yes | CR | N | No |
| Topatillo[3] | No | CR | None | No |
| Enmedio | Yes | S | N, I | No |
| Salmadina (Chopas Reef) | No | S | N | No |
| Blanca (Chopas Reef) | No | S | N | No |
| Cabezo | No | CR, R | None | No |
| **Campeche Bank Reefs** | | | | |
| Alacrán Reef | | | | |
| Perez | Yes | S | N, I | Yes |
| Chica (Cornezuelo, Blanca) | No | S | N | Yes |
| Pájaros (Larga) | No | S | N | Yes |
| Desertora (Muertos, Allison, Oeste) | No | S | N | Yes |
| Desterrada (Utowana) | No | S | N | Yes |
| Arenas Reef | | | | |
| Two unnamed islands (on northeast reef wall) | No | CR | None | No |
| Cayo Arenas (on west reef wall) | Yes | S, CR, R | N, I | Yes |
| Unnamed island (on southeast reef wall) | No | CR | None | No |
| Triángulo Oeste | Yes | S, CR, R | N, I | No |
| Triángulo Este | No | S, CR, R | N | Yes |
| Triángulo Sur | No | S, CR, R | N | Yes |
| Arcas Reef | | | | |
| Cayo del Centro | Yes | S, CR, R | N, I | Yes |
| Cayo del Oeste | No | S | N | No |
| Cayo del Este | No | S, CR, R | N | Yes |

[1] S = sand, CR = coral rubble, R = ramparts or coral "rocks."

[2] N = native vegetation; I = introduced vegetation.

[3] Topatillo Island, composed only of *Acropora cervicornis* rubble, disappeared in the mid-1990s, presumably due to the loss of protection by the former living *A. palmata* (windward) and *A. cervicornis* (leeward) reefs. These species died in the late 1970s and early 1980s (Tunnell 1992).

The flora of the Campeche Bank islands is more closely related to the flora of the shores of the Yucatán Peninsula and Caribbean islands rather than to that of the Mexican mainland, which shows relatively few affinities (Bonet and Rzedowski 1962). Dominant Campeche Bank island native vegetation are the grasses *Sporobolus virginicus* and *Cenchrus insularis;* the succulents *Sesuvium portulacastrum, Portulaca oleracea,* and *Batis maritima;* the perennials *Cakile edentula* var. *Alacranensis* and *Chamaesyce buxifolia;* and the shrubs *Suriana maritima* and *Tournefortia gnaphalodes* (Flores 1984, 1992). Other less common species are *Cyperus planifolius, Cenchrus pauciflorus, Tribulus alacranensis, Atriplex pentandra, Scaevola plumierii; Salicornia bigelovii,* and *Ipomoea pes-caprae* (Flores 1984, 1992). Small lagoons or saltwater ponds on some islands, such as Isla Perez and Cayo Centro at Cayos Arcas, have *Avicennia germinans* (black mangroves) (Flores 1992; Tunnell and Chapman 2001). *Rhizophora mangle* (red mangrove) has been reported on Isla Perez (Flores 1992; Tunnell and Chapman 2001). *Conocarpus erectus* (buttonwood) was reported on Isla Perez in 1899 (Millspaugh 1916) and Isla Pájaros (Bonet and Rzedowski 1962) in 1961, but it apparently no longer exists there. A mangrove lagoon described by Folk (1967) on Isla Pájaros no longer existed in 1986, the area being reduced to a "barren coral rubble spit" (Tunnell and Chapman 2001), again demonstrating the dynamic nature of these remote islands.

Introduced vegetation on the Campeche Bank islands is generally associated with those islands where human activity exists (lighthouses, weather stations, fishermen), which are Isla Perez (Alacrán Reef), Cayo Arenas, Triángulo Oeste, and Cayo Centro (Cayos Arcas). Some species were likely introduced intentionally for use as food, ornamentals, or protection from the sun as shade, for example, *Cocos nucifera* (coconut palm), *Cordia dodecandra* (orange cordial), *Crinum americanum* (swamp lily), *Terminalia catappa* (tropical almond), and *Casuarina equisetifolia* (Australian pine). Other species, like *Opuntia dillenii* (erect pricklypear), may have been accidentally introduced (Flores 1984; Tunnell and Chapman 2001). Collectively, approximately 43 species (35 native and 8 introduced; Flores 1992) of shoreline and upland vegetation have been reported from the Campeche Bank islands (see www.gulfbase.org for checklist).

No studies have focused specifically on island vegetation off the state of Veracruz in the southwestern Gulf. However, there are anecdotal accounts available in several papers and from field trips to some of the islands (Lot-Helgueras 1971; Villalobos 1971; Vargas-Hernández et al. 1993; J. W. Tunnell Jr., personal observation; P. Moreno-Casasola, personal communication). The higher rainfall in the southwestern Gulf of Mexico, compared to drier conditions on Campeche Bank islands, allows for denser and taller vegetation. When islands are present in the southwestern Gulf, they are typically located on the southwestern quadrant of the reef platform. The three largest islands, Lobos, Sacrificios, and Enmedio, have very important, long-established manned lighthouses, and as might be expected, considerable introduced vegetation, in addition to the native species. Isla Verde (see Plate 19c) is mostly native vegetation, except for a large stand of *Terminalia catappa,* introduced by university professor Dr. Alberto Vázquez de la Cerda (circa 1981) and his students to provide shade during their field trips to the island. Salmedina and Blanca islands on Chopas Reef off Antón Lizardo have only low, native vegetation. Interestingly, the coral reef islands off the city of Veracruz have native plant species that are similar in composition to Caribbean islands, most likely linked by the calcareous soils (coral reef derived sands; Moreno-Casasola 1988, 1999).

Isla de Lobos is the largest island in the southwestern Gulf, and it is the only island on the six reefs of the Tuxpan Reef System of northern Veracruz. Although a dense forest exists on the island (Plate 51), it has not been characterized. Due to oil and gas exploration and subsequent production, an earthen causeway was extended from the island northeastward to the windward reef crest, where eight producing wells, encased in a steel, concrete, and earthen platform, were built in the 1960s (Rigby and McIntire 1966; Tunnell 1992). Oil storage tanks were erected on the interior of the island and a dock was built to aid in petroleum operations, which continued through the late 1970s. Native vegetation was cleared from the southwestern part of the island to support facilities for petroleum workers, a small Mexican Navy detachment, a lighthouse, and a PEMEX (Petróleos Mexicanos) visitors' lodge. Considerable introduced vegetation existed there in 1973 (Tunnell 1974).

To the south, Villalobos (1971) reported three species of upland vegetation on La Blanquilla Reef: *Tournefortia gnaphalodes* (sea lavender), *Ipomoea stolonifera* (beach morning-glory), and *Sesuvium portulacastrum* (sea purslane). Today, La Blanquilla is only a small sandy cay without any terrestrial vegetation (Plate 19b).

While studying the marine flowering plants of the reef lagoons near the city of Veracruz, Lot-Helgueras (1971) briefly characterized some of the shoreline and upland flora associated with some of the islands. Twenty-six species were noted from Isla Verde, including the common species *Tournefortia gnaphalodes*, *Agave angustifolia* (century plant), *Chamaesyce buxifolia*, and *Sesuvium portulacastrum*. *Pandanus* sp. (screwpine) and *Randia laetevivens* (indigoberry) were also mentioned from one location on the island.

Islas Sacrificios (Plate 20b, c) and Enmedio are the most visited and have the most introduced species in the southern Veracruz area. Sacrificios is very popular, with many visitors daily, because it is only a short boat ride from the Veracruz city shoreline drive and people-friendly seawall (*malecón*). The famous lighthouse and island is depicted in many paintings, photos, and postcards of the Veracruz shoreline. Large introduced species, such as *Casuarina equisetifolia*, *Terminalia catappa*, *Cocos nucifera*, and *Psidium guajava* (guava), are common there (Vargas-Hernández et al. 1993). There are also a few tall and old native trees such as *Coccoloba barbadensis*, which is commonly found in tropical forests in mainland dunes in Veracruz (P. Moreno-Casasola, personal communication).

Enmedio Island has native vegetation (see Plate 24 and 52a–f), primarily *Sesuvium portulacastrum*, *Ipomoea stolonifera*, and *I. pes-caprae* (goat's foot morning-glory), and *Scaevola plumieri* (inkberry) on the north end, but the central portion of the island is covered by a dense canopy of tropical shade trees (Plate 52g). These trees, including primarily *Bursera simarubra* (gumbo limbo), *Terminalia catappa*, and *Plumeria sp.* (frangipani), were planted in the early 1950s by Francisco "Pancho" Velazquez Hidalgo, who nurtured and maintained them for 35–40 years as the lighthouse keeper on Enmedio. Other introduced species included *Crinum americanum* (the lilies), *Hymenocallis latifolia* (spiderlilly), *Cocos nucifera*, and *Casuarina equisetifolia*. After the death of the *Acropora palmata* (elkhorn coral) reef immediately southeast of the island in the early 1980s, the southern end of the island began eroding. Over the next two decades, approximately 30%–40% of the island was lost, and most of the large *Casuarina* and *Cocos* plants fell into the sea and were eventually washed away (see Plates 24, 53, and 54). Likewise, by the same process, it appears that over

50% of Salmedina Island on adjacent Chopas Reef was lost to wave erosion, due to lack of protection from the windward *A. palmata* reef.

Collectively, approximately 30 species of shoreline and upland vegetation are known from the southwestern Gulf coral reef islands. Most of these species are native to the islands or nearby mainland, but some species, such as *Casuarina equisetifolia*, *Cocos nucifera*, and *Terminalia catappa*, are ornamental transplants.

**Birds**

Ten (40%) of the 25 islands located on southern Gulf of Mexico emergent reef platforms have nesting seabird colonies (see Plates 47, 48, and 55). All of these are located on the remote islands of the Campeche Bank. None of the southwestern Gulf reef islands of Veracruz state have any current colonies, except possibly La Blanquilla Reef. Judging by the name, it is possible that Pájaros Reef (Veracruz) once had a nesting colony, but the island has disappeared. Past authors (Lot-Helgueras 1971[1] Vargas-Hernández et al. 1993) mention a small ephemeral island on Pájaros. Likewise, La Blanquilla Island has supported nesting of *Sterna albifrons* (little tern) in the past, and it has been suggested that the *S. anaethetus* (bridled tern) once nested there (Vargas-Hernández et al. 1993).

On the Campeche Bank, all four of the major coral reef-island complexes (Alacrán, Cayo Arenas, Triángulos, and Cayos Arcas) have significant seabird nesting colonies. Only two of the permanent islands (the larger ones with vegetation), Triángulos Oeste and Cayo del Oeste (Cayos Arcas), do not have historical nesting records. The last field survey of all these islands, except Triángulos Este and Sur, was conducted in 1986, and that survey was compared to all published literature for all of the islands (Tunnell and Chapman 2001). Eight of the 12 permanently emergent islands surveyed in 1986 had active seabird nesting colonies (Table 11.2). Nine species of colonial seabirds nested on the islands: *Sula dactylatra* (masked booby), *S. leucogaster* (brown booby), *S. sula* (red-footed booby), *Fregata magnificens* (magnificent frigatebird), *Larus atricilla* (laughing gull), *Sterna maxima* (royal tern), *S. sandvicensis* (sandwich tern), *S. fuscata* (sooty tern), and *Anous stolidus* (brown noddy).

The 1986 seabird nesting survey was conducted opportunistically during different months of the year (Alacrán in January and July, Arenas in March, and Arcas in April); however, as Table 11.2 reveals, it was a good example year for the number and species of birds nesting on particular islands, as well as for the significance of these rookery islands. The most common nesters were the masked booby (on five islands) and the magnificent frigatebird (on four island). The island with the most species, Desertora at Alacrán Reef, had five species nesting. The largest population of any species was the sooty tern on Isla Perez on Alacrán Reef, where 26,160 birds were counted in July 1986, the end of the nesting season. The brown noddy nested only on Isla Perez, and the red-footed booby was found nesting only on Isla Desertora. The latter is the only known nesting location in the Gulf of Mexico for the red-footed booby, as the nearest other colony is on Half Moon Cay, Belize, approximately 600 km to the south (Tunnell and Chapman 1988).

Most of the seabirds nesting on the Campeche Bank reef islands are ground nesters, but three species, the red-footed booby, magnificent frigatebird, and brown noddy, prefer elevated vegetation. The red-footed booby and the magnificent frigatebird nest primarily in *Tournefortia gnaphalodes*. The brown noddy apparently prefers *Suriana maritima*, but some nests were found in *Casuarina*

**Table 11.2.** *Number of seabird nests (n) or seabirds (b) on Campeche Bank coral reef islands during various times of the 1986 nesting season.*

| | Number of nests (n) or birds (b) per island (1986) | | | | | | | |
| | Alacrán Reef | | | | | Cayo Arenas | Cayos Arcas | |
| Species | Perez | Chica | Pájaros | Desertora | Desterrada | Cayo Arenas | Centro | Este |
|---|---|---|---|---|---|---|---|---|
| Masked booby | – | – | 3 (n) | 2,533 (n) | – | 258 (n) | 600 (n) | 98 (n) |
| Brown booby | – | – | – | – | 10 (n) | – | – | – |
| Red-footed booby | – | – | – | 2 (n) | – | – | – | – |
| Magnificent frigatebird | – | – | – | 206 (n) | 52 (n) | – | 1,712 (n) | 282 (n) |
| Laughing gull | – | 3 (n) | – | 10 (n) | 50 (n) | – | – | – |
| Royal tern | – | 28 (n) | – | – | – | – | – | – |
| Sanwich tern | – | 151 (n) | – | – | – | – | – | – |
| Sooty tern | 26,160 (b) | – | – | 10 (n) | – | – | – | – |
| Brown noddy | 1,357 (n) | – | – | – | – | – | – | – |

*Notes:* Dash (–) indicates no nests or birds found. Alacrán Reef islands were surveyed in January and July, Cayo Arenas in March, and Cayos Arcas in April (Tunnell and Chapman 2001).

*equisetifolia.* Interestingly, the brown noddy is known for utilizing molluskan shell fragments as part of its nest (Wright and Kornicker 1962; Tunnell and Chapman 2001). On Isla Perez, 90% of the shell fragments used were of the burrowing clam, *Codakia orbicularis,* a common inhabitant of the seagrass beds in the lagoon (Wright and Kornicker 1962).

The southern Gulf of Mexico coral reef islands are also important as stopovers, particularly during storms, for trans-Gulf migrating birds (Paynter 1953, 1955; Siebenaler 1954; Boswall 1978; Howell 1989), but little is known of their importance or significance in this area. A combined total of 106 species have been reported for the Campeche Bank islands (see www.gulfbase.org for checklist). The six most common species (over 100 individuals) observed during an eight-day study period in October 1984 (Howell 1989) on the Campeche Bank islands were *Bubulcus ibis* (cattle egret) (723), *Accipiter striatus* (sharp-shinned hawk) (120), *Arenaria interpres* (ruddy turnstone) (147), *Calidris alba* (sanderling) (100), *Hirundo rustica* (barn swallow) (879), and *Dendroica magnolia* (magnolia warbler) (408) (Howell 1989). Twelve less common species (10–99 individuals) over the eight-day period were *Pluvialis squatarola* (black-bellied plover) (50), *Catoptrophorus semipalmatus* (willet) (10), *Limnodromus griseus* (short-billed dowitcher) (20), *Stelgidopteryx serripennis* (northern rough-winged swallow) (17), *Riparia riparia* (bank swallow) (19), *Petrochelidon pyrrhonota* (cliff swallow) (14), *Vermivora peregrina* (Tennessee warbler) (12), *Dendroica virens* (black-throated green warbler) (33), *Dendroica palmarum* (palm warbler) (20), *Setophaga ruticilla* (American redstart) (13), *Geothlypis trichas* (common yellow-throat) (29), and *Passerina cyanea* (indigo bunting) (21). Sixty-five other species were observed during this brief survey, but all included nine or fewer total individuals (all species are listed at www.gulfbase.org).

Trans-Gulf migrants primarily use the islands for resting, but food and water, if available, can be important too. Midges and houseflies are common on Isla Perez near human habitations and may offer food for the migrants. Other insects, such as butterflies, dragonflies, lacewings, and grasshoppers, were noted in great numbers; they apparently migrate at the same time as the birds. Fresh water is scarce on these semiarid islands. Migrants are generally weak or tired and can often be easily approached without flying away. Some have been observed dead or dying (Boswall 1978).

The Campeche Bank islands, due to their greater distance from shore, are believed to be far more important as stopovers for trans-Gulf migrants than the Veracruz reef-islands. Although numerous fall migrants have been observed on Enmedio Island in October (J. W. Tunnell Jr., personal observation), all of the Veracruz islands are within sight of land.

**Other Fauna**

*Gecarcinus lateralis* (land crabs) are particularly abundant on the reef islands of the southwestern Gulf of Mexico off Veracruz. Their burrows are most abundant in the heavily vegetated, shady areas of Lobos, Sacrificios, and Enmedio islands. At night they can be observed all over the islands, as well as along the shore. The land hermit crab, *Coenobita clypeatus,* has been found on Lobos and Enmedio islands (Allen 1979, 1982), but it is rare there, which is its northwesternmost Caribbean distribution. Both of these crabs are also found on the Campeche Bank islands (Martínez-Guzmán and Hernández-Aguilera 1993).

Although little else is known about the terrestrial fauna of southern Gulf of Mexico reef-islands, more than 30 families of insects representing more than 10 orders are known from the islands of Alacrán Reef (Bonet and Rzedowski 1962; Fosberg 1962). More than 50 species of insects were collected, but only about 15 were identified to the species level and another 17 to the generic level (see www.gulfbase.org for checklist). In addition, 12 families of spiders representing four orders are known (Bonet and Rzedowski 1962). Only one of 17 species was identified to the species; four indeterminable families were noted.

Sea turtles are known to occur around all of the southern Gulf of Mexico coral reefs, and nesting occurs on some islands (Enmedio, Desertora, and Desterrada; J. W. Tunnell Jr., personal observation). Little published information is available on nesting, but sea turtles are known to be heavily exploited, both for eggs and meat (J. W. Tunnell Jr., personal observation). All five Gulf of Mexico turtles possibly occur around the reefs, but the most likely species are *Caretta caretta* (loggerhead), *Eretmochelys imbricata* (hawksbill), and *Chelonia mydas* (green) (Carr et al. 1982). The most likely nesters are the loggerhead and hawksbill. *Mabuya mabuya* (a skink) is the only lizard that has been reported from the Campeche Bank reef islands (Bonet and Rzedowski 1962; Fosberg 1962), and *Sceloporus* sp. (a spiny lizard) was commonly observed on Lobos Island in 1973 (Tunnell 1974).

*Monachus tropicalis* (the West Indian monk seal) is the only large mammal known to use any of the coral reef islands in the southern Gulf. Triángulo Este, and possibly other Campeche Bank islands, was used as a nesting and pupping location during the 1800s and earlier (Ward 1887). This species, now extinct, has not been seen on the Campeche Bank since the mid-1900s (Fosberg 1962).

# 12    Environmental Impacts

GUILLERMO HORTA-PUGA

The coral reefs in the southern Gulf of Mexico are subject to many natural and anthropogenic environmental stressors (Tunnell 1985, 1992; Chávez 1989; Botello et al. 1992; Chávez and Tunnell 1993; Lang et al. 1998). Natural threats include hurricanes, winter cold fronts, freshwater inflow carrying suspended sediments, bleaching, red tides, and massive die-offs. Coral reefs, especially those of the Campeche Bank, are in the path of hurricanes. The meteorological phenomenon known as *norte* (winter front) induces strong winds over the whole southern Gulf of Mexico and can be as destructive as hurricanes. The Gulf of Mexico is a semi-enclosed oceanic basin that receives the outflow of many river systems carrying a high load of suspended solids that settle down on the continental shelf. In the flood plumes of riverine systems, seawater turbidity increases and salinity decreases periodically with increased river flow volume.

Human activities, sometimes in concert with natural impacts, are an increasing threat to the natural environment. In general, the consequences of anthropogenic disturbances are decreased biodiversity, changes in community structure, increased concentrations and varieties of chemical pollutants, and landscape (reefscape) modification. The degree of environmental degradation is usually associated with distance from disturbance sources. Thus, the nearer the source, the greater the impact. Fortunately, the reefs of the Campeche Bank lie more than 50 km away from shore, and the primary threats to them are impacts from oil and gas exploration and production and overfishing. The Tuxpan Reef System (TRS), although located near the coast and the city of Tuxpan, is not heavily impacted, and anthropogenic threats are restricted to oil and gas activities on Isla de Lobos, the occasional presence of tourists, and overfishing. The reverse is true at the Veracruz Reef System (VRS) because it is offshore from the largest city in the southern Gulf of Mexico and the largest port in all of Mexico. Additionally, because it is under the influence of the flood plumes of at least two large river systems that drain municipal and industrial sewage waters from various inland cities, as well as from agricultural lands and paper pulp mills, the sources of environmental impact are numerous. Consequently, most impacts are in the vicinity of Veracruz city.

## Natural Disturbances

**Sediments and Low Salinity**  The VRS evolved on a terrigenous shallow continental shelf (Morelock and Koenig 1967). The main terrigenous sediment source was eroded materials transported by river flow from the nearby mainland. This condition does not apply on the Campeche Bank reefs (CBR), because they developed on a carbonate platform where river drainage is almost absent. There are many natural river systems that flow into the southwestern Gulf, including Grijalva-Usumacinta, Coatzacoalcos, Papaloapan-Blanco, Jamapa, Antigua, Nautla, Tuxpan and Candelaria, Cazones, and Pánuco (see Fig. 4.1). The joint hydrological basin of these rivers extends over ~263,000 km² (CNA 2000), and the mean annual precipitation is >1,500 mm (INEGI 1995). The mean annual discharge of these rivers to the ocean is ~5,200 m³/s (CNA 2000). The waters of these rivers have a high sediment load derived from eroded adjacent lands. In the Papaloapan River, which drains into the Gulf approximately 100 km south of the VRS, the mean annual load of suspended solids is 29 mg L⁻¹, with 695 mg L⁻¹ of dissolved solids (CNA 2000). These values probably are similar for the other rivers. With this high sediment load, turbidity increases, and consequently, visibility can be lowered from 10–12 m to less than 1 m (PEMEX 1987; Tunnell 1988).

During the rainy season (June–September), the amount of eroded particles in river waters increases (Plate 56), thus increasing turbidity of nearshore seawater and in the VRS. During this season of increased riverine discharge, live corals are covered by a thin layer of fine sediments (Plate 57), surface salinity is lowered, and at times, masses of freshwater plants such as water hyacinths, as well as terrestrial wood debris, can be found on the reefs (Plate 58). Tunnell (1988) recorded a surface salinity of 14 psu near in Antón Lizardo, 24 psu at Enmedio Reef, and 28 psu at Chopas Reef. Salinities of 28–32 psu are common in summer at the VRS (Secretaría de Marina 1978). A massive die-off of the coral *Acropora cervicornis* on Topatillo reef was observed after a major freshwater inflow event during the 1981 summer rainy season (Tunnell 1992).

**Winter Cold Fronts**   *Nortes* (winter cold fronts) are cold, high-pressure air masses derived from cyclonic waves from the United States and Canada that move from west to east across the Gulf of Mexico. When these cold air masses approach the sea and contact the warmer atmosphere over the ocean, they are forced to flow down, thereby increasing their wind speed up to 120 km/h (Davis 1978). Nortes affect all of the southern Gulf of Mexico, increasing turbidity by surge and wave action on shallow continental shelves (Plate 59), forming a surface current with a south-southeastly direction. Also, there is an associated thermal stress on reef biota on the most northerly reefs caused by low atmospheric and seawater temperatures (Tunnell 1992).

Another disturbance on coral reefs caused by the strong north winds is increased ocean surf, which produces waves of up to 6 m high. This strong surf is able to move boulders and coral heads that weigh more than 1 ton. During one severe norte in the winter of 1995–96, wind-generated waves moved a 1-ton buoy from the beach into the middle of the cay, some 50 m, at Isla Verde Reef (VRS). Waves can resuspend deposited sediments, increasing the erosive capability of the water on living and dead corals. The mechanical force of the wave may fragment coral colonies into smaller pieces, and these fragments then accumulate in the reef-crest zone.

**Tropical Storms and Hurricanes**   Hurricanes and tropical storms are other common atmospheric disturbances in the southern Gulf of Mexico. The impacts of these meteorological events are well documented for various reef localities in the Mexican Caribbean and include those discussed for the nortes, except for changes of water and air temperature (Jordán et al. 1981; Rodríguez-Martínez 1993). Many tropical storms and hurricanes in the western tropical Atlantic are formed in the Caribbean. Once formed, they often move on a northwest trajectory and enter the Gulf either through the Yucatán Channel, or by crossing the Yucatán Peninsula, and then make landfall in the northern or northwestern

Gulf (Jáuregui 2003). In an average season, five to seven hurricanes and tropical storms form in the tropical Atlantic, with one to three entering the Gulf. The Campeche Bank reefs lie in the path of almost all storms and hurricanes that enter the Gulf, so the potential for reef damage derived from heavy surge is high, although there are no published records of reef damage available.

Historical hurricane track records are available from the NOAA Coastal Services Center (http://hurricane.csc.noaa.gov/hurricanes). In the period from 1950 to 2001, several hurricanes passed near a reef location in the southern Gulf of Mexico at a distance of 120 km or less; 10 on or near Alacrán, 15 on or near Cayo Arcas, 5 on or near the VRS, and 15 on or near the TRS. Some of these hurricanes were classified as category 5, according to the Saffir-Simpson classification. These are intense hurricanes, with sustained wind speeds >250 km hr$^{-1}$, such as Hurricane Carla in 1961, Ines in 1966, Beulah in 1967, Allen in 1980, Gilbert in 1988, Ivan in 2004, and Katrina, Rita, and Wilma in 2005. Historical evidence of former hurricanes is seen in the storm-tossed boulders that are characteristic of windward reef flats, particularly on the Veracruz Reef System (Plate 60).

**Reef Species Die-Off**    Widespread die-off in the western tropical Atlantic of some reef species (e.g., the scleractinian corals *Acropora* spp. and the sea urchin *Diadema antillarum*) has significantly affected community structure of coral reefs in the the southern Gulf of Mexico. Climatically, severe winter seasons (1969–70, 1977, and 1981) caused a high mortality of *Acropora* species in shallow environments. Tunnell (1992) recorded the decline of shallow water communities, especially *Acropora*, from 100% of bottom cover to <5% in some selected reefs of the VRS (see Plates 26, 32, and 33). More recently, the relative abundance of *Acropora* spp. has been reduced to <2% in most areas 6 m or less (Horta-Puga 2003).

Effects of the absence of the *Acropora* zone are reef cay erosion and the loss of reef framework construction. The south ends of the emergent cays of Isla de Enmedio, Santiaguillo and Salmedina (Chopas Reef), have eroded by surge action (see Plate 24). The dead sparse stumps of *Acropora palmata* no longer provide protection from wave surge, allowing wave action to erode island shores. It has been estimated that 30%–40% of some cays (Isla de Enmedio and Salmedina) are gone because of this action (J. W. Tunnell Jr., personal communication). The small cay of Topatillo Reef completely disappeared in the late 1990s (J. W. Tunnell Jr., personal communication).

In the early 1980s the widespread mortality of *Diadema antillarum* throughout the Caribbean impacted reef environments (Lessios et al. 1984). This species was also abundant on southern Gulf reefs (Plate 61). However, today it is unusual to find even a single specimen. In a thorough ecological survey as a part of the AGRRA project in 1999 (Horta-Puga 2003), only two specimens of *D. antillarum* were observed along 124 belt-sampling transects (10 = 1 m) in the VRS. Density of other sea urchin species, *Echinometra* spp. (*E. lucunter* + *E. viridis*), was high, averaging 63 individuals per 100 m$^2$. It is likely that *Echinometra* (see Plate 29) is exploiting the empty ecological niche left by *D. antillarum*.

**Bleaching**    It is widely known that bleaching is a major threat to corals and coral reef ecology (Goldberg and Wilkinson 2004). Bleaching can be the result of loss of endozoic zooxanthellae from the coral host or loss of pigment from algae (Plate 62). Acute bleaching is a generalized stress response to various factors such as high or low temperatures, low light levels, high UV radiation, salinity shock, and/or chemical changes in seawater. The only massive bleaching event recorded in the southern Gulf coral reef system occurred in December 1994 in the VRS during a severe winter cold front. This event affected up to 50% of the colonies of *Colpophyllia natans, Diploria* spp., *Montastraea annularis,* and *M. cavernosa.* Each colony showed an average 40% of the surface bleached (J. P. Carricart, personal communication).

Although bleaching is inherently associated with widespread phenomena that affect zooxanthellate reef species, such as higher than normal salinity or temperature, partial and low-level bleaching also occurs in the absence of perceptible stress (Buddemeier and Fautin 1993). It is not uncommon to observe some bleached colonies on the reef at any time. Partial bleaching was documented for *Porites porites* in October 1990 on the Isla Verde reef flat, where all branch tips of this coral were pale or white. This condition lasted until summer 1992, but the cause and effect on the reef are unknown (Carricart-Ganivet 1993).

As part of a community-structure study, the portion of bleached specimens of various scleractinian species during a nonbleaching season was determined in the summer of 1989 on the La Blanquilla reef flat. The species affected and the portion of bleached colonies per species were *Diploria clivosa* (1.37%), *D. strigosa* (1.03%), *P. astreoides* (4.87%), *Siderastrea radians* (5.82%), and *Siderastrea siderea* (2.69%). *Porites branneri* was also sampled, but no bleached specimens were observed (Horta-Puga and Carricart-Ganivet 1989). Although low-level bleaching is not uncommon, the extent of population and/or community damage on Mexican reefs remains unknown.

**Red Tides**   Another natural disturbance that affects reef communities of the southern Gulf of Mexico is "red tide." This disturbance is a sudden bloom of various dinoflagellate genera such as *Gymnodinium, Gonyaulax,* and *Karenia.* Any time of year the reproduction rate of these organisms may increase by several orders of magnitude in response to known (nutrient influxes) and unknown environmental factors. The sea-surface layer becomes yellowish, brownish, or reddish, a color derived from the photosynthetic pigments of thousands of millions of organisms. The algae also release a neurotoxin that may kill reef biota, including scleractinians, gorgonians, mollusks, echinoderms, polychaetous annelids, and fishes.

Red tides may result in almost complete extirpations of shallow-water reef organisms, and several years may be required for the reestablishment of the reef community (Smith 1975). The first reliable record of an algal bloom for Veracruz was dated in 1853 (Magaña et al. 2003). Red-tide blooms were observed in the VRS in 1998, 1999, and 2002 (R. Cudney, personal communication). The red tide event of December 2001–January 2002 severely damaged reef-fish populations, as more than 50 tons of dead reef fishes found washed ashore (Fuentes et al. 2004).

## Anthropogenic Disturbances

**Mining**   In colonial times the use of stony corals, *piedra de múcar* (coralline rock), for building purposes was the primary threat to the VRS. All public buildings of the 17th and 18th centuries, such as fortresses, hospitals, churches, government offices, the customhouse, and hotels, as well as small houses and the rampart that surrounded the old city of Veracruz, were built with *piedra de múcar.* There are no records of the quantity of coral heads used, but it surely included thousands of tons, as more than 1,000 structures were built with coralline rock (Lerdo de Tejada 1858). Almost all the construction was accomplished using blocks of massive corals, which probably were obtained from the shallow adjacent reef areas of the VRS. The corals were also pulverized and mixed with sand to obtain a mortar used to join the construction blocks. Coral species used for construction were *Siderastrea radians*, *Porites astreoides*, *Diploria clivosa*, *Diploria strigosa*, *Colpophyllia natans*, *Montastraea annularis*, *Montastraea cavernosa* (Ganivet 1998), and *Acropora palmata* (Palacios-Coria 2001).

Fort San Juan de Ulúa was entirely built with *piedra de múcar* (Plate 63) (Ganivet 1998). Situated at the southeast end of La Gallega Reef, it was constructed in stages, beginning in the 16th century and continuing until the 19th century. The most common coral species used as building blocks in the construction were *Acropora palmata* (37%), *Diploria* spp. (35.5%), and *Colpophyllia natans* (18.7%). These corals were also the most abundant in shallow reef areas (Palacios-Coria 2001). Ancient maps of Veracruz from the 17th and 18th centuries show three apparently well-developed reefs: Ebreos, Gavias, and Caleta, all of which no longer exist.

The geographic position and morphology of Ebreos and Gavias reefs are ill-defined. It is not known whether they were isolated and well-developed small platform reefs or only small cays situated on the western reef flat of the Gallega Reef. It is very probable that the corals of these reef structures were used as construction blocks. Another possibility is that today they are buried below the terrace land-bridge that connects San Juan de Ulúa Island with the mainland (see next section). Reefs like Hornos and Gallega were severely disturbed by coral mining.

**Construction and Landfilling**    In the early 20th century, the port facilities of the city of Veracruz were extended to its present configuration (Plate 64). The small submerged patch reef La Lavandera, the fringing reef Hornos, and the southeast reef-flat area of the La Gallega Reef were severely disturbed by the construction of the breakwaters at the entrance of the port. Breakwaters were constructed using a rubblemound design in which small stones were discharged first over the bottom, then progressively larger (armor) stones were placed atop and aside the smaller stones to finish the structure. During the construction, reefs were damaged by falling rocks and gravel over the substrate and the resuspension of sediments in the water column. The docks in the harbor were constructed in a similar way.

The San Juan de Ulúa Island at the southwestern end of La Gallega Reef was the site chosen by Hernan Cortes to build the port of Villa Rica de la Veracruz. The dock was used as the main port facility until the end of the 19th century. The need for better, more efficient and safer docks for tying up freighters and the need to speed up ship loading and unloading maneuvers created the need for the construction of a land-bridge between the mainland and La Gallega Reef at the beginning of the 20th century (Rodríguez and Manrique 1991; García-Díaz 1992). The construction of this landfill closed the North Channel, which was the main entrance pass for centuries into the port from the Bay of Vergara to the north. Tons of fill materials were deposited in the channel. This fill covered the remains of the Caleta, Ebreos, and Gavias reefs, destroying them totally. Landfilling of La Gallega Reef reef flat was reinitiated in 2000 in order to extend the cargo area of the port. In 2005, this construction was stopped by the Mexican authorities.

**Dredging** The entrance channel of the Port of Veracruz is dredged every 6–8 months to permit the passage of large cargo ships. The dredge operations resuspend bottom sediments in the water column. Sediments are taken on board the dredge ship and then released off the port, some 10 km from the mainland (G. Horta-Puga, personal observation). Resuspended solids are distributed by local currents onto the reefs, where they accumulate over the reef substrate and corals. Unfortunately, there are no available studies of sedimentation rates on the VRS. Another threat associated with dredging is the resuspension of pollutants previously buried in the sediments.

**Ship Groundings** Ship groundings have occurred on the coral reefs of the southern Gulf of Mexico (Plate 65). The effects of this type of disturbance include destruction of shallow communities when vessels "crawl" over the reef bottom. As ships move by storm and tidal surge, the area of destruction of the reef increases. Additional damage is caused by cables and anchors that hold the ships in place, and by rescue maneuvers. In the last decade, there have been two freighter groundings on the reef flat of the Anegada de Adentro Reef (VRS). The Liberian ship *Morgan* in 1990 and the Russian ship *The USSR Reach 60 Years Old* in 1994 grounded on the reef flat and crest on the north and southeast parts of the reef, respectively. These freighters remained aground in the same place until it was decided to dismantle them after some unsuccessful rescue attempts. Although totally dismantled, some metal debris remains on site. In late 1990 the Panamanian vessel *New Hope* grounded on Chopas Reef (VRS). The *New Hope* was later pulled back to the sea off the reef by other ships.

In 2001 the Mexican ship *Halley* grounded on Alacrán Reef (CBR) and the German vessel *Rubin* impacted the reef front slope of Pájaros Reef (VRS). The impact on these reefs was evaluated by the Comisión Nacional de Áreas Naturales Protegidas (CONANP; Mexican National Commission on Natural Protected Areas). In the case of the *Rubin,* the impact affected an area of 4,150 m$^2$. It was calculated that ~1,735 coral colonies died, which covered ~141 m$^2$ of the reef bottom. Also important, though not evaluated, was the production of coralline rock debris that could increase damage when moved by surge (Horta-Puga and Vargas-Hernández 2003). More recently, in 2003 the ship *Paula Kay* grounded on the Tuxpan Reef (TRS), damaging ~177 m$^2$ of the reef flat, primarily affecting populations of the corals *Diploria clivosa* and *Millepora alcicornis* (Vargas-Hernández et al. 2003).

**Overfishing** Mexican reefs have been used as fishing areas since pre-Hispanic times. However, there are not enough available data on reef fisheries for the southern Gulf of Mexico to determine trends or impact. Some data gathered from various nonpublished manuscripts, as well as some national fishery yearbooks with very incomplete information, are the only sources of data.

The Port of Veracruz ranked as the 17th most important fishing port in Mexico in 1992. The total catch (in metric tons) for 1988, including all fished species, was 5,819 tons; for 1991 it was 9,021 tons, and for 1992 it was 9,130 tons. This represents 0.4% of the national annual catch for 1988 and 0.7% each for 1991 and 1992. The total annual catch in the Port of Veracruz increased 63.7% in the five-year period 1988–92).

Although the reports do not mention specific locations of capture, it is probable that an important percentage of the recorded 511 tons of marine snails, 38 tons of octopuses, and the six tons of *arbolitos* (ramose gorgonians) fished in the littoral waters off the state of Veracruz in 1988 were caught on or near the VRS. Almost all of the catch was caught using small boats (SEPESCA 1990b, 1992).

Despite the lack of suitable statistics, considerable fishing activity takes place in the VRS. Today, some mollusk species are fished in the reef lagoons, such as *almejas* or clams (*Codakia orbicularis, Asaphis deflorata*) and octopuses (*Octopus* spp). The clam fishing technique involves raking, fanning, or prop-washing the rhizomes of the seagrass *Thalassia testudinum* where clams are found (Tunnell 1992). The damage to bottom environments involve resuspension of sediments, overturning of coral heads (live or dead), and the exposing of infaunal organisms from the bottom to predators. Additionally, subsequent winter storms resuspend unbound sediments from 1 m to over 2–3 m deep, depositing them on southern reef slopes (J. W. Tunnell, personal communication).

Octopuses are fished using a hook and looking for them in crevices and cavities among corals. The gastropod *Strombus alatus* (*caracol canelo*) is another reef inhabitant caught for human consumption on the sand bottoms near reefs.

The most frequently captured fishes from the reefs and surrounding areas are cojinuda (*Caranx crysos*), pargo (*Lutjanus* spp.), robalo (*Centropomus* spp.), sargo (*Archosargus* spp.), trucha (*Cynoscion nebulosus*), cabrilla (*Cephalopholis* and *Epinephelus*), sierra (*Scomberomorus maculatus*), cazon (*Rhizopriondon terraenovae*), villajaiba (*Lutjanus synagris*), rubia (*Ocyurus chrysurus*), mojarra (*Diapterus* and *Eugerres*), jurel (*Caranx*), agujon (*Strongylura marina*), and barracuda (*Sphyraena barracuda*) (INEGI 1997b). Fish are captured using beach seines, gill nets, hand lines, spear guns, and *cimbras* (long bottom lines with hooks). Each reef is visited everyday by several small boats equipped with outboard engines and 2–4 fishermen from the towns of Antón Lizardo and Veracruz.

Recreational fishing is also a substantial activity in the VRS, and is done exclusively with hand lines. However, despite the substantial size of the catch, no data have been collected on catch composition or of catch and effort data. Local fishermen say that annual catches of all species are declining. It is important to mention that the spiny lobsters (*Panulirus argus*) and the queen conch (*Strombus gigas*), once abundant in the VRS, are now rarely seen in the area.

**Shell and Fish Collection**    As a consequence of the interest in maintaining tropical fauna in aquariums, there has been an increase in the collection and trade of coral reef fauna worldwide. Although reef organisms have been collected for years in the VRS to be sold locally, in recent times collected specimens have been traded to international distributors. Shells, skeletons, and dried or desiccated specimens or ornaments manufactured with them are sold in *El Malecón* craft market in downtown Veracruz city. The organisms most frequently collected for commercial purposes are corals (*Diploria, Colpophyllia, Montastraea, Porites, Mussa,* and *Oculina*); octocorals (*Eunicea* and *Pseudoplexaura*); gastropods (*Charonia, Strombus, Conus, Oliva, Cypraea, Cymatium, Cypreacassis, Tona,* and *Turbinella*); bivalves (*Dinocardium, Tellina, Donax,* and *Lima*); sea urchins (*Tripneustes ventricosus, Echinometra lucunter, Eucidaris tribuloides, Mellita quinquiesperforata,* and *Encope michelini*); and fishes (*Diodon hystrix, Hippocampus hudsonius, Lactophrys triqueter,* and *Rhynobatus lentiginosus*). Almost all of these species are now scarce in the VRS, due at least in part to overharvest (Vargas-Hernández 1992; Vargas-Hernández et al. 1994).

Reef fishes are also collected by aquarists (Vargas-Hernández, Carrera-Parra, et al. 1994). The small and colorful species such as damselfishes (*Eupomacentrus, Halichoeres*), sergeant majors (*Abudefduf saxatilis*), butterfly fishes (*Chaetodon*), and surgeonfishes (*Acanthurus*) are the most desired. There are neither records of capture nor regulation of this activity, and these species are becoming scarcer on the VRS. Aquarists also collect reef sand from the emergent cay beaches for use in aquaria (G. Horta-Puga, personal observation).

**Tourism and Recreational Aquatic Sports**  Coral reefs attract tourists everywhere, and the southern Gulf of Mexico coral reefs are no exception. People looking for a beautiful tropical marine environment, aquatic sports, or simply leisure choose reef destinations worldwide (Plate 66). Because the CBR and TRS are located far away from shore and from highly populated human settlements, these are visited infrequently and damage from tourism activities is negligible. In the VRS, however, tourism is a significant environmental threat. Every year more than 800,000 tourists visit the area, looking for beaches and aquatic recreational activities (INEGI 1995a). In reef habitats the calm waters of the shallow coral-reef lagoons are suitable for swimming and observing myriad marine organisms with just a mask and snorkel. Because the bottom has a depth of only 1.5 m or less, almost anyone can "walk" over the substratum, treading on corals, seagrasses, and bottom organisms. Corals also are overturned as visitors search for cryptic organisms.

The collection of shells, corals, and other reef inhabitants for souvenirs is a common activity. Some organisms are intentionally killed and used as bait. The main recreational destinations for tourists are Isla Verde, Isla de Enmedio, Punta Mocambo, and a small sand bank named *Cancuncito* in the reef lagoon of Pájaros, which emerges at low tide. Because these reefs are visited by thousands of tourists every year, the impact is severe and there is considerable destruction of reef habitat.

On a single weekend day there may be up to 30 boats anchored on the reef slopes and flats. Anchors crush, break, and dislodge corals, producing additional damage. In order to prevent anchoring of boats in the early 1990s, three mooring buoys were placed on the leeward slope of Isla Verde Reef, two in *Las Catedrales*, a beautiful dive destination in the northwest, and one in the southwest near the lighthouse. Unfortunately, no buoys were placed on other reefs, and those in Isla Verde are no longer there, so anchoring destruction of the reef bottom persists.

The VRS is also an important destination for scuba diving. This sport has been growing in Mexico and now there are at least six dive centers in the area of Veracruz and Antón Lizardo that accommodate thousands of divers every season (scuba shop managers, personal communication). Divers impact reefs nearly in the same way as tourists, extending the damage to the deeper reef slopes. The reefs most visited by divers are Santiaguillo, Anegada de Afuera, Anegada de Adentro, Isla de Enmedio, and Isla Verde. The damage caused by divers was so intense that at least one reef, Isla de Sacrificios, was closed to tourism and recreational activities from 1982 to the present by municipal and federal authorities.

**Military Maneuvers**  Isla Salmedina, on southeastern Chopas Reef, was used as a shooting range by the Mexican Navy during the summer of 1985 (G. Horta-

Puga, personal observation). The impact of bullets from machine guns and air-to-land missiles from military helicopters destroyed a small house that had been built for use as a target. Some bullets and missiles impacted the reef lagoon, damaging the bottom community, but the impact of this disturbance was not evaluated.

**Chemical Pollution**   One of the greatest threats to the southern Gulf of Mexico and its reefs is chemical pollution. Potentially toxic chemical pollutants enter the southern Gulf of Mexico through various means, as sewage effluents, terrestrial runoff, atmospheric fallout, wind currents, river outflow, seasurface currents, and accidental and intentional waste discharges (Sheets 1980). The kind and variety of chemical pollutants include pesticides, PCBs, PAEs, heavy metals, petroleum and its derivatives, detergents, suspended solids, and nutrients (Botello et al. 1992; Chávez and Tunnell 1993).

The concentrations of most pollutants are unknown for the southern Gulf of Mexico. An indirect measure of pollution in any area is pollutant levels recorded in sources and/or transport media (Tables 12.1, 12.2, and 12.3). Thus, the degree of pollution in adjacent environments (e.g., rivers, coastal lagoons, sewage effluents, and fallout) could indicate the extent of the problem in the southern Gulf of Mexico.

Riverine Input   Several rivers flow into the southern Gulf of Mexico, carrying assorted pollutants from the coastal Gulf states in Mexico. These rivers receive plant detritus, salts, silt, pesticide residues, and nitrogen- and phosphorous-rich fertilizers in runoff from agricultural practices, as well as from uncultivated and forest lands. The drainage basin of these rivers extends over an area of ~263,000 km² (INEGI 1988); these lands are cultivated with crops such as corn, beans, rice, potatoes, coffee, sugarcane (Plate 67), oranges, and bananas (INEGI 1995a, 1995b).

The most common pesticides used for agricultural purposes in Mexico are chlorpyrifos, carbaryl, diazinon, methamidophos, mancozeb, methyl parathion, and copper oxyclorides. Also, DDT has been used for the control of mosquitoes

**Table 12.1.** *Environmental levels (μg g⁻¹) of nonessential heavy metals in selected estuarine and riverine localities in the southern Gulf of Mexico.*

| State/Locality | Cr | | Pb | | Cd | | Hg | |
|---|---|---|---|---|---|---|---|---|
| | Sed | Org | Sed | Org | Sed | Org | Sed | Org |
| **Veracruz** | | | | | | | | |
| Rio Blanco | 83 | | 32 | | 1.6 | | | |
| Rio Coatzacoalcos | 67 | | 43 | | 1.6 | | | |
| **Tabasco** | | | | | | | | |
| Laguna Machona | | | | 0.2 | | | | 0.1 |
| Laguna Carmen | 31 | 4.6 | 6.5 | 3 | 0.3 | 7.1 | | 0.1 |
| **Campeche** | | | | | | | | |
| Laguna Términos | 47 | 6.7 | 34 | 5.8 | 1.4 | 3.7 | | |

*Notes:* Sed = bottom surficial sediments; Org = organisms. Data from Botello et al. (1992).

**Table 12.2.** *Environmental levels of pesticides (ng g⁻¹) and PCBs ($\mu g\ g^{-1}$) in selected estuarine and riverine localities in the southern Gulf of Mexico.*

| State/Locality | BHD | | Heptaclor | | Aldrin | | Dieldrin | | Endrin | | Endosulfan | | Chlordan | | DDT | | PCBs | |
|---|---|---|---|---|---|---|---|---|---|---|---|---|---|---|---|---|---|---|
| | Sed | Org | Sed | Org | Sed | Org | Sed | Org | Sed | Org | Sed | Org | Sed | Org | Sed | Org | Sed | Org |
| **Veracruz** | | | | | | | | | | | | | | | | | | |
| Laguna Pueblo Viejo | | | | | | | | | | | | 0.06 | | 0.1 | | 16 | | 75 |
| Laguna Tampamachoco | | | | | | | | 1.1 | | | | | | | | | | 20 |
| Laguna Alvarado | 1.1 | 2.4 | 3.9 | 2.9 | 2.1 | 6.6 | 2.1 | | 7.8 | 7.9 | 0.6 | 17.6 | | | 2.2 | 1.6 | | 72 |
| Laguna Ostión | 0.83 | | 0.33 | | 1.38 | | 0.75 | | 0.5 | | | | | | 0.3 | | | |
| Rio Coatzacoalcos | 0.5 | | 0.8 | | 0.2 | | 0.56 | | 0.27 | | | | | | 0.27 | | | |
| **Tabasco** | | | | | | | | | | | | | | | | | | |
| Laguna Machona | 0.3 | 0.9 | 2.3 | 1.8 | 1.2 | 1.6 | 0.6 | | 4.9 | 10 | | 8.8 | | | 0.9 | 5.6 | | |
| Laguna Carmen | 0.3 | 1.4 | 5.1 | 2.1 | 0.7 | 2.5 | 6.8 | | 2.7 | 1.5 | 0.1 | 14.9 | | | 1.4 | | | 90 |
| Laguna Mecoacán | 5.6 | | | | | | 36.7 | | | | | | | | 55.1 | | | |
| **Campeche** | | | | | | | | | | | | | | | | | | |
| LagunaTérminos | | 27.6 | | | | 286 | | 41.7 | | 203 | | 8.4 | | | 85 | | | 94 |

*Notes:* Sed = bottom surficial sediments; Org = organisms. Data from Botello et al. (1992).

**Table 12.3.** *Environmental levels of fecal coliforms (individuals per 100 mL⁻¹) and hydrocarbons (μg g⁻¹) in selected estuarine and riverine localities in the southern Gulf of Mexico.*

| State/Locality | Fecal coliforms | | | Total hydrocarbons | | |
| --- | --- | --- | --- | --- | --- | --- |
| | W | S | O | W | S | O |
| **Tamaulipas** | | | | | | |
| Laguna Madre | | | | | 26 | |
| **Veracruz** | | | | | | |
| Laguna Pueblo Viejo | | | | | 53 | |
| Laguna Tamiahua | 10 | | 18 | | 31 | |
| Laguna Alvarado | | | | | 18 | |
| Laguna Ostión | 1,121 | 3250 | 10 | 18.4 | 120 | 850 |
| Laguna Conchal | 370 | | | | | |
| Rio Coatzacoalcos | | | | | 680 | |
| **Tabasco** | | | | | | |
| Laguna Machona | 240 | | | 7 | 45 | |
| Laguna Carmen | | | | 4 | 45 | |
| Laguna Mecoacán | 300 | 300 | 10 | 5 | 88 | |
| Laguna Tupilco | | 980 | | | | |
| **Campeche** | | | | | | |
| LagunaTérminos | 240 | | | 48 | 37–85 | 2.3 |

*Notes:* W = water; S = bottom surficial sediments; O = organisms. Data from Botello et al. (1992).

(malaria disease) (Benítez et al. 1993). The use of pesticides in the region has increased in the last several decades in spite of their toxicity. In 1969, the demand for pesticides was 10,200 tons, but in 1980 the consumption increased to 26,700 tons, some of which was transported into aquatic systems by terrestrial runoff (Rosales-Hoz 1979). The levels of some organochlorine hydrocarbons, DDT (0.45 ppb) and dieldrin (0.87 ppb), have been determined in recent sediments of Alvarado Lagoon (Rosales-Hoz and Álvarez-León 1979). The ultimate destination of these pesticides is the ocean.

Municipal sewage effluents also are discharged directly from several important mainland cities: Matamoros, Tampico, Madero, Poza Rica, Cardel, Orizaba, Córdoba, Jalapa, Veracruz, Alvarado, Minatitlán, Coatzacolacos, Villahermosa, Ciudad del Carmen, and Campeche. Several chemical, textile, brewing, food processing, manufacturing, wood and paper, and steel industries also discharge their wastes (Rosales et al. 1986a, 1986b). These wastes are the main sources of nutrients, heavy metals and hydrocarbons found in water and sediment of rivers.

Coastal Lagoons  The levels of some heavy metals in sediment and water have been determined for various localities: Machona, Términos, Mandinga, La Mancha, and Alvarado coastal lagoons, and Blanco and Papaloapan rivers (Rosas et al. 1983; Rosales et al. 1986a, 1986b; Alvarez et al. 1986; Badillo

1986; Vargas-Hernández 1992). Heavy metal environmental values range widely among localities, with iron (Fe) having the highest values at almost all sites. Levels of the nonessential metals Cd, Hg, and Pb in the water from Mandinga Lagoon are higher than those levels considered as upper limit values in coastal waters (0.9, 0.02, and 6.0 $\mu$g L$^{-1}$, respectively) by Mexican environmental laws (SEDUE 1990) and for human consumption (0.13, 1.0, 0.2 $\mu$g L$^{-1}$, respectively; FDA 1996).

The metal levels in sediments and benthic fauna are also high. The contaminant levels of the continental aquatic areas near the VRS are high, and these may also be the sources of these metals in the VRS.

Hydrocarbons are also important pollutants released into continental aquatic environments. The levels of alkane, aromatic, and total hydrocarbon fractions were qualitatively evaluated in sediments and oyster tissue (*Crassostrea virginica*) from several coastal lagoons in the Gulf of Mexico, including Alvarado Lagoon (Botello 1979). These studies suggest the possibility that hydrocarbons could be transported by sea currents and reach the VRS. Hydrocarbons are also a source of various metals such as V, Ni, Fe, and Al (Echaniz-Hernández 1988).

Atmospheric Fallout    Another pathway of chemical pollutant entry is atmospheric fallout, both dry and wet, especially in zones with rainy climates like that of the VRS area. Air currents transport dust, toxic molecules (e.g., sulfur dioxide, nitrous oxide, radioisotopes), heavy metals (e.g., lead, cadmium, mercury), and smoke from manufacturing and smelter plants (Sheets 1980). Báez et al. (1980) recorded the levels of Cd, Cr, and Pb (0.068, 7.36 and 179.5 $\mu$g L$^{-1}$, respectively) in fallout in the city of Veracruz. These levels were higher than those recorded for other Mexican cities such as Cordoba and Puebla (not Mexico City) and some areas of the United States and the United Kingdom (Albert and Badillo 1991). They attributed the high concentrations to port activities.

Coastal Sewage    In the case of the VRS, sewage waters from the city of Veracruz, including wastewaters from the industrial area, are discharged into the sea at Playa Norte between the Gallega and Punta Gorda reefs. Although a sewage water treatment plant was opened in the early 1990s from which effluents flow out near Galleguilla Reef, it does not have the capability to treat all the wastewater produced by human activities; therefore, some is discharged without treatment (Vargas-Hernández et al. 1993). It is probable that the oxygen levels drop drastically and the conditions are eutrophic in the shallow areas nearest the outlet of the effluent. The unusual abundance of algae and the disappearance of some reef-lagoon biota, such as reef-building scleractinians in nearby La Gallega Reef, suggest high nutrient input. Corals tend to disappear in eutrophic environments, being displaced by algae, thus changing community structure and energy relationships in reefs (Smith et al. 1981; Hawker and Connell 1992), as is the case at La Gallega Reef.

The reef flat of Punta Mocambo receives small volumes of sewage waters. Prior to introduction of these effluents (1990) the population density of the sea cucumber *Holothuria grisea* was 3–5 per m$^2$ (G. Horta-Puga, personal observation), but today it is rarely found. The surface waters on the reef flat of La Gallega Reef contain considerable amounts of garbage, such as plastic bags, organic debris, pieces of paper, wood, and fecal material. The fringing reefs of Hornos and Punta Mocambo are affected in the same way but to a lesser extent.

Other evidence of high nutrient concentrations is the increase of the UV fluorescent bands in the coral skeleton of *Montastraea annularis* formed in the last two decades. Beaver et al. (1996) consider this phenomenon to be related to land clearing, habitat degradation, and high nutrient input from rivers and sewage effluents.

The presence of increased populations of some bacteria, such as *Escherichia, Streptococcus,* and *Clostridium,* in water and sediments is a clear indication of fecal contamination from sewage effluents (McNeill 1992). Seawater microbiological quality has been determined from various beaches of Veracruz. The concentration of fecal coliforms in seawater from five beaches (Boca del Río, Mocambo, Villa del Mar, Puerto, and Playa Norte) in the urban area of Veracruz City were evaluated for the period 1991–92. Almost all values found were higher than the maximum established by the Mexican environmental laws, 200 FC 100 m $L^{-1}$ (Norma Técnica Ecológica CE-CCA-001/89). These beaches are adjacent to coral reef areas and are a potential risk to human and environmental health (Medina and Ruiz 1991; Molina 1992). It is well known to the people of the city that some beaches are particularly dangerous to human health. Those beaches, like Playa Norte and El Playon, are usually avoided for tourism and recreational activities.

Coastal Runoff    Several small drainageways from the city of Veracruz, as well as terrestrial runoff, carry particulate matter and some dissolved substances that are washed from the streets of the city and unoccupied lands. Runoff is a source for many toxic and nontoxic pollutants (Vestal 1980). Some of these effluents discharge directly into reef areas, as in Hornos and Punta Mocambo reefs. The reef flat of the latter exists in almost the same conditions as those mentioned in the previous section for La Gallega Reef. Although the shallow-reef community is still present, algae are becoming dominant, suggesting a net influx of nutrients. The system is eutrophying (G. Horta-Puga, personal observation). These are all potential sources of pollutants to the VRS; however, there are no records of their chemical composition. The city of Veracruz is growing at a faster rate every year, and for this reason, the amount of pollutants in runoff waters will increase as land becomes impervious through the construction of streets, parking lots, houses, and buildings.

Ocean Currents    Ocean currents are another medium of transport of pollutants to the VRS. Dissolved and particulate matter can be carried long distances by sea-surface currents, coming from distant places such as the Campeche Bank (Grose et al. 1983). The southern Gulf of Mexico is one of the most productive areas of oil extraction in the world (see Plates 15 and 68). The joint crude oil production (land + offshore) for the year 2000 was 1100 = $10^6$ barrels from 4,300 oil drilling platforms (see Plate 15) (http://www.pemex.com). The Campeche Bank oil field area contributes 80% of the oil production in Mexico, and 90% of the oil processing plants are on adjacent coastal areas (Botello et al. 1992).

The drilling and extraction operations produce some losses of oil into the sea. In addition there are blowouts, ruptures of gathering lines, and other occurrences that result in significant spillage of petroleum. The estimated loss of petroleum from this source is 0.014% of the total production (Perry 1980). Some accidental oil spills occur every year, and in 1979 the major spill of the Ixtoc 1 well (Plate 69) released up to 630,000 gallons of petroleum per day to the sea from June through October (OSIR 1980). The oil from those accidental spills drifted as floating tar, moved by sea and wind currents to the north and up the coasts of the states of Veracruz and Tamaulipas in Mexico and Texas in the United States. Grose et al. (1983) developed a prediction model of surface transport of pollutants and predicted that oil spills resulting from operational discharges of ships navigating throughout the Gulf will tend to accumulate on the coast of the state of Veracruz and in the VRS.

It has been demonstrated that floating tars in the Gulf of Mexico include various chemical species such as aliphatic and aromatic hydrocarbons, naphthalenes, phenanthrenes, dibenzothiophenes, among others (Van Vleet et al. 1984). When the spilled oil arrives in the VRS, tar accumulates on sand beaches of the emerged reef cays and on coral blocks of the reef crest, forming a mat of up to 20 cm over the substratum on the intertidal zone (Tunnell 1992). This tar mat even extended out over the reef lagoon and covered the seagrass beds of *Thalassia testudinum* during the Ixtoc 1 oil spill in 1979, killing large numbers of bivalves (*Asaphis deflorata*) and sea urchins (*Lytechinus variegatus, Tripneustes ventricosus,* and *Echinometra lucunter*) (Tunnell and Dokken 1980). Subsequently, dense mats of green algae formed on some corals (Jernelov and Linden 1981). Oil can be also trapped by the thallus of benthic algae and the seagrass *Thalassia testudinum* (Echaniz-Hernández 1988). The tar crust prevents the attachment and development of benthic organisms, causing decreased bottom cover and diversity (Tunnell 1992; Chávez and Tunnell 1993).

Port Operations   Goods are loaded and unloaded from cargo ships on the docks of the Port of Veracruz. Usually there are 5–10 ships in the docks everyday, each spending three or more days at the dock. While in dock, maintenance activities such as fuel tank and deck washing and tank refueling and hull painting are performed, using detergents, abrasive liquids, oils, paints, and so on. Some wastes are discharged directly into the ocean without treatment. It is normal to see thin oil layers on the sea surface covering an area up to several hundred square meters. These oil layers prevent the ocean-atmosphere interaction, decreasing gas fluxes (e.g., oxygen and carbon dioxide) in and out the ocean. These oil layers may get out to the open ocean, increasing hydrocarbon concentrations and impacting shallow-water reef communities.

Some freighters must wait in the open sea near the VRS for several days before entering the port. In the meantime, some of the dockside activities mentioned above could be taking place offshore. Inside the port, oil, gasoline, and other fuels are loaded and discharged from oil tankers visiting the oil terminal of PEMEX, the Mexican petroleum company. Some small spills have occurred, but there are no records of these spillages. The dockyards of the port (Astilleros de Veracruz Co.) are used mainly for ship repair and maintenance. Some liquid wastes from the dockyard, as well as debris (metals and small welding fragments), are occasionally discarded into the sea.

There are few studies that determined the environmental levels of chemical pollutants in the Port of Veracruz despite the fact that it is one of the most important cargo ports in the Gulf. The levels of some hydrocarbons (Table 12.4) have been recorded for the VRS (Botello et al. 1981; Baca et al. 1982; Castro 1983; Celis et al. 1987; Echaniz-Hernández 1988). These studies recorded the concentration of total hydrocarbons in seawater, sediments, and the seagrass *Thalassia testudinum* from the Isla Verde, Enmedio, and Sacrificios reef lagoons (Castro 1983; Celis et al. 1987; Echaniz-Hernández 1988) and oceanic areas near the VRS (Botello et al. 1981). The high concentration of hydrocarbons, mainly in

**Table 12.4.** *Environmental levels of total hydrocarbons in the Veracruz Reef System.*

| Author | Seawater (ng g⁻¹) | Sediments (µg g⁻¹) | Thalassia testudinum (µg g⁻¹) |
|---|---|---|---|
| Botello et al. 1981 (Port of Veracruz) | 10.3 | 44.3 | |
| Baca et al. 1982 (Isla de Enmedio) | | | |
| Control area | | | 42.0 |
| Oiled area | | | 534.0 |
| Castro 1983 (coastal zone) | 29.2 | | |
| Celis et al. 1987 (coastal zone) | 14.0 | | |
| Echaniz-Hernández 1988 (Port of Veracruz) | 3.07 | 120.3 | 1,619.0 |

**Table 12.5.** *Heavy metal concentrations (µg g⁻¹) in reef corals and seagrasses from the Veracruz Reef System.*

| Species/Author | Metals | | | | | | | | |
|---|---|---|---|---|---|---|---|---|---|
| | Cd | Co | Cu | Cr | Fe | Mn | Ni | Pb | Zn |
| D. clivosa[1] | 3 | 26.1 | 17.3 | 7.1 | 223 | ND | 18.7 | 68.5 | 10.3 |
| D. strigosa[1] | 3.9 | 32.8 | 21.5 | 5.2 | 325 | 59.2 | 35.4 | 55.9 | 11.3 |
| S. radians[1] | 4.7 | 28.3 | 47.7 | 8.4 | 722 | ND | 53.9 | 44 | 79.3 |
| M. annularis[1] | 4.4 | 25.2 | 23.8 | 4.5 | 142 | 17.1 | 22.1 | 64.6 | 19.7 |
| M. annularis[2] | 7.2 | 35.3 | 6.9 | 80.7 | 76.9 | 8.2 | 81.9 | 62.2 | 18 |
| M. annularis[3] | | | | | | | | 62.4 | |
| Thalassia testudinum[4] | | | | | 533 | | | | |

*Note:* ND = no data.
[1]Horta-Puga (1991).
[2]Horta-Puga (1993).
[3]Horta-Puga and Ramírez-Palacios (1996).
[4]Duarte et al. (1995).

*Thalassia testudinum*, suggested that the VRS is a polluted zone where there is a continuous arrival of spilled oil (Baca et al. 1982; Echaniz-Hernández 1988).

Heavy metals are also pollutants that have been determined in the VRS. Only heavy metal levels in the skeleton (annual growth bands) of scleractinian corals and the seagrass *Thalassia testudinum* are recorded (Table 12.5). Levels of Co, Cr, Pb, and Zn were higher than those recorded in corals of other geographic areas, such as the Great Barrier Reef (Denton and Burdon-Jones 1986), Central America (Guzmán and Jiménez 1992), Florida (Glynn et al. 1989), and Phuket, Thailand (Howard and Brown 1986, 1987). Metal concentrations at Galleguilla Reef were found to be higher than those at Anegada and Isla Verde reefs. This situation was determined by the fact that La Galleguilla Reef is located near the waste treatment plant effluent and the docks of the port. Thus, corals that inhabit reefs near the port have a higher concentration of metals than those of the distant reefs (Horta-Puga 1993). Heavy metals determined in annual growth

**35.** Reef slot or cut in the Triángulo Oeste reef platform, May 1986. Photograph by J. W. Tunnell.

**36.** Cayo Arenas on the Campeche Bank, March 1986. **(a)** Coral ramparts. **(b)** Beach rock. **(c)** "Ceviche pile" of *Astraea caelata* shells. **(d)** Spur and groove zone on the southeastern windward reef. Photographs by J. W. Tunnell.

**37.** Alacrán Reef on the Campeche Bank. **(a)** Lagoon or anchorage east of Isla Perez. Note islands of Chica and Pájaros in the background, January 1986. **(b)** "The boilers" site: shipwreck on the southeastern windward reef crest, January 1986. **(c)** *Montas-* *traea faveolata* in the shallow lagoon, July 1986. **(d)** Abundant soft corals and sea fans in the shallow lagoon, July 1986. Photographs by J. W. Tunnell.

**38.** Cayos Arcas on the Campeche Bank. **(a)** Cayo Centro facilities for PEMEX and the Mexican Navy. Note tanker oil terminals in the background, April 1986. **(b)** Cayo Este looking toward Cayo Centro in the background, April 1986. Photographs by J. W. Tunnell.

**39.** Phase shift from healthy to declining coral reef at Topatillo windward forereef. **(a)** Healthy reef with good coral cover, June 1978. **(b)** Declining reef on exactly the same spot, with less coral cover and extensive fleshy macroalgae cover, June 1990. Photographs by J. W. Tunnell.

**40.** Feather duster worm (a polychaete, *Sabellastarte magnifica*) on Santiaguillo Reef, June 1989. Photograph by J. W. Tunnell.

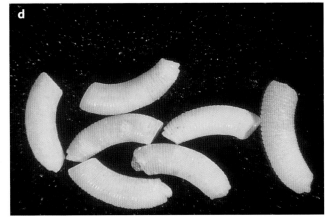

**41.** Seashell (mollusk) assemblages from Isla de Lobos Reef, June 1977. **(a)** Coral-rock-boring date mussels, clockwise from top: *Lithophaga antillarum, L. bisulcata, L. aristata,* and *L. nigra.* **(b)** Seagrass seashell species, clockwise from top: *Strombus raninus* (pair: smaller male on left, female on right), *Codakia orbicularis* (almeja), *Pinna rudis, P. carnea,* and *Strombus gigas. S. gigas* and *S. raninus* have been exterminated on Veracruz Shelf Reefs due to overfishing, and *Codakia* fishing is responsible for the destruc-tion of seagrass beds in the Veracruz Reef System. **(c)** Coral-associated species, clockwise from top left: *Lopha frons* (smaller one) and *Pteria colymbus* attached to soft coral branch; *Cyphoma gibbosum,* a soft coral predator; and three species of *Coralliophila,* all coral predators on soft and hard corals. **(d)** *Caecum pulchellum,* one of over 200 species of micromollusks (those under 10 mm in size). Photographs (a–c) by J. W. Tunnell. Photograph (d) by David W. Hicks.

45. (a) Almost 350 species of bony fishes, including many tropical fish like this blue angelfish (*Holocanthus bermudensis*, June 1978), and 29 species of sharks, rays, and skates, have been found on southern Gulf of Mexico coral reefs. (b) A significant artisanal shark fishery existed on Isla de Enmedio Reef and Alacrán Reef (June 1986) before they were overfished. (c) Shark fins are dried for the shark fin soup market in Japan, and filleted fish are salted and stacked on pallets (June 1986). Photographs by J. W. Tunnell.

46. Sea turtle track on beach dune on Isla Desterrada, Alacrán Reef, July 1986. Photograph by J. W. Tunnell.

**41.** Seashell (mollusk) assemblages from Isla de Lobos Reef, June 1977. **(a)** Coral-rock-boring date mussels, clockwise from top: *Lithophaga antillarum, L. bisulcata, L. aristata,* and *L. nigra.* **(b)** Seagrass seashell species, clockwise from top: *Strombus raninus* (pair: smaller male on left, female on right), *Codakia orbicularis* (almeja), *Pinna rudis, P. carnea,* and *Strombus gigas. S. gigas* and *S. raninus* have been exterminated on Veracruz Shelf Reefs due to overfishing, and *Codakia* fishing is responsible for the destruc-tion of seagrass beds in the Veracruz Reef System. **(c)** Coral-asso-ciated species, clockwise from top left: *Lopha frons* (smaller one) and *Pteria colymbus* attached to soft coral branch; *Cyphoma gib-bosum,* a soft coral predator; and three species of *Coralliophila,* all coral predators on soft and hard corals. **(d)** *Caecum pulchel-lum,* one of over 200 species of micromollusks (those under 10 mm in size). Photographs (a–c) by J. W. Tunnell. Photograph (d) by David W. Hicks.

**42.** Queen conch (*Strombus gigas*) was an important fisheries species on Alacrán Reef until they became overfished in the 1980s. **(a)** Shell of queen conch. The "foot" is removed, sold, and prepared in numerous popular food dishes, and the shell is sold as a curio. Photograph of shell from Majahual, Quintana Roo, Mexico, October 1985. **(b)** A conch fishing boat at anchor on Alacrán Reef. These boats were collecting 1,500–2,000 conch on a single fishing trip in July 1986. Photographs by J. W. Tunnell.

**43.** Land crab (*Gecarcinus latera-lis*), June 1977. **(a)** Mass movement at dusk on Isla de Lobos. **(b)** An individual in defensive stance. Photographs by J. W. Tunnell.

**44.** Sea urchin (*Echinometra lucunter*), which is abundant on the windward reef flats of the Veracruz Reef System and common in other shallow rocky areas on these reefs, June 1989. Photograph by J. W. Tunnell.

**45. (a)** Almost 350 species of bony fishes, including many tropical fish like this blue angelfish (*Holocanthus bermudensis*, June 1978), and 29 species of sharks, rays, and skates, have been found on southern Gulf of Mexico coral reefs. **(b)** A significant artisanal shark fishery existed on Isla de Enmedio Reef and Alacrán Reef (June 1986) before they were overfished. **(c)** Shark fins are dried for the shark fin soup market in Japan, and filleted fish are salted and stacked on pallets (June 1986). Photographs by J. W. Tunnell.

**46.** Sea turtle track on beach dune on Isla Desterrada, Alacrán Reef, July 1986. Photograph by J. W. Tunnell.

47. Colonial nesting seabirds on Campeche Bank reef islands. **(a)** Masked boobies, Cayo Arenas, March 1986. **(b)** Red-footed booby, Isla Desertora, Alacrán Reef, July 1986. **(c)** Magnificent frigatebirds, Isla Desertora, Alacrán Reef, January 1986. **(d)** Immature magnificent frigatebirds on Cayo Centro, Cayos Arcas, April 1986. Photographs by J. W. Tunnell.

**48.** Colonial nesting seabirds on Isla Perez, Alacrán Reef, July 1986. **(a)** Brown noddy in *Suriana maritima* bush at south end of the island. **(b)** Sooty terns on north end of the island. Over 25,000 have been observed on Isla Perez. Photographs by J. W. Tunnell.

**49.** Lighthouses of the Campeche Bank reef islands. **(a)** Isla Perez, Alacrán Reef, January 1986. **(b)** Cayo Arenas, March 1986. **(c)** Cayo Oeste, Triángulos Reef, May 1986. **(d)** Cayo Centro, Cayos Arcas, April 1986. Photographs by J. W. Tunnell.

**50.** Campeche Bank reef islands. **(a)** View looking northward along Isla Pájaros beach toward Isla Chica, Alacrán Reef, January 1986. **(b)** Cayo Oeste, Cayos Arcas, April 1986. **(c)** View to the north over low vegetation and nesting seabird colonies, Cayo Centro, Cayo Arenas, April 1986. **(d)** Unnamed small coral rubble cays on windward Cayo Arenas platform, March 1986. Photographs by J. W. Tunnell.

**51.** Dense tropical forest on Isla de Lobos, Tuxpan Reef System, June 1977. Photograph by J. W. Tunnell.

**52.** Selected vegetation on Isla de Enmedio. **(a)** Sea purslane (*Sesuvium portulacastrum*), June 1993. **(b)** Beach and low dune vegetation, October 1977. **(c)** Goat's-foot morning glory (*Ipomoea pes-caprae*), June 1990. **(d)** Close-up of (c). **(e)** Inkberry (*Scaevola plumieri*) in the foreground, and frangipani (*Plumeria* sp.) (pink flower), coconut palm (*Cocos nucifera*), and Australian pine (*Casuarina equisetifolia*) in the background, June 1978. **(f)** Close-up of inkberry, June 1989. **(g)** View from the lighthouse of the dense canopy of tropical ornamentals planted in the center of the island, June 1988. **(h)** Close-up of frangipani, June 1988. Photographs by J. W. Tunnell.

**53.** Erosion of Isla de Enmedio southern beaches. **(a)** View to the southwest toward the southern tip of the island. **(b)** Eroding frangipani root system that used to be centrally located on the island. Photographs by J. W. Tunnell.

**54.** Time series (1978–1993) of photographs looking southeast from the top of the lighthouse at the south end of Isla de Enmedio. Note the position of the palm tree relative to the beach: **(a)** 1978, **(b)** 1984, **(c)** 1988, **(d)** 1989, **(e)** 1990 (palm tree dying on beach), **(f)** 1991 (palm tree dead, only trunk remains), **(g)** 1993 (palm tree gone). Photographs by J. W. Tunnell.

**55.** Colonial nesting seabirds on Campeche Bank reef islands. **(a)** Masked booby, central Isla Desertora, Alacrán Reef, January 1986. **(b)** Magnificent frigatebirds in *Tournefortia gnaphalodes* on the northern part of Isla Desertora, Alacrán Reef, January 1986. **(c)** Immature magnificent frigatebirds on dead *T. gnaphalodes* (killed by excessive guano) on Cayo Centro, Cayos Arcas, April 1986. **(d)** Immature magnificent frigatebirds ground-nesting on Cayo Este, Cayos Arcas, April 1986. Photographs by J. W. Tunnell.

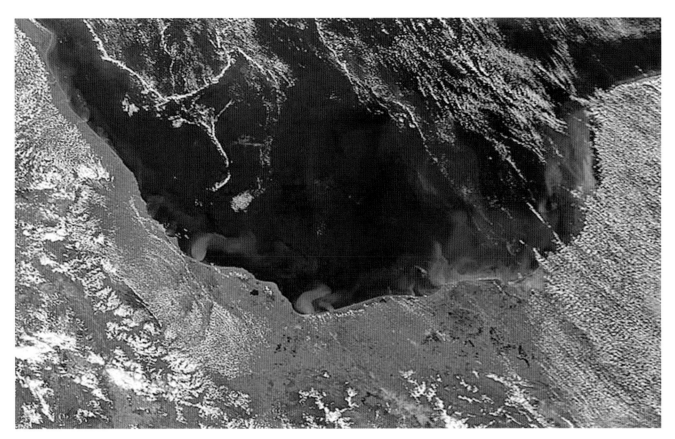

**56.** Sediment plumes at the outlets of the main river systems in the southern Gulf of Mexico. Left to right: Papaloapan-Blanco discharge from Laguna Alvarado, Coatzacoalcos, and Usuma-cinta-Grijalva. The Veracruz Reef System can be seen just west (left) of the Papaloapan-Blanco discharge. Image courtesy of NASA Visible Earth.

**57.** Example of reef rock **(a)** and algae **(b)** covered by sediment. Photograph by Gary Haralson (from Cozumel, 2002).

**58.** Freshwater inflow to Veracruz Reef System: **(a)** River discharge from Rio Jamapa, between Veracruz and Antón Lizardo reefs, September 2002; **(b)** terrestrial wood debris and trash, June 1993, and **(c)** freshwater hyacinths and wood debris, June 1983, on leeward shore of Enmedio Reef. Photographs by J. W. Tunnell.

**63**. Fort San Juan de Ulúa, which protects Veracruz harbor, was built between the 16th and 19th centuries completely from coral reef rock, known locally as *piedra de mucar* (July 1978). **(a)** View to the southwest across the port. **(b)** View to the southeast toward Isla Sacrificios. Photographs by J. W. Tunnell.

**58.** Freshwater inflow to Veracruz Reef System: **(a)** River discharge from Rio Jamapa, between Veracruz and Antón Lizardo reefs, September 2002; **(b)** terrestrial wood debris and trash, June 1993, and **(c)** freshwater hyacinths and wood debris, June 1983, on leeward shore of Enmedio Reef. Photographs by J. W. Tunnell.

**59.** Westward view from Isla de Enmedio lighthouse over the leeward reef platform. **(a)** Calm, clear water during the summer, June 1978. **(b)** High winds and significant turbidity during a winter *norte*, January 1979. Photographs by J. W. Tunnell.

**60.** Storm-tossed boulders, evidence of former hurricanes, on the windward reef flat of Isla de Enmedio Reef, June 1990. Photograph by J. W. Tunnell.

**61.** Long-spined sea urchin (*Diadema antillarum*), Flower Garden Banks National Marine Sanctuary, March 2006. The sea urchin were abundant throughout the Veracruz Reef System until the Caribbean and Gulf-wide 1983 die-off. Photograph by Gary Haralson.

**62.** Bleached coral that has lost its symbiotic algae (zooxanthellae), due to an environmental stress of some kind (e.g., elevated temperature). (Photo example unavailable for southern Gulf of Mexico; this example is from the Dry Tortugas in 2004, courtesy of the Florida Marine Research Institute).

**63.** Fort San Juan de Ulúa, which protects Veracruz harbor, was built between the 16th and 19th centuries completely from coral reef rock, known locally as *piedra de mucar* (July 1978). **(a)** View to the southwest across the port. **(b)** View to the southeast toward Isla Sacrificios. Photographs by J. W. Tunnell.

**64.** Earthen landfill on Gallega Reef platform, which forms the Port of Veracruz. **(a)** View to the southeast, including the harbor entrance and the drydock and shipyard, August 2002. **(b)** View to the southwest over container dock toward downtown Veracruz, August 2002. **(c)** Ground view of the earthen landfill rubble, November 1987. Photographs by J. W. Tunnell.

**65.** Ship groundings on reefs of the Veracruz Reef System. **(a)** Southwest leeward side of Isla de Lobos, 8 m, June 1976. **(b)** Southeast windward forereef of Anegada de Adentro, August 2002. Photographs by J. W. Tunnell.

**66.** Extensive shoreline development at Punta Mocambo. **(a)** View looking northwest toward Veracruz city. **(b)** View looking westward just north of Punta Mocambo, August 2002. Photographs by © Kip Evans, National Geographic Society.

**67.** Sugarcane, which requires high applications of fertilizers and pesticides, is an important agriculture crop in central and southern coastal Veracruz. **(a)** Sugarcane fields in the San Andres Tuxtlas area south of Veracruz city, July 1980. **(b)** Sugar "refinery," July 1976. Photographs by J. W. Tunnell.

**68.** PEMEX operations for petroleum products at Isla de Lobos, June 1976. **(a)** Production platform sitting on top of the windward reef flat. **(b)** Docking facilities and dredged channel leading to the well platform. Photographs by J. W. Tunnell.

**69.** Ixtoc 1 oil spill impacts on the Veracruz Reef System, October 1979. **(a)** Floating oil and water hyacinths between Isla de Enmedio and Antón Lizardo. **(b)** Tar mat 0.3 m deep on the leeward subtidal beach of Isla de Enmedio, showing footprints. Photographs by Q. R. Dokken.

bands of *M. annularis* from 1974 through 1991 showed no indication of an increase in the skeletal concentrations of any metal through time. Thus, metal concentrations in coral skeletons have been more or less without significant change through the period of observations. Iron also has been determined in leaves of the seagrass *Thalassia testudinum* from Hornos and Punta Mocambo reefs. The levels are at least 2–5 times higher than those recorded for other Mexican localities (Duarte et al. 1995). There are no metal records in sediments and water in the area. Therefore, from the coral data, it may be considered that the VRS is a heavy metal–contaminated area.

# 13  Conservation and Management

ERNESTO A. CHÁVEZ AND JOHN W. TUNNELL JR.

Coral reef ecosystems in the southern Gulf of Mexico provide services (e.g., fishery support, storm protection) and revenue (e.g., fishing, tourism, oil exploration) in a variety of ways to adjacent coastal communities. Loss of these coral reef resources would have tremendous social impacts related to loss of work, income, and potentially, an important food source for many artisanal fishing communities. The value of natural capital like coral reefs is determined by estimating how changes in the services they provide will affect human welfare (Costanza et al. 1997). The value of coral reefs has been estimated at $6,075.00 ha$^{-1}$ yr$^{-1}$. The coral reefs of the southern Gulf of Mexico cover an area of approximately 33,024 ha, with a total annual value of $200,622,471 (Table 13.1). Because of the value of these ecosystems and because the activities that provide much-needed income and/or food to coastal communities have great potential to disturb or destroy the reefs, it is crucial to understand the threats to the health of these ecosystems so that workable management strategies for conservation and sustainable use can be formulated.

Natural and anthropogenic threats to coral reefs in the southern Gulf of Mexico were detailed by Horta-Puga in chapter 12 (this volume). Briefly, natural disturbances to these reefs are sedimentation and low salinity due to river inflow (Veracruz reefs only), meteorological events (winter cold fronts, tropical cyclones), reef species die-off (especially the long-spined sea urchin *Diadema* and scleractinian corals in the genus *Acropora*), increased sea-surface temperatures, coral bleaching and disease, and algal blooms, including red tides (Table 13.2). Anthropogenic disturbances that affect the reefs are coastal construction, dredging and filling, including mangrove destruction, point and nonpoint source pollution, especially organic enrichment from untreated sewage effluent, watershed deforestation and concomitant increased sedimentation and freshwater inflow, boat traffic (anchoring, ship grounding), tourism (littering, trampling, diver damage, coral collection), fishing and overfishing, and historically, coral mining for building materials. Many natural disturbances can be exacerbated by anthropogenic disturbances, such as algal blooms (organic enrichment) and sedimentation impacts (deforestation).

The reefs in the Gulf of Mexico have been moderately to severely impacted by human activities (Chávez and Hidalgo 1988, 1989; Chávez and Tunnell 1993, Tunnell 1992; Vergara et al. 2000). The Veracruz reefs have suffered the greatest damage, due to their proximity to the coast and coastal drainages and to important population centers and ports such as Veracruz, Tuxpan, and Coatzacoalcos. Coral cover on Veracruz reefs has been reduced to 17% or less (Horta-Puga 2003), primarily due to increased sedimentation resulting from changing land use upstream and due to fishing and tourism activities. Coastal development, especially near the city of Veracruz, has significantly impacted the reefs

**Table 13.1.** *Annual value of services that the coral reef systems of the southern Gulf of Mexico provide to society as a part of the life support systems contributing to human welfare.*

| Reef zone | Hectares | Value (U.S. dollars) |
|---|---|---|
| Blanquilla-Medio-Lobos | 67.9 | 412,493 |
| Tanguijo-Medio-Tuxpan | 37.5 | 227,813 |
| Veracruz northern reefs | 906.4 | 5,506,608 |
| Veracruz southern reefs | 3,612.4 | 21,945,558 |
| Arcas-Arenas-Nuevo-Obispos-Triángulos | 2,000.0 | 12,150,000 |
| Alacrán | 26,400.0 | 160,380,000 |
| **Total** | 33,024.3 | 200,622,471 |

*Note:* Based on estimates of annual value per year from Costanza et al. (1997).

through increased turbidity and organic loading. Deforestation of upper ridges of the Sierra Madre Oriental has led to erosion, causing significant siltation of these reefs, and this problem is often aggravated by the input of fertilizers, pesticides, and other pollutants from agricultural practices on the coastal plains. Less than 10% of wastewater receives treatment before being discharged into coastal waters, causing eutrophication and accelerated algal growth. In addition, tourist-related threats have increased tremendously. Both commercial and recreational fishing pressures and spear fishing have led to significant declines in fish, lobster (*Panulirus* spp.), conch (*Strombus* spp.), and coral populations.

The Campeche Bank reefs are in better condition due to greater distance from shore, low human population on adjacent coastlines, and no freshwater inflow. However, the oil terminal near Cayo Arcas, associated construction activities, tanker traffic, and offshore oil reserves adjacent to the reefs as well as tourism-related activities are potential threats.

The reefs in the southern Gulf of México have also been impacted by natural damage from hurricanes. Prolonged algal blooms followed the Caribbean-wide mass mortalities of the long-spined sea urchin in 1983. Reduced herbivory, due to the loss of long-spined sea urchin and chronic overfishing of herbivorous fishes (e.g., parrotfish), has allowed algae to replace coral in many areas (T. J. Nelson 1991). In addition, outbreaks of coral diseases, possibly exacerbated by human-induced stress and global warming, have become a concern during the last few years (Jordán-Dahlgren 2004).

## Current Management Status and Issues

Several initiatives have been put forth for the protection and management of coral reefs in the southern Gulf of Mexico and the Caribbean (González de la Parra et al. 1984; Dirección General de Flora y Fauna Silvestre 1985; SEDUE 1985; Vargas-Hernández, Hernández-Guitérrez, et al. 1994; Ardisson and Durán-Nájera 1997; ICRI 2003). Most coral reefs in the southern Gulf of Mexico are within Marine Protected Areas (MPAs) and/or marine parks established by the Mexican government (Table 13.3; Fig. 13.1). Although management plans exist for all these areas, there is a serious lack of scientific information on which to base these plans, and little money to implement them. Several species of coral and other reef invertebrates are listed as endangered in the Norma Oficial Mexi-

**Table 13.2.** *Natural and human impacts to the coral reef resources of the southern Gulf of Mexico, with selected references.*

| Impacts | Comment (selected reference) |
| --- | --- |
| **Natural** | |
| Freshwater inflow | Southern Veracruz reefs (Tunnell 1988). Nearshore Veracruz reefs (E. Chávez, personal observation). Inflow from the Jamapa, Papaloapan, and Tuxpan rivers. |
| Winter fronts | |
|   Wind, waves, and turbidity | Nearshore Veracruz reefs |
|   Cold thermal stress | Mostly northern Veracruz reefs |
| Hurricanes | All reefs; low frequency; storm tossed boulders on most windward reef crests (Rigby and McIntire 1966) |
| *Diadema* die-off | Concurrent with Caribbean-wide die-off in the 1980s; slow recovery |
| Bleaching | Moderate and localized, not widespread |
| Black-band disease | Not widespread but increasing in recent years |
| **Anthropogenic** | |
| *Oil and gas activities* | |
|   Deballasting chronic small spills | La Blanquilla Reef (Santiago 1977), Cayos Arcas (Chávez and Hidalgo 1988) |
|   Large oil spills | Ixtoc I impacts over most southern Gulf reefs (Jernelov and Linden 1981, Chávez and Hidalgo 1988) |
|   Exploration | Northern Veracruz reefs and Arcas (Chávez and Hidalgo 1988) |
| *Overfishing* | |
|   Clams (*almejas*) | Seagrass beds being destroyed by this fishery on nearshore southern Veracruz reefs |
|   Conch | Exterminated from Veracruz reefs in the 1970s, overfished on Alacrán Reef with 500–2,000 taken per fishing boat per 2-week trip in 1986. |
|   Fish | Snapper and grouper almost depleted on southern Veracruz reefs; commercial spear fishermen now taking many other species (e.g., parrotfish, angelfish, and surgeonfish). |
|   Lobster | Seldom seen on southern Veracruz reefs; overfished on Alacrán and other Campeche Bank reefs. |
|   West Indian seal | Exterminated from Campeche Bank reef islands (Ward 1887, Fosberg 1962). The Caribbean monk seal was formally declared extinct in the 1996 IUCN Red List of Threatened Animals (Baillie and Groombridge 1996). |
| *Municipal and industrial pollution and activities* | Greatest around large cities of Veracruz and Coatzacoalcos |
|   Urban sewage | Nearshore city of Veracruz |
|   Agricultural chemical | Uninvestigated, but potential because of crops in southern state of Veracruz (tobacco, sugarcane, pineapple) |
|   Dredging/Excavation | Channel dredging for oil exploration and production, Lobos Reef (Rigby and McIntire 1966); construction of Fort San Juan de Ulúa, city of Veracruz, La Gallega Reef. |
|   Poor land and river management | Clearing of mangroves from river mouths (Jamapa and Papaloapan rivers) and poor inland practices have increased nearshore sediment load and runoff. |
|   Coral collecting | La Blanquilla (Santiago 1977) and other Veracruz area reefs; many curio shops with local corals in city of Veracruz. |

*(continued)*

**Table 13.2.** (*continued*)

| Impacts | Comment (selected reference) |
|---|---|
| *Commercial wildlife trade* | |
| Personal souvenirs | Mainly nearshore Veracruz reefs |
| *Tourism activities* | |
| Sport diving and tourism | Large numbers of divers on Antón Lizardo reefs on weekends, 2–6 busloads per weekend from Mexico City. |
| Anchor and propeller damage | Mainly from small boats, on reefs and in lagoons (Santiago 1977), especially in the reefs most visited by tourists. |
| *Shipwrecks and groundings* | Several large vessels on Alacrán and Arenas reefs; late 1990 grounding of *New Hope* from Panama on western Chopas Reef; removed mid-1990s. |

*Note:* From Tunnell (1992), with additions and updates.

**Table 13.3.** *Marine Protected Areas where coral reefs of the southern Gulf of Mexico are included.*

| Category | Reef area | | |
|---|---|---|---|
| National park | Veracruz Reef System Alacrán Reef | | |
| Area of protection of natural resources | Port of Veracruz | | |
| Zone for refuge of marine flora and fauna | La Blanquilla Reef (Veracruz Reef System) | | |
| **Marine Protected Area*** | **Characteristics**** | | |
| 47　Pueblo Viejo–Tamiahua | AB | AA | AU |
| 49　Laguna Verde–Antón Lizardo | AB | AA | AU |
| 56　Cayos Campeche | AB | AA | |
| 58　Arrecife Alacranes | AB | AA | AU |
| 59　Sonda de Campeche | AB | AA | AU |

*Note:* From Cabrera et al. (1998); CONABIO (2004).

　* Numbers correspond to locations of Marine Protected Areas on Figure 13.1.

　**AB = areas of high biodiversity; AA = areas whose biodiversity is threatened; AU = areas in use by some sectors of activity (CONABIO 2004).

cana (Mexican code of laws and regulations), despite the fact that their bathymetric distributions are essentially unknown and there are few resources available for their protection.

An environmental survey has been conducted on the Caribbean Meso-American Barrier Reef System (MBRS; Sale et al. 1999). The MBRS survey evaluated environmental monitoring activities and made recommendations for regionwide monitoring of ecosystem "health," the implementation of a regional environmental information system, a regional research program to provide baseline information on the MBRS, improved techniques for monitoring water quality, and improvements to collecting fishery catch statistics. It was expected that enhanced monitoring and protection of this area would help Mexico strengthen and coordinate its national policies, regulations, and institutional arrangements

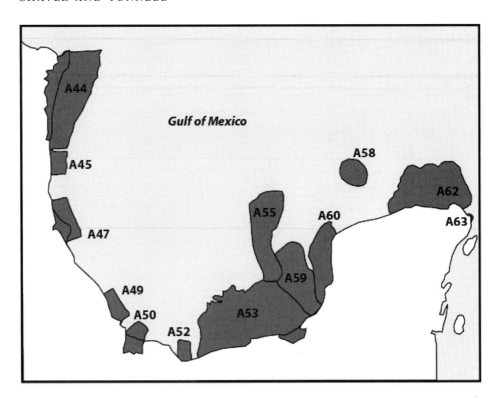

**Figure 13.1.** Marine regions with high diversity and marine protected areas identified by the Mexican Commission for the Knowledge and Use of Biodiversity (CONABIO), where priority conservation efforts are proposed within a framework of integrated coastal management (modified from Cabrera et al. 1998). Areas containing coral reefs are A47 (Pueblo Viejo-Tamiahua); A49 (Laguna Verde-Antón Lizardo); A56 (Cays of Campeche); A58 (Alacran Reef); and A59 (Campeche Bank). See also Table 13.3 and CONABIO (2004).

for marine ecosystem conservation so that sustainable use could be achieved. In Mexico, there is strong concurrence among these topics and those adopted by the International Coral Reef Initiative (ICRI), a partnership among governments and international and nongovernmental organizations that strives to preserve coral reefs and related ecosystems. In addition, among the three actions proposed in the MBRS report (Sale et al. 1999), one is particularly pertinent and should be adopted for the Gulf of Mexico. It states that there is a need to "implement an interdisciplinary regional . . . collection of synoptic data on physical oceanography and ecological connections among reefs, and between reefs and adjacent ecosystems, including coastal watersheds."

A research program similar to that conducted on the MBRS (Sale et al. 1999) is needed for the coral reefs of the southern Gulf of Mexico. Any national research program that would develop conservation strategies for coral reefs of the Gulf of Mexico must address the problem of too little recent or historical data on these reefs, particularly with regard to reef management and the effects of current reef impacts. These data are critical for conservation, management, and decision making within the MPAs and marine parks in the southern Gulf of México. The goals of this research program should be as follows:

- Determine baseline conditions (e.g., water quality, species diversity, fishing effort) that exist at reefs and adjacent coastlines and watersheds.
- Characterize the ecology of reefs and surrounding areas, including trophic structure and community organization.
- Identify and prioritize conservation issues.
- Identify and prioritize threats, impacts, and already stressed areas.
- Determine if available legal protections and legislative tools are adequate.
- Determine the funding needs of already established MPAs and marine parks in the southern Gulf of México.

- Provide recommendations for the management and conservation of the coral reefs of the southern Gulf of Mexico and adjacent coastlines and ecosystems.

In addition, the proposed research program should adopt the Cartagena Convention's Protocol on Specially Protected Areas and Wildlife (SPAW), which calls for the establishment of a regional network of protected areas in order to conserve, maintain, and restore ecosystems, and in particular, to maintain the "ecological and biological processes essential to the functioning of the Wider Caribbean ecosystems." Strategies that support this purpose include the establishment of networks of MPAs and the development of management plans, which have been implemented to some extent in the southern Gulf of Mexico, monitoring of environmental trends (including pollution) in fragile ecosystems and threatened species, which would be accomplished through the research program described above, and training in coastal zone management.

An effort in this direction was the national consultation (Cabrera et al. 1998) completed under the auspices of the Comisión Nacional para el Conocimiento y Uso de la Biodiversidad (Mexican National Commission for the Knowledge and Use of Biodiversity) (CONABIO 2004). This document proposed development of priority conservation efforts within a framework of integrated coastal management for marine protected areas and marine regions with high diversity. For each such area, a "technical fiche" was developed that contained general information on the area's geographic location, climatic characteristics, geology, and oceanographic features, as well as biological data, use of resources, economic aspects, and problems of use and conservation. The report recommended several coral reef ecosystems of the southern Gulf of Mexico for priority conservation efforts (see Fig. 13.1): regions A47 (Pueblo Viejo–Tamiahua), A49 (Laguna Verde–Antón Lizardo), A56 (Cayos Campeche), A58 (Arrecife Alacranes), and A62 (Dzilam-Contoy).

## Future Considerations

Major current and future conservation issues for coral reefs in the southern Gulf of Mexico are the following:

- Insufficient scientific monitoring of coral reef health due to a lack of resources and/or regional capacity.
- Insufficient information about the location of biodiversity "hot spots," recruitment sources and sinks for corals, fishes, and other community components, and "at risk" areas.
- Lack of both funds and personnel to enforce regulations that limit overfishing and other activities that are detrimental to reef areas.
- Unabated sedimentation and eutrophication in coral reef areas due to the lack of wise land-use practices in coastal watersheds and of integrated coastal zone management plans.
- Lack of coral reef management plans that are based on ecosystem functioning, and few funds for their implementation, once formulated.
- Lack of public education aimed at alerting stakeholders to the consequences of anthropogenic impacts.

A vast amount of information, both printed and electronic, concerning coral reef programs, initiatives, and organizations is now available to assist countries in the management and restoration of coral reefs. Because our intent is not just to point out the problems but to offer a framework for management and conservation solutions for the reefs in the southern Gulf of Mexico, we offer information on two leading programs that exist in the United States and Australia.

In the United States, the U.S. Coral Reef Task Force (CRTF), established by Presidential Executive Order in 1998, leads U.S. efforts to preserve and protect coral reef ecosystems. The National Coral Reef Action Strategy was developed in 2002 based on the U.S. National Action Plan to Conserve Coral Reefs. This strategy was produced by the National Oceanic and Atmospheric Administration (NOAA) in cooperation with the U.S. CRTF to fulfill the requirements of the Coral Reef Conservation Act of 2000 (NOAA 2002a). The strategy is divided into two fundamental themes and 13 goals essential to addressing and reducing the threats to coral reefs around the world:

THEME 1: UNDERSTAND CORAL REEF ECOSYSTEMS    Better understanding of complex coral reef ecosystems will improve management and conservation of these valuable resources. The strategy outlines the following major goals to increase understanding of coral reef ecosystems:

1. Create comprehensive maps of all U.S. coral reef habitats.
2. Conduct long-term monitoring and assessments of reef ecosystem condition.
3. Support strategic research to address the major threats to reef ecosystems.
4. Increase understanding of the social and economic factors of conserving coral reefs.

THEME 2: REDUCE THE ADVERSE IMPACTS OF HUMAN ACTIVITIES    Reducing the impacts of human activities is essential to conserving coral reef ecosystems. The strategy outlines the following major goals to reduce the adverse impacts of human activities:

5. Improve the use of marine protected areas to reduce threats.
6. Reduce adverse impacts of fishing and other extractive uses.
7. Reduce impacts of coastal uses.
8. Reduce pollution.
9. Restore damaged reefs.
10. Improve education and outreach.
11. Reduce international threats to coral reef ecosystems.
12. Reduce impacts from international trade in coral reef species.
13. Improve coordination and accountability.

For full information on this strategy, see http://www.coralreef.noaa.gov. For more extensive information about coral reefs (mapping, biodiversity studies, biological population surveys, climate studies, monitoring, and coral bleaching forecasts), refer to NOAA's Coral Reef Information System (CoRIS) at http://www.coris.noaa.gov.

In Australia, the Global Coral Reef Monitoring Network (GCRMN) provides the largest and most systematic monitoring network for coral reefs in the world. Under the leadership of Clive Wilkinson, GCRMN has produced four global reports on the *Status of Coral Reefs of the World* (Wilkinson 1998,

2000, 2002, 2004). The latest report contains recommendations from more than 80 countries for specific actions that can be taken to halt the decline in coral reef destruction. Most countries and organizations agree with and support the action agenda of the International Coral Reef Initiative:

- Using Integrated Coastal Management (ICM) to reduce land-based sources of pollution from poor land-use practices that deliver excess sediments and nutrients onto coral reefs (e.g., from deforestation, unsustainable agriculture, and untreated domestic and industrial wastes).
- Reducing or diverting fishing effort to avoid overexploitation and specifically stopping destructive practices such as bomb and cyanide fishing.
- Developing interconnected networks of MPAs to support the effective flow of larvae from coral reefs and the maintenance of vital ecosystem processes.
- Ensuring that the current MPAs are effectively managed with adequate financial logistic and, especially, human resources.
- Focusing on developing MPAs that have higher resilience and resistance to global threats such as coral bleaching and disease and also on protecting reefs with healthy and reproducing populations of coral reef species.
- Developing alternative livelihoods for coastal communities to reduce the need to exploit reef resources (e.g., ecotourism, sustainable aquaculture of food and aquarium species, more effective agriculture, and community industries based on traditional cultures).
- Expanding research and monitoring capacity in more countries, especially small, developing states, and undertaking the fundamental research needed for sound and adaptive management of coral reefs.
- Improving the capacity of governments and nongovernmental organizations for monitoring, enforcement, and surveillance in support of coral reef management and implementing integrated ocean governance.

Most recently, the United States Commission on Ocean Policy (USCOP) released its final report, *An Ocean Blueprint for the 21st Century* (http://www .oceancommission.gov), on September 20, 2004, and President George W. Bush provided his response, *U.S. Ocean Action Plan*, on December 17, 2004. Both of these documents call for a strengthened U.S. Coral Reef Task Force and also note that the United States should be a leader in providing coral management at an international level. All of the following "guiding principles" of the USCOP report are pertinent for consideration for management and conservation of the southern Gulf of Mexico coral reefs:

- Sustainability: Ocean policy should be designed to meet the needs of the present generation without compromising the ability of future generations to meet their needs.
- Stewardship: The principle of stewardship applies both to the government and to every citizen. The U.S. government holds ocean and coastal resources in the public trust—a special responsibility that necessitates balancing different uses of those resources for the continued benefit of all Americans. Just as important, every member of the public should recognize the value of the oceans and coasts, supporting appropriate policies and acting responsibly while minimizing negative environmental impacts.
- Ocean-Land-Atmosphere Connections: Ocean policies should be based on the recognition that the oceans, land, and atmosphere are inextricably inter-

twined and that actions that affect one Earth system component are likely to affect another.

- Ecosystem-based Management: U.S. ocean and coastal resources should be managed to reflect the relationships among all ecosystem components, including humans and nonhuman species and the environments in which they live. Applying this principle will require defining relevant geographic management areas based on ecosystem, rather than political, boundaries.
- Multiple Use Management: The many potentially beneficial uses of ocean and coastal resources should be acknowledged and managed in a way that balances competing uses while preserving and protecting the overall integrity of the ocean and coastal environments.
- Preservation of Marine Biodiversity: Downward trends in marine biodiversity should be reversed where they exist, with the desired end of maintaining or recovering natural levels of biological diversity and ecosystem services.
- Best Available Science and Information: Ocean policy decisions should be based on the best available understanding of the natural, social, and economic processes that affect ocean and coastal environments. Decision makers should be able to obtain and understand quality science and information in a way that facilitates successful management of ocean and coastal resources.
- Adaptive Management: Ocean management programs should be designed to meet clear goals and provide new information to continually improve the scientific basis for future management. Periodic reevaluation of the goals and effectiveness of management measures, and incorporation of new information in implementing future management, are essential.
- Understandable Laws and Clear Decisions: Laws governing uses of ocean and coastal resources should be clear, coordinated, and accessible to the nation's citizens to facilitate compliance. Policy decisions and the reasoning behind them should also be clear and available to all interested parties.
- Participatory Governance: Governance of ocean uses should ensure widespread participation by all citizens on issues that affect them.
- Timeliness: Ocean governance systems should operate with as much efficiency and predictability as possible.
- Accountability: Decision makers and members of the public should be accountable for the actions they take that affect ocean and coastal resources.
- International Responsibility: The United States should act cooperatively with other nations in developing and implementing international ocean policy, reflecting the deep connections between U.S. interests and the global ocean.

In addition to these overarching guiding principles, one chapter was devoted in its entirety to coral reefs. Although most of the five recommendations were specific to U.S. legislation and action, Recommendation 21–1 proposed the establishment of a "Coral Protection and Management Act" that enhances research, protection, management, and restoration of coral ecosystems. The recommendation suggested that the new legislation should include the following elements (in part):

- Mapping, monitoring, assessment, and research programs to fill critical information gaps.

- Increased protections for vulnerable coral reefs, including the use of marine protected areas.
- Liability provisions for damages to coral reefs with flexibility to use funds in a manner that provides maximum short- and long-term benefits to the reef.
- Support for state-level coral reef management.
- Outreach activities to educate the public about coral conservation and reduce human impacts.
- Support for U.S. [and Mexican] involvement, particularly through the sharing of scientific and management expertise, in bilateral, regional, and international coral reef management programs.

Similar legislation in Mexico would establish a conservation and protection plan so that these reefs and their associated resources will remain viable for the long term. The needs of the resource are clear. The strategies to accomplish its conservation are available. Together, we must now act.

# Acronyms

| | |
|---|---|
| ALC | Alacrán Reef |
| CAC | Cayos Arcas (reefs) |
| CAE | Cayo Arenas (reef) |
| CBR | Campeche Bank Reefs |
| CINVESTAV | Centro de Investigación y Estudios Avanzados (Center of Research and Advanced Studies) |
| CNA | Comisión Nacional del Agua (National Commission on Water) |
| CONABIO | Comisión Nacional Para el Conocimiento y Uso de la Biodiversidad (National Commission for the Knowledge and Use of Biodiversity) |
| CONANP | Comisión Nacional de Áreas Naturales Protegidas (National Commission on Natural Protected Areas) |
| CoRIS | Coral Reef Information System |
| CRTF | Coral Reef Task Force |
| DDT | dichlorodiphenyl trichloroethane |
| ECOSUR | El Colegio de la Frontera Sur (College of the Southern Border) |
| ENSO | El Niño–Southern Oscillation |
| FAO | Food and Agriculture Organization (UN) |
| FDA | Food and Drug Administration (U.S.) |
| Ga | billion years before present |
| GCRMN | Global Coral Reef Monitoring Network |
| GCW | Gulf Common Water |
| HRI | Harte Research Institute for Gulf of Mexico Studies |
| ICM | Integrated Coastal Management |
| ICRI | International Coral Reef Initiative |
| INEGI | Instituto Nacional de Estadística Geografía e Informática (National Institute of Geographical Statistics and Computer Science) |
| ITCZ | Intertropical Convergence Zone |
| ka | thousand years before present |
| K-T | Cretaceous-Tertiary |
| LC | Loop Current |
| Ma | million years before present |
| MBRS | Meso-American Barrier Reef System |
| MJO | Madden-Julian Oscillation |
| MN | Mexican Navy |
| MPA | Marine Protected Area |
| MSY | maximum sustainable yield |
| MY | maximum yield |
| NACEC | North American Commission of Economic Cooperation |

| | |
|---|---|
| NGO | nongovernmental organization |
| NOAA | National Oceanic and Atmospheric Administration |
| OSIR | Oil Spill Intelligence Report |
| PAE | phthalate acid ester |
| PCB | polychlorinated biphenyl |
| PEMEX | Petróleos Mexicanos (Mexican Petroleum) |
| psu | practical salinity units |
| SAGARPA | Secretaría de Agricultura, Ganadería, Desarrollo Rural, Pesca, y Alimentación (Secretary of Agriculture, Cattle Ranching, Rural Development, Fisheries, and Food) |
| SAT | surface air temperature |
| SEDUE | Secretaría de Desarrollo Urbano y Ecología (Secretary of Urban Development and Ecology) |
| SEPESCA | Secretaría de Pesca (Secretary of Fisheries) |
| SGM | Southern Gulf of Mexico |
| SPAW | Specially Protected Areas and Wildlife |
| SSE | Sustainable Seas Expedition |
| SST | sea surface temperature |
| SUW | Caribbean Subtropical Underwater |
| TAMU | Texas A&M University |
| TAMU-CC | Texas A&M University–Corpus Christi |
| TRI | Triángulos Reef |
| TRS | Tuxpan Reef System |
| USCOP | United States Commission on Ocean Policy |
| USF | University of South Florida |
| USN | U.S. Navy |
| VRS | Veracruz Reef System |
| VSR | Veracruz Shelf Reefs |
| WGAG | Western Gulf Anticyclone Gyre |
| WCS | World Conservation Strategy |

# Literature Cited

Adey, W. H., and T. Goertemiller. 1987. Coral reef algal turfs: Master producers in nutrient poor seas. *Phycologia* 26 (3): 374–86.

Agassiz, A. 1888. *Three Cruises of the United States Coast and Geodetic Survey Steamer "Blake," in the Gulf of Mexico, in the Caribbean Sea, and along the Atlantic Coast of the United States, from 1877 to 1880,* vol. 1. Boston: Houghton, Mifflin.

Aguayo, S. M., 1965. Notas preliminares en la distribución de copépodos de Veracruz, Veracruz. *Anales de Instituto del Biología* (Universidad Nacional Autónoma de México) 36 (1–2): 161–71.

Alandro-Lubel, M. A., and M. E. Martínez-Murillo. 1999. Epibiotic protozoa (Ciliophora) on a community of *Thalassia testudinum* ex König in a coral reef in Veracruz, Mexico. *Aquatic Botany* 65:239–54.

Albert, L. A., and F. Badillo. 1991. Environmental lead in Mexico. *Reviews of Environmental Contamination and Toxicology* 117:1–48.

Allen, R. L. 1979. *Coenobita clypeatus* (Herbst, 1791) in the western Gulf of Mexico (Decapod, Anomura). *Crustaceana* 36 (1): 109.

———. 1982. The reptant decapods of Enmedio and Lobos coral reefs, Southwestern Gulf of Mexico. M.S. thesis, Corpus Christi State University, Corpus Christi, Tex.

Alvarez, L. W., W. Alvarez, F. Asaro, and H. V. Michel. 1980. Extraterrestrial causes for the Cretaceous-Tertiary extinction. *Science* 208:1095–1108.

Alvarez, R. U., L. Rosales, and A. Carranza-Edwards. 1986. Heavy metals in Blanco River sediments, Veracruz, Mexico. *Anales del Instituto de Ciencias del Mar y Limnologia* (Universidad Nacional Autónoma de México) 13 (2): 1–10.

Andrade, M. G. (*see also* Garduño and Garduño-Andrade). 1989. Distribución de la ictiofauna asociada a los arrecifes coralinos. In *Proceedings of the Workshop Australia-Mexico on Marine Science,* ed. E. A. Chávez, 63–74. Mérida, México: Centro de Investigación y de Estudios Avanzados del Instituto Politécnico Nacional.

Aranda, D. A., E. B. Cárdenas, I. M. Morales, A. Z. Zárate, and T. Brulé. 2003. A review of the reproductive patterns of gastropod mollusks from Mexico. *Bulletin of Marine Science* 73 (3): 629–41.

Ardisson, P. L., and J. J. Durán-Nájera. 1997. *Programa de Manejo del Parque Marino Nacional Arrecife Alacranes.* Mérida, Mexico: Centro de Investigación y de Estudios Avanzados del IPN, Unidad Mérida, Programa Nacional de Apoyo para las Empresas de Solidaridad y el Instituto Nacional de Ecología.

Aronson, R. B., and W. F. Precht. 2001. Evolutionary paleoecology of Caribbean coral reefs. In *The Ecological Context of Macroevolutionary Change,* ed. W. D. Allmon, and J. Bottjer, 171–233. New York: Columbia University Press.

Aronson, R. B., W. F. Precht, T. J. T. Murdoch, and M. L. Robbart. 2005. Long-term persistence of coral assemblages on the Flower Garden Banks, northwestern Gulf of Mexico: Implications for science and management. *Gulf of Mexico Science* 23 (1): 84–94.

Baca, B. J., T. M. Schmidt, and J. W. Tunnell. 1982. IXTOC oil in the seagrass beds surrounding Isla de Enmedio. Paper presented at the Simposio Internacional IXTOC-I, June 2–5, Mexico City.

Báez, A., F. Gonzalez, F. Solorio, and R. Belmont. 1980. Determinacion de plomo, cadmio y cromo en la precipitacion pluvial de alcunos lugares de la Republica Mexicana. *TIT, Medio Ambiente*, no. 21, 35–46.

Badillo, G. J. F. 1986. Evaluacion preliminary de la contaminacion por metales pesados en el Rio Blanco, Veracruz. Tesis Lic. Biol., Universidad Nacional Autónoma de México, ENEPI.

Baillie, J., and B. Groombridge, comps. and eds., 1996. *1996 IUCN Red List of Threatened Animals*. Gland, Switzerland, and Cambridge, UK: International Union for the Conservation of Nature (IUCN).

Baker, F. C. 1891. Notes on a collection of shells from southern Mexico. *Proceedings of the Academy of Natural Sciences of Philadelphia* 43:45–55.

Bakker, R. T. 1986. *The Dinosaur Heresies*. New York: William Morrow.

Basurto, M., O. Cruz, D. Martínez, and P. Cadena. 2002. Caracol del Caribe *Strombus gigas*. In *Sustentabilidad y Pesca Responsable en México, Evaluación y Manejo 1999–2000*, ed. M. A. Cisneros-Mata, L. F. Meléndez-Moreno, E. Zárate-Becerra, M. T. Gaspar-Dillanes, L. C. López-González, C. Saucedo-Ruiz, and J. Tovar-Avila, 727–44. CD edition. México, D.F.: Instituto Nacional de la Pesca.

Baughman, J. L. 1952. The marine fisheries of the Mayas as given in Diego de Landa's "Relacion de las cosas de Yucatan" with notes on the probable identification of fishes. *Texas Journal of Science* 4:433–58.

Bautista-Gil, M. L., and E. A. Chávez. 1977. Contribución al conocimiento de los foraminíferos del arrecife de Lobos, Veracruz. In *Memorias del V Congreso Nacional de Oceanografía, Guaymas, Sonora, México, 22–25 de Octubre 1974*, ed. F. Manrique, 90–103. n.p.

Beaver, C. R., K. J. P. Deslarzes, J. H. Hudson, and J. W. Tunnell. 1996. Fluorescent banding in reef corals as evidence of increased (organic) runoff into the southern Veracruz coral reef complex (Abstract). *Eighth International Coral Reef Symposium* (Panama City, Panama, June 24–29, 1996), 14.

Beaver, C. R., S. A. Earle, E. F. Evans, A. V. de la Cerda, and J. W. Tunnell Jr. 2004. Mass spawning of reef corals within the Veracruz Reef System, Veracruz, Mexico. *Coral Reefs* 23 (3): 324.

Behringer, D. W., R. L. Molinari, and J. R. Festa. 1997. The variability of anticyclonic current patterns in the Gulf of Mexico. *Journal of Geophysical Research* 82:5469–76.

Beltrán-Torres, A., and J. P. Carricart-Ganivet. 1993. Skeletal morphologic variation in *Montastraea cavernosa* (Cnidaria: Scleractinia) at Isla Verde Coral Reef, Veracruz, México. *Revista de Biología Tropical* 41 (3): 559–62.

———. 1999. Lista revisada y clave para los corales pétreos zooxantelados (Hydrozoa: Milleporina; Anthozoa: Scleractinia) del Atlántico mexicano. *Revista de Biología Tropical* 47 (4): 813–29.

Benítez, J. A., C. Barcenas, and L. Albert. 1993. Patterns of pesticide use in coastal zones of the Gulf of Mexico. In *First World Congress, Society of Environmental Toxicology and Chemistry (SETAC), 28–31 March*, 134–35. Lisbon, Portugal: n.p.

Berner, T. 1990. Coral-reef algae. In *Coral Reefs*, vol. 25 of *Ecosystems of the World*, ed. Z. Dubinsky, 253–64. Amsterdam: Elsevier.

Blaha, J., and W. Sturges. 1981. Evidence for wind-forced circulation in the Gulf of Mexico. *Journal of Marine Research* 39:711–34.

Blanchon, P., and C. T. Perry. 2004. Taphonomic differentiation of *Acropora palmata* facies in cores from Campeche Bank Reefs, Gulf of México. *Sedimentology* 51:53–76.

Bonet, F. 1967. Biogeología subsuperficial del Arrecife Alacranes, Yucatán. *Boletín del Instituto de Geología* (Universidad Nacional Autónoma de México) 80:1–192.

Bonet, F., and J. Rzedowski. 1962. La vegetación de las islas del Arrecife Alacranes, Yucatán (México). *Anales de la Escuela Nacional de Ciencias Biológicas* (México) 6 (1–4): 15–59.

Bosellini, F. R., A. Russo, and A. Vescogni. 2001. Messinian reef-building assemblages of the Salento Peninsula (southern Italy): Palaeobathymetric and palaeoclimatic significance. *Palaeogeography, Palaeoclimatology, Palaeoecology* 175:7–26.

Bosscher, H., and W. Schlager. 1992. Computer simulation of reef growth. *Sedimentology* 39:503–12.

Boswall, J. 1978. The birds of Alacran Reef, Gulf of Mexico. *Bulletin of the British Ornithologists' Club* 98 (3): 99–109.

Botello, A. V. 1979. Niveles actuales de hidrocarburos fósiles en ecosistemas estuarinos del Golfo de México. *Anales del Instituto de Ciencias del Mar y Limnologia* (Universidad Nacional Autónoma de México) 1:7–14.

Botello, A. V., S. Castro, L. Celis, and J. Cortes. 1981. Concentración de hidrocarburos fósiles en sedimentos marinos recientes de las cercanías al Puerto de Veracruz, México. Unpublished technical report, Instituto de Ciencias del Mar y Limnología, Universidad Nacional Autónoma de México.

Botello, A. V., G. P. Veléz, A. Toledo, G. D. González, and S. Villanueva. 1992. Ecología, recursos costeros y contaminación en el Golfo de México: Ciencia y desarrollo. *CONACYT* 17 (102): 28–48.

Boudreaux, W. W. 1987. Comparisons of molluscan reef flat assemblages from four reefs of the Campeche Bank, Yucatan, Mexico. M.S. nonthesis project, Corpus Christi State University, Corpus Christi, Tex.

Briggs, J. C. 1974. *Marine Zoogeography.* New York: McGraw-Hill.

Britton, J. C., and B. Morton. 1989. *Shore Ecology of the Gulf of Mexico.* Austin: University of Texas Press.

Brooks, D. A., and R. V. Legeckis. 1982. A ship and satellite view of hydrographic features in the western Gulf of Mexico. *Journal of Geophysical Research* 87:4195–4206.

Brulé, T., X. Renán, T. Colás-Marrufo, Y. Hauyon, and A. N. Tuz-Sulub. 2003. Reproduction in the protogynous black grouper (*Mycteroperca bonaci* [Poey]) from the southern Gulf of Mexico. *Fishery Bulletin* 101:463–75.

Bryant, W. R., J. Lugo, C. Cordova, and A. Salvador. 1991. Physiography and bathymetry. In *Gulf of Mexico Basin,* ed. A. Salvador, 13–30. Vol. J of *The Geology of North America.* Boulder, Colo.: Geological Society of America.

Buddemeier, R. W., and D. G. Fautin. 1993. Coral bleaching as an adaptive mechanism: A testable hypothesis. *BioScience* 43 (5): 320–26.

Bunge, L., J. Ochoa, A. Badan, J. Candela, and J. Sheinbaum. 2002. Deep flows in the Yucatan Channel and their relation to changes in the Loop Current extension. *Journal of Geophysical Research* 107 (C12): 3233, doi:10.1029/2001JC001256.

Burke, L., and J. Maidens. 2004. *Reefs at Risk in the Caribbean.* Washington, D.C.: World Resources Institute.

Busby, R. F. 1966. *Sediments and Reef Corals of Cayo Arenas, Campeche Bank, Yucatan, Mexico.* Technical report TR-187. Washington, D.C.: U.S. Naval Oceanographic Office.

Cabrera, L. A., E. Vázquez-Domínguez, J. González-Cano, R. J. Rosenberg, E. M. López, and V. A. Sierra, coordinators. 1998. *Regiones Prioritarias Marinas de México.* México, D.F.: Comisión Nacional para el Conocimiento y Uso de la Biodiversidad.

Cabrera J., J. A. 1965. Contribuciones Carcinológicas I: El primer estadio zoea en *Gecarcinus lateralis* (Freminville) (Brachyura Gecarcinidae) procedente de Veracruz, México. *Anales del Instituto de Biología* (Universidad Nacional Autónoma de México) 36:173–87.

Cairns, S. D. 1982. Stony corals (Cnidaria, Hydrozoa, Scleractinia) of Carrie Bow Cay, Belize. *Smithsonian Contributions in Marine Science* 12:271–302.

Carpenter, R. C. 1990. Mass mortality of *Diadema antillarum,* I: Long-term effects on sea urchin population-dynamics and coral reef algal communities. *Marine Biology* 104:67–77.

Carr, A. F., A. Meylan, J. Mortimer, K. Bjorndal, and T. Carr. 1982. *Surveys of Sea Turtle Populations and Habitats in the Western Atlantic.* NOAA Technical memorandum NMFS-SEFC-91. Panama City, Fla.: U.S. Department of Commerce, National Oceanic and Atmospheric Administration, National Marine Fisheries Service.

Carranza-Edwards, A., L. Rosales-Hoz, and A. Monreal-Gomez. 1993. Suspended sediments in the southeastern Gulf of Mexico. *Marine Geology* 112:257–69.

Carricart-Ganivet, J. P. (*see also* Ganivet). 1993. Blanqueamiento parcial en *Porites porites* (Cnidaria: Scleractinia) en el Arrecife de Isla Verde, Veracruz, México. *Revista de Biología Tropical* 41 (3): 495–98.

———. 1994. Distribución de zooxanthelas y pigmentos clorofílicos en el coral hermatípico *Montastraea cavernosa* (Linneo, 1767) en relación con la profundidad y época del año en un arrecife veracruzano. Tesis de maestría,

ENEP, Iztacala, Universidad Nacional Autónoma de México, México, D.F.

———. 2004. Sea surface temperature and the growth of the West Atlantic reef-building coral *Montastraea annularis*. *Journal of Experimental Marine Ecology* 302:249–60.

Carricart-Ganivet, J. P., and A. U. Beltrán-Torres. 1993. Zooxanthellae and chlorophyll *a* responses in the scleractinian coral *Montastraea cavernosa* at Triangulos-W. Reef, Campeche Bank, Mexico. *Revista de Biología Tropica* 41 (3): 491–94.

———. 1994. Relación entre la clorofila*a* y la densidad de zooxantelas en *Montastraea cavernosa* en el Arrecife de Isla Verde, Veracruz, México. *Revista de Investigaciones Marinas* 15 (3): 191–96.

———. 1997. Lista de corales pétreos (Hydrozoa: Milleporina, Stylasterina: Anthozoa: Scleractinia) de aguas someras del Banco de Campeche, México. *Revista de Biología Tropical* 44/45:619–22.

Carricart-Ganivet, J. P., and G. Horta-Puga. 1993. Arrecifes de coral en México. In *Biodiversidad Marina y Costera de México*, ed. S. I. Salazar-Vallejo and N. E. González, 80-90. México, D.F.: Comisión Nacional para la Biodiversidad y Centro de Investigaciones de Quintana Roo.

Carricart-Ganivet, J. P., G. Horta-Puga, M. A. Ruiz-Zárate, and E. Ruiz-Zárate. 1994. Tasas retrospectivas de crecimiento del coral hermatípico *Montastrea annularis* (Scleractinia: Faviidae) en arrecifes al sur del Golfo de México. *Revista de Biología Tropical* 42 (3): 515–21.

Carricart-Ganivet, J. P., and M. Merino. 2001. Growth responses of the reef-building coral *Montastraea annularis* along a gradient of continental influence in the southern Gulf of Mexico. *Bulletin of Marine Science* 68 (1): 133–46.

Caso, M. E. 1961. Los equinodermos de México. Tesis doctoral, Universidad Nacional Autónoma de México, México, D.F.

Castro, S. 1983. Hidrocarburos disueltos en costas mexicanas 1980–1983. Unpublished report, Instituto de Ciencias del Mar y Limnología, Universidad Nacional Autónoma de México.

Castro-Aguirre, J. L., and A. Márquez-Espinoza. 1981. Contribución al conocimiento de la ictiofauna de la Isla Lobos y zonas adyacentes, Veracruz. Instituto Nacional de la Pesca, Serie Científica, México, no. 22.

Celis, L., A. V. Botello, M. Mendelewicsz, and G. Diaz. 1987. Actividades del proyecto CARIPOL en la zona costera del Golfo de Mexico, I: Hidrocarburos disueltos. *Caribbean Journal of Science* 23 (1): 11–18.

Chamberlain, C. K. 1966. Some Octocorallina of Isla de Lobos, Veracruz, Mexico. *Brigham Young University, Geological Studies* 13:47–54.

Chávez, E. A. 1973. Observaciones generales sobre las comunidades del arrecife de Lobos, Veracruz. *Anales de la Escuela Nacional de Ciencias Biológicas* (México) 20:13–21.

———. 1994. Los recursos marinos de la Península de Yucatán. In *Recursos Faunísticos del Litoral de la Península de Yucatán*, ed. A. Yáñez-Arancibia, 1–12. Universidad Autónoma de Campeche (México). EPOMEX Serie Científica, 2.

———. 1997. Sampling design for the study of Yucatan reefs, Northwestern Caribbean. In *Proceedings of the Eighth International Coral Reef Symposium* (Panama City, Panama, 24–29 June 1996), ed. H. A. Lessios and I. G. Macintyre, 2:1465–70.

———. 1998. Estrategias óptimas de explotación del pulpo de la Sonda de Campeche, México. *Hidrobiológica* 8 (2): 97–105.

Chávez, E. A., and E. Hidalgo. 1988. Los arrecifes coralinos del Caribe noroccidental y Golfo de México en el contexto socioeconómico. *Anales del Instituto de Ciencias del Mar y Limnología* (Universidad Nacional Autónoma de México) 15 (1): 167–76.

———. 1989. The human impact on the coral reef environment in Mexico. In *Proceedings of the Workshop Australia-Mexico on Marine Sciences*, ed. E. A. Chávez, 81-86. Mérida, Mexico: Centro de Investigación y de Estudios Avanzados del IPN.

Chávez, E. A., E. Hidalgo, and M. A. Izaguirre. 1985. A comparative analysis of Yucatan Coral Reefs. In *Proceedings of the Fifth International Coral Reef Congress: Tahiti, 27 May–1 June 1985*, ed. C. Gabrie and V. M. Harmelin, 6:355–61. Moorea, French Polynesia: Antenne Museum-Ephe.

Chávez, E. A., E. Hidalgo, and M. L. Sevilla. 1970. Datos acerca de las comunidades bentónicas del arrecife de Lobos, Veracruz. *Revista de la Sociedad Mexicana de Historia Natural* 31:211–80.

Chávez, E. A., and J. W. Tunnell Jr. 1993. Needs for management and conservation of the Southern Gulf of Mexico. In *Coastal Zone '93: Proceedings of the Eighth Symposium on Coastal and Ocean Management* (July 19–23, 1993, New Orleans, Louisiana), ed. O. T. Magoon, W. S. Wilson, H. Converse, and L. T. Tobin, 2:2040–53. New York: American Society of Civil Engineers.

Chávez, H. 1966. Peces colectados en el Arrecife Triángulos Oeste y en Cayo Arenas, Sonda de Campeche, México. *Acta Zoológica Mexicana* 8 (1): 1–12.

Choucair, P. C. 1992. A quantitative survey of the ichthyofauna of Arrecife de Enmedio, Veracruz, Mexico. M.S. thesis, Corpus Christi State University, Corpus Christi, Tex.

Christensen, V., and D. Pauly. 1993. *Trophic Models of Aquatic Ecosystems.* ICLARM Conference Proceedings, vol. 26. Manila: International Center for Living Aquatic Resources Management; Copenhagen: International Council for the Exploration of the Sea, Danish International Development Agency.

CNA (Comisión Nacional del Agua). 2000. *Compendio Basico del Agua.* CNA, SEMARNAP, Mexico.

Cochrane, J. D. 1963. *Yucatan Current.* Technical Report, Texas A&M University, Ref. 63–18A, 6 -11.

———. 1972. Separation of an anticyclone and subsequent developments in the Loop Current (1969). In *Contributions on the Physical Oceanography of the Gulf of Mexico*, Texas A&M University Oceanographic Studies, ed. L. R. A. Capurro and J. L. Reid, 2:91–106. Houston: Gulf Publishing Co.

CONABIO (Comisión Nacional para el Conocimiento y Uso de la Biodiversidad). 2004. Regiones terrestres prioritarias de México, Sierra de Picachos, RTP76. http://www.conabio.gob.mx/conocimiento/regionalizacion/doctos/Mlistado.html.

Cortés, J. 2003. *Latin American Coral Reefs.* Amsterdam: Elsevier Science.

Costanza, R., R. d'Arge, R. de Groot, S. Farber, M. Grasso, B. Hannon, K. Limburg, S. Naeem, R. V. O'Neill, J. Paruelo, R. G. Raskin, P. Sutton, and M. van den Belt. 1997. The value of the world's ecosystem services and natural capital. *Nature* 387:253–60.

Coto, C. F. (*see also* Flores-Coto). 1965. Notas preliminares sobre la identificación de las apendicularias de las aguas Veracruzanas. *Anales del Instituto de Biología, Serie Hidrobiología* (Universidad Nacional Autónoma de México) 36:293–96.

Cowen, R. 2000. *History of Life,* 3rd ed. Boston: Blackwell Scientific.

Cruz-Piñon, G., J. P. Carricart-Ganivet, and J. Espinoza-Avalos. 2003. Monthly skeletal extension rates of the hermatypic corals *Montastraea annularis* and *Montastraea faveolata*: Biological and environmental controls. *Marine Biology* 143:491–500.

Dahlgren, E. J. (*see also* Jordán-Dahlgren). 1989. Coral reef studies in Mexico. In *Proceedings of the Workshop Australia-Mexico on Marine Sciences,* ed. E. A. Chávez, 29–35. Mérida, Mexico: Centro de Investigación y de Estudios Avanzados del IPN.

———. 1993. El ecosistema arrecifal coralino del Atlántico mexicano. *Revista de la Sociedad Mexicana de Historia Natural* (Mexico City) 44:157–75.

Dampier, W. 1699. *Voyages and Descriptions.* Vol. 2, pt. 2 of *Two Voyages to Campeachy,* 2nd ed. (microfiche). London: James Knapton.

Darwin, C. 1842. *Structure and Distribution of Coral Reefs.* London: Smith Elder.

Da Silva, A., A. C. Young, and S. Levitus. 1994. *Atlas of Surface Marine Data 1994, Volume 1: Algorithms and Procedures.* NOAA, National Environmental Satellite, Data, and Information Service, Atlas 6. Washington, D.C.: U.S. Department of Commerce.

Davis, R. A. 1978. *Principles of Oceanography.* Boston: Addison-Wesley.

Davis, R. A. Jr. 1964. Foraminiferal assemblages of Alacran Reef, Campeche Bank, Mexico. *Journal of Paleontology* 38 (2): 417–21.

Dawes, C. J. 1998. *Marine Botany.* New York: John Wiley and Sons.

De la Campa, S. 1965. Datos preliminares de la flora marina del Estado de Veracruz. *Contribución del Instituto Nacional de Investigación Biológico-*

*Pesqueras al II Congreso Nacional de Oceanografía,* 1 14. n.p.

Delorme, L. D. 2001. Ostracoda. In *Ecology and Classification of North American Freshwater Invertebrates,* ed. J. A. Thorp and A. P. Covich, 2nd ed., 811–49. San Diego: Academic Press.

Dennis, G. D., and T. J. Bright. 1988. Reef fish assemblages on hard banks in the Northwestern Gulf of Mexico. *Bulletin of Marine Science* 43 (2): 280–307.

Denton, G. R. W., and C. Burdon-Jones. 1986. Trace metals in algae from the Great Barrier Reef. *Marine Pollution Bulletin* 17 (3): 98–107.

Díaz, M. C., and K. Rützler. 2001. Sponges: An essential component of Caribbean coral reefs. *Bulletin of Marine Science* 69:535–46.

Díaz-Ruiz, A., A. Aguirre-León, and J. E. Arias-González. 1998. Habitat interdependence in coral reef ecosystems: A case study in a Mexican Caribbean reef. *Aquatic Ecosystem Health and Management* 1:387–97.

Dingle, R. V., I. K. McMillan, S. Majoran, and L. Bisset. 2001. Palaeo-oceanographical implications of early-middle Miocene subtropical ostracod faunas from the continental shelf of the SE Atlantic Ocean. *Palaeogeography, Palaeoclimatology, Palaeoecology* 173:43–60.

Dirección General de Flora y Fauna Silvestre. 1985. *Alternativas de Manejo para los Arrecifes de Veracruz,* no. 139. México, D.F.: Dirección General de Flora y Fauna Silvestre.

Duarte, C. M., M. Merino, and M. Gallegos. 1995. Evidence of iron deficiency in seagrass growing above carbonate sediments. *Limnology and Oceanography* 40:1153–58.

Echaniz-Hernández, V. 1988. Determinación de los niveles de hidrocarburos en agua, sedimentos recientes y hojas del pasto marino *Thalassia testudinum* (Köning, 1805) en tres islas arrecifales del Puerto de Veracruz, Veracruz. B.Sc. thesis, Universidad Nacional Autónoma de México, México, D.F. ENEP, Iztacala.

Edwards, G. S. 1969. Distribution of shelf sediments, offshore from Anton Lizardo and the Port of Veracruz, Veracruz, Mexico. M.S. thesis, Texas A&M University, College Station, Department of Oceanography Report 69–10-T.

Elliott, B. A. 1979. Anticyclonic rings and the energetics of the circulation of the Gulf of Mexico. Ph.D. diss., Texas A&M University, College Station.

———. 1982. Anticyclonic rings in the Gulf of Mexico. *Journal of Physical Oceanography* 12:1292–1309.

Emery, K. O. 1963. Coral reefs off Veracruz, Mexico. *Geofísica Internacional* 3:11–17.

Enfield, D. B., and D. A. Mayer. 1997. Tropical Atlantic SST variability and its relation to El Niño-Southern Oscillation. *Journal of Geophysical Research* 102:929–45.

Ewing, T. E. 1991. Structural framework. In *Gulf of Mexico Basin,* ed. A. Salvador, 31–52. Vol. J of *The Geology of North America.* Boulder, Colo.: Geological Society of America.

Fairbanks, R. G. 1989. A 17,000-year glacioeustatic sea level record: Influence of glacial melting rates on the Younger Dryas event and deep-ocean circulation. *Nature* 342:637–42.

FAO (Food and Agriculture Organization of the United Nations). 2004. FAO-STAT data. http://apps.fao.org/faostat/notes/citation.htm.

Farrell, T. M., C. F. D'Elia, L. Lubbers, and L. J. Pastor. 1983. Hermatypic coral diversity and reef zonation at Cayo Arcas, Campeche, Gulf of Mexico. *Atoll Research Bulletin,* no. 270.

FDA (Food and Drug Administration). 1996. Fish, shellfish, crustaceans, and other aquatic animals—fresh, frozen or processed—methyl mercury (CPG 7108.07). Sec. 540.600 (rev. 3/95). *Compliance Policy Guides,* August 1996. Washington, D.C.: Department of Health and Human Services, Food and Drug Adminstration.

Fenical, W. H. 1980. Distributional and taxonomic features of toxin-producing marine algae. In *Pacific Seaweed Aquaculture,* ed. I. A. Abbott, M. S. Foster, and L. F. Eklund, 144–51. La Jolla: California Sea Grant Program.

Ferré-D'Amaré, A. R. 1985. Coral reefs of the Mexican Atlantic: A review. In *Proceedings of the Fifth International Coral Reef Congress, Tahiti, 27 May–1 June 1985,* ed. C. Gabrie and V. M. Harmelin, 6:349–54. Moorea, French Polynesia: Antenne Museum-Ephe.

Flores, J. S. 1984. Dinámica de emersion del suelo y sucesión de la vegetación en el arrecife Alacranes del Canal de Yucatán. *Biótica* 9 (1): 41–63.

———. 1992. *Vegetacion de Las Islas de La Peninsula de Yucatán: Floristica y Etnobotanica*. Etnoflora Yucatanense, Fascículo 4. Mérida: Universidad Autónoma de Yucatán.

Flores-Coto, C. F. (*see also* Coto). 1965. Notas preliminares sobre la identificación de las apendicularias de las aguas Veracruzanas. *Anales del Instituto de Biología, Serie Hidrobiología* (Universidad Nacional Autónoma de México) 36:293–96.

Folk, R. L. 1962. Sorting in some carbonate beaches of Mexico. *Annals of the New York Academy of Sciences* 25:222–44.

———. 1967. Sand cays of Alacran Reef, Yucatan, Mexico: Morphology. *Journal of Geology* 75:412–37.

Folk, R. L., and A. S. Cotera. 1971. Carbonate sand cays of Alacran Reef, Yucatan, Mexico: Sediments. *Atoll Research Bulletin*, no. 137.

Folk, R. L., and R. Robles. 1964. Carbonate sands of Isla Perez, Alacran Reef Complex, Yucatan. *Journal of Geology* 72 (3): 255–92.

Fosberg, F. R. 1961. Atoll news and comments. *Atoll Research Bulletin* 84:6–9.

———. 1962. A brief study of the cays of Arrecife Alacran, a Mexican atoll. *Atoll Research Bulletin*, no. 93.

Freeland, G. L. 1971. Carbonate sediments in a terrigenous province: the reefs of Veracruz, Mexico. Ph.D. diss., Rice University, Houston, Tex.

Frenzel, P., and I. Boomer. 2005. The use of ostracods from marginal marine, brackish waters as bioindicators of modern and Quaternary environmental change. *Palaeogeography, Palaeoclimatology, Palaeoecology* 225:68–92.

Fuentes, V. A., L. Jiménez-Badillo, J. M. Vargas-Hernández, and L. López-de Buen. 2004. Algunos efectos del evento de marea roja en el Sistema Arrecifal Veracruzano (diciembre 2001-enero, 2002). *XIII Reunion Nacional de la SOMPAC, Sixth International Meeting of the Mexican Society of Planktology, Nuevo Vallarta, Nayarit*, resumenes 109.

Furnas, M. J., and T. J. Smayda. 1987. Inputs of subthermocline waters and nitrate onto the Campeche Bank. *Continental Shelf Research* 7: 161–75.

Ganivet, J. P. C. (*see also* Carricart-

Ganivet). 1998. Corales escleractinios, "piedra mucar" y San Juan de Ulúa, Veracruz. *Ciencia y Desarrollo* 24 (141): 70–73.

García-Díaz, B. 1992. *Puerto de Veracruz*. Veracruz: Archivo General del Estado de Veracruz.

Garduño, M. (*see also* Andrade and Garduño-Andrade). 1989. Distribución de la ictiofauna asociada a los arrecifes coralinos. In *Proceedings of Workshop Australia-Mexico on Marine Sciences*, ed. E. A. Chavez, 63–74. Mérida, Mexico: Centro de Investigación y de Estudios Avanzados del IPN.

Garduño, M., and E. A. Chávez. 2000. Fish resource allocation in coral reefs of Yucatan Peninsula. In *Aquatic Ecosystems of Mexico: Status and Scope*, ed. M. Munawar, S. G. Lawrance, I. F. Munawar, and D. F. Malley, 367–81. Leiden: Backhuys Publishers.

Garduño-Andrade, M. (*see also* Andrade and Garduño). 1988. Distribución de la ictiofauna asociada a los arrecifes del Caribe Mexicano. M.S. thesis, Centro de Investigación y de Estudios Avanzados del IPN, Unidad Mérida, Yucatán.

Giannini, A., Y. Kushnir, and M. A. Cane. 2000. Interannual variability of Caribbean rainfall, ENSO and the Atlantic Ocean. *Journal of Climate* 13:297–311.

Gili, J.-M., and R. Coma. 1998. Benthic suspension feeders: their paramount role in littoral marine food webs. *Trends in Ecology and Evolution* 13:316–21.

Gladfelter, W. B., J. C. Ogden, and E. H. Gladfelter. 1980. Similarity and diversity among coral reef fish communities: a comparison between tropical Western Atlantic (Virgin Islands) and tropical central Pacific (Marshall Island) patch reefs. *Ecology* 61 (5): 1156–68.

Glynn, P. W. 1973. Aspects of the ecology of coral reefs in the western Atlantic region. In *Biology and Geology of Coral Reefs*, ed. O. A. Jones and R. Endean, 271–324. New York: Academic Press.

Glynn, P. W., A. M. Szmant, E. F. Corcoran, and S. V. Cofer-Shabica. 1989. Condition of coral reef cnidarians from the northern Florida reef tract: Pesticides, heavy metals and histopathological examination. *Marine Pollution Bulletin* 20 (11): 568–76.

González-Cano, J., G. V. Ríos, C. Zetina, A. Ramírez, P. Arceo, C. Aguilar, K. Cervera, J. Bello, I. Martínez, D. de Anda, and M. Cobá. 2002. Langosta espinosa del Caribe. In *Sustentabilidad y Pesca Responsable en México, Evaluación y Manejo 1999–2000*, ed. M. A. Cisneros-Mata, L. F. Meléndez-Moreno, E. Zárate-Becerra, M. T. Gaspar-Dillanes, L. C. López-González, C. Saucedo-Ruiz, and J. Tovar-Avila, 631–54. CD edition. México, D.F.: Instituto Nacional de la Pesca.

González de la Parra, A., L. M. Guzmán, and M. R. Sánchez. 1984. *Manejo de la Zona Arrecifal de Antón Lizardo, Veracruz*. México, D.F.: Servicio Social, Universidad Autónoma Metropolitana.

González-Gándara, C. 2001. Las comunidades de peces del Arrecife Alacranes, Yucatan: variaciones espaciotemporales. Tesis de doctorado, Centro Investigación y Estudios Avanzados–IPN, Unidad Mérida.

González-Gándara, C., and J. E. Arias-González. 2001a. Lista actualizada de los peces del arrecife Alacranes, Yucatán, México. *Anales del Instituto de Biología, Serie Zoología* (Universidad Nacional Autonóma de México) 72 (2): 245–58.

———. 2001b. Nuevos registros de peces en el Arrecife Alacrán, Yucatán, México. *Revista de Biología Tropical* 49:770–71.

González-Gándara, C., N. Membrillo-Venegas, E. Nuñez-Lara, and J. E. Arias-González. 1999. The relationship between fish and reefscapes in the Alacranes Reef, Yucatan, Mexico: A preliminary trophic functioning analysis. *Vie et Milieu* 49 (4): 275–86.

González-Gándara, C., Pérez-Díaz, L. Santos-Rodriguez, and J. E. Arias-González. 2003. Length-weight relationships of coral reef fishes from the Alacranes Reef, Yucatan, Mexico. *Naga* 26 (1): 14–16.

Gónzalez-Solís, A., E. A. Chávez, G. de la Cruz, and D. Torruco. 1991. Patrones de distribución de Gasterópodos y Bivalvos en la Península de Yucatán, México. *Ciencias Marinas* 17 (3): 147–72.

Goreau, T. F. 1959. The ecology of Jamaican coral reefs, I: Species composition and zonation. *Ecology* 40:67–90.

Goreau, T. F., and N. I. Goreau. 1973. The ecology of Jamaican coral reefs, II: Geomorphology, zonation, and sedimentary phases. *Bulletin of Marine Science* 23:399–464.

Goreau, T. F, N. I. Goreau, and T. J. Goreau. 1979. Corals and coral reefs. *Scientific American* 241 (2): 124–36.

Goreau, T. F., and J. M. Wells. 1967. The shallow-water scleractinia of Jamaica: revised list of species and their vertical distribution range. *Bulletin of Marine Science* 17:442–53.

Goreau, T. F., and L. S. Land. 1974. Fore-reef morphology and depositional processes, North Jamaica. In *Reefs in Time and Space*, ed. L. F. Laporte, 77–89. Special Publication 18. Tulsa: Society of Economic Paleontologists and Mineralogists.

Granados-Barba, A., V. Solís-Weiss, M. A. Tovar-Hernández, and V. Ochoa-Rivera. 2003. Distibution and diversity of the Syllidae (Annelida: Polychaeta) from the Mexican Gulf of Mexico and Caribbean. *Hydrobiologia* 496:337–45.

Graus, R. R., I. G. Macintyre, and B. E. Herchenroder. 1984. Computer simulation of the reef zonation at Discovery Bay, Jamaica: Hurricane disruption and long-term physical oceanographic controls. *Coral Reefs* 3:59–68.

Green, G. 1977. Sinopsis taxonómica de trece especies de esponjas del arrecife La Blanquilla, Veracruz, México. *Anales del Centro de Ciencias del Mar y Limnología* (Universidad Nacional Autónoma de México) 4 (1): 79–98.

Grose, P., F. Everdale, and L. Katz. 1983. Predicting the surface transport of oil pollutants in the Gulf of Mexico. *Marine Pollution Bulletin* 14 (10): 372–77.

Gulland, J. A. 1983. *Fish Stock Assessment: A Manual of Basic Methods*. FAO/Wiley Series on Food and Agriculture, vol. 1. Chichester:Wiley-Interscience.

Gutiérrez, D., C. García-Sáez, M. Lara, and C. Padilla. 1993. Comparación de arrecifes coralinos: Veracruz y Quintana Roo. In *Biodiversidad Marina y Costera de México*, ed. S. I. Salazar-Vallejo and N. E. González, 787–806. México, D.F.: Comisión Nacional para la Biodiversidad y Centro de Investigaciones de Quintana Roo.

Gutiérrez de Velásco, G., S. Shull, P. J. Harvey, and N. A. Bray. 1992. Gulf of Mexico experiment: Meteorological, moored instrument, and sea level observations. Data Report 1: August 1990 to July 1991, SIO Ref. 92–26, Scripps Institute of Oceanography, University of California, San Diego.

———. 1993. Gulf of Mexico experiment: Meteorological, moored instrument, and sea level observations. Data Report 2: August 1991 to July 1992, SIO Ref. 93–31, Scripps Institute of Oceanography, University of California, San Diego.

Gutiérrez de Velásco, G., and C. D. Winant. 1996. Seasonal patterns of wind stress and wind stress curl over the Gulf of Mexico. *Journal of Geophysical Research* 101:18127–40.

Guzmán, H. M., and Jiménez C. E. 1992. Contamination of coral reefs by heavy metals along the Caribbean Coast of Central America. *Marine Pollution Bulletin* 24 (11): 554–61.

Hallam, A. 1992. *Phanerozoic Sea-Level Changes.* New York: Columbia University Press.

Hallock, P. B., H. Lidz, E. M. Cockey-Burkhard, and K. B. Donnelly. 2003. Foraminifera as bioindicators in coral reef assessment and monitoring: the FORAM Index. *Environmental Monitoring and Assessment* 81:221–38.

Hammer, W. M., M. S. Jones, J. H. Carleton, I. R. Hauri, and D. M. Williams. 1988. Zooplankton, planktivorous fish and water currents on a windward reef face: Great Barrier Reef, Australia. *Bulletin of Marine Science* 42 (3): 459–79.

Hammond, L. S., and C. R. Wilkinson. 1985. Exploitation of sponge exudates by coral reef holothuroids. *Journal of Experimental Marine Biology and Ecology* 94:1–9.

Hansen, T. A., R. B. Farrand, H. A. Montgomery, H. Billman, and G. Blechschmidt. 1987. Sedimentology and extinction patterns across the Cretaceous-Tertiary boundary interval in east Texas. *Cretaceous Research* 8:229–52.

Harte, J. 2003. Tail of death and resurrection. *Nature* 424:1006–1007.

Hawker, D. W., and D. W. Connell. 1992. Standards and criteria for pollution control in coral reef areas. In *Pollution in Tropical Aquatic Systems*, ed. D. W. Connell and D. W. Hawker, 169–91. Boca Raton, Fla.: CRC Press.

Heilprin, A. 1890. The corals and coral reefs of the western waters of the Gulf of Mexico. *Proceedings of the Academy of Natural Sciences of Philadelphia* 42:303–16.

Henkel, D. H. 1982. Echinoderms of Enmedio Reef, southwestern Gulf of Mexico. M.S. thesis, Corpus Christi State University, Corpus Christi, Tex.

Hernández, L. R. 1997. Estructura de la comunidad faunística asociada a la esponja *Iricinia strobilina* (Lamark, 1816) Porifera: Demospongiae: Thoredtidae, del arrecife Triángulo Oeste, Banco de Campeche, México. Tesis profesional, Universidad Veracruzana, Xalapa, Veracruz.

Hernandez, R. C. 1987. *Primer Informa del Estudio de Caracterización de los Sedimentos en el Sistema Arrecifal Veracruzano.* México, D.F.: Secretaría de Marina, Dirección General de Oceanografía.

Hernández-Rosario, C., and D. Tinoco-Blanco. 1988. *Sedimentos del Sistema Arrecifal Veracruzano (Primera Parte: Caracterización).* Veracruz, México: Secretaría de Marina, Dirección General de Oceanografía, Estación de Investiaciones Oceanografía, Veracruz.

Hernández-Tabares, I., and P. R. Bravo-Gamboa. 2002. Pesquería de pulpo. In *La Pesca en Veracruz y sus Perspectivas de Desarrollo*, ed. P. Guzmán, C. Quiroga, C. Díaz, D. Fuentes, C. Contreras, and G. Silva, 217–28. Veracruz: Instituto Nacional de la Pesca, Universidad Veracruzana, México.

Hidalgo, E., and E. A. Chávez. 1967. Prospección ecológica en el arrecife de Lobos, Veracruz. *Contribución del Instituto de Investigaciones Biológico-Pesqueras al III Congreso Nacional de Oceanografía.* Campeche, Camp.: n.p.

Hildebrand, A. R., M. Pilkington, M. Connors, C. Otiz-Aleman, and R. E. Chavez. 1995. Size and structure of the Chicxulub crater revealed by horizontal gravity gradients and cenotes. *Nature* 376:415–17.

Hildebrand, H. H., H. Chávez, and H. Compton. 1964. Aporte al conocimiento de los peces del Arrecife Alacranes, Yucatán, México. *Ciencia, México* 23 (3): 107–34.

Hillis-Colinveaux, L. 1980. *Ecology and Taxonomy of Halimeda: Primary Producer of Coral Reefs.* Advances in Marine Biology, no. 17. London: Academic Press.

Hixon, M. A., and B. P. Beets, 1993. Predation, prey refuges and the structure of coral reef fish communities. *Ecological Monographs* 63:77–101.

Hopcroft, R. R., and J. C. Roff. 1995. Zooplankton growth rates: Extraordinary production by the larvacean *Oikopleura dioica* in tropical waters. *Journal of Plankton Research* 17: 205–20.

———. 1998. Production of tropical larvaceans in Kingston harbour, Jamaica: Are we ignoring an important secondary producer? *Journal of Plankton Research* 20:557–69.

Horta, G. 1991. Concentración de diversos metales pesados en Corales Scleractinios en Veracruz, Ver. *XI Congreso Nacional de Zoología, Octubre de 1991.* Resúmenes 27. n.p.

Horta-Puga, G. 1993. Metales pesados en esqueleto de *Montastraea annularis* (Cnidaria: Scleractinia), del Sistema Arrecifal Veracruzano: Un análisis retrospectivo. *V Congreso Latinoamericano sobre Ciencias del Mar, La Paz.* B.C.S., México. Resúmenes 0–176.

Horta-Puga, G. 2003. Condition of selected reef sites in the Veracruz Reef System (stony corals and algae). *Atoll Research Bulletin* 496:360–69.

Horta-Puga, G., and J. P. Carricart-Ganivet. 1985. Corales scleractinos de Isla de Enmedio, Ver. *Memorias del VIII Congreso Nacional de Zoología,* 310–21. Saltillo, Coahuila, México.

———. 1989. Estudio ecologico del blanqueamiento en corales escleractinios del arrecife La Blanquilla, Veracruz. *XII Simposio Biología Campo,* Universidad Nacional Autónoma de México–Iztacala, Tlalnepantla, Mexico. Resúmenes 1.

———. 1990. *Stylaster roseus* (Pallas, 1766): First record of a stylasterid (Cnidaria: Hydrozoa) in the Gulf of Mexico. *Bulletin of Marine Science* 47 (2): 575–76.

———. 1993. Corales pétreos recientes (Milleporina, Stylasterina y Scleractinia) de México. In *Biodiversidad Marina y Costera de México,* ed. S. I. Salazar-Vallejo and N. E. González, 66–80. México, D.F.: Comisión Nacional para la Biodiversidad y Centro de Investigaciones de Quintana Roo.

Horta-Puga, G., and R. Ramírez-Palacios. 1996. Niveles de plomo en el esqueleto del coral arrecifal *Montastrea annu-*

*laris.* In *La Situación Ambiental en México,* ed. O. Rivero-Serrano, 823–30. México, D.F.: Universidad Nacional Autónoma de México.

Horta-Puga, G., and J. M. Vargas-Hernandez. 2003. Impacto del encallamiento del buque *Rubin* en el Arrecife Pajaros, Sistema Arrecifal Veracruzano, I: Cambios en la comunidad de corales hermatipicos. *II Congreso Mexicano Sobre Arrecifes,* Universidad del Mar, Puerto Angel, Oaxaca, 5–7 Noviembre 2003. Resúmenes 2.

Hoskin, C. M. 1962. Recent carbonate sedimentation on Alacran Reef, Mexico. Ph.D. diss., University of Texas at Austin.

———. 1963. Recent carbonate sedimentation on Alacran Reef, Yucatan, Mexico. Publication no. 1089. Washington, D.C.: National Academy of Sciences/National Research Council.

———. 1966. Coral pinnacle sedimentation, Alacran Reef Lagoon, Mexico. *Journal of Sedimentary Petrology* 36 (4): 1055–74.

———. 1968. Magnesium and strontium in mud fraction of recent carbonate sediment, Alacran Reef, Mexico. *Bulletin of the American Association of Petroleum Geologists* 52:2170–77.

Howard, L. S., and B. E. Brown. 1986. Metals in tissues and skeleton of *Fungia fungites* from Phuket, Thailand. *Marine Pollution Bulletin* 17 (12): 569–70.

———. 1987. Metals in *Pocillopora damicornis* exposed to tin smelter effluent. *Marine Pollution Bulletin* 18 (8): 451–54.

Howell, S. N. G. 1989. Additional information on the birds of the Campeche Bank, Mexico. *Journal of Field Ornithology* 60:504–509.

Huerta M., L. (*see also* Múzquiz and Huerta-Múzquiz). 1960. Lista preliminar de las algas marinas del litoral del estado de Veracruz. *Anales del Instituto de Biología, Serie Botánica* (Universidad Nacional Autónoma de México) 25:39–45.

Huerta M., L., and A. G. Barrientos. 1965. Algas marinas de la Barra de Tuxpan y de los arrecifes Blanquilla y Lobos. *Anales de la Escuela Nacional de Ciencias Biológicas, México* 13 (1–4): 5–21.

Huerta M., L., M. L. Chávez, and M. E. Sánchez. 1977. Algas marinas de la Isla de Enmedio, Veracruz. In *Memorias* de V Congreso Nacional de Oceanografía, Guaymas, Sonora, México, 22–25 de Octubre 1974, ed. F. A. Manrique, 314–25. n.p.

Huerta-Múzquiz, L. (see also Huerta M. and Múzquiz), A. C. Mendoza-González, and L. E. Mateo-Cid. 1987. Avance sobre el estudio de las algas marinas de la Península de Yucatán. Phytologia 62 (1): 23–31.

Hughes, T. P., B. D. Keller, J. B. C. Jackson, and M. J. Boyle. 1985. Mass mortality of the echinoid Diadema antillarum Philippi in Jamaica. Bulletin of Marine Science 36:377–84.

Humm, H. J. 1964. Epiphytes of the seagrass, Thalassia testudinium, in Florida. Bulletin of Marine Science of the Gulf and Caribbean 14:307–41.

Hurlburt, H. E., and J. D. Thompson, 1980. A numerical study of loop current intrusions and eddy shedding. Journal of Physical Oceanography 10:1611–51.

Ichiye, T., 1962. Circulation and water-mass distribution in the Gulf of Mexico. Geofisica Internacional 2:47–76.

ICRI (International Coral Reef Initiative). 2003. ITMEMS2 Action Statement. Second International Tropical Marine Ecosystems Management Symposium. Manilla, Philippines: ICRI.

INEGI (Instituto Nacional de Estadística Geografía e Informática). 1988. Sintesis Geografica, Nomenclator y Anexo Cartografico del Estado de Veracruz. Aquascalientes, México: INEGI.

———. 1995a. Anuario Estadístico del Estado de Veracruz. Aquascalientes, México: INEGI.

———. 1995b. Estadísticas Históricas de México Tomol, 1994. Aquascalientes, México: INEGI.

———. 1997a. Conteo De Poblacion y Vivienda 1995. Aquascalientes, México: INEGI.

———. 1997b. Cuaderno Estadístico Municipal. Boca del Rio, Estado de Veracruz. Aquascalientes, México: INEGI.

Ives, J. E. 1890. Echinoderms from the northern coast of Yucatan and the harbor of Veracruz. Proceedings of the Academy of Natural Sciences of Philadelphia 42:317–40.

———. 1891. Crustacea from the northern coast of the Yucatan, the harbor of Veracruz, the west coast of Florida and the Bermuda Islands. Proceedings of the Academy of Natural Sciences of Philadelphia 1891:176–207.

Jackson, J. B. C. 1992. Pleistocene perspectives on coral-reef community structure. American Zoologist 32 (6): 719–31.

James, N. P. 1983. Reef. In Carbonate Depositional Environments, ed. P. A. Scholle, D. G. Bebout, and C. H. Moore, 345–440. AAPG Memoir 33. Tulsa, Okla.: American Association of Petroleum Geologists.

Jameson, S. C. 1995. Morphometric analysis of the Poritidae (Anthozoa: Scleractinia) off Belize. Ph.D. diss., University of Maryland.

———. 1997. Morphometric analysis of the Poritadae (Anthozoa: Scleractinia) off Belize. In Proceedings of the Eighth International Coral Reef Symposium (Panama City, Panama, 24–29 June 1996), ed. H. A. Lessios and I. G. Macintyre, 2:1591–96.

Jáuregui, E. 2003. Climatology of land-falling hurricanes and tropical storms in Mexico. Atmósfera 4:193–204.

Jernelov, A., and O. Linden. 1981. IXTOC I: A case study of the world's largest oil spill. Ambio 10 (6): 299–306.

Johnson, D. R., J. D. Thompson, and J. D. Hawkins. 1992. Circulation in the Gulf of Mexico from Geosat altimetry during 1985–1986. Journal of Geophysical Research 97:2201–14.

Jordán-Dahlgren, E. (see also Dahlgren). 1992. Recolonization patterns of Acropora palmata in a marginal environment. Bulletin of Marine Science 51 (1): 104–17.

———. 2002. Gorgonian distribution patterns in coral reef environments of the Gulf of Mexico: Evidence of sporadic ecological connectivity. Coral Reefs 21:205–15.

———. 2004. Los arrecifes coralinos del Golfo de México: Caracterización y diagnóstico. In Diagnóstico ambiental del Golfo de México, ed. M. Caso, I. Pisanty, and E. Ezcurra, 555–71. México, D.F.: Instituto Nacional de Ecología.

Jordán-Dahlgren, E., and R. E. Rodríguez-Martínez. 2003. The Atlantic coral reefs of Mexico. In Latin American Coral Reefs, ed. J. Cortés, 131–58. Amsterdam: Elsevier Science.

Joubin, M. L. 1912. Carte des bancs et récifs de Coraux (Madrépores).

Annales de L'Institut Océanographique 4, no. 2.

Kauffman, E. G. 1979. The ecology and biogeography of the Cretaceous-Tertiary extinction event. In *Cretaceous-Tertiary Boundary Events II*, ed. K. Christen and T. Birkelund, 29–37. Copenhagen: University of Copenhagen.

Kauffman, E. G., and N. F. Sohl. 1974. Structure and evolution of Antillean Cretaceous Rudist frameworks. *Verhandlungen Naturforschende Gesellschaft in Basel* 84:399–467.

Keller, G. 1989. Extended period of extinctions across the Cretaceous/Tertiary boundary in planktonic foraminifera of continental-shelf sections: Implications for impact and volcanism theories. *Geological Society of America Bulletin* 101:1408–19.

Kennedy, J. N. 1917. A little-known bird colony in the Gulf of Mexico. *Ibis* 10 (5): 41–43.

Kier, P. M., and R. E. Grant. 1965. Echinoid distribution and habits, Key Largo Coral Reef Preserve, Florida. *Smithsonian Miscellaneous Collections* 149, no. 6.

Kornicker, L. S., and D. W. Boyd. 1962a. Bio-geology of a living coral reef complex on the Campeche Bank. In *Guide Book Field Trip to Peninsula of Yucatan*, ed. G. E. Murray and A. E. Weidie Jr., 73–84. New Orleans: New Orleans Geological Society.

———. 1962b. Shallow-water geology and environments of Alacran Reef Complex, Campeche Bank, Mexico. *Bulletin of the American Association of Petroleum Geologists* 46 (5): 640–73.

Kornicker, L. S., R. Bonet, R. Cann, and C. M. Hoskin. 1959. Alacran Reef, Campeche Bank, Mexico. *Publications of the Marine Science Institute* (University of Texas) 6:1–22.

Krutak, P. R. 1974. *Standing Crops of Modern Ostracods in Lagoonal and Reefal Environment, Veracruz, Mexico*. Special Publication 6:11–14. St. Croix, U.S. Virgin Islands: West Indies Laboratory Fairleigh Dickinson University.

Krutak, P. R., and S. E. Rickles. 1979. Equilibrium in modern coral reefs, Western Gulf of Mexico: Role of the ecology and Ostracod microfauna.

*Transactions Gulf Coast Association of Geological Societies* 29:263–74.

Krutak, P. R., S. E. Rickles, and R. Gío-Argáez. 1980. Modern ostracod species diversity, dominance, and biofacies patterns, Veracruz-Anton Lizardo reefs, Mexico. *Anales Centro Ciencias del Mar y Limnología* (Universidad Nacioznal Autónoma de México) 7 (2): 181–98.

Kühlmann, D. H. H. 1975. Charakterisierung der korallenriffe von Veracruz, Mexico. Museum für naturkunde on der Humboldt Universitat zu Berlin. *Internationale Revue der gesamten Hydrobiologie* 60 (4): 495–521.

Land, L. S. 1974. Growth rate of a West Indian (Jamaican) reef. *Proceedings of the Second International Coral Reef Symposium* (Brisbane, Australia) 2:409–12.

Landsea, C. W., R. A. Pielke, A. Mestas-Nunez, and J. A. Knaff. 1999. Atlantic basin hurricanes: Indices of climatic changes. *Climatic Change* 42:89–129.

Lang, J., P. Alcolado, J. P. Carricart-Ganivet, M. Chiappone, A. Curran, P. Dustan, G. Gaudian, F. Geraldes, S. Gittings, R. Smith, W. Tunnell, and J. Wiener. 1998. Status of coral reefs in the northern areas of the wider Caribbean. *Status of Coral Reefs of the World: 1998*, ed. C. Wilkinson, 123–34. Australian Institute of Marine Science on behalf of the Global Reef Monitoring Network, Australia.

Lara, M., C. Padilla, C. García, and J. J. Espejel. 1992. Coral reefs of Veracruz Mexico, I: Zonation and community. In *Proceedings of the Seventh International Coral Reef Symposium* (22–26 June 1992, Mangilao, Guam), ed. R. H. Richmond, 1:535–44. Mangilao: University of Guam Press.

Lehman, R. L. 1993. Field and laboratory investigations of the macroalgae of Enmedio coral reef, with specific taxonomic reference to the genus *Caulerpa*. Ph.D. diss., Texas A&M University, College Station, Tex.

Lehman, R. L., and J. W. Tunnell Jr. 1992a. A topographic description of Enmedio Reef, Veracruz, Mexico. Abstract. Gulf Estuarine Research Society Annual Meeting, Port Aransas, Tex., April 2–4, 1992.

———. 1992b. Species composition and ecology of the macroalgae of Enmedio

Reef, Veracruz, Mexico. *Texas Journal of Science* 44 (4): 445–57.

Leipper, D. F. 1970. A sequence of current patterns in the Gulf of Mexico. *Journal of Geophysical Research* 75:637–57.

Lerdo de Tejada. 1858. *Apuntes historicos de la Heroica Ciudad de Veracruz: San Juan de Ulua*. Veracruz: Comisión Federal de Electrica.

Lesser, M. P. 2006. Benthic-pelagic coupling on coral reefs: feeding and growth of Caribbean sponges. *Journal of Experimental Biology and Ecology* 328:277–88.

Lessios, H. A., D. R. Robertson, and J. D. Cubit. 1984. Spread of *Diadema* mass mortality through the Caribbean. *Science* 226:335–37.

Liceaga-Correa, M. A., and J. I. Euan-Avila. 2002. Assessment of coral reef bathymetric mapping using visible Landsat Thematic Mapper data. *International Journal of Remote Sensing* 23 (1): 3–14.

Liddell, W. D., and S. L. Ohlhorst. 1988. Hard substrata community patterns, 1–120 m, north Jamaica. *Palaios* 3:413–23.

Lidz, L., and B. Lidz. 1966. Foraminiferal biofaces of Veracruz reefs. *Bulletin of the American Association of Petroleum Geologists* 50 (7): 1514–17.

Lighty, R. G., I. G. Macintyre, and R. Stuckenrath. 1982. *Acropora palmata* reef framework: A reliable indicator for sea level in the western Atlantic for the past 10,000 years. *Coral Reefs* 1:125–30.

Littler, D. S., and M. M. Littler. 2000. Caribbean reef plants. Washington, D.C.: Offshore Graphics, Inc.

Littler, D. S., M. M. Littler, K. E. Bucher, and J. N. Norris. 1989. *Marine Plants of the Caribbean*. Washington, D.C.: Smithsonian Institution Press.

Littler, M. M., and D. S. Littler. 1984. Models of tropical reef biogenesis: The contribution of algae. In *Progress in Phycological Research*, ed. F. E. Round and D. J. Chapman, 3:323–63. Bristol: Biopress Ltd.

———. 1988. Structure and role of algae in tropical reef communities. In *Algae and Human Affairs*, ed. C. A. Lembi and J. R. Waaland, 29–56. Cambridge: Cambridge University Press.

Littler, M. M., D. S. Littler, and E. A. Titlyanov. 1991. Comparisons of N- and P-limited productivity between high

granitic islands versus low carbonate atolls in the Seychelles Archipelago: A test of the relative-dominance paradigm. *Coral Reefs* 10:199–209.

Logan, B. W. 1962. Submarine topography of the Yucatan Platform. In *Guide Book Field Trip to Peninsula of Yucatan*, ed. G. E. Murray and A. E. Weidie Jr., 101–104. New Orleans: New Orleans Geological Society.

———. 1969a. Part 1: Late Quaternary carbonate sediments of Yucatan Shelf, Mexico. In *Carbonate Sediments and Reefs, Yucatan Shelf, Mexico*, ed. B. W. Logan, J. L. Harding, W. M. Ahr, J. D. Williams, and R. S. Snead, Pp. 1–128. AAPG Memoir 11. Tulsa, Okla.: Association of Petroleum Geologists.

———. 1969b. Part 2: Coral reefs and banks, Yucatan Shelf, Mexico (Yucatan Reef Unit). In *Carbonate Sediments and Reefs, Yucatan Shelf, Mexico*, ed. B. W. Logan, J. L. Harding, W. M. Ahr, J. D. Williams, and R.S. Snead, 129–98. AAPG Memoir 11. Tulsa, Okla.: American Association of Petroleum Geologists.

Logan, B. W., J. L. Harding, W. M. Ahr, J. D. Williams, and R.S. Snead, eds. 1969. *Carbonate Sediments and Reefs, Yucatan Shelf, Mexico*. AAPG Memoir 11. Tulsa, Okla.: American Association of Petroleum Geologists.

López-Urrutia, Á., J. L. Acuña, X. Irigoien, and R. Harris. 2003. Food limitation and growth in temperate epipelagic appendicularians (Tunicata). *Marine Ecology Progress Series* 252:143–57.

Lot-Helgueras, A. 1971. Estudios sobre fanerógamas marinas en las cercanías de Veracruz, Veracruz. *Anales del Instituto de Biología, Serie Botánica* (Universidad Nacional Autónoma de México) 42 (1): 1–48.

Lubel, M. A. A. 1984. Algunos ciliados intersticiales de Isla Enmedio, Veracruz, México. *Anales Instituto de Biología, Serie Zoología* (Universidad Nacional Autónoma de México) 55 (1): 1–59.

MacDougall, J. D. 1988. Seawater strontium isotopes, acid rain, and the Cretaceous-Tertiary Boundary. *Science* 239:485–87.

Macías-Zamora, V., J. Villaescusa-Celaya, A. Muñoz-Barbosa, and G. Gold-Bouchot. 1999. Trace metals in sediment cores from the Campeche shelf, Gulf of Mexico. *Environmental Pollution* 104:69.

Macintyre, I. G., R. B. Burke, and R. Stuckenrath. 1977. Thickest recorded Holocene reef section Isla Perez core hold, Alacran Reef, Mexico. *Geology* 5:749–54.

Magaña, H. A., C. Contrenas, and T. A. Villareal. 2003. A historical assessment of *Karenia brevis* in the western Gulf of Mexico. *Harmful Algae* 2:163–71.

Maloney, E. D., and D. L. Hartmann. 2000. Modulation of hurricane activity in the Gulf of Mexico by the Madden-Julian oscillation. *Science* 287:2002–2004.

Margalef, R. 1974. *Ecología*. Barcelona: Editorial Omega.

Marion, A. F. 1884. Excursion aux isles Alacrans. *Bulletin of Société Academique de Brest* (France, Serie 2) 9:5–21.

Márquez-Espinoza, A. 1976. Peces de importancia económica del Arrecife de Lobos, Veracruz, México. In *Memorias de la Reunión Sobre Recursos de la Pesca Costera de México*, ed. J. L. Castro-Aguirre, 133–40. n.p.

Marshall, J., Y. Kushnir, D. Battistini, P. Chang, A. Czaja, R. Dickson, J. Hurrell, M. McCartney, R. Saravan, and M. Visbeck. 2001. North Atlantic climate variability: Phenomena, impacts, and mechanisms. *International Journal of Climatology* 21:1863–98.

Martínez-Guzmán, L. A, and J. L. Hernández-Aguilera. 1993. Crustáceos estomatópodos y decápodos del Arrecife Alacrán, Yucatán. In *Biodiversidad Marina y Costera de México*, ed. S. I. Salazar-Vallejo and N. E. Gonzalez, 609–29. Comisión Nacional para la Biodiversidad y Centro de Investigaciones de Quintana Roo, México.

Mateo-Cid, L. E., A. C. Mendoza-González, and C. G. Garcia. 1996. Algas marinas de Isla Verde, Veracruz, Mexico. *Acta Botanica Mexicana* 36:59–75.

Maul, G. A. 1977. The annual cycle of the Gulf Loop Current, 1: Observations during a one-year time series. *Journal of Marine Research* 35:29–47.

Maul, G. A., D. A. Mayer, and S. R. Baig. 1985. Comparison between a continuous three-year current meter observation at the sill of the Yucatan Strait, satellite measurements of Gulf Loop Current area, and regional sea level. *Journal of Geophysical Research* 90:9089–96.

Maul, G. A., and F. M. Vukovich. 1993. The relationship between variations in the Gulf of Mexico Loop Current and Strait of Florida volume transport. *Journal of Physical Oceanography* 23:785–96.

McKee, E. D., and W. C. Ward. 1983. Eolian environment. In *Carbonate Depositional Environments*, ed. P. A. Scholle, D. G. Bebout, and C. H. Moore, 131–70. AAPG Memoir 33. Tulsa, Okla.: American Association of Petroleum Geologists.

McNeill, A. R. 1992. Recreational water quality. In *Pollution in Tropical Aquatic Systems*, ed. D. W. Connell and D. W. Hawker, 193–216. Boca Raton: CRC Press.

Medina, J., and A. Ruiz. 1991. Caracterizacion del grado de contaminacion bacteriana producida por el hombre en cuerpos de agua destinados para la recreacion en las zonas costeras del Estado de Veracruz. *XV Simposio Biología Campo*, Universidad Nacional Autónoma de México–Iztacala, Tlalnepantla, Mexico. Resúmenes 20.

Melosh, H. J., N. M. Schneider, K. J. Zahnle, and D. Latham. 1990. Ignition of global wildfires at the Cretaceous/Tertiary boundary. *Nature* 343:251–54.

Mendoza-González, A., and L. E. Mateo-Cid. 1985. Contribucion al conocimiento de la flora marina benionica de las Islas Sacrificios y Santiaguillo, Veracruz, México. *Phytologia* 59 (1):9–16.

Merino, M. 1997. Upwelling on the Yucatan Shelf: Hydrographic evidence. *Journal of Marine Research* 13:101–21.

Merino, M., S. Czitrom, E. Jordán, E. Martin, P. Thomé, and O. Moreno. 1990. Hydrology and rain flushing of the Nichupté Lagoon System, Cancún, México. *Estuarine, Coastal and Shelf Science* 30:223–37.

Merrell, W. J. Jr., and J. M. Morrison. 1981. On the circulation of the western Gulf of Mexico with observations from April 1978. *Journal of Geophysical Research* 86:4181–85.

Merrell, W. J. Jr., and A. M. Vázquez de la Cerda. 1983. Observations of changing mesoscale circulation patterns in the western Gulf of Mexico. *Journal of Geophysical Research* 88:7721–23.

Millspaugh, C. F. 1916. Contributions to North American Euphorbiaceae: Vegetation of Alacran Reef. *Field Museum of Natural History Publication, Botanical Series* 2 (11): 421–31.

Molina, G. 1992. Caracterizacion del grado de contaminacion bacteriana en cinco playas de uso recreativo en Puerto de Veracruz. *XVI Simposio Biología Campo,* Universidad Nacional Autónoma de México–Iztacala, Tlalnepantla, México. Resúmenes 2.

Molinari, R. L., D. W. Behringer, G. A. Maul, S. Baig, and R. Legeckis. 1977. Winter intrusions of the Loop Current (water circulation in Gulf of Mexico). *Science* 198:505–507.

Molinari, R. L., and J. Morrison. 1988. The separation of the Yucatan Current from the Campeche Bank and the intrusion of the loop current into the Gulf of Mexico. *Journal of Geophysical Research* 93 (C9): 10645–54.

Monreal-Gómez, M. A., and D. A. Salas de León. 1997. Circulación y estructura termohalina del Golfo de México. In *Contribuciones a la Oceanografía Física en México,* ed. M. F. Lavín, 183–99. Monografía no. 3. Ensenada: Unión Geofísica Mexicana.

Monreal-Gómez, M. A., D. A. Salas de León, A. R. Padilla-Pilotze, and M. A. Alatorre-Mendieta. 1992. Hydrography and estimation of density currents in the southern part of the Bay of Campeche, México. *Ciencias Marinas* 18:115–33.

Monroy, C., V. Moreno, A. Hernández, and M. Garduño. 2002. Mero *Epinephelus morio.* In *Sustentabilidad y Pesca Responsable en México, Evaluación y Manejo 1999–2000,* ed. M. A. Cisneros-Mata, L. F. Meléndez-Moreno, E. Zárate-Becerra, M. T. Gaspar-Dillanes, L. C. López-González, C. Saucedo-Ruiz, and J. Tovar-Avila, 585–614. CD edition. Instituto Nacional de la Pesca, México.

Montes, J. J. E. 1991. Aspectos geológicos y ecológicos de la distribución de escleractinios en los arrecifes coralinos de Antón Lizardo y el Puerto de Veracruz, Golfo de México. Tesis de maestría, Universidad Nacional Autónoma de México.

Moore, D. R. 1958. Notes on Blanquilla Reef, the most northerly coral formation in the Western Gulf of Mexico. *Publications of the Institute of Marine Science* (University of Texas) 5:151–55.

Morales-García, A. 1986. *Estudio de los Crustáceos Estomatópodos y Decápodos de Isla Verde, Veracruz, México.* México, D.F.: Secretaría de Marina, Dirección General de Oceanografía.

———. 1987. *Estudio de los Crustáceos Estomatópodos y Decápodos de Isla Sacrificios, Veracruz, México.* Report no. 87. Secretaría de Marina, Estación Veracruz, México.

Morelock, J., and K. J. Koenig. 1967. Terrigenous sedimentation in a shallow water coral reef environment. *Journal of Sedimentary Petrology* 37 (4): 1001–1005.

Moreno-Casasola, P. 1988. Patterns of plant species distribution on coastal dunes along the Gulf of Mexico. *Journal of Biogeography* 15:787–806.

———. 1999. Dune vegetation and its biodiversity along the Gulf of Mexico, a large marine ecosystem. In *The Gulf of Mexico Large Marine Ecosystem,* ed. H. Kumpf, K. Steidinger, and K. Sherman, 593–612. Malden: Blackwell Science, Inc.

Moyle, P. B., and J. J. Cech Jr. 1988. *Fishes: An Introduction to Ichthyology,* 2nd ed. Englewood Cliffs, N.J.: Prentice-Hall.

Múzquiz, L. H. (*see also* Huerta M. and Huerta-Múzquiz). 1961. Flora marina de los alrededores de la isla Pérez, Arrecife Alacranes, sonda de Campeche, México. *Anales de la Escuela Nacional de Ciencias Biológicas* (México) 10 (14): 11–22.

Nehring, R. 1991. Oil and gas resources. In *Gulf of Mexico Basin,* ed. A. Salvador, 445–94. Vol. J of *The Geology of North America.* Boulder, Colo.: Geological Society of America.

Nelson, T. H. 1991. Salt tectonics and lystric-normal faulting. In *Gulf of Mexico Basin,* ed. A. Salvador, 73–89. Vol. J of *The Geology of North America.* Boulder, Colo.: Geological Society of America.

Nelson, T. J. 1991. A quantitative comparison of the community structure of two forereefs in the southwestern Gulf of Mexico. M.S. thesis, Corpus Christi State University, Corpus Christi, Tex.

Nelson, T. J., T. L. Stinnett, and J. W. Tunnell. 1988. Quantitative assessment of an unusually dense octocoral community in the southwestern Gulf of Mexico. In *Proceedings of the Sixth International Coral Reef Symposium*

(Townsville, Queensland, Australia, 8–12 August 1988), ed. J. H. Choat, D. Barnes, M. A. Borowitzka, J. C. Coll, P. J. Davies, P. Flood, B. G. Hatcher, D. Hopley, P. A. Hutchings, D. Kinsey, G. R. Orme, M. Pichon, P. F. Sale, P. Sammarco, C. C. Wallace, C. Wilkinson, E. Wolanski, and O. Bellwood, 2:791–96. Townsville: Sixth International Coral Reef Symposium Executive Committee.

Nipper, M., J. A. Sánchez-Chávez, and J. W. Tunnell Jr., eds. 2004. GulfBase: Resource database for Gulf of Mexico research. Harte Research Institute for Gulf of Mexico Studies, Texas A&M University–Corpus Christi. http://www.gulfbase.org.

NOAA (National Oceanographic and Atmospheric Administration). 2002a. Regional perspectives: Tropical America. http://www.ogp.noaa.gov/misc/coral/sor/soramericas.html.

———. 2002b. NOAA's Coral reef activities. http://www.coris.noaa.gov.

———. 2002c. International agreements concerning living marine resources of interest to NOAA Fisheries. International Fisheries Division (F/SF4) Office of Sustainable Fisheries. http://www.nmfs.noaa.gov/sfa/international/2002International_agree.htm#CA.

Nobre, P., and J. Shukla. 1996. Variations of sea surface temperature, wind stress, and rainfall over the tropical Atlantic and South America. *Journal of Climate* 9:2464–79.

Novak, M. J. 1992. Sedimentology and community structure of reefs of the Yucatan Peninsula, Mexico. M.S. thesis, Utah State University, Logan.

Novak, M. J., W. D. Liddell, and D. Torruco. 1992. Sedimentology and community structure of reefs of the Yucatan Peninsula. In *Proceedings of the Seventh International Coral Reef Symposium* (22–26 June 1992, Mangilao, Guam), ed. R. H. Richmond, 1:265–72. Mangilao: University of Guam Press.

Nowlin, W. D., and J. M. Hubertz. 1972. Contrasting summer circulation patterns for the eastern Gulf Loop Current versus anticyclonic ring. *Contributions on the Physical Oceanography of the Gulf of Mexico*, ed. L. R. A. Capurro and J. L. Reid, 91–106. Houston: Gulf Publishing Co.

Nuñez-Lara, E., and J. E. Arias-González, E. 1998. The relationship between reef fish structure and environmental variables in the Southern Mexican Caribbean. *Journal of Fish Biology* z53 (A): 209–21.

Opitz, S. 1996. *Trophic Interactions in Caribbean Coral Reefs*. Technical report 43. Manila, Philippines: International Center for Living Aquatic Resources.

OSIR (Oil Spill Intelligence Report). 1980. *Special Report on Ixtoc I*, vol. 3, no. 1. Cambridge, MA: Center for Short-Lived Phenonena.

Palacios-Coria, E. 2001. Composición de especies de macrocorales hermatípicos de zonas arrecifales someras de Veracruz, Veracruz: Su uso como material de construcción en el Castillo de San Juan de Ulua. Bsc. tesis, Universidad Nacional Autónoma de Mexico.

Palmer, A. R., and J. Geissman. 1999. 1999 Geologic time scale. Geological Society of America. http://www.geosociety.org.

Paynter, R. A. Jr. 1953. Migrants on Campeche Bank. *Auk* 70:338–49.

———. 1955. *The Ornithogeography of the Yucatán Peninsula*. Bulletin of Peabody Museum, no. 9. New Haven, Conn.: Peabody Museum of Natural History, Yale University.

Pech-Paat, J. A., V. S. Echeverría, and E. Cruz. 2002. Pesquería de caracol. In *La Pesca en Veracruz y sus Perspectivas de Desarrollo,* ed. P. Guzmán, C. Quiroga, C. Díaz, D. Fuentes, C. Contreras, and G. Silva, 233–34. Instituto Nacional de la Pesca, Universidad Veracruzana, México.

PEMEX (Petroleos Mexicanos). 1987. Evaluacion de los corales escleractinios del sistema arrecifal del Puerto de Veracruz. GPTA-E_01/87. México, D.F.: PEMEX and SECMAR (Secretaría de Marina).

Perry, J. J. 1980. Oil in the biosphere. In *Introduction to Environmental Toxicology,* ed. F. E. Guthrie and J. J. Perry, 198–209. New York: Elsevier.

Quintana y Molina, J. 1991. Resultados del programa de investigaciones en Arrecifes Veracruzanos del laboratorio de Sistemas Bentónicos litorales. *Hidrobiológica* 1 (1): 73–86.

Randall, J. E. 1967a. Food habits of reef fishes of the West Indies. *Studies in Tropical Oceanography* (Miami) 5:665–847.

———. 1967b. Food habits of reef fishes of the West Indies. In *Proceedings of the International Conference on Tropical Oceanography* (November 17–24, 1965), ed. F. M. Bayer, C. P. Idyll, J. I. Jones, F. F. Koczy, A. A. Myrberg, C. R. Robins, F. G. Walton Smith, G. L. Voss, E. J., E. J. Ferguson Wood, and A. C. Jensen, 665–847. Miami: Institute of Marine Sciences, University of Miami.

———. 1983. *Caribbean Reef Fishes.* London: T. F. H. Publications, Inc.

Rannefeld, J. W. 1972. The stony corals of Enmedio Reef off Veracruz, Mexico. M.S. thesis, Texas A&M University, College Station, Tex.

Ray, J. P. 1974. A study of the coral reef crustaceans (Decapoda and Stomatopoda) of two Gulf of Mexico reef systems: West Flower Garden, Texas and Isla de Lobos, Veracruz, Mexico. Ph.D. diss., Texas A&M University, College Station, Tex.

Reid, R. O. 1972. A simple dynamical model of the Loop Current. *Contributions on the Physical Oceanography of the Gulf of Mexico,* ed. L. R. A. Capurro and J. L. Reid, 157–60. Texas A&M University Oceanographic Studies.

Reséndez-Medina, A. 1971. Peces colectados en el Arrecife La Blanquilla, Veracruz, México. Anales del Instituto de Biología (Universidad Nacional Autónoma de México), 42. *Serie Ciencias del Mar y Limnología* 1:7–30.

Rezak, R., and G. S. Edwards. 1972. Carbonate sediments of the Gulf of Mexico. In *Contributions on the Geological and Geophysical Oceanography of the Gulf of Mexico,* Texas A&M University Oceanographic Studies, ed. R. Rezak and V. J. Henery, 263–80. Houston: Gulf Publishing Co.

Rezak, R., T. J. Bright, and D. W. McGrail. 1985. *Reefs and Banks of the Northwestern Gulf of Mexico: Their Geological, Biological, and Physical Dynamics.* New York: Wiley and Sons.

Rice, W. H., and L. S. Kornicker. 1962. Mollusks of Alacran reef, Campeche Bank, Mexico. *Publications of the Institute of Marine Science* (University of Texas) 8:366–403.

———. 1965. Addendum to 1962 publication: Mollusks of Alacran reef, Campeche Bank, Mexico. *Publications of the Institute of Marine Science* (University of Texas) 10:108–72.

Rickles, S. E. 1977. Ecology, taxonomy and distribution of Holocene reefal ostracods, Veracruz, Mexico. M.S. thesis, University of Nebraska, Lincoln.

Rickner, J. A. 1975. Notes on members of the Family Porcellanidae (Crustacea: Anomura) collected on the east coast of Mexico. *Proceedings of the Biological Society of Washington* 88 (16): 159–66.

———. 1977. Notes on a collection of crabs (Crustacea: Brachyura) from the east coast of Mexico. *Proceedings of the Biological Society of Washington* 90 (4): 831–38.

Ricono, N. A. 1999. Seasonal water quality impacts of riverine and coastal waters on coral reefs of Veracruz, Mexico. M.S. thesis, Texas A&M University–Corpus Christi, Corpus Christi, Tex.

Rigby, J. K., and W. G. McIntire. 1966. The Isla de Lobos and associated reefs, Veracruz, Mexico. *Brigham Young University Geology Studies* 13:3–46.

Riley, C. M., and G. J. Holt. 1993. Gut contents of larval fishes from light trap and plankton net collections at Enmedio Reef near Veracruz, Mexico. *Revista de Biologia Tropical* 41:53–57.

Risk, M. J. 1972. Fish diversity on a coral reef in the Virgin Islands. *Atoll Research Bulletin* 153:1–7.

Roberts, K. A. 1981. Polychaetes of Lobos Reef, Veracruz, Mexico. M.S. thesis, Corpus Christi State University, Corpus Christi, Tex.

Rodriguez, D. G. L. 1965. Distribución de pterópodos en Veracruz, Ver. *Anales del Instituto de Biología, Serie Hidrobiología* (Universidad Nacional Autónoma de México) 36:249–51.

Rodríguez, F. V. 1965. Distribución de Chaetognatha en Veracruz, Ver. *Anales del Instituto de Biología, Serie Hidrobiología* (Universidad Nacional Autónoma de México) 36:229–47.

Rodríguez, F. V., and V. A. Fuentes. 1965. Resultados preliminares sobre la distribución de plancton y datos hidrográficos del arrecife La Blanquilla, Veracruz, Veracruz. *Anales del Instituto de Biología, Serie Hidrobiología* (Universidad Nacional Autónoma de México) 36:53–59.

Rodríquez, H., and J. A. Manrique. 1991. *Veracruz, la Ciudad Hecha de Mar*

*1519–1821*. Instituto Veracruzano de Cultura, H. Ayuntamiento de Veracruz, Secretaría de Agricultura, Pesca, y Aquacultura.

Rodríguez-Gil, L. 1994. Análisis de la evolución de la pesquería de caracol en dos estados de la Península de Yucatán, México y en una cooperativa de pescadores. In *Queen Conch Biology, Fisheries and Mariculture*, ed. R. S. Appeldoorn and B. Rodríguez, 113–24. Caracas, Venezuela: Fundacion Cientifica Los Roques.

Rodriguez-Martinez, R. E. 1993. Efectos de un ciclon en la estructura comunitaria de corales escleractinios. Tesis profesional, ENEP Iztacala, Universidad Nacional Autónoma de México, México, D.F.

Rosales, H. L., E. A. Carranza, and R. U. Alvarez. 1986a. Sedimentological and chemical studies in sediments from Alvarado Lagoon System, Veracruz, Mexico. *Anales del Instituto de Ciencias del Mar y Limnologia* (Universidad Nacional Autónoma de Mexico) 13:19–28.

———. 1986b. Sedimentological and chemical studies in sediments from Papaloapan River, Mexico. *Anales del Instituto de Ciencias del Mar y Limnologia* (Universidad Nacional Autónoma de Mexico) 13: 263–72.

Rosales-Hoz, M. T. L. 1979. Sobre la dispersion de compuestos organoclorados en el medio ambiente marino: Nota científica. *Anales del Instituto de Ciencias del Mar y Limnologia* (Universidad Nacional Autónoma de Mexico) 6 (2): 33–36.

Rosales-Hoz, M. T. L., and R. Álvarez-León. 1979. Niveles actuales de hidrocarburos organoclorados en sedimentos de lagunas costeras del Golfo de México. *Anales del Instituto de Ciencias del Mar y Limnologia* (Universidad Nacional Autónoma de Mexico) 6 (2):1–6.

Rosas, P. I., A. Baez, and R. Belmont. 1983. Oyster (*Crassostrea virginica*) as indicator of heavy metals pollution in some lagoons of the Gulf of Mexico. *Water, Air, and Soil Pollution* 20:127–35.

Ruiz, R., M. L. Gonzalez-Regalado, J. I. Baceta, and J. M. Muñoz. 2000. Comparative ecological analysis of the ostracod faunas from low- and high-polluted southwestern Spanish estuaries: A multivariate approach. *Marine Micropaleontology* 40:345–76.

Ruppert, E. E., and R. D. Barnes. 1994. *Invertebrate Zoology*, 6th ed. Fort Worth: Saunders College Publishing.

SAGARPA (Secretaría de Agricultura, Ganadería, Desarrollo Rural, Pesca, y Alimentación). 2006. Regulations for fisheries species. http://www.sagarpa.gob.mx/cgcs/.

Salas de León, D. A., M. A. M. Gómez, and J. A. Ramirez. 1992. Periodos característicos en las oscilaciones de parámetros meteorológicos en Cayo Arcas, México. *Atmósfera* 5:193–205.

Sale, P., E. A. Chávez, B. G. Hatcher, C. Mayfield, and J. Ciborowski. 1999. *Guidelines for Developing a Regional Monitoring and Environmental Information System: Final Report to the World Bank*. Hamilton, Canada: United Nations University.

Sale, P. F. 1982. The structure and dynamics of coral reef fish communities. In *Theory and Management of Tropical Fisheries*, ed. D. Pauly and G. I. Murphy, 9:41–53. ICLARM Conference Proceedings. Manila, Philippines: International Center for Living Aquatic Resource Management (ICLARM).

———. 1997. Visual census of fishes: How well do we see what is there? *Proceedings of the Eighth International Coral Reef Symposium* (Panama City, Panama, 24–29 June 1996), ed. H. A. Lessios and I. G. Macintyre, 2: 1435–40.

Sale, P. F., and W. A. Douglas. 1984. Temporal variability in the community structure of fish in coral patch reefs and the relation of community structure to reef structure. *Ecology* 65 (2): 409–22.

Salvador, A. 1991a. Introduction. In *Gulf of Mexico Basin*, ed. A. Salvador, 1–12. Vol. J of *The Geology of North America*. Boulder, Colo.: Geological Society of America.

———. 1991b. Triassic-Jurassic. In *Gulf of Mexico Basin*, ed. A. Salvador, 131–80. Vol. J of *The Geology of North America*.Boulder, Colo.: Geological Society of America.

———. 1991c. Origin and development of the Gulf of Mexico Basin. In *Gulf of Mexico Basin*, ed. A. Salvador, 389–444. Vol. J of *The Geology of North America*. Boulder, Colo.: Geological Society of America.

Santiago, V. 1977. Algunos estudios sobre las madréporas del Arrecife "La Blanquilla" Veracruz, México. Tesis profesional, Universidad Autónoma Metropolitana.

Saravanan, R., and P. Chang. 2000. Interaction between tropical Atlantic variability and El Niño–Southern Oscillation. *Journal of Climate* 13:2177–94.

Schirripa, M. J., and C. M. Legault. 1999. The red grouper fishery of the Gulf of Mexico. Assessment 3.0. Miami, Fla.: Southeast Fisheries Science Center, Miami Laboratory, National Marine Fisheries Service.

Secretaría de Marina. 1978. Temperatura y salinidad en los puertos de México en el Golfo de México y Mar Caribe. D.H./M-02-78. México, D.F.: Dirección General de Oceanografía Naval.

SEDUE (Secretaría de Desarrollo Urbano y Ecología). 1985. *Alternativas de Manejo para los Arrecifes de Veracruz.* México, D.F.: Dirección General de Flora y Fauna Silvestre.

———. 1990. Secretaría de Desarrollo Urbano y Ecologia. *Gaceta Ecológica* 2 (6): 1–64.

SEPESCA (Secretaría de Pesca). 1990a. *Aquaculture in Mexico.* Mexico City: Mexican Investment Board.

———. 1990b. *Anuario Estadistico de Pesca.* México, D.F.: Direccion General de Informatica y Registro Pesqueros, Secretaría de Pesca.

———. 1992. *Anuario Estadistico de Pesca.* México, D.F.: Direccion General de Informatica y Registro Pesqueros, Seceretaría de Pesca.

Sevilla, M. L., E. Hidalgo, and A. M. Bolívar de Carranza. 1983. Distribución de algunos moluscos de la superfamilia Rissoacea (Clase Gastrópoda) en sedimentos del arrecife Isla Lobos, Veracruz, México. *Anales de la Escuela Nacional de Ciencias Biológicas* (México) 27:39–53.

Sheets, T. J. 1980. Transport of pollutants. In *Introduction to Environmental Toxicology,* ed. F. E. Guthrie and J. J. Perry, 154–60. New York: Elsevier.

Siebenaler, J. B. 1954. Notes on autumnal trans-Gulf migration of birds. *Condor* 56:43–48.

Slutz, R. J., S. J. Lubker, J. D. Hiscox, S. D. Woodruff, R. L. Jenne, D. H. Joseph, P. M. Steuer, and J. D. Elms. 1985. *Comprehensive Ocean-Atmosphere Data Set: Release 1.* Boulder, Colo.: NOAA Environmental Research Laboratory.

Smith, G. B. 1975. The 1971 red tide and its impact on certain reef communities in the mid-eastern Gulf of Mexico. *Environmental Letters* 9:141–52.

Smith, S. V., W. J. Kimmerer, E. A. Laws, R. E. Brock, and T. W. Walsh. 1981. Kaneohe Bay sewage diversion experiment: Perspectives on ecosystem responses to nutritional perturbation. *Pacific Science* 35:279–395.

Smith, T. 1838. Description of Alacran and Cay Arenas, in the Gulf of Mexico. *Nautical Magazine* 7:804–805.

Smith, W. F. G. 1954. Gulf of Mexico Madreporaria. In *Gulf of Mexico and Its Origin, Waters, and Marine Life,* ed. P. S. Galstoff, 291–95. Fish and Wildlife Service Fishery Bulletin 89. Washington, D.C.: U.S. Government Printing Office.

Solís, W. R. S. R. 1990. Estructura de la comunidad bentonica de la parte sur del Arrecife Alacranes, Yucatán, México. M.S. tesis, Recursos del Mar del Centro de Investigación y Estudios Avanzados del IPN, Unidad Mérida.

Sorokin, Y. I. 1991. Parameters of productivity and metabolism of coral reef ecosystems off central Vietnam. *Estuarine, Coastal and Shelf Science* 33:259–80.

Spalding, M. D., C. Ravilios, and E. P. Green. 2001. *World Atlas of Coral Reefs.* Berkeley: University of California Press.

Sparre, P., and S. C. Venema. 1992. *Introduction to Tropical Fish Stock Assessment,* pt. 1: *Manual.* FAO Fisheries Technical Paper 306/1. Paris: United Nations.

Stanley, S. M. 1984. Marine mass extinction: A dominant role for temperature. In *Extinction,* ed. M. H. Nitecki, 69–117. Chicago: University of Chicago Press.

———. 1987. *Extinction.* New York: Scientific American Library, W.H. Freeman and Co.

Stehli, F. G., and J. W. Wells. 1971. Diversity and age patterns in hermatypic corals. *Systematic Zoology* 20: 115–26.

Stemann, T. A. 1991. Evolution of the reef-coral family Agariciidae (Anthozoa: Scleractinia) in the Neogene through Recent of the Caribbean. Ph.D. diss., University of Iowa, Ames.

Stinnett, T. L. 1989. Species composition and ecological zonation of the sponge fauna of Enmedio Reef, Veracruz, Mexico. M.S. thesis, Corpus Christi State University, Corpus Christi, Tex.

Sturges, W. 1993. The annual cycle of the western boundary current in the Gulf of Mexico. *Journal of Geophysical Research* 98:18053–68.

Sturges, W., and J. P. Blaha. 1976. A western boundary current in the Gulf of Mexico. *Science* 92:367–69.

Sturges, W., and J. C. Evans. 1983. On the variability of the Loop Current in the Gulf of Mexico. *Journal of Marine Research* 41:639–53.

Sturges, W., and R. Leben. 2000. Frequency of ring separations from the Loop Current in the Gulf of Mexico: A revised estimate. *Journal of Physical Oceanography* 30:1814–19.

Súarez-Caabro, J. 1965. Datos meteorológicos, hidrográficos y planctónicos del litoral de Veracruz, Veracruz. *Anales del Instituto de Biología* (Universidad Nacional Autónoma de México) 36 (12): 25–46.

Torruco, D., M. A. González, W. D. Liddell. 1993. Integracion ecologica de grupos funcionales en la laguna arrecifal de Alacranes, Yucatan, Mexico. *Brenesia* 39/40:37–49.

Tunnell, J. W. 1974. Ecological and geographical distribution of Mollusca of Lobos and Enmedio coral reefs, Southwestern Gulf of Mexico. Ph.D. diss., Texas A&M University, College Station, Tex.

———. 1977. Coral reef mollusks of the southwestern Gulf of Mexico. *Bulletin of the American Malacological Union* 43:91.

———. 1985. Environmental stresses of the Veracruz coral reefs, southwestern Gulf of Mexico. *Proceedings of the Fifth International Coral Reef Congress,* Abstracts 2:384.

Tunnell, J. W. Jr. 1988. Regional comparison of southwestern Gulf of Mexico to Caribbean Sea coral reefs. In *Proceedings of the Sixth International Coral Reef Symposium* (Townsville, Australia, 8th–12th August 1988), ed. J. H. Choat, D. Barnes, M. A. Borowitzka, J. C. Coll, P. J. Davies, P. Flood, B. G. Hatcher, D. Hopley, P. A. Hutchings, D. Kinsey, G. R. Orme, M. Pichon, P. F. Sale, P. Sammarco, C. C. Wallace, C. Wilkinson, E. Wolanski, and O. Bellwood, 3:303–308. Townsville:

International Coral Reef Symposium Executive Committee.

———. 1992. Natural versus human impacts to Southern Gulf of Mexico coral reef resources. In *Proceedings of the Seventh International Coral Reef Symposium* (22–26 June 1992, Mangilao, Guam), ed. R. H. Richmond, 1:300–306. Mangilao: University of Guam Press.

Tunnell, J. W., and B. R. Chapman. 1988. First record of Red-footed Boobies nesting in the Gulf of Mexico. *American Birds* 42:380–81.

———. 2001. Seabirds of the Campeche Bank islands, southeastern Gulf of México. *Atoll Research Bulletin* 482:1–50.

Tunnell, J. W., and Q. R. Dokken. 1980. Observations on IXTOC I oil impact of southwestern Gulf of Mexico coral reefs. Paper presented at the Congreso Sobre Problemas Ambientales de México, Instituto Politecnico Nacional, Mexico, D.F.

Tunnell, J. W., J. Jones, and K. Withers. In prep. Stony coral depth zonation and decline within and between reefs, Veracruz Reef System.

Tunnell, J. W., and T. J. Nelson. 1989. A high density-low diversity octocoral community in the southwestern Gulf of Mexico. In *Diving for Science . . . 1989: Proceedings of the American Academy of Underwater Sciences, Ninth Annual Scientific Diving Symposium* (Woods Hole, Mass.), ed. M. A. Lang and W. C. Jaap, 325–35.

Turner, J. R., and E. Granéli. 1992. Zooplankton feeding ecology: Grazing during enclosure studies of phytoplankton blooms from the west coast of Sweden. *Journal of Experimental Marine Biology and Ecology* 157:19–31.

Universidad Veracruzana. 2003. Area de protección de flora y fauna silvestre "Sistema Arrecifal Lobos-Tuxpan." Documento téchnico justificativo para la creación de un area natural protegida en el sistema arrecifal Lobos-Tuxpan. Tuxpan, Veracruz, Mexico.

van Oppen, M. J. H., B. L. Willis, H. W. J. A. Van Vugt, and D. J. Miller. 2000. Examination of species boundaries in the *Acropora cervicornis* group (Scleractinia, Cnidaria) using nuclear DNA sequence analyses. *Molecular Ecology* 9:1363–73.

van Vleet, E. S., W. M. Sackett, S. B. Reinhardt, and M. E. Mangini. 1984. Distribution, sources, and fates of floating oil residues in the eastern Gulf of Mexico. *Marine Pollution Bulletin* 15:106–10.

Vargas-Hernández, J. M. 1992. El uso de animales marinos con fines artesanales y su repercusión en el sistema arrecifal Veracruzano. *Boletin Sociedad Veracruzano Zoologia* 2 (1): 6–9.

Vargas-Hernández, J. M., M. L. J. Badillo, and V. A. Fuentes. 2002. El sistema arrecifal Veracruzano y las pesquerias asociadas. In *La Pesca en Veracruz y Sus Perspectivas de Desarrollo*, ed. P. G. Amaya, C. Q. Brahms, C. D. Luna, D. F. Castellanos, C. M. Contreras, and G. Silva-López, 13–16. México: Secretaría de Agricultura, Ganadería, Desarrollo Rural, Pesca y Alimentación and Universidad Veracruzana.

Vargas-Hernández, J. M., L. F. Carrera-Parra, R. Bravo-Sanchez, and Sanchez-Domiguez. 1994. Artesanias con fauna marina en el sistema arrecifal Veracruzano. *El Jarocho Verde, Red de Informacion Ambiental del Estado de Veracruz* 7:3–4.

Vargas-Hernández, J. M., A. Hernández-Gutiérrez, and L. F. Carrera-Parra. 1993. Sistema arrecifal Veracruzano. In *Biodiversidad Marina y Costera de Mexico*, ed. S. I. Salazar-Vallejo and N. E. González, 559–75. México, D.F.: Comisión Nacional para la Biodiversidad y Centro de Investigaciones de Quintana Roo.

Vargas-Hernández, J. M., A. Hernández-Guitérrez, and M. I. Sánchez-Vall. 1994. La problemática del Sistema Arrecifal Veracruzano: Aagunas propuestas para su uso y conservación. *El Jarocho Verde, Red de Informacion Ambiental del Estado de Veracruz* 7:4–7.

Vargas-Hernández, J. M., M. A. Lozano-Aburto, and M. A. Roman-Vives. 2003. Impacto causado por el encallamiento del barco de transprote PAULA KAY al "Bajo Tuxpan." *II Congreso Mexicano Sobre Arrecifes,* 5–7 Noviembre 2003, Universidad del Mar, Puerto Angel, Oaxaca. Resúmenes 25.

Vargas-Hernández, J. M., G. Nava-Martínez, and M. A. Román-Vives. 2002. Peces del sistema arrecifal Veracruzano. In *La Pesca en Veracruz y Sus Perspectivas de Desarrollo*, ed. P. G. Amaya, C. Q. Brahms, C. D. Luna, D. F. Castellanos, C. M. Contreras, and G. Silva-López, 17–29. Mexico: Secretaría de Agricultura, Ganadería, Desarrollo Rural, Pesca y Alimentación and Universidad Veracruzana.

Vargas-Hernández, J. M., and M. A. Román-Vives. 2002. *Corales Pétreos de Veracruz, México: Guía de Identificación*. México, D.F.: Publicacion de Acuario de Veracruz, A.C.

Vaughan, T. W. 1901. *Some Fossil Corals from the Elevated Reefs of Curacao, Aruba and Bonaire*. Leiden: Rijks Geologisches Mineralogisches Museum Sammlungen.

Vázquez de la Cerda, A. M. 1975. Currents and waters of the upper 1200 m of the southwestern Gulf of Mexico. M.S. thesis, Texas A&M University, College Station, Tex.

———. 1993. Bay of Campeche cyclone. Ph.D. diss., Texas A&M University, College Station, Tex.

Veracruz ReefMonitor Update. 2001. Tuxpan coral reefs: Prime site for marine protected area. Miami: Reef-Keeper International.

Vergara, S. G., J. W. McManus, K. N. Kesner-Reyes, L. A. B. Meñez, R. Z. Funk, R. C. Evangelista, M. Noordeloos, A. M. B. Serrano, M. F. Rull, V. L. Alarcón, A. B. T. Meneses, and J. R. Glorioso. 2000. *ReefBase2000: Improving Policies for Sustainable Management of Coral Reefs,* ver. 2000. CD-ROM and guide. Manila, Philippines: International Center for Living Aquatic Resources.

Veron, J.E.N. 1993. *A Biogeographic Database of Hermatypic Corals, Species of the Central Indo-Pacific, Genera of the World*. Monograph Series 9. Townsville: Australian Institute of Marine Science.

———. 1995. *Corals in Space and Time: The Biogeography and Evolution of the Scleractinia*. New York: Cornell University Press.

———. 2000. *Corals of the World*. Townsville: Australian Institute of Marine Science.

Vestal, J. R. 1980. Pollution effects of storm-related runoff. In *Introduction to Environmental Toxicology*, ed. F. E. Guthrie and J. J. Perry, 450–56. New York: Elsevier.

Vidal, V. M. V., F. V. Vidal, and J. M. Pérez-Molero. 1994a. Baroclinic flows, transports, and kinematic properties in a cyclonic-anticyclonic-cyclonic ring triad in the Gulf of Mexico. *Journal of Geophysical Research* 99:7571–7597.

Vidal, V. M. V., F. V. Vidal, A. F. Hernández, E. Meza, and L. Zambrano. 1994b. *Atlas Oceanográfico del Golfo de México*, vol. 3. Cuernavaca, México: Instituto Investigaciones Electrica.

———. 1994c. Winter water mass distributions in the western Gulf of Mexico affected by a colliding anticyclonic ring. *Journal of Oceanography* 50:559–88.

Vidal, V. M. V., F. V. Vidal, and J. M. Perez-Molero. 1992. Collision of a loop current anticyclonic ring against the continental shelf slope of the western Gulf of Mexico. *Journal of Geophysical Research* 97:2155–72.

Villalobos, A. (*see also* Villalobos-Figueroa). 1971. Estudios ecológicos en un arrecife coralino en Veracruz, México. In *Symposium on Investigations and Resources of the Caribbean Sea and Adjacent Regions*, 531–45. Willemstad, Curacao.

Villalobos-Figueroa, A. 1980. Informe del programa de arrecifes coralinos. In *Anales del Instituto de Biología*. México, D.F.: Universidad Nacional Autónoma de México.

———. 1981. *Evaluación de los Efectos del Derrame del IXTOC-I Sobre la Cominidad Arrecifal de Veracruz y Campeche*. Informe al Programa Coordinado de Estudios Ecológicos en la Sonda de Campeche. México, D.F.: Universidad Autónoma de México.

Vokes, H. E., and E. H. Vokes. 1983. *Distribution of Shallow-Water Marine Mollusca, Yucatan Peninsula, Mexico*. Publication no. 54. New Orleans: Middle American Research Institute, Tulane University.

Vollmer, S. V., and S. R. Palumbi. 2002. Hybridization and the evolution of reef coral diversity. *Science* 296:2023–25.

Voss, G. L., and N. A. Voss. 1955. An ecological study of Soldier Key, Biscayne Bay, Florida. *Bulletin of Marine Science of the Gulf and Caribbean* 5:203–29.

Vukovich, F. M., and B. W. Crissman. 1986. Aspects of warm rings in the Gulf of Mexico. *Journal of Geophysical Research* 91:2645–60.

Ward, H. L. 1887. Notes on the life-history of *Monachus topicalis*, the West Indian seal. *American Naturalist* 21:257–64.

Ward, W. C. 1985a. Recent carbonate sediments of the inner shelf. In *Geology and Hydrogeology of the Yucatan and Quaternary Geology of Northeastern Yucatan Peninsula*, ed. W. C. Ward, A. E. Weidie, and W. Back, 24–61. New Orleans: New Orleans Geological Society.

———. 1985b. Upper Pleistocene limestones. Geology and Hydrogeology of the Yucatan and Quaternary Geology of Northeastern Yucatan Peninsula, ed. W. C. Ward, A. E. Weidie, and W. Back, 62–73. New Orleans: New Orleans Geological Society.

Weil, E. 1992a. Genetic and morphological variation in Caribbean and eastern Pacific *Porites* (Anthozoa, Scleractinia). Preliminary results. In *Proceedings of the Seventh International Coral Reef Symposium* (22–26 June 1992, Mangilao, Guam), ed. R. H. Richmond, 2:643–56. Mangilao: University of Guam Press.

———. 1992b. Genetic and morphological variation in *Porites* (Cnidaria, Anthozoa) across the Isthmus of Panama. Ph.D. diss., University of Texas at Austin.

Weil, E., and N. Knowlton. 1994. A multi-character analysis of the Caribbean coral *Montastraea annularis* (Ellis and Solander, 1786) and its two sibling species, *M. faveolata* (Ellis and Solander, 1786) and *M. franksi* (Gregory, 1895). *Bulletin of Marine Science* 55:151–75.

Wells, J. W. 1956. Scleractinia. In *Treatise on Invertebrate Paleontology, Part F: Coelenterata*, ed. R. C. Moore, F328–F444. Lawrence: University of Kansas Press.

———. 1957. Coral reefs. In *Treatise on Marine Ecology and Paleoecology*, ed. J. W. Hedgpeth. Geological Society of America Ecological Memoirs 67 (1): 1087–1104.

Wells, J. W., and J. C. Lang. 1973. Systematic list of Jamaican shallow-water Scleractinia. *Bulletin of Marine Science* 23:55–58.

Wells, S. M., ed. 1988. *Coral Reefs of the World*, vol. 1: *Atlantic and Eastern Pacific*. Gland, Switzerland: International Union for Conservation of Nature and Natural Resources.

White, R. B. 1982. A study of the natantid decapod crustaceans collected from

Enmedio Reef, Veracruz, Mexico. M.S. thesis, Texas A&I University, Kingsville, Tex.

Wilkinson, C. 1998. *Status of Coral Reefs of the World: 1998.* Townsville: Australian Institute of Marine Science.

————. 2000. *Status of Coral Reefs of the World: 2000.* Townsville: Australian Institute of Marine Science.

————. 2002. *Status of Coral Reefs of the World: 2002.* Townsville: Australian Institute of Marine Science.

————. 2004. *Status of Coral Reefs of the World: 2004.* Townsville: Australian Institute of Marine Science.

Williams, D. 1982. Patterns in distribution of fish communities across the central Great Barrier Reef. *Coral Reefs* 1:35–43.

Williams, D., and A. I. Hatcher. 1983. Structure of fish communities on outer slope of inshore, midshelf and outer shelf reefs of the Great Barrier Reef. *Marine Ecology Progress Series* 10:239–50.

Wright, T., and L. S. Kornicker. 1962. Island transport of marine shells by birds on Perez Island, Alacran Reef, Campeche Reef, Mexico. *Journal of Geology* 70 (5): 616–18.

Wulff, J. L. 2006. Rapid diversity and abundance decline in a Caribbean coral reef sponge community. *Biological Conservation* 127:167–76.

Wynne, M. J. 1998. *A Checklist of Benthic Marine Algae of the Tropical and Subtropical Western Atlantic,* 1st rev. Berlin: Gebrüder Borntraeger.

Zavala-Hidalgo, J., S. L. Morey, and J. J. O'Brien. 2003a. Cyclonic eddies northeast of the Campeche Bank from altimetry data. *Journal of Physical Oceanography* 33:623–29.

————. 2003b. Seasonal circulation on the western shelf of the Gulf of Mexico using a high-resolution numerical model. *Journal of Geophysical Research* 108 (C12): 3389, doi:10.1029/2003JC001879.

Zavala-Hidalgo, J., A. Parés-Sierra, and J. Ochoa. 2002. Seasonal variability of the temperature and heat fluyes in the Gulf of Mexico. *Atmósfera* 15:81–104.

Zlatarski, V.N., and N. Martínez-Estalella. 1982. *Les Scleractiniares de Cuba, avec des Donnés sur les Organismes Associés.* Sofia: Editions de l'Académie Bulgare des Sciences.

# List of Contributors

**Carl R. Beaver, Ph.D. (1959–2006)**
University of South Florida, College of
Marine Science, 140 7th Avenue S.,
St. Petersburg, Florida 33701

**Juan Pablo Carricart-Ganivet, Ph.D.**
Departamento de Ecología Acuática,
ECOSUR, Zona Industrial No. 2, Carr.
Chetumal-Bacalar, Apartamento Postal
424, Cancun, Quintana Roo, México
77000

**Laura Carrillo, Ph.D.** Departamento de
Ecología y Taxonomia del Zooplancton
Marino, El Colegio de la Frontera
(ECOSUR), Av. del Centenario Km. 5.5,
Chetumal, Quintana Roo, México, 77900

**Ernesto A. Chávez Ortiz, Ph.D.** Centro
Interdisciplinario de Ciencias Marinas,
Instituto Politécnico Nacional, Av.
Instituto Politécnico Nacional s/n, Col.
Sta. Rita, Playa El Conchalito, La Paz,
BCS, México, 23000

**Guillermo Horta-Puga** Universidad
Nacional Autónoma de México, Av.
de los Barrios 1, Los Reyes Iztacala,
Tlalnepantla, México 54910

**W. David Liddell, Ph.D.** Department of
Geology, 1400 Old Main Hill, Utah State
University, Logan, Utah 84322

**John W. (Wes) Tunnell Jr., Ph.D.**
Center for Coastal Studies, Harte
Institute for Gulf of Mexico, Texas A&M
University–Corpus Christi, 6300 Ocean
HRI 318C, Corpus Christi, Texas 78412

**Kim Withers, Ph.D.** Center for Coastal
Studies, Texas A&M University–Corpus
Christi, 6300 Ocean NRC 3200, Corpus
Christi, Texas 78412

**Juan Manuel Vargas-Hernández**
Universidad Veracruzana, Departamento
de Biología, Xalapa, Veracruz, México
91090

# Index

ISBN-13: 978-1-58544-617-9
ISBN-10: 1-58544-617-3